P9-DUJ-185

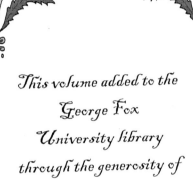

This volume added to the
George Fox
University library
through the generosity of

Deborah Gerner

INTERNATIONAL NEGOTIATION

ACTORS, STRUCTURE/PROCESS, VALUES

Edited by

PETER BERTON, HIROSHI KIMURA,
AND I. WILLIAM ZARTMAN

St. Martin's Press
New York

INTERNATIONAL NEGOTIATION

Copyright © Peter Berton, Hiroshi Kimura, I. William Zartman, 1999. All rights
reserved. Printed in the United States of America. No part of this book may be
used or reproduced in any manner whatsoever without written permission
except in the case of brief quotations embodied in critical articles or reviews. For
information, address St. Martin's Press, 175 Fifth Avenue, New York, N.Y. 10010.

ISBN 0-312-21778-1

Library of Congress Cataloging-in-Publication Data

International negotiation / actors, structure/process, values / edited
  by Peter Berton, Hiroshi Kimura, and I. William Zartman.
      p.   cm.
  Includes bibliographical references and index.
  ISBN 0-312-21778-1 (cloth)
    1. International relations.   2. Negotiation—Cross-cultural
studies.   I. Berton, Peter, 1922- .   II. Kimura, Hiroshi, 1936- .
III. Zartman, I. William, 1932- .
JZ1305.I574   1999
327.1'7—dc21   98-51658
        CIP

Design by Letra Libre, Inc.

First edition: July, 1999
10 9 8 7 6 5 4 3 2 1

For
Joan, Noriko, and Daniele

CONTENTS

Part III: Values

ACKNOWLEDGMENTS

The Editors wish to express their appreciation to coauthor Professor Robert FRIEDHEIM for his kind assistance and advice; to the School of International Relations, University of Southern California, for clerical support; to Theresa Taylor SIMMONS of the School of Advanced International Studies, Johns Hopkins University, in Washington, DC; SUENO Maki of the International Research Center for Japanese Studies in Kyoto; and especially to XU Feng of the USC School of International Relations, who helped prepare this book manuscript for publication—no mean feat considering the fact that there were fourteen contributions by scholars from six nations on three continents, written in six different computer programs (some of them no longer in use), with references in half a dozen languages. The work of Professors Spector and Zartman was made possible, in part, through the support of the Jacob and Hilda Blaustein Foundation.

Acronyms

APEC	Asia-Pacific Economic Cooperation
BATNA	best alternative to a negotiated agreement
BWU	Blue Whale Unit
CPSU	Communist Party of the Soviet Union
EC	European Community
EEZ	Exclusive Economic Zones
EU	European Union
GATT	General Agreement on Tariffs and Trade
ICRW	International Convention for the Regulation of Whaling
ICSU	International Council of Scientific Unions
IGC	Intergovernmental Conference
IMF	International Monetary Fund
INC	Intergovernmental Negotiating Committee for a Framework Convention for Climate Change
INF	Intermediate-Range Nuclear Forces
IPCC	Intergovernmental Panel on Climate Change
IRA	Irish Republican Army
IWC	International Whaling Commission
MBFR	Mutual and Balanced Force Reductions
MITI	Ministry of International Trade and Industry (Japan)
NAFTA	North American Free Trade Agreement
NATO	North Atlantic Treaty Organization
NGO	non-governmental organization
OECD	Organization for Economic Cooperation and Development
PLO	Palestine Liberation Organization
RMA	Rice Millers Association (Japan)
SALT	Strategic Arms Limitation Talks
START	Strategic Arms Reduction Talks
SWAPO	South-West African Peoples Organization

UN	United Nations
UNCED	United Nations Conference on Environment and Development
UNCTAD	United Nations Conference on Trade and Development
UNECE	United Nations Economic Commission for Europe
UNEP	United Nations Environmental Program
UNESCO	United Nations Educational, Scientific and Cultural Organization
USTR	U.S. Trade Representative
WMO	World Meteorological Organization
WTO	World Trade Organization

PREFACE

HIROSHI KIMURA

Whether we like it or not, we are always negotiating—with our boss, colleagues, friends, or even family members. We are constantly engaged, tacitly or not, in negotiating, bargaining, or making a deal. Our work, for example, whether it be for the government or a private company, is determined by a contract that is a result of negotiation. A housewife's shopping, or a daughter's decision to accept an invitation for a date from her boyfriend, as well as almost all of her conduct during dating—all these are acts that have something to do with negotiation, bargaining, and making deals. Negotiation is necessary in a situation where there are two people or more. Robinson Crusoe (the hero of Daniel Defoe's novel), after living for a long time in complete isolation on an island, a situation in which naturally no negotiating activity was needed, suddenly discovered the necessity of negotiation when "Friday" arrived on the scene.

Negotiations take place at various levels—among individuals, groups, and states. Negotiations are necessary not only among rivals, opponents, and enemies—be they potential or actual—but even between close friends and allies. In other words, even among people whose objectives, tasks, and interests are identical, negotiations are still necessary for the purpose of adjusting their differences in approach, method, division of labor, and burden- or cost-sharing. Naturally, negotiations are even more necessary among people, groups, or states with conflicting interests.

The methods to resolve conflicts of interest can be largely classified into two kinds: those that resort to force and those that use peaceful means. Negotiation constitutes a typical example of the latter method (Israelian & Lebedeva, 1991; Kohler, 1958). Resolution of conflicts by force, such as military means, may appear to be efficient, but resolution by force is, in fact, often more costly and time-consuming, because it may lead to a vicious circle of counterforce. The forceful method is thus not regarded as an appropriate way to reach a long-lasting settlement. It does not succeed in providing a resolution that is acceptable to all parties concerned (Putman & Roloff, 1992). Consequently, no matter how much time, energy, and other resources may be consumed, we have no practical alternative but to choose the peaceful solution of a conflict, relying upon negotiation as the best means.

Negotiation, the central theme of this book, is a universal human behavior, whose origin can be traced back to the very beginning of history. Negotiation is also the main means for resolving conflicts, thereby serving as an important tool of diplomacy. With the end of the Cold War, the significance of negotiation in international politics has increased. Let us elaborate on these points.

The end of the Cold War has led to a situation in which certain types of local wars (national, ethnic, territorial, or religious) erupt more easily than they did previously. On the one hand, the end of the Cold War greatly softened the confrontation between the two superpowers—the United States and the former Soviet Union—over ideology and nuclear weaponry, which in turn contributed to the solution of certain kinds of local war. For example, proxy wars between the two superpowers (for example, in Angola) have ceased, and are now much less likely to occur. On the other hand, there are other kinds of local wars, arising not from ideological confrontation or differences in politico-economic systems, but from national, ethnic, racial, or religious differences; economic poverty and social discrimination; or dissatisfaction over existing borders. During the Cold War, such conflicts were restrained and successfully contained, largely because of the firmly established hegemonic control by the former Soviet Union over its satellites; the solidarity among the Western camp countries; and the general apprehension that events might escalate to a nuclear war. However, with the decline of communist ideology, the breakup of the Eastern bloc, and the collapse of the Soviet Union, such conflicts suddenly became prominent, like magma that had been contained under the surface.

Another reason for the recent increase in the role of negotiation in international affairs is the emergence of disparities in opinions and interests in the Western camp since the end of the Cold War. Although such disparities existed during the Cold War, the most important task for Western countries at that time was to unite against their actual or potential enemies—the former Soviet Union, China, and other Communist states. With the end of the Cold War and the disappearance of common enemies, however, differences in views and interests in the Western camp emerged as important issues. In the world of politics, once one enemy has gone, new enemies tend to appear, or have to be discovered or even created (Arendt, 1951). This argument is best illustrated by Samuel Huntington's popular theory of "the Clash of Civilizations" (1993).

Although all of this seems to be almost self-evident, it has not been sufficiently appreciated and recognized that it will continue in the future. The well-known axiom of Carl von Clausewitz that "war is a mere continuation of policy by other means" (1971) must now be changed, into a dictum that "negotiation is a continuation of policy by other means" (Winham, 1987).

REFERENCES

Arendt, H. 1951. *The Origins of Totalitarianism*. Cleveland: The World Publishing Company.

Gaddis, J. L. 1992. "The Cold War, the Long Peace, and the Future." In Michael, *The End of the Cold War: Its Meaning and Implications*. Cambridge: Cambridge University Press.

Huntington, S. P. 1993. "The Clash of Civilizations?" *Foreign Affairs*, 72 (3).

Israelian, V., & Lebedeva, M. 1991. "Peregovory iskusstvo dlia vsekh." *Mezhdunarodnaia zhizn'*, November.

Kohler, F. D. 1958. "Negotiation as an Effective Instrument of American Foreign Policy." *U.S. Department of State Bulletin*, 38, June 2.

Putnam, L. L., & Roloff, M. E. 1992. *Communication and Negotiation*. Newbury Park, CA: Sage.

von Clausewitz, C. 1971. *On War*. London: Penguin Books.

Winham, G. R. 1987. "Multilateral Economic Negotiation." *Negotiation Journal*, 3 (2).

NEGOTIATING CULTURES

I. WILLIAM ZARTMAN

Around the world, people negotiate: It is the only way they have to make collective decisions when there must be unanimity and there is no decision rule. They have negotiated from the beginning of time and are in no danger of stopping. But like any other social activity, negotiation exhibits both universal patterns determined by the finite possibilities of its nature and local variations determined by cultural practices and differences among its practitioners. In principle, universalities predominate if one digs deep enough, and peculiarities abound in surface manifestations. But this general observation does not indicate how deep is deep enough and how shallow the surface, or where the meeting line between depth and surface is located, or whether that meeting line is indeed an even isotherm or a jagged relief where the surface sometimes plunges to the bottom and the bottom sometimes erupts to the surface. Those are empirical questions that demand greater study.

These questions have important implications for the achievement and analysis of negotiated outcomes. Where does one look for explanations of negotiated outcomes, and therefore where does one focus practices to produce them? Are the best analyses, and therefore the most fruitful efforts, situated on the level of universal behavioral characteristics or of cultural variations? How similarly and how differently do people negotiate the world around anyhow?

Although it would be nice to have clear answers to such questions, they are too broad to yield conclusive findings; any attempt to answer them in bulk would be a denial of the delicacy and complexity of the operations. Answers need to be focused on analytical targets so that, in avoiding overly broad generalizations, they do not become just idiosyncratic accounts of a historical moment without relevance to future strategies of analysis and policy. Three such components of negotiation stand out for focus: actors, structures/processes, and goal values. Which of the three explains most about the determination of outcomes? Are the negotiating actors stronger vehicles of universalist or particularist behaviors that determine outcomes? Do structures and processes exhibit local or universal patterns that explain results? Can goal values be better understood as a universal or particularist phenomenon that defines solutions?

ACTORS

An analysis of actors as a focus for explanations most immediately brings to fore the matter of culture (Faure & Rubin, 1994). While actors could be studied individually, by their psychological traits, or operationally, by the roles they play, the data requirements and analytical assumptions of both these approaches pose significant problems. But their collective behavioral traits, grouped as national delegations or subnational representatives, provide intriguing targets of study. Commonly it is assumed that different people negotiate differently, and that assumption tends to become an attribution, so that people disappoint when they do not conform. But like any caricature, this one—if it is one—merely accentuates traits that are present, at least to some extent, and it is the extent as much as the existence of the trait that becomes interesting.

The stage is then set for some creative analysis, a taking apart of the subject. How "Japanese" are the Japanese in their negotiations? In other words, what are the characteristics that would enable a blind (but sharply listening) observer to identify an unlabeled group of negotiators as Japanese, and therefore not something else, and how widely spread are these characteristics among this group? The subject is examined in chapter 2 by Michael Blaker.

Then, how "Russian" are the Russians, another cultural collectivity, and how much of their Russianness is Russian and how much Communist? In other words, how does the snapshot of defining traits change over time, and what is the effect of discreet components that are added and removed (and, indeed, if they can be added and removed, how and why)? This complex matter is studied by Hiroshi Kimura. Finally, how different are these

Japanese from these Russians and Chinese in their negotiating behavior, and does that behavior make it possible for the blind auditor to distinguish one from the other? In other words, are the identifying traits of one culture distinct from those of each of the others, and why can we tell them apart? This inquiry is the subject of the study by Peter Berton.

These three examinations of specific cultures are introduced by a general presentation of the cultural effects on negotiation by Guy Olivier Faure. Differences in actors' behavior are to be observed in every component of negotiation—structure, strategy, process, and outcome—but the challenge comes in systematizing these differences into reliable and distinguishing effects, as the case examinations attempt to do. Only when one is sure how much of the cultural portrait of the actor is real and how much caricature can the other party turn culture from an obstacle to a bridge that facilitates negotiation.

STRUCTURE AND PROCESS

Structure and process are usually opposed to culture as the universalist modes of analysis, but it need not be so. Structure refers to a distribution of elements, usually elements of power (or means) but also elements of value (ends), giving rise to structuralist or power explanations and strategic or game theoretic analyses of negotiation (Zartman, 1991). It is reasonably clear by now that structure matters, but only as it affects process, which matters too (Dupont & Faure, 1991). The two necessarily combine, in reality and in analysis, as symmetric, asymmetric, and ambiguous structures open different processual possibilities for the parties, possibilities that can be catalogued as finite and universal opportunities open to all negotiators (Zartman & Rubin, 1999). But there are many sources of structures.

Culture also can provide its own structures, and so its own processes, opening an analytical potential that has rarely been utilized. Different types of cultural actors may well exhibit different negotiating behaviors, but in interaction with each other those behaviors may well change, determined now by the response of the other rather than by the actor's own internal components. An explanation that considers this distribution and interaction is more comprehensive than one that only analyzes an actor's theoretically preferred behavior. It is the former type of analysis that John Graham supplies, examining the interactive behavior of two cultures in relation to each other, looking not at the "Japaneseness" of Japanese behavior, but at the "Japaneseness" versus the universality of the Japanese position with respect to the Americans, and vice versa. Not surprisingly, perhaps, it turns out that what was "Japanese" about the Japanese was their universal reactions in many types of dealings with the Americans, a characteristic shared by the Americans.

Another type of structure is that which contains the actors rather than that which exists between them, referring to the distribution of positions and channels within governmental institutions. Cultures themselves operate within national structures of power and behavior and therefore are at least shaped by their context, although the relation is irresolvably circular, since internal structures are themselves part of or at least determined by internal cultures. Is it the "Japaneseness" of the Japanese negotiators, their universal-type responses as rational actors, or the national structures within which they operate which best accounts for their negotiating behavior? This comparative search for explanations is undertaken by Robert Friedheim in his subsequent chapter, with results that bring out the role of governmental structures but that then leave open the question, in turn, of *their* explanation.

The same type of analysis can also be applied to the level of international structures. Where there is an established setting, such as a regime or an organization, there is an additional layer over the internal structures of the parties and the structure of their lateral encounters. Indeed, in such cases, more clearly than in the case of national institutions, such multilateral or multinational structures are often observed to create their own cultures. The homogenizing socializing culture of the United Nations often seems to override component national cultures and to be a creation of its own, not just a larger sum of its parts. The same occurs within the European Union, where the networking imposed by the forming structures engenders its own modus operandi and dominates the effects of component cultures. This structural effect is analyzed in detail by Frank Pfetsch in chapter 7.

In the end, it is the situation itself that provides the structure for negotiations, returning the analytical and practical understanding of the event to three basic variations: symmetry, asymmetry, and ambiguity. Each structural variation has its own appropriate behaviors and counterbehaviors, applicable without distinction of race, creed, color, or previous condition of servitude. But even here, the situation, and the opportunities it offers, is not subsumed simply in a distinction between equality and inequality of the parties. Equality is extremely difficult to identify and even more difficult to maintain (Zartman & Rubin, 1998). Inequalities predominate but multiply, as the weaker party seeks to introduce another inequality in its favor.

Negotiation is a game of one-upmanship, of outbidding or *surenchère,* at best conducted constructively and constrained by the mutual satisfaction of both parties.

But there are also situations in which the parties do not play their structurally assigned roles, where the stronger does not come on strong or the weaker act submissively (Rubin & Brown, 1975). Recognition of such situations is the first step toward creative negotiations, and the second step is the adoption of appropriate but counterintuitive behaviors. In multilateral regime-forming negotiation, in the presence of a hegemon who does not act like one, can the smaller parties fill the role vacuum and provide the leadership necessary to manage the structure's inherent complexity (Zartman, 1994)? The question is the subject of very policy-relevant analysis by Gunnar Sjöstedt. At best, in this situation, cultural descriptions may add some gloss on the ability of each party to play its new role (and may explain, necessarily ambiguously, why the hegemon is a cowardly lion).

VALUES

Negotiators negotiate to achieve their particular goals, but they also negotiate within the constraints of larger values, beginning with the basic processual assumption of reciprocity (Larson, 1992). The role of equality as a processual and structural characteristic has already been discussed. But it also becomes a value that hovers over both process and outcome. Negotiations take place when one party cannot impose its will over the other or do without the other's assent; if it could, there would be no need for negotiations. If interaction and assent are therefore involved, they involve countervailing efforts operating within some sort of normative constraints; only if the power exercised were completely unilateral would normative restraints not obtain. There is therefore something other than unalloyed power—deployed structurally or processually—that is involved in an explanation and achievement of outcomes.

Normative considerations are only beginning to reenter discussions about negotiation, and the relation between structural and moral notions or equality as power and as justice, respectively, requires examination. Just as justice has some capacity to resist the imposition of power, power is likely to have some capacity to influence a determination of justice. Once again, there is a question of the boundary between two effects. Once again, too, there is a question about the universality vs. the particularity of definitions of justice, or, in more specific terms, the degree of equality and its terms or reference—how much equality, and equality of what? These questions are laid out in the presentations of both Cecilia Albin and I. William Zartman, the first arguing for a mixture of the two determining elements, power and justice, and the second for a more absolute consideration of the neglected element of justice. In fact, the two discussions are not that far apart.

While arguing for the universality of the role of justice, however, both discussions indicate the multiplicity of principles and references covered by the general concept. Thus, there is plenty of room for particularist inputs under the universal umbrella, in addition to the inputs derived from the parties' different power and interests. These elements are the bases of the difficulty in negotiating a common sense of justice to govern the ensuing deliberations. Sometimes, however, these notions of justice are so absolute as to be purposefully irreconcilable. This is the case of villains and pariahs. Some parties' sense of justice inspires their actions as true believers, putting them beyond the pale of other parties' sense of legitimacy. How can such cultural absolutes be overcome? How do parties defined as outlaws become redefined as legitimate negotiating partners (or at least adversaries) even when they do not change their defining behavior? This is the problem examined by Bertram Spector. Both redefinition of the actors and reframing of the issue are means for making matters negotiable.

Finally, beyond objective referents and notions of justice as aids and obstacles to negotiation are the subjective feelings of the parties. Since negotiations are conducted by humans, their emotions, including anger, are always present to some extent. These too are related to notions of justice: Parties get mad because of the other's injustice and their own righteousness. Sometimes it helps, sometimes it gets in the way. ("Never lose your temper," said Philip Jessup, "unless you intend to." [Zartman & Berman, 1982, p. 23]). Such considerations are not conceptual determinants of outcomes or even cultural idiosyncrasies but the most epiphenomenal of occurrences that, nonetheless, can have an important impact on the results. Fred Iklé highlights this effect in the last chapter.

IN THE END, AS THE BEGINNING

Thus the discussion about negotiation comes full circle, back to actors. In the round-the-word voyage, it has explored two crosscutting questions, about the roles of universal versus cultural inputs into negotiations and about the effectiveness of actions and explanations centered on actors, structures and processes, and values. The most important discovery at the end is that, in regard to the first, both universal patterns of behavior and their particularistic variations need to be taken into account. To amend the words (but follow the works) of Clifford Geertz (1983, p. 11), "[t]he question is . . . [indeed] whether art (or anything else) is universal; it is whether one can talk about West African carving, New Guinea palm-leaf painting, quattrocento picture making, and Moroccan versifying in such a way as to cause them to shed some sort of light on one another"—and one could for present purposes substitute "negotiation styles" for the four cited art forms—if only because the particularist variations cannot be discussed independent of an understood and underlying universality.

In regard to the second issue too, there are no trumps. Justice and its variations, in the face of power, is crucial to the production and analysis of negotiated outcomes. Structure matters, and channels process in its multiple options. Actors seek ends and pursue process within structures, each in their own way (within the limits imposed by the elements they encounter). None of these aspects of negotiation is dominant because all are necessary, to analysis as to practice—practice being all there is to analyze.

REFERENCES

Dupont, C., & Faure, G. O. 1991. "Process." In Kremenyuk, *International Negotiation*. San Francisco: Jossey-Bass.

Faure, G. O., & Rubin, J. Z., eds. 1994. *Culture & Negotiation*. Newbury Park, CA: Sage.

Geertz, C. 1984. *Local Knowledge*. New York: Basic Books.

Larson, D. 1988. "The Psychology of Reciprocity in International Relations." *Negotiation Journal*, IV (3), 281–302.

Rubin, J. Z., & Brown, R. 1975. *The Social Psychology of Bargaining and Negotiation*. New York: Academic Press.

Zartman, I. W. 1991. "Structure." In Kremenyuk, *International Negotiation*.

Zartman, I. W., ed. 1994. *International Multilateral Negotiation*. San Francisco: Jossey-Bass.

Zartman, I. W., & Berman, M. 1982. *The Practical Negotiator*. New Haven: Yale University Press.

Zartman, I. W., & Rubin, J. Z., eds. 1999. *Power and Negotiation*. Ann Arbor: University of Michigan Press.

PART I

ACTORS

CHAPTER 1

CULTURAL ASPECTS OF
INTERNATIONAL NEGOTIATION

GUY OLIVIER FAURE

Modern society with its technological development has brought men considerably closer to each other, suppressed distances, and increased opportunities for communicating and interacting. With the collapse of the ideological division of the world, the development of third world economies, the multiplication of foreign investments, and the huge growth of exchanges, the world economy has gone one step further in achieving a higher degree of integration. Even countries that were for so long out of the global trend are now strongly part of this movement. As a consequence, opportunities for negotiations dramatically increase. It also means that more and more individuals meet around the negotiation table and, thus, provide conditions for cultural encounters. Concerns for the common inheritage of our planet, such as scarce resource management, threats to the environment, and danger of wars, also contribute to getting people of all countries to meet and negotiate on related issues.

The growing interdependence between nations has increased the visibility of national cultures. In turn, two contrasting trends could be considered: either this interdependence will lead to relationships' transcending the bounds of culture or to people's being more sensitive towards the differentiating effects of culture. The enhanced global interdependence has also increased the likelihood of conflicts of all kinds, and the instruments of diplomacy and negotiations could become more useful than ever. Organizations in which negotiations are a basic activity, such as the European Union's Commission or the World Trade Organization secretariat, have already developed a kind of negotiating culture appropriate to handling thorny problems and conflicts that may arise among its members, paving the way for other cultural evolution. These among other reasons display why negotiation and culture are and will be more and more on the foreground of the international stage.

To understand a negotiation is to grasp the sense that actors attach to their moves and the meaning they give to their perceptions. Many events that take place in a negotiation cannot be explained by a monorational approach, for some negotiators may appear to act in a non-understandable way, to the extent that they may do the opposite of what should be in their own interest. First of all, negotiators are human beings, and they bring into the interaction all attributes linked to their human condition, including culture with its ambiguities and its complexity. Culture does influence negotiations, no doubt, in a number of cases. Carnevale (1995), considering research on negotiation in general, concludes that the traditional paradigm is "overly simplistic" because it does not come to grips with the social context. The current intellectual challenge is to grasp the quicksilver concept of culture, to analyze under which circumstances it becomes a key variable, and to understand how and with what kind of consequences this is done. The encounter between two cultures adds to this questioning: what may come out of this chemistry, of this "correlation of cultures"?

This search for the role of culture and its distinctive effects may bear another fruit than mere knowledge. It could help to build predictive instruments concerning negotiators' behaviors and provide means for a better control of the negotiation process and subsequently its outcome.

CULTURE AND CULTURES

Edouard Herriot, a French writer and politician, has defined culture as what remains when one has forgotten everything. This paradoxical proposition captures one of the most salient properties of culture: the fact that it is not a matter of substance but a way of thinking or acting of which the individual is usually unaware. If one wants to be more specific on the topic, culture could be defined as "a set of shared and enduring meanings, values, and beliefs that characterize national, ethnic, or other groups and orient their behavior" (Faure & Rubin, 1993). Culture may be understood as a system of widely accepted beliefs and assumptions that are transmitted from one generation to the next through a learning process. They pertain to people and their interaction, the relationship between them and their environment as well as the way people consider nature, space, time, or major events of one's life. Clearly people are constrained both by reality and by their perception of reality. They tend to act according to beliefs and values provided by their culture. "The role of culture is to answer questions even before they are raised" observes a French sociologist (Akoun, 1989). However, culture cannot just be defined as software in a computer, for it not only provides orientations for action but meanings as well, and it contributes to establish, assert, and preserve identity. In a short-term perspective, culture can be viewed as a kind of structural component conditioning human behavior, operating in a deterministic way, and leaving an enduring print on people. In a long-term perspective it is a dynamic social phenomenon that provides changes through the integration of new values and eviction of former ones.

From a qualitative viewpoint, Demorgon (1994) suggests a way to capture the significant aspects of a culture by combining three different perspectives: a synchronic approach defining the fundamental questions that express the real or symbolic system in action; a strategic approach focusing on people's projects while confronted with contextual events; and a diachronic approach aimed at explaining the production of sustainable cultural answers through history.

Hofstede (1980) distinguishes four basic dimensions of culture that may be used to classify the behavior of negotiators. One dimension concerns the power distance between actors. Another measures the tendency to avoid uncertainty, which is narrowly related to stress, stability, and desire for rules enforcement. A third dimension, individualism, deals with the relationship between the individual and the collectivity. The last dimension, masculinity, relates to ambition defined as the desire to achieve something and to earn more. The behavior of social actors such as negotiators may be ranked in each of these categories. In a comparative mode, national cultural profiles may be characterized with the help of these indicators. For instance, the Japanese have more respect for authority than the Israelis (with a score of 54 to 13), are much more collective minded than the Americans (46 to 91 on the scale of individualism), develop a much stronger tendency to avoid uncertainty than the Americans (92 to 46), and emphasize much more masculine values than the Swedes (95 to 5).

Language is a cultural product that may help to understand how cultural factors influence social action. A basic function of language is to structure reality and organize experience. Language provides categories to capture what is perceived and to turn it into thinking. Any particular language has its own set of categories to interpret reality. These categories may differ considerably from one society to another. For instance, the Eskimo have more than twenty words to differentiate among types of snow, while the Aztecs put snow, ice, and frost under the same broad denomination. European languages divide the spectrum into six basic colors, whereas the Jale of New Guinea recognize only two colors, warm and cold. Similarly, language also reflects society values and ways of behaving.

Culture leaves its print in the most unsuspected places. This is as true for the labeling of common objects as it is for the construction of very specific concepts. If we take, for instance, an object such as the octopus, its very name narrowly depends on the way it is perceived by each culture. In the Anglo-Saxon and the French cultures, the octopus is described by its shape: "eight feet" and "many feet." In the Chinese culture it is similarly called the "spider with long legs." Germans and Swedes put the focus on one of its functions—"ink fish," the fish that produces ink. In other cultures it is named according to a behavioral characteristic: in dialectical Arabic, the octopus is the "cunning," and in colloquial German, it is "the one that grasps." Names are based on perception. The cultural process behind labeling relies on the selection of significant traits and their interpretation, and the perception dramatically changes from one culture to another.

National ethnic cultures strongly contribute to shaping what is usually referred to as a national negotiating style by combining its own influence with that of history, of the political system, and of the geographic and economic position of the country.

Subcultures such as corporate culture may also influence negotiation behavior by providing their own norms of conduct, symbols, and meanings. A subculture may complement or contradict the national ethnic culture, for it can favor values that may be very different. Hofstede (1991) isolates six dimensions of organizational culture: process or results orientation, employee or job orientation, parochial or professional dominance, open or closed system, loose or tight control, normative or pragmatic tendencies. Martin (1992) distinguishes among three cultural approaches of an organization: an integration view referring to egalitarianism, homogeneity, harmony, well-being of the employees, consistency, and clarity; a differentiation perspective focusing on separation and conflict, contradiction, and cultural clusters within the organization; and a fragmentation view based on concepts such as multiplicity, flux of interpretations that do not coalesce, complexity, absence of visible order, and unpredictability. A corporate culture may also retain a transnational quality if, for instance, the company is a multinational enterprise operating in many countries at the same time.

Professional culture, a subculture narrowly linked with the activity of the negotiator in his own company where he can be, for instance, an engineer, a manager, a lawyer, an accountant, or a salesperson, functions in a similar way. The task itself provides people with specific norms of behavior and values that may complement or oppose the other subcultures involved in the interaction. The knowledge shared by all the members of a profession through education and field experience link people together by producing a common frame of reference. This elicits specific ways to structure problems and to deal with them.

Each professional culture tends to promote a particular set of values while practicing its skills and interacting with other cultures. Negotiating styles are narrowly connected with the way professionals see themselves. Lang (1993, p. 42) provides on this topic some significant observations: engineers see themselves as builders and problem-solvers, lawyers as defenders of justice, economists as planners and policy advisers, and politicians as defenders of the public interest.

In an organization, the extreme variety of professional cultures may turn it into a Tower of Babel if there is no integrative dimension at work such as, for instance, the organizational culture. Other groupings, such as generation, religion, social class, region, and gender, express as well specific cultures and may add their own touch to the cultural concert. It is extremely difficult to assess the relative influence of each of those subcultures in the negotiating behavior of the participants. The uncertainty grows when the cultural subsystems embody competing or conflicting values. What takes place, then, is a highly complex interplay between these various subcultures.

A number of international organizations have produced an organizational culture powerful enough to counterbalance the influence of national cultures. The main activity of its members can also entail similar effects. Thus, the European Union Commission has throughout decades created a genuine culture of its own, a combination of the organizational system, the legal background of most of its members, and their negotiation practice: a European negotiator culture.

The culture of a society evolves and changes over time. Its dynamics can be captured by defining culture not as a coherent and stable system of values but as a "bundle of cultural norms" that are subject to "dialectic tension" (Janosik, 1987). The outcome of the cultural management of these tensions may vary according to time and the people involved. Thus, Blaker (1977, cited by Janosik) distinguishes between two very different domestic ideals of conflict resolution within the Japanese culture, the "harmonious cooperation" and the "warrior ethic." The ideals are rather incompatible but at the same time they are strongly embedded in the Japanese tradition. According to the circumstance, one or the other can be legitimate. These tensions between values provide some internal dynamics for change, and as a consequence the related behaviors become much less predictable than they are in the Hofstede model.

In the same fashion, French culture has always been articulated around conflicting values such as liberty and equality. According to the period, one or the other would dominate, eliciting a change in priorities. This variation on the scale of preferences can be viewed as an indicator of the cultural dynamics.

RESEARCH ON CULTURAL ISSUES

Systematic comparisons between cultures are uneasier than it would appear a priori because behind similar words, there can be very different realities. For instance, the Chinese concept of negotiation does not strictly overlap with the Anglo-Saxon concept (Faure, 1995a). This observation also applies to exercises and simulations, for a cooperative game in one culture can be viewed as a competitive game in another. Cooperation and competition correspond to semantic sets that vary according to cultures. As a consequence, the implicit rules of the game will be understood differently by experimental subjects. It will, then, not be totally relevant in comparing performances.

Research on international negotiation is also influenced by the cultural conditions of its development. Ways to look at objects and ideas are culturalized, framed by given concepts and current problematiques. Are the scientific means we possess today adapted to identically study a negotiation carried out in Manhattan and in Timbuktu? Nothing is less certain.

The current bulk of research on cultural issues in negotiation is predominantly North American and demonstrates very little interest for non-U.S. literature on the subject (Dupont, 1994). Again culture comes into the picture to influence researchers on negotiation behaviors as well as negotiators' behaviors. As underlined by Weiss (1996), bodies of work on negotiation have developed outside the United States, for example in France. Indigenous research on international negotiation has even been carried out in unexpected places, such as China (Faure, 1995c).

Research on international negotiation focusing on cultural variables or integrating cultural components in its models and paradigms has developed only recently and is still largely in the making. Four main streams linked to specific approaches can be distinguished: the structural-processual approach, the behavioral approach, the cognitive-strategic approach, and the stages approach. The works fitting into these categories have been developed by a number of researchers. Some names will be attached to each of these approaches as an indication for reference to specific publications.

Inherited from the Sawyer and Guetzkow social-psychological model (1965) defining five categories of variables intervening in a negotiation at various stages, the structural-processual approach offers several constructions refining and adapting the initial model. The resulting analytical framework combines the main factors, be they contextual or situational, processual or behavioral, strategic or related to the outcome. Culture is either integrated among contextual factors (Fayerweather & Kapoor, 1976; Tung, 1988), or assumed as operating directly within each of the analytical categories (Faure & Rubin, 1993; Weiss, 1993).

A second type of approach focuses on the negotiator's behavior as a fundamental component in producing negotiation dynamics. According to the analytical tools and methodology used, two different traditions have been established. The first one aims at testing the impact of cultural elements on a number of behavioral variables in order to assess the reality of their influence (Carnevale, 1995; Graham, 1983, 1984, 1994; Kirkbride, Tang & Westwood, 1991). The second tradition is based on surveys and aims at describing the impact of culture on negotiators' behaviors and at analyzing its consequences (Campbell, 1988; De Paw, 1981; Frankenstein, 1986; Kimura, 1980). Most of the collected data comes from practitioners of intercultural negotiation who convey some of their personal experience by filling out, for instance, a questionnaire.

The cognitive-strategic approach aims to capture the main elements of a negotiator's action and to link them to the actor's cognition in order to explain the logics implemented during the negotiation. In comparing national cultural profiles of negotiators, Casse (1982) and Weiss and Stripp (1985) describe negotiation conception, cultural dispositions, and typical ways of acting for each negotiator. Focusing on one group, the Chinese, Faure (1998), basing his work on interviews and field observations, presents the major elements of the cognitive map of the Chinese negotiator and establishes a relation with the most typical strategic actions undertaken by this negotiator in terms of cultural causation. Thus, negotiation dynamics are captured, made explicit, and explained.

The fourth mode of structuration for international negotiation is the stages approach. Borrowing from Zartman and Berman (1984), Salacuse

(1991) divides the negotiation process into three phases, each having a particular objective and specific rationale. Satisfying the requirements of each stage will allow an effective adjustment of the different sequences and the reaching of an agreement.

CRITICAL VIEWS

Zartman (1993, p. 17) considers the current state of research on international negotiation and draws four observations, all fed on an obvious skepticism about the importance of culture in the understanding of negotiation processes: "culture is cited primarily for its negative effects. Yet even the best understanding of any such effect is tautological, its measure vague, and its role in the process basically epiphenomenal."

The first argument aims to oppose culturalists who claim that ignoring culture is a major cause of failure in negotiations. For Zartman, culturalists do not seriously substantiate their assertions, and in no case set out a culturally distinct process that could shed light on the matter. In addition, they are no more able to prove the reverse, that the successful end of a negotiation is due to the influence of the cultural aspects. Such a comment does make sense but far from rendering the hypothesis void, calls for more work in this area. Rubin and Brown (1975) already underlined the relative scarcity of scholarly works, assuming that the cause could be the methodological problems inherent in such studies. For instance, laboratory experiments concerning culture tend to have one negotiator for each side and one variable to test. In a real world negotiation between a Western company and its Chinese counterpart for the setting up of a joint venture, two to three Westerners face fifteen to thirty Chinese and discuss during several years over a hundred issues, putting on the stage dozens of variables. It becomes difficult to transfer findings extracted from the former situation to the latter. A number of researchers have recently carried out fieldwork and analysis to provide more insights on this topic, showing how shared norms and specific cultural combinations may facilitate negotiation, or how the creation of a professional negotiator's culture may strengthen the dynamic of the process (Elgström, 1990; Dupont, 1993; Lang, 1993; Kremenyuk, 1993).

Culture tends to be defined tautologically. When culture is related to independent variables, these variables end up being cultural too. If, for instance, social structure is claimed to determine culture, at the same time, it is a cultural product. In fact, as shown by Faure and Rubin (1993), culture relates to problems of different kinds—communication, perception and identity—that enable the researcher to formulate hypotheses on its relative importance as compared to other types of causation. What is at stake is not really the weakness of culture as an influencing factor but rather the complexity of the interaction process and its consequences.

Culture is a vague concept and if it is viewed as the sum of the behavioral traits of a collectivity, the significance of the "cultural basket" is never clearly defined. This observation is obviously quite accurate and relevant but does not lead to the conclusion that the influence of culture should be smaller than formerly hypothesized. The essential lesson to draw from this criticism is that research should be more narrowly focused on specific and well defined objects in order to avoid this problem in the future. Works such as those of Hofstede (1980, 1991), distinguishing four dimensions of culture, or those of Carnevale and Radhakrishnan (1994), using attitude scales to characterize a cultural trait, demonstrate possibilities and potentialities.

Zartman's last critique is that culture is epiphenomenal and, as a consequence, his statement does not substantially help in understanding the negotiation process itself. The epiphenomenal character assigned to culture is a judgment that is not backed by a demonstration. It bears the same weakness that was underlined in the first criticism, which stated that culturalists have never been able to prove what they assume. In fact, as underlined by Elgström (1994), who raised the issue of the "internal validity" of culture as the relevant determinant, it is extremely difficult to precisely assess the relative influence of each major variable operating in the negotiation process. Outcomes can also be determined by other variables, such as structural or process variables, and it would not make sense to turn culture into the unique explanatory variable of a whole and often complex process. As shown by Druckman et al. (1976) in a study of bargaining behavior of Indians, Argentineans, and Americans, culture does matter in determining behavior but other factors such as age, gender, and environment also play an important role, paving the way to multicausal models. In addition, what is often observed is that culture's effect on negotiation is subtle; this subtlety, however, does not reduce the importance of culture but only makes it less visible. Again, it only calls for more attention, more research.

Another strong objection to the importance of culture in negotiation is raised by a number of psychologists who tend to consider that individual variables are by far the most important, and that personality is the leading force in the interaction process. The answers to this can only be found in real case studies and might even provide a different answer each time. In addition, and this restriction cannot be easily lifted, it is sometimes very difficult to draw a line between cultural variables and personality variables. If we consider, for instance, risk-taking behavior, it may belong to both sets, and only a specific investigation within a case study will enable the researcher to draw an accurate conclusion.

HOW CULTURE IMPACTS ON NEGOTIATIONS

"What is it that cannot quite be seen but follows us around constantly? . . . The answer . . . is culture" (Faure & Rubin, 1993, p. xi). The subtle influence of culture has to be grasped in an organized way to disclose some of its content. Its distinctive effects can be related to the key components of a negotiation: actors, structure, strategies, process, and outcome.

ACTORS

First, culture is brought into the negotiation by the actors, be they individuals, groups, or organizations. It conditions how they view the negotiation, the kind of game they perceive to be going on. Is it, for instance, a power confrontation, a cooperative exercise, a debate, a ritual, a human venture, etc.? For Americans negotiation is mainly a give-and-take exercise, but for the Japanese it is far from that (Kimura, 1980, p. 65). Negotiation is affected by actors' stereotypes of others, intentions, and values. How negotiators understand the topic under consideration is influenced by culture. For instance, Americans will view a set of issues as a list of items to be discussed sequentially, while the Japanese will see the same set as a system of interconnected elements to be approached in a holistic way (Graham & Sano, 1984, p. 29).

Issues may also carry a symbolic value that defy simple, rational understanding. Underlying symbolic meanings, memories from past experiences, and occasionally historical memory may strongly influence behaviors and become true explanatory variables.

Ethics are also brought into the interaction by the negotiators themselves. The cultural line drawn between what should not be done, or tolerated, varies from one culture to another. In some cultures, people easily resort to means of action such as lies, deception, or bribes that are considered absolutely unacceptable in other cultures.

Culture does not need to have a visible impact, or be consciously perceived to be influential. Moreover, to belong to a highly dominant culture may amplify this phenomenon of cultural insensitivity. Often negotiators who belong to nondominant cultures show higher sensitivity to this dimension and see it as a major component of the relation.

STRUCTURE

Structural components of a negotiation are not culture free. External constraints, such as the legal framework and the organizational setting of a negotiation, are social products. Other typical structural factors include the number of parties involved, the number of issues at stake, the distribution of power between the parties, and the degree of transparency of the process for external observers such as the media.

Again, culture may influence some of the structural aspects. For instance, the number of negotiators representing one party in the negotiation is largely related to cultural habits. In business negotiations in China, a foreign team negotiates not only with its Chinese counterpart but indirectly with other parties such as the local authorities and government as well. This displays how Chinese culture and society imprint on the negotiation structure.

Concerning power distribution, culture tends to legitimize some types of situational power and to disavow others. In China, it is quite legitimate for the strongest to impose his own views. In the former USSR, the party could not be wrong. In traditional African villages, the eldest always has the final word in a discussion. Such a priori judgments will influence the whole process by weighing on negotiators' behaviors.

The organizational culture of an international institution provides another example of culture becoming a structural component, for instance, in the way the institution deals with decision making or conflict handling.

STRATEGY

Negotiating is a global action, and the overall orientation given by an actor to achieve his goal is a strategy. Strategic choices are led by values which, in turn, relate to culture. In some cultures action will be direct, conflict widely accepted, and problems met head on; in others, action will be indirect, conflict not openly acknowledged, and problems only dealt with through allusions. Russians, for instance, tend to negotiate from a position of strength and do not mind resorting to aggressive tactics such as threats, whereas the Japanese are highly reluctant about direct confrontation (Kimura, 1980).

Goal setting is also, to some extent, influenced by culture. For instance, Westerners are strongly driven by the idea of fairness and respect to basic principles, rules, etc. The Chinese are much more concerned with preserving harmony among the participants of a negotiation or saving face than with abiding by rules and abstract principles, and sometimes even act at the expenses of these rules.

Culture may also influence the way negotiators operate to reach an agreement. Some cultures, such as the French or German, favor a deductive approach, looking first for acceptable principles, then applying them to concrete issues. Other cultures, such as the American, would rather adopt an inductive approach, dealing pragmatically with encountered difficulties, while the underlying principles will become discernible only in the end.

In multilateral negotiations, culture may have its word to say when building coalitions. Some actors will be willing to join forces with people who have common interests regardless of who they are, others will only cooperate with people who share the same values. In the first case, one could speak about a Machiavellian culture, and in the second case, of a principled culture.

PROCESS

The core of the negotiation, that is the interaction between the actors, is made up of moves or tactics of all kinds designed to divide a resource, exchange information and concessions, or create new options.

These behaviors are value related, and what can be seen as legitimate in one culture can be totally rejected in another culture. For instance, not sticking to one's word or deceiving the other party about a deadline can be viewed from very different angles, for being polite is in some cultures more important than telling the truth. Bluffing and issuing threats can be seen in some societies as a common tool of the negotiator. In other societies it is a sufficient reason for breaking off the relationship.

The way behaviors are perceived and understood is also highly cultural. A significant example of this is described in a letter sent at the beginning of the century by a Chinese man traveling in the West to one of his friends. "I have seen two white men meeting on the deck of a ship. Each one offers his right hand and holds the other's. I thought they were trying to throw each other into the water, for I believe they were engaging themselves in a fight. In fact, it was their way to greet each other: they were friends!" (Chih, 1962, p. 203). Thus, it was inconceivable for a Chinese person to see shaking hands as an expression of politeness or friendship. It is culture that provides the meaning of the gestures.

Communication is another major component of the negotiation process. Its effectiveness may be considerably affected by cross-cultural dissimilarities. When communication is indirect, content ambiguous, and feedback scarce, negotiation has to become mainly a decoding exercise in which culture and context provide the two main keys to an accurate perception of signals sent by the other party. Differences do not only lie in what is said but in how it is said and also in the social context of the discussions. Drawing conclusions from a field study on U.S./Japanese negotiations, Graham (1993, p. 139) observes that "Americans are unable to read Japanese expressions and wrongly describe Japanese as expressionless."

The meaning of the Japanese smile is an interesting and significant case with which to illustrate the complexity of the task. A Japanese smile can be perceived as a mask of politeness, an opaque wall behind which observation of the other takes place. It can express cooperation or denial, joy or anger, certainty or total ignorance, trust or distrust, pleasure or embarrassment. Only some knowledge of the Japanese culture and the current context of the smile may enable access to its real meaning. It is a necessary access in a negotiation where signals are often scarce.

Cross-cultural differences in the description of time may also affect the negotiation process. In the West, time is conceived as a commodity that has a cost and should be used with parsimony. In contrast, in the East, time is viewed as an unlimited resource like the air we breathe. As a consequence, time pressure will have very little effect on Asian negotiation behavior. As it has been said by a Chinese negotiator to his Western counterpart who was pushing him to quickly come to an agreement: "China has been able to do without your technology for 5,000 years. We can wait for a few more years."

Humor may be used as a facilitation device but what is funny in one culture may be viewed as nonsense or as a quite unpleasant remark in another culture. Differences existing between Voltairian irony and the form of criticism conventionally called "English humor," are more than a matter of shade, but reveal intellectual constructs of a very distinct nature.

OUTCOME

The outcome is the function of the other key elements of negotiation and, as a consequence, the influence of culture on these elements will indirectly bear upon it. As it happens with power, culture may under certain circumstances impact on the outcome. Culture operates a selection among the various types of possible agreements, modifies the zone of potential agreements by restructuring it according to compatible combinations, and by doing so changes the global value of the game. There are also more direct linkages between cultures and outcome. For instance, some cultures prefer an agreement in which each word has been carefully assessed, others may do with more loosely formulated agreements. Thus, a joint venture contract in Japan conceived by the Western side can be several hundred pages long, whereas the Japanese would be satisfied with ten pages. What is included in the outcome is not always written down, and varies according to cultures. Besides the usual provisions, numbers, and figures that are mentioned in a business contract, Westerners would consider the time spent (or saved) reaching the agreement part of the outcome. Japanese would systematically put trust and quality of the relationship as major components of the outcome.

Culture may also influence how the parties interpret the outcome. In some societies, an agreement is a final decision carved in marble that has to be strictly implemented. In others, an agreement is a written paper that was valid the day it was signed and that may be modified if the external conditions prevailing at the time of the signing have changed. For a Chinese, for instance, signing a contract is not closing a deal but substantiating a relationship.

To be concluded, agreements normally have to meet some norm of fairness. Perceived fairness can be narrowly linked with cultural differences (Roth et al., 1991). Behind such a concept one can find different, sometimes conflicting principles of justice narrowly connected with social values. Some cultures would favor equality of concessions or gains as a basic norm of fairness; others would, for instance, prefer unequal gains distributed according to the specific needs of each party.

Once an agreement has been reached, the challenge is to make sure both parties will respect its provisions. In the Western mind, this is done through institutional mechanisms such as courts and international arbitration. In some cultures, these mechanisms are viewed as a signal of distrust, and additional negotiation or mediation is preferred.

Concerning the substance of the agreement, the Westerner would consider abiding by the mentioned principles as an absolute necessity whereas the Chinese would pay more attention to the consequences of not respecting what has been decided and consider the related cost as the first criteria in making a decision. If the latter were himself victim of someone who did not implement all the terms of a contract, he would first assess the losses and, if they were relatively small, remain silent to avoid looking mean and losing face.

CULTURE'S EFFECTS ON NEGOTIATION

During World War II, a small group of American officers were taken prisoner by the Japanese army. They were kept in wooden barracks on a small island in the middle of the Pacific Ocean. One evening, conscious about the humiliation that these American officers had to stand, their jailers discreetly left some razors at their reach. The next morning, to the surprise of the Japanese, the officers had restored their dignity in a very unexpected way, by carefully shaving themselves. Whether true or fictitious, such a story sharply illustrates the influence of culture on proper behavior within a certain set of constraints.

Culture impacts on negotiation in a number of ways and this leads to consequences at four different levels: cognition, belief, behavior, and identity. As underlined by Rubin and Sander (1991), some of the most important effects of culture are felt even before the negotiation starts. This is typically the case with these four levels where, silently and unconsciously for the actors, culture leaves its invisible trail.

Cognition relates to ways of perceiving and understanding what is at stake in a negotiation: money, power, technology, status, goods, face concerns, etc. Cognition also relates to how the negotiation itself is perceived—the nature of the game that the actors are playing: a test of strength, a relationship, a search for justice, a palabra, a game of seduction, a construction exercise, etc. Cognition also concerns what one party knows about the other party. Driving perceptions include stereotypes, historical memory, past personal experiences, and other factors. Stereotyping by bringing together various traits reduces cognitive complexity to simple terms, which are easier to handle during the preparation of the action.

Cognitive aspects are essential for framing the problems and subsequently making choices in terms of strategy and behaviors. When Magellan, in the year 1521, made the first circumnavigation of the world, reaching an island in the Pacific Ocean, he met the king and offered him presents. He wanted to establish relationships on an equal basis and explained that he looked at him as a brother, but the king sharply objected to the idea and told him he could only be considered a father. In this early cultural encounter, what was at stake was precisely the framing of the relationship to be developed. In a current example of Westerners doing business in Japan, what is viewed as a conflictual negotiation by the Japanese may not be seen as such by the Americans. Similarly, what is often seen by American negotiators as a delaying device can simply be for a Japanese the time needed to get to know the other party.

The general approach to the negotiation is typically conditioned by actors' cultures. The Cartesian-analytical approach implemented in the West can be opposed to the holistic approach shared by the Japanese and Chinese. The first approach aims to segment the problem and solve the difficulties as and when required; the second tends to assess the entire situation and to learn how to accommodate the relative influence of the many forces involved (Redding, 1990).

Language, a classical cultural product, is a major instrument in cognitive activities. Problems can only be defined within existing categories as has already been emphasized. If your only tool is a hammer, then every problem is a nail (Faure, 1995a). Labeling is, thus, a major cultural activity that conditions and, to some extent, structures social action.

The second level, that of beliefs, puts forth a set of values coming from the cultural background of the negotiator. These values, stating what is desirable and what is not, operate as instrumental goals and directly orient the behavior of the actors. If only national cultures were at play, as a set of shared values, culture would generate a highly predictable pattern of negotiating behavior. With the corporate culture and the professional culture, the assumption of a homogeneity loses its relevance, and common values become more difficult to discern. In turn, combined with personality variables within strategic behaviors, the final attitude would become much less predictable, if at all.

If cognition deals with the type of game to be played and beliefs deal with what should be achieved in this game, behaviors concern the way to play. This is done in selecting a range of acceptable behaviors and defensible arguments. Tactics such as "take it or leave it" or issuing direct threats are part of the American culture. The Asian-Pacific cultures would better be illustrated by the use, for instance, of the "salami tactic" (nibbling) or just keeping silent and not answering. Each culture has some sense of what level of risk should be taken, and this level can differ widely between cultures (Faure, 1995b). The uncertainty-avoidance scale, on which Hofstede (1980) ranks 53 cultures, goes for instance from 8 to 112. Behaviors as part of the experience gained in the course of the negotiation may, in turn, influence cognition. Cultural learning is an ongoing process throughout the interaction.

A number of publications address the behavioral aspects of negotiation, emphasizing cultural differences under the heading of "negotiating styles."

They tend to describe the typical ways in which negotiators behave when they are, for instance, Japanese (Van Zandt, 1970), Chinese (Pye, 1982), and Arab (Alghanim, 1976). Conclusions are sometimes drawn in terms of advise to the practitioner such as "do not call your Chinese counterpart by his first name," "while sitting in a tent do not show the sole of your shoes to your Arab counterpart," "do not give a Japanese a slap on the shoulder to show him sympathy," and "when you meet a Latin-American negotiator, do not suggest getting to work before getting well acquainted." These rather anecdotal observations may sometimes be useful to the practitioner but bear limitations as they do not really help to understand the culture of the negotiator across the table, if ever there is a table.

Identity is the last level of intervention, the deepest and the most difficult to deal with. It can be critical in some negotiations, such as those between Israelis and Palestinians over Jordanian river waters (Lowi & Rothman, 1993), or between Northern-Arab Sudanese and Southern African Sudanese over the Jonglei canal (Deng, 1993). When identity is not built by differentiation but mainly through opposition to the other party, any change likely to improve the conditions for a settlement may appear as a betrayal. Modifying the elements that comprise one's identity is a denial of oneself and can be viewed, at the symbolic level, as a destructive attempt. Difficult to grasp, highly complex to manipulate, identity aspects remain the untouchable core of culture.

IMPLICATIONS FOR PRACTITIONERS

Culture may operate in many ways in the negotiation process, but mainly it acts as an obstacle or a facilitator. Salacuse (1993) describes the practical effects of culture as being those of either a weapon, a fortress, or a bridge. If both parties' cultures are seen as incompatible, each negotiator may perceive the other's culture as a weapon aimed against his own values and beliefs, and may become extremely defensive. One common way to resist this threat is to build a cultural fortress by, for instance, demonizing the other side on the basis of alleged cultural traits. The culturally assertive weapon of one party as it is perceived, elicits the cultural fortress of the other party. The more assertive the former appears, the more defensive the latter becomes. This weapon-and-fortress phenomenon is often triggered by an attitude interpreted as a sign of cultural arrogance. For instance, the suggestion from an American to structure a negotiation in a very specific way because it is "the way it is done in America" may not be taken as a constructive proposal. Far from being convinced, the other party may become highly defensive and start building up his fortress.

Culture has too often been described as a barrier and used as an explanatory variable for failures. Besides its scapegoat function, it definitely can serve as a bridge between the two negotiating sides. One party can rely on certain elements of the other's culture to start building that bridge. From this common basis, these shared values, the overall relationship can benefit from this kind of synergy. For instance, when parties spend a long time negotiating together in international organizations such as the European Union, they develop a common negotiation culture made up of well-understood symbols and shared habits that could be attributed to a mixing between professional and organizational cultures (Lang, 1993; Hofstede, 1989; Sjöstedt, 1994). This new culture can be quite effective in handling divergences because they are framed in a similar way.

Building a bridge is, to some extent, a risky venture, and one has to feel secure when beginning this task, although it's not always easy. To this regard, learning about the other party's culture is a way of paying respect and avoiding a defensive response. Thus, it paves the road to establishing complementarities and, eventually, enriches the joint potential.

From a very different angle, addressing the prescriptive issues, Weiss (1994) has designed eight cultural strategies among which the negotiator may choose according to his level of familiarity with another's culture. Among these strategies are employing an agent, adapting to the counterpart's script, inducing the counterpart to follow one's own script, and transcending either home culture by improvising a new script "effect symphony."

Implicit in both approaches is the idea that culture is not just an external constraint negotiators have to bear, but an active element that can take a conclusive part in the reaching of an agreement if actors can make a proper use of it.

CONCLUSION

International negotiation is a cross-cultural exploration, but, as underlined by Hall, all cross-cultural exploration begins with the experience of being lost. Fortunately, it is a long lasting process, and one has opportunities to find his or her way again. This ambivalent activity leads to the grasping of more knowledge but at the same time, may naturally elicit doubts, an unavoidable psychological consequence of cultural investigation. International negotiation gets people around the same table and, thus, does more than confront cultural differences by producing a combination that should be made as effective as possible. On each side of the table, national culture and organizational culture unite while professional cultures divide. Across the table, national and organizational cultures divide whereas professional cultures establish bridges. The overall outcome is more than a minimum sound, a kind of smallest common denominator, it is a global cultural orchestration with richness and variety in the sounds that are produced. In this process, to lift barriers means to clear up misunderstandings and misperceptions, to reduce discrepancies in the ways of framing a common problem. Eventually a major task is to avoid the "Babel effect" (Gauthey, 1995), which, described in the Bible (Genesis 10) as a total confusion of languages leading to paralysis, sharply illustrates the fact that generalized incomprehension can only produce failures.

The constructive orientation can, on the contrary, generate a communicational phenomenon, a kind of highly productive multicultural interaction. In the day-to-day negotiations, building bridges is already developing the embryo of a common culture but without giving up one's own identity. Instead of looking first for what is different and probably wrong with the other, the point is rather to look for complementarities and synergies; to turn the cultural encounter into a source of creativity to feed negotiation dynamics; and, as a consequence, to raise the level of efficiency of the overall system.

REFERENCES

Akoun, A. 1989. *L'illusion sociale.* Paris: P.U.F.

Alghanim, K. 1976. "How to Do Business in the Middle East." *Management Review,* 65 (8).

Blaker, M. 1977. *Japanese International Negotiating Style.* New York: Columbia University Press.

Campbell, N. 1989. *A Strategic Guide to Equity Joint Ventures.* Oxford: Pergamon Press.

Carnevale, P. 1995. "Property, Culture, and Negotiation." In Kramer & Messick, *Negotiation as a Social Process.* Newbury Park, CA: Sage.

Carnevale, P., & Radhakrishnan, P. 1994. *Group Endowment and the Theory of Collectivism.* Urbana-Champaign: University of Illinois, Department of Psychology.

Casse, P. 1982. *Training for the Multicultural Manager.* Washington, DC: Society of Intercultural Education, Training, and Research.

Chih, A. 1962. *L'Occident chrétien vu par les Chinois (1870–1900).* Paris: P.U.F.

Cohen, R. 1993. "An Advocate's View." In Faure & Rubin, *Culture and Negotiation*.

De Pauw, J. 1981. *U.S. - Chinese Trade Negotiations*. New York: Praeger.

Demorgon, J. 1994. "Histoires et cultures." *Intercultures* (Paris), 25/26.

Deng, F. 1993. "Northern and Southern Sudan: the Nile." In Faure & Rubin, *Culture and Negotiation*.

Druckman, D. et al. 1976. "Cultural Differences in Bargaining Behavior: India, Argentina, and the U.S." *Journal of Conflict Resolution*, 20 (3).

Dupont, C. 1993. "Switzerland, France, Germany, the Netherlands: the Rhine." In Faure & Rubin, *Culture and Negotiation*.

Dupont, C. 1994. *La négociation: conduite, théorie, applications*. Paris: Dalloz.

Elgström, O. 1990. "Norms, Culture, and Cognitive Problems in Foreign Aid Negotiations." *Negotiation Journal*, 6 (2).

Elgström, O. 1994. "National Culture and International Negotiations." *Cooperation and Conflict*, 29 (3).

Faure, G. O. 1995a. "Conflict Formulation: The Cross Cultural Challenge." In Bunker and Rubin, *Conflict, Cooperation, and Justice*. San Francisco: Jossey-Bass.

Faure, G. O. 1995b. "Nonverbal Negotiation in China." *Negotiation Journal*, 11 (1).

Faure, G. O. 1995c. "Research on Negotiation in China." *PIN Points* (Laxenburg, Austria), No. 8.

Faure, G. O. 1998. "Negotiation: The Chinese Concept." *Negotiation Journal*, 14 (2).

Faure, G. O. 1999. "Joint Ventures in China and their Negotiation." In Kremenyuk & Sjöstedt, *International Economic Negotiation*. London: Edward Elgar.

Faure, G. O., & Rubin, J., eds. 1993. *Culture and Negotiation*. Newbury Park, CA: Sage.

Fayerweather, J., & Kapoor, A. 1976. *Strategy and Negotiation for the International Corporation*. Cambridge, MA: Ballinger.

Frankenstein, J. 1986. "Trends in Chinese Business Practices: Changes in the Beijing Wind." *California Management Review*, 29 (1).

Gauthey, F. 1995. "Au-delà de la malédiction de Babel." *A.N.D.C.P. Personnel*, No. 360.

Graham, J. 1983. "Brazilian, Japanese, and American Business Negotiations." *Journal of International Business Studies*, Spring/Summer.

Graham, J. 1984. "A Comparison of Japanese and American Business Negotiations." *International Journal of Research in Marketing*, 1.

Graham, J. 1993. "The Japanese Negotiating Style: Characteristics of a Distinct Approach." *Negotiation Journal*, 9 (2).

Graham, J., Mintu, A., & Rodgers, W. 1994. "Explorations of Negotiation Behavior in Ten Foreign Cultures Using a Model Developed in the United States." *Management Science*, 40 (1).

Graham, J., & Sano, Y. 1984. *Smart Bargaining: Doing Business with the Japanese*. Cambridge, MA: Ballinger.

Hall, E. 1976. *Beyond Culture*. New York: Doubleday.

Hofstede, G. 1980. *Culture's Consequences*. Beverly Hills, CA: Sage.

Hofstede, G. 1989. "Cultural Predictors of National Negotiating Styles." In Mautner-Markhof, *Processes of International Negotiation*. Boulder, CO: Westview.

Hofstede, G. 1991. *Culture and Organizations: Software of the Mind*. London: McGraw-Hill.

Janosik, R. 1987. "Rethinking the Culture-Negotiation Link." *Negotiation Journal*, 3.

Kimura, H. 1980. "Soviet and Japanese Negotiation Behavior: The Spring 1977 Fisheries Talks." *Orbis*, 24 (1).

Kremenyuk, V. 1993. "A Pluralistic Viewpoint." In Faure & Rubin, *Culture and Negotiation*.

Lang, W. 1993. "A Professional's View." In Faure & Rubin, *Culture and Negotiation*.

Lowi, M., & Rothman, J. 1993. "Arabs and Israelis: The Jordan River." In Faure & Rubin, *Culture and Negotiation*.

Martin, J. 1992. *Cultures in Organizations*. New York: Oxford University Press.

Redding, G. 1990. *The Spirit of Chinese Capitalism*. Berlin: W. de Gruyter.

Roth, A. et al. 1993. "Bargaining and Market Behavior in Jerusalem, Ljubljana, Pittsburgh, and Tokyo: An Experimental Study." *American Economic Review*, 81.

Rubin, J., & Brown, B. 1975. *The Social Psychology of Bargaining and Negotiation*. New York: Academic Press.

Rubin, J., & Sander, F. 1991. "Culture, Negotiation, and the Eye of the Beholder." *Negotiation Journal*, 7.

Salacuse, J. 1991. *Making Global Deals*. Boston: Houghton Mifflin.

Salacuse, J. 1993. "Implications for Practitioners." In Faure & Rubin, *Culture and Negotiation*.

Sawyer, J., & Guetzkow, H. 1965. "Bargaining and Negotiation in International Relations." In Kelman, *International Behavior: A Social-Psychological Analysis*. New York: Holt, Rinehart and Winston.

Sjöstedt, G. 1994. "Negotiating the Uruguay Round of the G.A.T.T." In Zartman, *International Multilateral Negotiation*. San Francisco: Jossey-Bass.

Tung, R. 1982. *U.S. - China Trade Negotiations*. New York: Pergamon Press.

Weiss, S. 1993. "Analysis of Complex Negotiations in International Business: The RBC Perspective." *Organization Science*, 4 (2).

Weiss, S. 1996. "International Business Negotiations Research: Bricks, Mortar, and Prospects." In Punnett & Shenkar, *Handbook for International Management Research*. Cambridge, MA: Blackwell Business, 1996.

Weiss, S., & Stripp, W. 1985. *Negotiating with Foreign Businesspersons*. Working Paper 85–6, New York University Graduate School of Business Administration.

Zartman, I. W. 1993. "A Skeptic's View." In Faure & Rubin, *Culture and Negotiation*.

Zartman, I. W., & Berman, M. 1982. *The Practical Negotiator*. New Haven: Yale University Press.

CHAPTER 2

Japan Negotiates with the United States on Rice: "No, No, a Thousand Times, No!"*

MICHAEL BLAKER

Introduction

Negotiating skills are one key facet of the multifaceted art of diplomacy. Scholarly studies of Japanese and other national negotiating "styles" rest on three basic arguments: first, that a particular country's diplomatic representatives' style of negotiating is identifiable; second, that these identifiable negotiating styles differ; and, third, that these identifiable, country-specific styles significantly affect negotiating outcomes.

While particular bargaining moves are not unique to any country, the mix of moves provides a distinctive composite portrait for any country's diplomatic behavior. Japan is no exception. Enough has been written by Japanese and other analysts to permit one to offer a portrait of the Japanese style of negotiation. The behavior—what may be labeled "coping"—is consistently evident both at the loftier plateau of diplomacy and down in the trenches at the level of direct negotiations (Blaker, 1993).

"Coping" captures the go-with-the-flow essence of the Japanese bargaining approach: cautiously appraising the external situation; methodically weighing and sorting each and every option; deferring action on contentious issues; crafting a domestic consensus on the situation faced; making minimal adjustments or concessions in order to block, circumvent, or dissolve criticism; and adapting to a situation with minimum risk. This negotiating style mirrors the vaunted low-key, low-profile, risk-minimizing, defensive, damage-limiting patterns in Japan's overall foreign-relations conduct.

Ever since Commodore Matthew Perry's "black ships" sailed into Edo Bay in 1853, piercing the curtain of Japan's centuries of virtual isolation from the outside world, matters of diplomatic negotiations have divided the nation and stirred controversy and crisis among its leaders. Japanese newspapers have scrutinized in microscopic detail any topic or official decision relating to the government's handling of negotiations. Japanese leaders have regarded diplomacy and diplomatic negotiations as formidable, face-threatening undertakings. They have trod warily when diplomatic problems led to the negotiating table. The Japanese themselves dwell upon the hardships and complexities of diplomatic negotiations. Most Japanese today would no doubt still agree with a remark made by Okubo Toshimichi[1] over a century ago. "Dealing with foreigners," the Meiji-era statesman observed, "can be a troublesome and difficult task."

Drawing from the extensive literature on the topic, we can identify the "top ten" characteristics of Japanese bargaining behavior:

1. use of vague, ambiguous, noncommittal language in framing negotiating proposals;
2. heavy stress on process-related elements of negotiation (such as person-to-person communication and back-channel contacts);
3. few initiatives, especially on political, security, and controversial economic topics;
4. avoidance of front-line, assertive, visible, leadership positions and roles;
5. slowness in reaching negotiating positions, after lengthy deliberations among domestic interests affected by subject(s) to be discussed;
6. preference for adaptive, short-range, ad-hoc, case-by-case approaches over comprehensive, integrated plans;
7. preference for bridging, mediating, go-between role when faced with highly adversarial situations;
8. concessions presented slowly, in small increments;
9. significant compromises offered only when conditions have become highly politicized and a "crisis" stage has been reached; and
10. relatively great weight given to instruments bolstering commitment to Japanese positions as against arguments and techniques to persuade or convince others to change their views or positions.

Based on the sheer consistency of these and other traits over time, Japanese negotiating style has lent itself to a variety of characterizations. "Probe, push, panic, and postpone" is one. "Silence, smiling, and sleeping" is another. "Deny, delay, defer, deadlock, and discontinue" could be yet another. While Japanese analysts are uncomfortable with the rather mocking tone of such descriptions, few have disputed their general accuracy in portraying the behavior of Japanese negotiators.

FACTORS SHAPING THE "JAPANESE" NEGOTIATING STYLE

Attitudes, Psychology, and Cultural Traits (Berton, 1996)
Most relevant to Japan's negotiating style is a core of beliefs widely shared among Japanese—notably an uneasiness toward the outside world, an ultra-sensitivity to foreign opinions and criticism, and a near-obsessive concern with Japan's weakness and vulnerability.

Such verities are less than eternal and at best have loose connections to observable behavior in international negotiations. Could the much-vaunted, culturally rooted precept of *wa* (harmony) tell us why Japanese negotiators have stood firmly against compromise on the Northern Islands for nearly half a century? Are not other countries' government officials just as inclined as Tokyo's to keep their true feelings *(honne)* to themselves when they deliver official statements for public consumption?

Political Institutions and Processes
In addressing government-to-government negotiating behavior, variables relating to domestic Japanese political processes, institutions, and decision making exert a direct, significant, and demonstrable impact upon visible behavior. Japan is a highly pluralistic society. Reaching public policy decisions is an intensely combative, heavily bureaucratized, consensus-driven process of accommodating diverse interests and viewpoints. Typically, negotiating decisions are reached ("arranged" is the preferred term) from the bottom up, via informal, give-and-take, consensus-based processes stressing personal relationships and networks.

A Second-Tier Power in a Defensive Position
In addition to the direct and indirect impact of domestic political structures and processes, Japanese negotiating style is heavily conditioned by Japan's position as a secondary or second-tier power in global affairs. Japan's rapid postwar economic growth raised foreign expectations that Japan could, would, and should play an enlarged international role. These expectations

turned into demands during the late 1970s and 1980s that Japan act in ways thought commensurate with its economic superpower status.

Beginning in the occupation era, the pattern of Japanese defensive, reactive, minimalist diplomacy was established, and it made sense at the time. After all, what choice did Japanese officials have? When asked to "jump," they would reply, "How far?" When asked "What does Japan want to do?" they would answer, "What do you want us to do?"

Throughout the postwar era, Japanese representatives have negotiated with foreign counterparts who have asked Japan to do more, take action, participate more actively, and compromise, or face the consequences. Faced with such demands, the Japanese side has sought to limit, avoid, circumvent, weaken, blunt, or reduce the level of these demands. Typically, Japan's negotiators have worked from a borrowed or reflected bargaining agenda—an imported wish list drawn up by other governments. This study emphasizes the impact of Japan's defensive position in negotiations.

The analytical difficulty of rating the effectiveness of the Japanese bargaining approach is highlighted in negotiations to open Japan's domestic market to foreign-grown rice. Over seven long years, the Japanese government resisted foreign demands to sell rice in Japan. Japanese negotiating behavior was quintessentially "Japanese" on rice. Moving from an adamant "not a single grain of foreign rice will enter Japan" position, the Japanese side gradually succumbed to a combination of American and GATT-centered multilateral pressure, finally accepting a "minimum access" or "partial access" formula for step-by-step increases in Japanese rice imports. Was the final outcome a Japanese bargaining victory? Was it a defeat? Objectively, the Japanese government had conceded in principle but had compromised only a little on substance. At bottom, when the dust had settled, the much-maligned Japanese approach seemed to have worked.

Or had it? If Japan's core concern is averting or containing foreign criticism, then its negotiating "victory" on rice was outweighed by its obvious "defeat" in the ongoing battle to dodge foreign flak. Just as Japan's whopping $13 billion contribution to the U.S.-led forces in the Persian Gulf was lost in the wave of anti-Japanese criticism of Tokyo's reluctant, "too little, too late" response, Japan's stubbornness to budge on the rice issue invited heavy, and probably lasting, foreign resentment and criticism.

No matter whether one rates Japanese negotiating performance positively or negatively, it is interesting that the behavior is capable of such sharply divergent interpretations. Tokyo University political scientist Inoguchi Takashi (Inoguchi, 1993) labels Japanese diplomacy as iridescent (*tamamushiiro*). It is this iridescence which enables observers to see what they choose to see, to interpret the behavior in ways they prefer, depending on their mood swings or endorphin levels at a given moment.

In assessing Japanese negotiating behavior and performance, this study seeks to define *Japanese* objectives. After all, should not Japanese negotiators be judged on the basis of *Japanese* goals? While this may seem an obvious point, it is not, because Japanese goals are typically opaque and therefore must be inferred from behavior. Moreover, as mentioned above, Japan is typically on the defensive side in negotiations, and the Japanese side deals with an imported agenda. Also, even though Japanese negotiators often draw criticism for failing to take initiatives, to articulate Japanese positions clearly, to assume political risks, or to respond quickly to changes in the bargaining situation, one may well ask whether or not the Japanese were interested in such matters at all. Identifying Japan's "medium of exchange" is therefore critical to grasping correctly the Japanese style.

THE RICE NEGOTIATIONS

THE SUBJECT OF RICE

For Japan, rice is a near-sacred product, deeply embedded in history, culture, economics, politics, and symbolism. For the Japanese, rice is "our Christmas tree," and rice-producing land is reverently called "our holy land." In Japanese eyes, rice—far more than beef, citrus fruit, or textiles—represents the ultimate non-negotiable market-access topic. "Not a single grain of foreign rice shall ever enter Japan," was the solemn vow of Japanese politicians of all stripes, backed by public opinion, the press, the business community, academics, and the bureaucracy. Opposition to imported rice reflected a national consensus.

Small wonder that American demands in 1986 for opening the Japanese rice market were seen as a frontal assault on Japanese culture itself. There is some irony in the Americans' criticizing Japan's inefficient rice-farming system. After all, it was the American-led Occupation that had broken up existing large land holdings into the small tracts that would become the bastions of rice farmers whose votes politicians rewarded with generous subsidies perpetuating these economically inefficient plots.

PRELIMINARY PHASE

U.S. pressure on Japan to open its rice market to foreign rice began with the U.S. complaint in 1986 that Japanese restrictions on imports of twelve agricultural products, including rice, were in violation of GATT rules. The U.S. complaint stemmed from prodding from a well-organized American lobbying group, the Rice Millers Association (RMA).

Over seven years would pass, and six prime ministers would hold office, before a negotiated settlement was reached in December 1993.

The Japanese goal on the issue of rice imports was simple: keep foreign rice from Japanese mouths. On an opposition-to-liberalization scale of one to ten, with oranges rating a "3" and beef about a "5," rice would have registered a perfect "10." Along with the heavy value Japanese attached to the subject was the virtually universal Japanese perception of the domestic rice market as sacrosanct. Permitting foreign rice to enter Japan was tantamount to letting foreign firms build condos inside the walls of the Imperial Palace. The Japanese response to American demands for opening the domestic market was akin to "how dare you!"

During the pre-negotiating period on rice, Japan's basic objective was negative, to block entirely the subject from being placed on the bargaining agenda, at either the bilateral or the multilateral GATT level. Once the RMA's petition was filed, and U.S. Trade Representative (USTR) Clayton Yeutter had to decide how to deal with the petition, Tokyo unleashed a defensive counterattack with every weapon at its disposal.

Both houses of the Diet voted unanimously in favor of a resolution binding Japan to self-sufficiency in rice production. Politicians, the press, big business, academic experts, and of course farm lobby groups voiced a single message: "no" on rice imports. In order to communicate this resolve to the Americans—to make Washington "understand" the Japanese situation and to prevent it from pressing rice liberalization upon Japan—letters were sent, envoys were dispatched, meetings were arranged, and demonstrations were organized.

"The List"—Japanese Arguments against Rice Imports
Among the long list of reasons cited in support of the Japanese position in the various pre-bargaining communications to the American side were the following:

- rice is historically significant in Japan;
- rice is culturally significant to Japan;
- other countries also award preferential treatment to certain economic sectors;
- Japan is the world's top importer of foreign agricultural products;

- Japan's National Food Control Law establishes rice as a "basic food," and self-sufficiency in rice as essential to national-security interests;
- the Japanese Diet will never accept rice liberalization;
- the Japanese public will not accept rice liberalization;
- Japan's situation on rice is "unique," "special," and "different";
- if Japan is forced to import rice, Japanese-American relations will suffer;
- rice is a domestic issue of no concern to other countries;
- Japan needs more time to consider the subject, so other governments should be "patient"; and
- rice liberalization is not a bilateral but a multilateral subject.

Arguably, presentation of two of the above reasons proved to be a mistake for the Japanese in their preliminary jousting on the issue. When negotiations on the subject subsequently switched to the multilateral level, Tokyo rejected the idea of liberalization because, for Japan, rice (unlike steak and oranges, staples of the Japanese daily diet) was a basic food. Japan's multilateral-level approach was to seek an exception for Japan's rice producing sector.

In 1988, with a second Rice Millers' petition under consideration at USTR, Ambassador Matsunaga met Yeutter. In that conversation, after urging Yeutter to reject the petition, Matsunaga communicated Japan's willingness to include rice on the Uruguay Round negotiating agenda. Based on the ambassador's assurance, Yeutter turned down the RMA request (Sanger, 1988; Darlin, 1988; *Yomiuri,* October 30, December 5, 1988), on the condition that Japan deliver on its stated commitment by addressing the issue multilaterally.

As Yeutter was putting the Japanese commitment on public record, multilateral pressures were beginning to build on Japan. In October 1988, the "Cairns Group" at the Uruguay Round asked for "minimum access" for imported rice into Japan. In December, Japan assembled a mammoth delegation to the Uruguay Round negotiations in Montreal, including a bloated *oendan* ("support group") of party politicians, as is typical for Japanese multilateral delegations, to gain information, score political points by having been at the scene, demonstrate commitment to the Japanese cause in the negotiations, and, perhaps, keep a watchful eye on Japanese bureaucrats in the event they might be inclined to compromise excessively.

By the Montreal meetings, Japan had crossed the line: Tokyo was on record as supporting the liberalization of agricultural products and was irreversibly enmeshed in the negotiating process. There would be no turning back.

Communication—Static and Shifting Goal Posts

During the course of the 1988 U.S.-Japan negotiations over renewal of the beef and citrus fruit agreement, Yeutter had told Japanese Minister of Agriculture Sato Takashi that the United States would not press Japan bilaterally to liberalize its rice market. Rice, to Japanese the dreaded "r" word, was taken by Tokyo officials as off limits at the bilateral level, according to this mutual understanding.

Also important, in Japanese eyes, was Agriculture Secretary Richard E. Lyng's statement later that year that the United States would be willing to accept a percentage-based "partial access" *(bubun kaiho)* arrangement for Japanese rice imports. (*Yomiuri,* May 16, 1990, October 24, 1991)

Through the summer of 1990, in fact, the heated Japanese domestic political debate over the rice question was based upon this understanding, namely, that the Americans would allow the issue to be addressed at the GATT on the basis of "partial access"—a gradual opening of Japan's rice market—without tariffication.

Not surprisingly, in light of this belief, Japanese officials were jolted in mid-1990 when Deputy Secretary of State Lawrence R. Eagleberger informed the Japanese that "partial access" would not satisfy Washington but, instead, tariffication of rice imports would be required. Overnight, the rug had been yanked from under Japanese assumptions as to what type of Japanese compromise on rice would be necessary to meet American desires.

Throughout the rice negotiations, but especially after this shift in U.S. expectations, Japanese bargaining behavior was finely attuned to, and directly shaped by, American policies and American officials' statements, as well as by Japanese interpretations of the meaning behind explicit and implicit American positions taken on the rice issue (*Yomiuri,* October 24, 1991).

One element in Japan's defensive bargaining strategy was active involvement in negotiations on the issue at the multilateral level. Tokyo's multilateralization of the rice import question no doubt stemmed from a conviction that action could be thereby avoided, given the GATT's impoverished past record in reining in protection-minded governments. As they conducted a holding pattern at the Uruguay Round, Japanese officials concentrated their focus on the real target, the United States government. Consistently, the Japanese goal was to ferret out by whatever means possible what the Americans meant by their proposals, what they expected, and what minimum level of Japanese rice-related concessions they would accept.

THE MIDDLE PHASE: TO THE BRINK OF COMPROMISE AND BACK

Miyazawa Kiichi became prime minister in November 1991. He quickly assigned top priority to working toward the successful conclusion of the Uruguay Round. His personal commitment to that process, however, did not imply that he supported rice imports based on a tariffication formula. The most likely explanation was that his Liberal Democratic Party had lost its majority in the upper house of the Japanese Diet in mid-year elections. Tariffication of rice imports would mean revising the Food Control Law. Upper house approval would be required for revising the Law. Thus, as the prime minister told Secretary of State James Baker in Tokyo that month, "It's impossible to accept tariffication-based rice imports, because that would require revising the Food Control Law" (*Asahi,* December 14, 1993).

Japan's negotiating stance on rice thus shifted *(kome shifuto)* with Miyazawa's assuming office. Now it was focused on locating areas of possible Japanese compromise without changing the Food Control Law. Miyazawa, anticipating release of the GATT secretary general's draft proposal (the "Dunkel Paper") on December 20, sent former ambassador to the United States Matsunaga Nobuo to sound out the American side. Among others, Matsunaga met Brent Scowcroft, who expressed firmly to the envoy the American hard-line "no exceptions on tariffication" position on the issue (*Asahi,* December 14, 1993).

As it happened, the Dunkel proposal fell short of gaining enough support to succeed in Geneva. But the presentation of the 450-page Dunkel "take it or leave it" proposal—with its "no exceptions" prohibition against special treatment for any nation's domestic agricultural sector—forced the Japanese government to confront the issue of liberalization. With Tokyo now prepared to deal seriously with the rice import issue, the presentation of Dunkel's document marked the beginning of the middle phase of the process of bargaining on the subject.

The Dunkel proposal also hardened the American side's "no exceptions" position and shaped the approach it would adopt in discussions on the issue during the ensuing year. American officials began what would later become a chorus of criticism aimed at Japanese "intransigence" that threatened to derail the Uruguay Round process.

Japan's early–1992 response to the Dunkel draft had raised the hackles of American negotiators, for the document excluded rice tariffication entirely. In light of the hostile U.S. reception to the Japanese proposal, Miyazawa directed Gaimusho (Foreign Ministry) and Agriculture Ministry officials to work out a policy plan that would be acceptable to the United States and would not require changing the Food Control Law. Operating under these two general guidelines, Foreign Ministry bureaucrats prepared several drafts but Agriculture Ministry officials defiantly planted their feet against any compromise. One impassioned Agriculture bureaucrat even invoked the fighting spirit of those stalwart defenders of Edo against rebel forces over a century before: "we are the white tiger battalion. We'll fight to the death. It's the only way we can survive" (*Asahi,* December 14, 1993; Noguchi, 1994, p. 138).

A frustrated Miyazawa then summoned Owada Hisashi and Hamaguchi Yoshiharu, respectively the top-ranking career officials in the Foreign and Agriculture ministries to "talk" about the rice problem. Owada was willing to discuss the topic during the meeting, but Hamaguchi was not, because he considered management of the Food Control Law to be Agriculture's responsibility.

The Agriculture Ministry Softens its Stance

Ministry of Agriculture intransigence softened in July 1992, with the appointment of Kyotani Akio as administrative vice-minister. Four years before, Kyotani, as Livestock Production Bureau chief, had participated in the beef and citrus negotiations with the United States. He favored liberalization. A highly influential official, Kyotani was revered by his bureaucratic brethren in the ministry. Why? Kyotani had a particular gift, a personal quality much prized in Japanese officialdom, of "being able to respond to the situation correctly" *(jokyo ni tekikaku ni taio dekiru)* (*Asahi,* December 14, 1993).

In the fall of 1992, Kyotani warned a group of Liberal Democratic Party agriculture group members that negotiations with the United States would "go nowhere" unless Japan was prepared to "set forth specific numbers." According to a later newspaper account of the meeting, Kyotani asked the politicians to "give me the responsibility to handle this" (*Asahi,* December 14, 1993, May 21, 1990; George, 1988).

Reading between the lines, the Japanese side, and even Agriculture Ministry officials, were now willing to use the "t" word (tariffication) as well as the dreaded "r" word in policy planning for the negotiations. From the Ministry of Agriculture's perspective the shift was extraordinary. After all, until just a few years before, no official interested in long-term employment at the ministry would have dared utter the "r" word, much less discuss the idea of tariffication. Thus, Japan's one-dimensional "we won't accept tariffication" approach had now changed.

Shortly thereafter, Agriculture officials started sounding out the American side on possible tariffication of wheat and dairy products. Apparently, the idea was that by accepting tariff-based arrangements on these two lesser items, the Japanese side could then pull their wagons in a circle to protect the main issue—rice imports.

Moreover, several influential Liberal Democratic Party agriculture-issue tribe *(zoku)* members had been working behind the scenes to orchestrate a way for Miyazawa to be able to reach a politically viable decision on rice imports. This trio of conservative politicians—Okawara Taichiro, Kato Koichi, and Yamamoto Tomio—had enough clout, earned by years of experience dealing with farm-related problems, for them to risk the wrath of farmers' groups and Agriculture Ministry bureaucrats by raising the possibility of opening Japan's rice market.

In December 1992, at a press conference after his cabinet was reshuffled, Miyazawa hinted at the softening of Japan's negotiating stance: "we don't want to ruin the [Uruguay Round] negotiations and yet we don't want to ruin rice farming in Japan. How can we satisfy both goals?" (*Asahi*, December 14, 1993).

Miyazawa's impromptu remarks (not included in the press conference briefing materials aides had prepared) were taken to mean the Japanese side was on the brink of compromise on rice. According to insiders' accounts published in the press (*Asahi*, December 14, 1993), Miyazawa had reached the conclusion that tariffication was "unavoidable" *(yamu o ezu)*.

Behind Miyazawa's significant statement was the fact that Japan had found itself in an untenable position in the multilateral negotiations. As long as the EC and the United Sates remained at loggerheads on agricultural imports, Japanese leaders seemed quite content merely to watch from the sidelines, to let others take the heat for continued deadlock and the blame if the Uruguay Round talks collapsed. But the United States and the EC had announced an agreement on November 24. Miyazawa evidently was amazed that the French, who "disliked" the Americans, could have buckled to Washington's pressure on the agricultural issue (*Asahi*, December 14, 1993).

In addition, Washington was strongly urging Tokyo to open its rice market by the end of 1992. Japan's Agriculture and Fisheries minister, Tanabu Makoto, had visited Washington to meet USTR Carla Hills and others to probe how firmly American trade officials were committed to the "no exceptions" stance. Finding the United States to be quite firmly committed, Tanabu returned to Tokyo where he reported his assessment to Miyazawa. At about the same time, Miyazawa received a report on the multilateral situation from two of his party's leading agricultural affairs politicians, Okawara Taichiro and Hori Kosuke, who had just arrived back in Tokyo from Geneva. In addition, Miyazawa heard from his close friend Matsunaga that a settlement was imminent in Geneva (*Asahi,* November 27, 1993).

Based on information from these sources, Miyazawa was now prepared to take decisive action on the rice problem. Anticipating a U.S.-EC accommodation in December 1992, which would have isolated Japan as the lone holdout on agricultural imports, the Miyazawa government, backed by ranking agricultural Diet members in his party and top Agriculture Ministry bureaucrats, was ready—however reluctantly—to compromise on the rice issue.

As it happened, however, and fortunately for the Japanese side, the EC-U.S. confrontation had not ended but continued to persist, giving Tokyo a respite, at least until the new Clinton administration took office in January. Miyazawa's earlier readiness to compromise on rice imports, albeit at the final hour, as well as his subsequent readiness to postpone taking action on the issue, underline the extent to which the Japanese side's position varied according to fluctuations in U.S. policy and in circumstances at Geneva.

Japanese leaders were troubled by several potential repercussions if Japan maintained its uncompromising posture on rice imports: the possibility Japan would "become isolated" *(koritsuka)* at the Uruguay Round; the likelihood that Japan would become the scapegoat if the negotiations were to fail; and the chance that the United States might retaliate in some fashion, threatening other Japanese economic sectors and even the stability of the Japanese-American relationship itself. These were not far-fetched concerns; they seemed based on an accurate assessment of actual conditions at the multilateral level and of repeatedly expressed American expectations of Japan.

These factors gradually increased in significance during the middle phase of negotiations on rice, raising the pressure on Japan's negotiators to compromise. These same factors, over time, helped to splinter the once-unanimous Japanese domestic consensus against rice imports.

By 1992, the once impregnable dike against imported rice was about to give way. Only the party politicians from rural districts and Agriculture Ministry bureaucrats still had fingers in the dike. As happened during the earlier orange negotiations, the bureaucrats at Agriculture proved themselves ahead of the politicians in accepting the need for compromise. Ministry officials thus turned willing, even eager, to have the ministry negotiate the best deal possible under the circumstances. Once the ministerial fingers were pulled from the dike, the vote-conscious politicians surrendered, permitting Agriculture bureaucrats negotiating authority. By this point, the rice-import issue no longer was "whether or not" but "when" and "how much."

THE FINAL PHASE OF THE NEGOTIATIONS

The Bush years ended with a standoff on the subject of rice imports, with Washington standing firmly behind its "no exceptions" position and Tokyo doggedly continuing to seek preferential treatment on rice. The new Clinton administration trade team, working against the backdrop of the looming deadline for wrapping up the Uruguay Round multilateral negotiations, moved aggressively—in both style and substance—to resolve the issue. When he met Clinton at a bilateral summit session on April 16, Miyazawa recited the standard Japanese script, that tariffication of rice would require changing the Food Control Law, which would be impossible. Instead of responding with the American "no exceptions" argument, as Bush had done repeatedly, Clinton chose to avoid a harsh response.

The multilateral negotiations revived in May when a quadrilateral (United States, Canada, Japan, EC) trade ministers' meeting agreed to open comprehensive negotiations in the fall, a decision that intensified pressure on Japan to face and force resolution of the rice problem.

The O'Mara-Shiwaku Connection

An American initiative provided the catalyst for advancing the rice negotiations to the final stage. In June 1993, Charles J. O'Mara, chief agricultural negotiator in the Department of Agriculture, arranged a meeting with his counterpart in the Ministry of Agriculture, Shiwaku Jiro (O'Mara, 1996; *Asahi,* December 14, 1993).

Shiwaku and others in the Agriculture Ministry believed that with tariffication and free competition in the domestic Japanese rice market, U.S.-grown rice would be at a serious disadvantage to rice grown in Thailand where labor costs were significantly lower. Shiwaku thought, as had proved to be the case with wheat, nation-based set amounts of imports would be more advantageous to the United States than an open-market approach. Agriculture Ministry officials also thought that the Clinton administration, being more interested in results-oriented, managed trade than devotion to free-trade ideology, would be receptive to applying the wheat precedent to resolution of the rice issue on a non-tariffication basis. Shiwaku ran this argument by the U.S. side, which listened. After all, thanks to a decade of preferential import treatment, compliments of the Ministry of Agriculture, half the wheat sold in Japan was American grown.

The U.S. side did more than listen. In June 1993, O'Mara submitted a compromise draft proposal to Shiwaku that suggested deferring tariffication on rice for six years, during which period rice would be imported into Japan according to a "minimum access" formula. In a personal interview (O'Mara, 1996; *Asahi,* December 14, 1993), O'Mara confirmed the accuracy of reports published in the Japanese press regarding his private meetings with Shiwaku, including the fact that the offer was an American initiative. According to the formula that O'Mara submitted, tariffication of rice would only begin in the year 2000, after the six-year "minimum access" period.

Joe O'Mara's plan, which allowed Japan to avoid immediate tariffication of rice, was a welcome surprise to the Japanese team. "It was more than we expected," was the reaction of one delighted Japanese negotiator (*Asahi,* December 14, 1993).

In July, Agriculture Ministry officials assembled to review the O'Mara draft. The bureaucratic lineup and relatively receptive thinking of officials in the ministry continued even through the domestic political chaos of mid-1993, the end of the thirty-eight-year reign of the Liberal Democrats, and the beginning of a series of multiparty coalition governments. Despite the tumble of domestic political events in Japan, these were the officials whose views mattered most in determining the Japanese side's negotiating position. These officials promptly decided to accept the American draft.

On the other hand, the Liberal Democratic Party politicians ready to accept rice liberalization a year before, when their party was in power, had become members of the "opposition." Now they were unfettered by concerns about shouldering the burden, and the blame, associated with making a decision to open the rice market.

The American side was closely monitoring the dramatically changing internal political environment, with an eye to the implications these changes, particularly the Liberal Democrats' fall from power, would have on Japanese negotiating policy. Had the Liberal Democrats altered their earlier stance? Accordingly, in early August, American trade officials invited Iwakura Guzo, a savvy agricultural affairs specialist and longtime party staff official, to Washington to learn the "opposition" party's thinking on the subject of rice. In the meeting, O'Mara asked Iwakura how the Liberal Democrats would respond to the draft proposal (O'Mara, 1996). "Even though we're the opposition party now, we'll respond by putting national interests first," was Iwakura's reassuring reply, which O'Mara and the Americans interpreted to mean the party would support, or at least not oppose, the compromise plan (*Asahi*, December 14, 1993).

In August, as Japan commenced emergency imports of foreign rice, Ministry of Agriculture officials secretly approached the Rice Millers Association. That meeting brought yet another surprise to the Japanese side, as RMA officers expressed their willingness to go along with the deferred-tariffication approach. In fact, following their discussion with the Agriculture Ministry representatives, the RMA sought Department of Agriculture guarantees on rice imports to Japan.

Thus, by the beginning of September the two sides had crafted the basis for an agreement on rice, a compromise arrangement that seemed acceptable to the most vociferous American lobbying protagonist and to the principal antagonists in the Japanese ministries and political parties. Meanwhile, the indefatigable Shiwaku continued to toil in the trenches on the details of an accord, for the most part side by side with his American counterpart, O'Mara. From September on, Shiwaku—who reportedly had "virtually complete" negotiating authority over the rice issue (*Asahi*, December 14, 1993), was abroad, engaged in discussions in Washington and Europe. He met secretly at a small hotel in France with O'Mara, using a rental car, but not using a pager or cellular phone. No record of these meetings appear in the Gaimusho records; only a small number of Agriculture Ministry officials were aware the meetings were in progress (*Asahi*, December 14, 1993).

The Shiwaku-O'Mara meetings focused on several specific issues, including coming up with an acceptable translation for the key word *yuyo* (which means "postponement" or "delay"): Shiwaku balked at this English translation, favoring more ambiguous language. In the end the problem was averted through a circumlocution. The two officials also dealt with details on handling the period after the "minimum access" framework terminated following six years, and the exact percentage amounts of imported rice to be set for the six-year "minimum access" period. The Dunkel draft had set forth a staggered percentage increase of 3 percent (year one) to 5 percent (year six). Japan pushed for the Dunkel figures; the United States countered with percentages twice as high (6–10 percent over six years). In the end, the sides landed squarely in the middle, agreeing on a 4–8 percentage formulation (O'Mara, 1996; *Asahi*, December 14, 1993).

His task virtually completed, Shiwaku returned to Tokyo on October 10. He and O'Mara had worked out a mutually satisfactory arrangement that achieved Washington's goal of accessing the Japanese rice market and met Tokyo's desire to avert immediate tariffication. The final deal: in exchange for raising the amount of rice imported under the "minimum access" formulation (beyond the original Dunkel percentages), Japan won postponement of tariffication until the year 2000. Thus, the U.S. initiative of mid-1993 (the O'Mara plan) had proved the breakthrough in the negotiations on rice, providing the Japanese side with a face-saving path of retreat.

The negotiated deal had several pluses: it met the minimum acceptable to the central player (the United States); it seemed to meet the expectations of Japan at the Uruguay Round; it would, for a time, postpone resolution of the still politically iffy matter of rice tariffication; it committed Japan to a rice import structure that other rice importing countries would follow; it entailed a politically and economically manageable process of step-by-step increases in imports; and it only required Japan to import comparatively modest amounts of rice.

The final compromise solution made sense, but would it survive the formidable political obstacles in Japan? Of the many obstacles to rice liberalization that Japanese officials and politicians had listed repeatedly before and during negotiations (see "The List," p. xxx), several were rooted in hard political reality. One was the Diet resolution on self-sufficiency in rice, which remained in effect and which was taken seriously as a commitment. Another constraint stemmed from the long-term and unchanged public statements of many politicians and political parties opposing the importation of a single grain of rice, much less tariffication. This was the main barrier to winning acceptance of the compromise draft, one that caused the premier to be *ganjigarame,* or "tied up in a rope" (*Asahi,* October 23, November 7, 1993).

Was disagreement within his governing coalition serious enough to threaten its continuation in power? Hosokawa's whopping 70 percent public support rating obscured his government's inner frailty; his popularity did not translate into the political clout to overcome opponents in his multiparty government, especially on a subject as touchy as rice. The coalition was not unified on rice liberalization. Hosokawa himself supported liberalization and had told associates he would open the rice market (*Asahi,* November 7, 1993). At the same time, in a conversation with a top policy advisor a month earlier, he expressed the opinion that Japan should not liberalize rice without getting something in return. "If Japan can get conditions attached to liberalization, we should do so" (*Asahi,* November 7, 1993).

After his meeting with Clinton in New York in September he stated Japan's commitment to the December Uruguay Round deadline. Ozawa Ichiro, a Nakasone-esque political weathervane and former Liberal Democrat of the Tanaka-Takeshita factional line, from a major rice-producing prefecture of Iwate in northeastern Japan, was a born-again reformist willing to accept rice liberalization. His party, the Japan New Party, consisted mostly of breakaway Liberal Democrats. Komeito, another coalition member party whose support centers on urban constituencies, accepted liberalization. To persuade the New Party Sakigake to join the coalition, Hosokawa had promised its leader, Takemura Masayoshi (also a former Liberal Democrat), that the coalition would oppose tariffication of rice (*Asahi,* November 7, 1993).

Because the compromise plan offered deferred tariffication, some analysts reasoned, there was technically no breach of Hosokawa's pledge to Takemura. Some hard-liners in Ozawa's New Life Party (Shinseito) also staunchly opposed tariffs, but Ozawa seemed able to contain his troops and kept them in the party and the coalition.

In his late-stage efforts to hammer out a consensus in his coalition on the compromise rice-imports plan, Hosokawa's most daunting challenge came from the Socialists. Although political reform was the pivotal issue to the Socialist party—as it was to all parties—during 1993, the rice issue was highly volatile as well. Socialist party leaders had stated repeatedly their willingness to bolt from Hosokawa's coalition rather than accede to a decision allowing rice imports. In one illustration of the extreme reaction the inflammable rice problem elicited in Japanese politics, some Socialist leaders even spoke of forging an alliance with conservative Liberal Democrats after their party had left the coalition.

Contrary to conventional wisdom, the Socialists were as dependent on rural district support as the Liberal Democrats, a support base that party leaders desperately wished to maintain. As late as the first week of December, the Socialist leadership clung to an anti-liberalization line and even called for additional debate on the topic in the Diet. The Socialists, known for nearly four decades as a party in perpetual opposition, were still playing that adversarial role—to the point of posing hostile queries about the status of the rice liberalization negotiations directly to the prime minister on the Diet floor. In the end, the negativistic politics of the Socialists left them out of the loop, the odd men out in contributing to the resolution on the rice-imports issue.

However irrelevant the Socialists may have been to the negotiating process on rice, they remained a major—albeit the weakest—part of Hosokawa's jerry-built coalition.

Multilateral Pressure

In mid-October, GATT director general Peter Sutherland trekked to Tokyo where he spent two exhausting days trying to convey to Japan's leaders the urgency of the imminent deadline for finishing up the Uruguay Round. During his stay he conferred with bureaucrats, Liberal Democrats, and Socialist party leaders who, to a surprised and exasperated Sutherland, seemed determined just to state Japan's unrelenting commitment against rice imports and to recite from "The List" (including "Japan's cultural heritage" and "Japan's food security imperatives"). Perhaps because he was less used to Japanese-style arguments on the issue than were Americans, Sutherland reacted with surprise, and even astonishment, that the Japanese leaders he met seemed indifferent to the fact that agriculture was but one of fifteen other major negotiating group topics at the Uruguay Round, including subjects of trade-in-services and intellectual property rights that he expected would have been of concern to his Japanese hosts. Aside from leaders of Keidanren, who were "the only people I could talk to," he noted in a sarcasm-laced statement to the press, "the only thing anyone seems interested in talking about is rice." "They seem to think rice imports mean the end of the world," he went on, "but they are not" (*Asahi*, October 23, 1993).

Sutherland's comments had repercussions. For instance, once the outspoken Sutherland had left town, Hosokawa felt compelled to reassure the press that, "I told him [Sutherland] Japan would not accept tariffication" (*Asahi*, October 23, 1993).

"Final" Final-Stage Events

The prime minister's defensive and evasive public statements stemmed from the tightrope he was walking in domestic politics. Caught between his own preferences and commitments stated and these die-hard political opponents, Hosokawa was frustrated and cautious. He also was pessimistic about the usefulness of continued Japanese stonewalling. He told one coalition party leader that Japan's merely saying "we oppose, we oppose" *(hantai, hantai)* will "not work" (*Asahi*, November 1, 1993).

The hostile political and press backlash to reports of his remarks led Hosokawa to avoid comment on the subject. He fended off a barrage of questions on the Diet floor concerning rumored Japanese compromises with such comments as "such reports haven't reached me," or "you can't believe every story you hear," or "diplomatic negotiations should be handled secretly" (*Asahi*, October 27, 1993).

His disclaimers aside, former GATT secretary general Dunkel, in Tokyo for a conference, commented that there were no major differences between the secrecy-shrouded compromise plan and the overall draft plan, a statement that substantiated the rumors being circulated (*Asahi*, October 28, 1993).

Another Sutherland remark while in Tokyo had later repercussions and may have affected Japanese handling of negotiations during the final month of the process. In November, Minister of Agriculture Hata Eishiro decided to travel to Europe for a week of meetings with Sutherland and EC trade officials. His last-minute trip apparently was inspired by an ambiguous remark Sutherland had made during his eventful stay in Japan the month before. While in Tokyo, Sutherland had confessed, "What I want is an agreement. As long as the involved countries agree, even if they want to say white is black, that's all right by me" (*Asahi*, November 1, 1993).

Thus, even as the terms of the final agreement seemed settled upon, the Japanese side still was grasping at straws that might somehow improve rice-related provisions of the accord. Sutherland's remark was such a straw, one that Japanese leaders seized upon as a possible opening to be exploited.

Whether or not Sutherland's ambiguous remark had actually prompted Hata's final-hour foray to the other side of the world, the agriculture minister's goal was clear enough. His approach: "Having already swallowed the stick, we'll try to make it less painful" (*Asahi*, November 1, 1993).

By "less painful," Hata seemed to have in mind an improved deal for Japan, one that would postpone rice tariffication to some unspecified future time instead of beginning the process in the seventh year, as the then existing compromise plan required.

In Tokyo, Hosokawa launched a preemptive strike against opponents of the compromise plan. Aware that a domestic backlash might jeopardize chances of an agreement, Hosokawa turned to two veteran Foreign Ministry officials, Sato Yukio and Owada Hisashi, who then dealt with Agriculture Ministry bureaucrats. Agriculture officials virtually never met with the prime minister himself at his residence over this period (*Asahi*, December 14, 1993).

Hosokawa's near-obsession with secrecy and worries that the rice problem might spill over to affect the U.S.-Japan relationship itself spurred him to ask the Americans (through Ambassador Walter Mondale) not to make the rice import topic an issue at the upcoming APEC meeting in Seattle.

Apparently, the U.S. side appreciated Hosokawa's precarious position and agreed to downplay the subject at the November summit (*Asahi*, December 14, 1993). The APEC meeting went as expected, with the rice issue given the low-key treatment arranged beforehand.

Hosokawa returned to Tokyo where he began arrangements for a final round of consultations among his party allies in the coalition. His personal choice for undertaking this delicate task was Ogura Kazuo, Economic Bureau chief in the Foreign Ministry. Perhaps Ogura had instructions to be especially tight lipped in his comments and especially narrow in his circle of briefing contacts. Perhaps not. In any case, he did not touch base with farm lobbying organizations. Moreover, his briefings to the politicians and officials he did meet covered only information already published in the newspapers.

Hosokawa was certainly using his best spin-doctoring skills to obscure what had really been happening in the final stage of the negotiations on rice imports. Just a week before the Uruguay Round ended, Japanese government officials not only were denying reports of a compromise settlement but were asserting, in fact, that Tokyo was still engaged in final-hour attempts that somehow might improve rice-import-related terms in the document. As late as December 9, days before conclusion of the Uruguay Round was announced, Hosokawa himself publicly rejected reports of a final agreement.

The Japanese leader's claim strained credulity. One person who responded publicly about Hosokawa's statement was the ever-quotable GATT director, Peter Sutherland. Sutherland, who was obviously quite aware of the facts, seemed unable to resist likening Hosokawa's remark to "calling 'white' 'black'" (*Asahi*, December 14, 1993).

Nor did the prime minister's claims do anything to reassure skittish Japanese politicians. From that point until the December settlement, the frantic maneuverings of Japanese politicians did not stem from their concern with a foreign audience or with influencing the negotiations. Their target was domestic, namely, their electoral constituents and party rivals. At the same time, no politician seemed willing to go up against the international "system" *(taisei)* with Japan isolated in opposing a standard set by the international community (*Asahi*, December 21, 1993).

The vast majority of Diet members of all parties were on record as having deemed rice liberalization to be "inevitable." A sizable minority had declared rice tariffication to be "unavoidable." These same politicians were now frantically scurrying about, seeking refuge from being held accountable for the reported Japanese concessions on rice. Most politicians blamed the bureaucrats. Liberal Democratic politicians blamed the Hosokawa coalition. Ironically, it was the Liberal Democrats who Iwakura had assured O'Mara and other American negotiators some months earlier would put the national interest first. In the crunch, it seemed, his party colleagues were less interested in acting on that belief by lending their support to a beleaguered prime minister and the negotiated compromise plan, than they were in jockeying for political advantage in advance of possible elections and pledging unaltered loyalty to the "no foreign rice" slogan.

Politicians hoped to demonstrate that they had exerted sufficiently "great efforts" and had tried their best, albeit in a losing cause. By the same token, government leaders' *ex post facto* statements are properly viewed as merely damage-control tactics to minimize the potential political impact of what were—to Japanese minds—wholly unsatisfactory final terms. A mere handful of politicians stood behind Hosokawa (and the vaunted "national interest"), willing to shoulder the risks and responsibilities associated with supporting the final agreement.

Events between December 1992 and December 1993 merely furthered previous trends toward Japanese acceptance of the inevitability of compromise on rice imports. Apart from the factors already discussed, one should mention the 1992 shortfall in Japan's domestic rice crop and subsequent decision to import rice from several countries on an emergency basis.

Of course, the Japanese government's decision to settle the rice problem stemmed from other reasons and incentives. At the same time, the emergency rice imports undermined yet further whatever credibility remained in the Japanese side's adherence to the principle of national self-sufficiency in rice. Japanese representatives' attempts to rationalize these as "one-time only" purchases were ineffectual (*Asahi,* March 30, 31; November 1, 3, 1993).

Some Japanese leaders feared that, in the wake of the emergency rice imports, the Japanese side would be criticized for hypocrisy and opportunism if it were to continue to stonewall on the compromise agreement. The emergency importing of rice was merely one more factor leading the Japanese government to realize the hopelessness of its defensive, watch-and-wait negotiating approach.

Only after seven years of haggling had Tokyo relented, grudgingly, incrementally, minimally, to a strings-attached settlement. Japan's behavior during the rice negotiations was consistently self-centered, narrow-minded, and parochial. In light of that dismal bargaining record, it seems ironic, indeed, that when announcing their decision to accept the final agreement, Japanese leaders explained the decision as motivated by

Japanese devotion to free-trade principles, dedication to the GATT process, and commitment to fulfilling their nation's responsibilities as a global economic power.

SUMMARY ANALYSIS

What does the rice case suggest about the "Japanese style" of conducting international negotiations?

NEGOTIATING STRUCTURE AND PROCESS

Centrality of the Bilateral Process
The heart of the negotiating process in both cases was bilateral. Bargaining over rice imports (quota-based and tariff-based) began at the bilateral U.S.-Japan level. Subsequently, even while farm product issues were addressed multilaterally at the Uruguay Round trade negotiations, the process axis on rice continued to be the U.S.-Japan connection. Final resolution of the rice issue was achieved via negotiations between the two governments within the structural umbrella of the Uruguay Round.

Japanese diplomacy buffs refer to such bilateral-in-a-multilateral-framework interactions as *maruchi-bi*. In the rice example, the critical process level was clearly *bi*, with not much *maruchi*-type impact until an impending global trade accord provided isolation-conscious Japanese leaders with a final-hour incentive to accept the previously arranged U.S.-Japan compromise formula.

The United States Plays "Offense"
The American side played the "offensive" role: Washington established the bargaining agenda, issued direct and indirect threats, undertook the significant initiatives, set the deadlines, and, at the multilateral level, acted to mobilize other governments to buttress its negotiating stance vis-à-vis Japan.

Japan Plays "Defense"
In sharp contrast, the Japanese played a "defensive" role: Japanese negotiators did not frame the initial bargaining agenda, but reacted within the framework of a U.S.-dominated bargaining agenda and process. Its proposals were counterproposals. Its conditions were attached as strings to accepting American demands. Its bargaining game plan was executed upon an American playing field—with an American rule book, American referees, an American

scorekeeper, and an American crew adjusting the height of the goal posts. No matter at which level negotiations took place—bilateral, multilateral, or bilateral within multilateral—the policies, approach, and behavior of Japanese negotiators were conditioned by Japan's defensive position.

This is not to say the Japanese were passive, for they were actively engaged in the bargaining process. Their active involvement in the process, however, took place in an externally defined context. Their initiatives were not designed to replace or fundamentally alter the existing, made-in-America negotiating agenda. Throughout negotiations on rice, the Japanese negotiating team was in the position of reacting and adapting to other governments'—notably the American government's—initiatives, proposals, statements, demands, pressures, and expectations.

STRATEGIES AND TACTICS

In interviews with the author, several Gaimusho officials have described Japanese bargaining strategy as "a strategy of no strategy." While few in number, perhaps, compared to other countries, there were Japanese bargaining strategies and tactics—shaped in form and nuance by the Japanese defensive orientation described above.

For analytical purposes, the strategies and tactics that were adopted and pursued by the Japanese side during the rice negotiations can be arranged into two general types: "issue avoidance" and "issue minimization."

"Issue-Avoidance" Behavior

The Japanese government's fundamental goal in the rice case was not to enter into negotiations on the issues in the first place. Accordingly, a variety of "issue-avoidance" techniques were used, to block or defer consideration of what to the Japanese side were off-limits subjects from the bilateral and/or multilateral agendas. A sampling of the behavior drawn from the rice example:

- Gaining prior understandings or promises (through personal meetings with American officials) that topics will be off limits or that Japan will receive exceptional, special, or preferential treatment;
- Seeking to "multilateralize" negotiations, thus side-stepping the United States and averting action;
- Adopting a watch-and-wait posture at the multilateral level;
- Blocking and/or delaying multilateral-level action in GATT panels based on unanimity rule;

- Using available tools to demonstrate the Japanese side's commitment to its basic stance (as against stressing techniques to persuade
  others to change their positions); and
- Repeatedly maintaining subject(s) as "off limits" (tariff-based imports).

"Issue-Minimization" Behavior

Once "avoidance" efforts had failed, the Japanese side turned to ways to reduce the scope and content of compromises required to resolve the issues
involved. These are a few illustrations from the rice negotiations:

- Conceding less significant items (wheat and dairy products, tomato
  paste, and the like in these cases) to minimize concessions on more
  important items;
- Offering minor concessions and postponing further compromise
  until American response was received and assessed;
- Avoiding explicit pledges; and
- Expressing Japanese proposals in ambiguous language (notably during the preliminary and early phases).

DOMESTIC INSTITUTIONS AND POLITICS

Decision making in Japan's political culture requires the expenditure of
enormous energy and time in consensus-building tasks. Only by a politically correct process—extensive discussions, behind-the-scenes consultations, formal and formal conferences—can a viable decision be arranged.
According to Japanese norms of politics, all relevant opinions must be
heard and be taken into consideration when reaching policy decisions.
Japan's fractious, fragmented political processes extend to international negotiations and shape Japanese bargaining style in direct ways.

Nongovernmental Actors

The extensive involvement of unofficial actors on both sides reflects the
diversity, complexity, and intensely interrelated quality of relationships between the two societies. In the rice case the Japanese negotiators' consensus-building (nemawashi) efforts included a visit to RMA offices to test the
waters on the final compromise plan.

Similarly, dispatching missions, delegations, and personal envoys to the United States was a *nemawashi*-type tactic employed for domestic political reasons. These visits facilitated the softening of the Japanese stance and thus were a critical part of the process of reaching final agreements.

Manipulating "Outside Pressure"

In the rice case, various Japanese official and non-official actors used external pressure—real, imagined, expected, and typically American—to provide added support for policies they personally espoused but might not have been able to accomplish without a dash of *gaiatsu* (foreign pressure).

Time-Consuming Policy-Making

In the rice case, the Japanese side typically took two to three months to prepare and present its positions at the negotiating table. The lengthy response time did not stem from intentional delaying or stalling tactics by the Japanese side but from the snail-like pace of consensus-building toward lowest-common-denominator decisions among all parties having a stake in the issues being considered.

Japanese News Media and Negotiating Secrecy

The Japanese newspapers' relentless pursuit of "scoops" and information make bargaining secrecy difficult. Newspaper and magazine reporting on the Uruguay Round focused almost exclusively on rice, prospects for rice, problems with rice, foreign demands on rice, and foreign leaders' statements on rice.

If details of private discussions (for example, the Shiwaku-O'Mara rice-related conversations during 1993) can be kept from the press the domestic decision-making process is smoothed considerably, which, in turn, may help produce a politically sustainable final agreement. Given the fiercely combative political environment and a scoop-driven army of Japanese journalists, Hosokawa (like any Japanese leader) performed a balancing act. On the one hand, his secretive approach seems to have allowed the O'-Mara-Shiwaku talks to achieve results that publicity might have nullified. On the other hand, keeping details of the final compromise plan from the public (and some domestic parties) even after the deal had been negotiated left him vulnerable to political attack when terms of the final agreement became known.

ATTITUDES AND PERCEPTIONS

One Issue - ism

Japanese negotiating behavior on the rice issue, and particularly its role in the Uruguay Round bargaining process, was molded consistently and heavily by the extraordinary weight of the topic of rice liberalization in the Japanese mind. It is no exaggeration to say that the Japanese viewed the Uruguay Round process through a rice-clouded lens. In Japanese eyes, concluding the Uruguay Round meant an avalanche of foreign rice into Japan. The Japanese newspapers freeze-dried their reporting on Uruguay Round happenings to a simple question: what about rice?

This preoccupation with the single and, to Japanese, non-negotiable subject of rice had repercussions on Japanese negotiating conduct. For one thing, the mindset virtually ruled out objective policy debate on the topic. Rice liberalization was a taboo topic, even at the highest levels of the Japanese government, until negotiations neared completion.

Only by appreciating this Japanese outlook on the topic can one explain the otherwise baffling intensity of the Japanese side's efforts—at each stage and at both the bilateral and multilateral levels—to explain Japan's situation, gain special treatment for Japan's rice sector, and escape compromise, on a matter of peripheral consequence to all but a few other governments. Many foreign critics and government officials were both bewildered and unconvinced by Japan's one-dimensional negotiating performance at the Uruguay Round.

JAPANESE COMPROMISE BEHAVIOR

Beyond a rock-hard commitment to its minimum position, what was acceptable to the Japanese side depended on what was acceptable to the Americans. Japanese concessions were seen as giving up less of what the Americans were asking, rather than winning more from the Americans.

What prompted Japanese concessions in these two cases? Significant Japanese compromises (in the final stage) were offered only when circumstances surrounding negotiations had become heavily politicized, a "crisis" stage had been reached, and the Japanese side had come to see itself to be in a "no-choice" position.

A significant, final-stage source of pressure to concede was multilateral, if unanimous agreement there, and the possibility of being isolated, criticized, and blamed for the collapse of the Uruguay Round. Japanese fears of American retaliation for noncompliance with its proposals (and consequent threat to other, relatively more significant sectors of the Japanese economy) constituted another major, final-stage reason for Japanese compromise.

The apparent Japanese sense of relief when Washington dropped its more ambitious demands (for example, its demand for immediate tariffication of rice imports in mid-1993) seemed to make the Japanese side more willing to accept earlier American proposals it had rejected. In what must be a uniquely Japanese way of rationalizing compromise, Japanese final concessions in both cases were justified because they permitted a final agreement with better terms than those Washington had been demanding earlier!

In light of the actual, as against stated or indirect, reasons why the Japanese side accepted the minimum-access-cum-deferred-tariffication formula, it therefore made little, if any, difference which single party or coalition of parties happened to be heading the Japanese government when the final-stage decisions were reached in the fall of 1993.

AMERICAN BARGAINING STYLE AS A FACTOR

Japanese Complaints
At various times during the years of negotiating agreements on rice, Japanese negotiators and officials complained about Washington's negotiating conduct. Among these alleged American shortcomings were the following:

1. unannounced shifts in position;
2. unexplained, sudden escalation of demands;
3. discrepancies between American positions expressed at multilateral and bilateral meetings;
4. violation of previous Japanese-U.S. "understandings" or "promises";
5. excessive use of pressure and threats; and
6. repeated submission of demands known to the American side as "off limits," clearly beyond Japan's maximum concession range.

Impact on the Negotiations
The escalation of American demands in both cases clearly imposed added hardships on the consensus-driven Japanese domestic decision-making process, making the process even more time consuming. American shifts in position during negotiations had similar effects.

Such American behavior had a particularly striking impact on the Japanese side's conduct of the negotiations, precisely because Japan's bargaining "menu" was provided by the United States. When the American side changed or added items to that agenda, the existing Japanese internal consensus disintegrated. Tokyo then had to arrange a fresh consensus, more or less from scratch, on the basis of the latest U.S. plan.

Aside from these domestic political effects, what impact did such American behavior have upon the Japanese side? One example: in the case of mixed signals sent to the Japanese from different officials on the U.S. side, Japanese negotiators, always on the alert for any sign of softness on the Americans' part, would seize upon the most conciliatory among the statements received (for instance, Ambassador Mansfield's remark that he "understood" Japan's refusal to import rice [*The Washington Post,* October 22, 1988; *Yomiuri,* February 11, 1988]) and use them in subsequent talks with U.S. negotiators as supporting evidence for the Japanese position.

While Japan was not able to exploit effectively these conflicting messages from the American side to its advantage, the frequently different and occasionally contradictory messages added static to the communication process.

Whether the U.S. demands were artificially inflated ("phony") or not, their later withdrawal affected the bargaining process (by hastening settlement between the sides) and the final outcome (by improving final terms in favor of the U.S. side). However loudly and often Japanese officials cried foul over this violation of bargaining norms by the Americans, from the U.S. perspective the tactic (if it was, in fact, intentional) of submitting and then retracting especially harsh conditions was an effective tool. Why the American "ploy" worked so well is explained, again, by Japan's place in a fundamentally defensive bargaining structure and by the Japanese side's view of its position within that framework as weak, vulnerable, and necessarily reactive (see "Reasons for Japanese Compromise," p. xxx).

Japanese bargaining style in the rice case is "classic." The "style" mirrored the "coping" or "go-with-the-flow" approach described earlier. Japanese negotiators sought, to the greatest extent possible, to avoid losses, to limit damage, and to avoid mistakes. Their bargaining behavior in these instances fits one American observer's (Gibney, 1971, p. 101) apt likening of Japan's diplomatic style to that of "an interested bridge partner, waiting to follow the first good bid from the American side."

NOTES

* This chapter is part of a larger forthcoming study *Japanese Negotiating Behavior*, undertaken under the auspices of the United States Institute of Peace. The views expressed here are solely those of the author and not necessarily of the Institute.

1. Japanese names are given with the surname first.

REFERENCES

Berton, P. 1996. "The Psychological Dimensions of Japanese Negotiating Behavior." *Kyoto Conference on Japanese Studies, 1994* (Vol. I, pp. I-273-I-284). [Kyoto]: International Research Center for Japanese Studies, The Japan Foundation.

Blaker, M. 1993. "Evaluating Japanese Diplomatic Performance." In Curtis. *Japanese Foreign Policy after the Cold War* (pp. 1–42). New York: M. E. Sharpe.

Darlin, D. 1988. "Japan Firmly Resists US Pressure on Rice." *The Wall Street Journal,* November 12.

Gibney, F. 1971. "The View from Japan." *Foreign Affairs,* 50 (3).

Inoguchi, T. 1993. *Japan's Foreign Policy in an Era of Global Change.* London: Pinter Publishers.

Noguchi, H. 1994. "Kome sakokuron: seijika to chihoshi." *Shokun!,* 1.

O'Mara, J. 1996. Interview.

Sanger, D. 1988. "Japan's Sensitivity on Rice Issue." *The New York Times,* October 28.

CHAPTER 3

THE RUSSIAN WAY OF NEGOTIATING*

HIROSHI KIMURA

This chapter discusses features of the Russian way of negotiating as perceived by Western observers. The following three questions are examined. (1) How do Russians tend to view the human conduct of negotiating? (the question of "Russian perception of negotiations"); (2) What kind of behavior do Russians tend to adopt in negotiating? (the question of "Russian negotiating behavior"); and (3) What kind of techniques do Russians tend to use to achieve their objectives in negotiation? (the question of "Russian negotiating strategy and tactics").

These questions will be addressed within the context of a larger underlying question: Are the post-Soviet perceptions, behavior, and techniques the same as those identified in the Soviet (and pre-Soviet) period, how do we know, and why? To address these questions, Soviet and pre-Soviet images will be reviewed and further questions asked about the current post-Soviet Russian period. These questions concerning perception, behavior, and techniques of negotiations are inseparably linked to each other. However, they are not one and the same thing. At least on the theoretical level, they are three different, independent entities. For this reason, I will discuss each of them separately, distinguishing the three dimensions, while at the same time recognizing their close interrelation.

Before discussing these questions, I would like to make two important caveats. The first concerns the role that culture plays in negotiations. Do people from different cultures negotiate differently? Or, to what extent do differences in national culture affect negotiations? Among the specialists in negotiation studies, there are two contrasting answers to this question (Faure & Rubin, 1993).

One school of thought argues that negotiation is a universal process for which one can find a more or less similar behavioral pattern that can thus be generalized across cultures. Using an excellent analogy, in his book coauthored with Maureen R. Berman, I. William Zartman (1982, p. 10) writes: "there may be a number of air routes to Boston, but they all involve the phase of takeoff, cruising, and landing, and in that order." Likewise, it is possible to develop a generalized pattern of negotiation. The model to clarify the nature of the process of negotiation proposed by Zartman identifies three stages in the negotiation process: (1) diagnosing the situation and deciding whether to enter into negotiations; (2) negotiating a formula or common definition of the conflict in terms amenable to a solution; and (3) negotiating the details to implement a formula on the points of dispute. Zartman and Berman (Ibid.) conclude: "Cultural differences are simply differences in style and language—much as one could say that there are a limited number of basic game patterns, and the differences between basket-ball and hockey are simply variations of a basic theme." This is the view held by scholars who are interested in developing a general theory of negotiations, including economists, game theorists, sociologists, and experimental psychologists. In other words, these people believe that the study of negotiation is a science (Brady, 1991, pp. 12–19). The most important implication of their argument for the context of this article is that there are no unique features in a Russian way of negotiating.

The second school of thought, on the other hand, regards negotiation as an art (Brady, pp. 12–19). Historians, diplomats, and practitioners of negotiations tend to hold such a view. They view negotiation as a form of human behavior that is hard to replicate due to its unique qualities. They emphasize the specific peculiarities in terms of their historical context. Environment, situation, and timing also greatly influence the content of negotiations. Likewise, differences in culture also affect negotiations; each culture has its own concept of negotiation and its own "negotiation style." (Faure & Rubin, pp. 5, 108) Such factors as cultural differences, national life styles, and the personalities of individual negotiators have a great impact on the conception, process, and tactics of negotiations (Brady, p. 9). If one goes back to the analogy of air routes to Boston, although the starting and arrival place are the same, the in-between process varies from case to case. It is thus almost impossible to establish a theoretical generalization or pattern of negotiation; at best, one can only provide individual case studies. If the second school of thought on negotiation is accepted, then the Russian way of negotiating can be considered unique and worth studying.

To which school do I myself subscribe? My position is a middle-of-the-road view, as I consider both arguments have their own strengths and weaknesses. On the one hand, despite the differences in negotiating actors, negotiating behavior has factors that can be generalized, such as bargaining, compromise, and give and take. These are elements that can be seen in almost all negotiations. On the other hand, however, there are also differences in national negotiating styles. Thus, negotiation is a combination of two elements: universal and unique (Sloss & Davis, 1986).

I strongly believe that Russian negotiating behavior consists of two aspects: those similar to and those different from other nationalities. Their differences are often a matter of degree, since many of the traits discussed are used to varying extents by all negotiators. This chapter will deal with aspects of Russian negotiating behavior that to many observers appear as characteristically Russian, leaving analysis of the similar aspects to other scholars.

The second caveat I would like to make is that the question of historical change in Russian culture, character, and mentality is still open to investigation. Cultures change over time, and Russian culture is no exception to this general rule. Russian culture has actually undergone tremendous historical transformation, from tsarist Russia to Soviet Russia to present-day Russia. Yet many of the Soviet characteristics were Russian, carrying over from the pre-Soviet period, and many of the current Russian characteristics are Soviet, instilled by the communist experience. How can they be separated? There are not enough data to define a separate Russian way of negotiating since 1991. All that can be done is to present the generally accepted analysis of the Soviet and pre-Soviet Russian characteristics as hypotheses in regard to the post-Soviet Russian period, and ask if these characteristics still obtain and if any causes or evidence of change exists.

PERCEPTIONS OF NEGOTIATIONS

The first question concerns the significance and values Russians attach to the aspect of human behavior called "negotiations." Why is it necessary to become engaged in such a troublesome task as negotiation in the first place? One of the reasons that makes negotiating with Russians a lengthy and difficult task lies in Russians' own answer to this basic question, which does not necessarily accord with the concept of negotiation held by other nations.

At the outset, it should be noted that there is an extreme lack of Russian-language literature on this subject.[1] Even those papers that have been written by Russian authors on negotiations only deal with the subject in a very abstract and general fashion (Jönsson, 1979, p. 42). This lack of discussion and studies on negotiation in Russia is candidly admitted by Russian scholars themselves. One of few articles on negotiation, published in November 1991 (in the midst of the transitional period from Gorbachev to Yeltsin) by Victor Israelyan and Marina Lebedeva, recognizes that negotiation played a very minor role in the Communist one-party dictatorship and centralized-command economic system in the Soviet Union. However, the article also points out that "the situation is radically changing," due to the transition from a "socialist" system to a multiparty political and a market economic system, and particularly to the continuous eruption of ethnic and other kinds of conflicts (Israelian & Lebedeva, 1991, p. 48). The article concludes that in the long history of the Soviet Union, negotiations have finally obtained a chance to play a role, and that the role is increasing—another hypothesis to be examined.

Naturally in Russia, as in other countries, the extent to which negotiation is used to resolve conflicts varies depending on political, economic, and systematic differences. Therefore, to a certain degree I share the view held by these Russian authors. Still, I do not fully understand why in the Soviet era there was so little study on the subject, resulting in a state of underdevelopment in negotiation studies in the Soviet Union. This is puzzling, since one can assume that even in Soviet days there was some need for bargaining or negotiation, both domestically among institutions and organizations and internationally with foreign countries. Such internal and external necessities exist in almost any countries, regardless of differences in their political and economic systems.

Israelian and Lebedeva (p. 53) gave the following three reasons for the lack of studies on negotiations in the Soviet era: (1) In domestic decision-making fields, the Communist Party (CPSU) dictatorship system based on Marxist-Leninist ideological principles, which is tantamount to a one-man dictatorship, allowed no room for negotiating, and negotiation was considered to be a matter concerning external affairs only. Such a conception was naturally not conducive to serious negotiation study. (2) Foreign policy - making was conducted secretly behind the curtain in the Kremlin, and any external intervention in foreign-policy decisions was shut out. Such conditions made negotiation studies difficult. (3) The academic community was organized in a vertical hierarchical compartmentalized fashion, divided according to disciplines totally unrelated to each other. This situation prevented negotiation study from developing into a high-level interdisciplinary subject.

For these and other reasons, it is a fact that even after the breakup of the Soviet system there has been little study by Russians themselves on

Russian negotiating behavior. This situation has meant that our attention is focused on what Russians have actually done in their negotiations rather than what they themselves may be writing about negotiations. Even if Russians had written a great deal on negotiations in general and on their own negotiating behavior, we would still probably be focusing more on their actual behavior, since what Russians wrote about themselves in the Soviet era cannot always be taken at its face value (a problem that also troubles Western scholarship during the Cold War). This is reflected in the words of former U.S. secretary of state Dean Acheson (1969, p. 378): "The Soviets negotiate by acts rather than words." Although the following analysis concords with the rare contemporary Russian writings, the paucity of Russian self-analysis means that we will have to rely on Western studies from the past and hold them up for testing as the new data come in.

Judging from contemporary Russian attitudes and behaviors, what is their perception of negotiations? As portrayed by the analysis of the Soviet and pre-Soviet eras, the following four constitute salient characteristics of a Russian perception of negotiations.

NEGOTIATION IS A STRUGGLE

Russians regard negotiations as a struggle. The term "struggle" may even be somewhat of an understatement. Some Western observers have gone so far as to suggest that Russians consider negotiations in a Clausewitzian inversion as a form of "war" in peacetime.

Maxim Litvinov, Soviet people's commissar for foreign affairs under Stalin, once stated: "The Soviet diplomat tries in peacetime to perform the task which the Red army would have to perform in wartime" (Pope, 1943, p. 190). This, he explained, was a reversal of the famous statement by Clausewitz: "War is a continuation of politics by other means" (Ibid.). Russians have a broad conception of negotiation. They see it as part of a larger effort designed to achieve their objectives. As pointed out by Helmut Sonnenfeldt, for them, negotiating does not necessarily mean simply "sitting down and haggling over language at the bargaining table," but rather trying to achieve national goals "by one means or another including the use of threats, agitation, bribery, inducements, or any number of things" (Sloss & Davis, p. 24). James J. Wadsworth (1962, pp. 21–22), another observer of Russian concepts of negotiations, went as far as to say: "To a Western nation, the basic purpose of negotiation is to reach an agreement by compromise," but "to communists, at least to date, negotiation is part of a grand strategy aimed at the eventual total defeat of the other side."

Russian national goals, of course, include domestic as well as foreign objectives. Secretary Mikhail S. Gorbachev, by taking a bold initiative and making compromises and even primary concessions in the field of arms controls vis-à-vis the United States, astonished the world, which had been used to watching only a very conservative, noncompromising side of Soviet diplomatic behavior. However, even such an innovative action taken by Gorbachev may not be an exception of the Russian concept of negotiations. Gorbachev took such preemptive diplomatic actions in order to achieve his domestic objective, perestroika, for which he regarded an externally peaceful environment and above all good relations with the United States, as an important prerequisite. One reason why Gorbachev considered perestroika so badly needed was because of his conviction that without perestroika his country would no longer be powerful enough to compete with the United States. Such a correlation between international competition and internal reform is described best by the following sentences of an astute Kremlin watcher, Martin Malia (1994, p. 413): "Throughout his career, Gorbachev always insisted on his country's dignity as a great state. What was involved in perestroika was a change of priorities: a revived Soviet economy was the indispensable precondition for maintaining superpower status. Thus the Soviet Union needed a 'breathing space' from international competition, in order to recoup internally before returning to the contest with capitalism."

This type of thinking does not view diplomacy, negotiation, and war as separate or independent concepts, but instead sees them as a part of a broader theme—struggle (von Clausewitz, 1968, pp. 401–402). Such a concept of negotiations is called by Nathan Leites (1953, p. 60) "a struggle by negotiation" or "war by negotiation." With the grand strategy concept gone in the collapse of Communism, the notion of a struggle may still remain, much as it did in third world anticolonialism after independence had been won.

EMPHASIS ON POWER

The second characteristic of the Russian concept of negotiation is the view that power is one of its most important determining factors (Whelan, 1979, p. 528). In negotiation, although other factors such as eloquence, goodwill, and morality also play a significant role, for Russians the role of power outweighs any other factor. Power—and thus the "correlation of forces" *(sootnoshenie sil)* in Soviet terms and the "balance of power" in Western terms—is the principal criterion in Russians' perception of negotiation. In order to achieve their goal of surviving in a struggle, Russians may at times resort to military force, while at other times they may not, or at least not directly. If they decide not to resort to war, they must turn to negotiations. In a nutshell analysis, the Russian concept of negotiations seems to boil down to this line of thinking. When Josef Stalin heard that the Pope's authority was quite great, he reportedly asked: "How many divisions does he have?" Over a century earlier, when discussing the impending congress at Vienna, a Russian general boasted in 1814, "One does not need to worry much about negotiations when one has 600,000 men under arms" (Nicolson, 1946, p. 119).

On this point, Western experts on Russian affairs have little disagreement. For example, Sir William Hayter, former British ambassador to the Soviet Union, wrote that "the Russians rely on what Stalin used to call the proper basis of international policy, the calculation of forces" (Acheson, 1969, p. 275). Making a similar observation, John R. Deane wrote that "we are dealing with people who respond only to strength" (1946, pp. 300, 304) and that "Soviet leaders have respect only for strength." Russians tend to view human relations through a hierarchical lens (R. Smith, 1989, pp. 7–24). They do not conceive human relationships as being equal, but rather polarized between superiors and subordinates. Ronald Hingley illustrates this Russian characteristic, citing Anton Chekhov's well-known short story, *Fat and Thin*. Two old school friends meet accidentally after many years. While exchanging hearty and intimate greetings, they discover that the fat one has reached the higher echelons of the Table of Ranks, while his thin friend is still sulking in the lower reaches. As soon as this becomes clear, "friendly communion abruptly gives way to condescension on one side and awed sycophancy on the other" (Hingley, 1977, p. 172). Many specialists on Russia have pointed out that Russian domestic society is based upon a hierarchical order of domination and submission. Russians have tended to almost automatically project such a hierarchical view of human relations at home into the international arena as well.

Power is invisible, a relative concept, and varies over time. Therefore, it is necessary for negotiators to gauge and test power (R. Smith, 1989, pp. 14–24). Geoffrey Gorer and John Rickman wrote in *The People of Great Russia* (1950, p. 174): In the Russians "there seems to be a general tendency to 'test' authority; if authority is not firm and consistent, it will be first disregarded and then cast off." Hedrick Smith, former *New York Times* correspondent in Moscow (1976, p. 264), also underlined that "for the Russians the instinctive question is: who is the stronger and who is the weaker."

When it turns out that their opponents are superior or more powerful than themselves, Russians do not mind retreating. When it turns out to be the other way around, however, they continue to move forward. The

Russian expansionist impulse toward the outside can be compared to the movement of an amoeba, which instinctively keeps moving toward the area where there is not much hindrance, but stops moving in an area where it finds strong resistance. Lenin once advocated: "If you strike steel, pull back; If you strike mush, push forward." In short, if your opponents show signs of making a compromise, probe until you find their limit. One of Nikita Khrushchev's motivations in making his decision to bring Soviet missiles into Cuba in 1962 was his assessment of John F. Kennedy's personal qualities as president and statesman. The Soviet leader saw his American counterpart as a man of "wishy-washy behavior" without a "strong backbone" or "the courage to stand up to a serious challenge" (Schevchenko, 1985, p. 117). However, when Kennedy unexpectedly demonstrated strong willpower and leadership capability to counter Khrushchev's test, Khrushchev did not hesitate to back off (or retreat) (R. Smith, 1989, p. 264.).

COMPROMISES AND CONCESSIONS AS SIGNS OF WEAKNESS

For Russians who view negotiation as a form of struggle for survival, the most important thing is the outcome of the battle, namely, victory or defeat. Hayter (1960, p. 28) thus wrote: "The Russians always negotiate for victory. It never seems to occur to them that the proper object of a negotiation is not to defeat your opposite number but to arrive at an agreement with him which will be mutually beneficial." Put in another way, in the Russian perception of negotiations, such concepts as compromise and concession are not highly evaluated, because such actions are regarded in the Russian view as surrendering to the opponent's demands.

There is no disagreement among Western specialists on Russian affairs that the term "compromise" *(kompromiss)* is not of native Russian origin, but imported from the West. Hedrick Smith (1976, p. 264), for instance, wrote: "Compromise is an Anglo-Saxon concept that assumes a rough equality. It does not arise instinctively in the soul of Russian officialdom." The word *"kompromiss"* carries even a negative connotation (Sloss & Davis, 1986, p. 46; Binnendijk, 1987, p. 26). The traditional Russian reluctance to make compromises was reinforced further by the Marxist-Leninist doctrine of class struggle. In his masterful article on Soviet negotiating style and techniques, Philip E. Mosely (1960, p. 32) wrote: "Compromise for the sake of getting on with the job is natural to American and British people, but it is alien to the Bolshevist way of thinking and to the discipline which the Communist Party has striven to inculcate in its members. . . . To give up a demand once presented in even a very minor or formalistic point," Mosely continued, "makes a Bolshevik-trained negotiator feel that he is losing control of his own will and is becoming subject to an alien will."

Russians, who show reluctance to compromise, naturally do not like either its similar or almost identical concept of concessions (Jönsson, 1979, p. 46; Wedge & Muromcew, 1965, p. 33; Binnendijk, 1987, p. 36). Like compromise, a concession is regarded as a sign of weakness, contributing only to the opponent's demands. Khrushchev stated that "we do not have to make any concessions because our proposals have not been made for bartering" (Craig, 1962, p. 368). Confirming this, Arthur M. Schlesinger (1965, p. 362), who during the Kennedy administration carefully watched Soviet conduct in foreign policy, remarked: "Khrushchev objected to the language of commercial bargaining so often used in dealings with the Soviet Union—you give this and we'll give that."

DISREGARD FOR RHETORIC AND COMMITMENT

Such elements as eloquence and morality, which are usually considered to play an important role in negotiations, are not greatly appreciated by Russians. The Russians' tendency to disregard rhetoric and commitment is a corollary of their emphasis on power in the negotiating process—they are two sides of the same coin. Summing up the Russian idea of negotiating, Hayter wrote: "The Russians are not to be persuaded by eloquence or convinced by reasoned arguments" (Acheson, 1969, p. 275). Likewise, Charles B. Marshall, former member of the U.S. policy planning staff (1960, p. 5), advised a Western negotiator not to overestimate the role that debate plays in negotiations with Russians, since Russians do not pay much attention to the outcome of such debate. He writes: "One current view of negotiation compares it to an intercollegiate debate—an exercise in histrionics and logic, with the decision going to the side scoring best in presentation. It is as if at a certain point in the argument across the table, [Mr.] Khrushchev might say to Mr. Dulles, 'All right, you've got me! I can't answer that one. So what are your terms?'"

U.S. ambassador Lawrence Steinhardt expressed this perception to U.S. Secretary of State Cordell Hull by writing:

My observation of the psychology of the individuals who are conducting Soviet foreign policy has long since convinced me that they do not and cannot be induced to respond to the customary amenities, that it is not

possible to create "international goodwill" with them, that they will always
sacrifice the future in favor of an immediate gain, and that they are not affected by ethical or moral considerations, nor guided by the relationships
which are customary between individuals of culture and breeding. Their
psychology recognizes only firmness, power and force, and reflects primitive instincts and reactions entirely devoid of the restraints of civilization. I
am of the opinion that they must be dealt with on this basis and on this
basis alone (cited by Whelan, 1979, p. 85).

It will take long and different experiences based on different underlying
attitudes to change these perceptions in Russia in the post-Soviet period.

NEGOTIATING BEHAVIOR

Based on those perceptions of negotiations described above, what patterns
of negotiating behavior have been ascribed to Russians? The following
three behavioral patterns, while not exclusive to Russians, seem to be particularly significant.

LACK OF INITIATIVES

"Initiative is punishable." This is a saying in Russia, according to Raymond
F. Smith (1989, p. 85), author of one of the best books on Soviet negotiating behavior. Russian negotiators rarely take an initiative, but rather prefer
the opponent to take initiatives, to which they respond. This characteristic
has been well known since the time of Litvinov. Robert Browder (1953,
p. 128) noted that Litvinov did not lay down any detailed proposals on the
negotiating table but rather only reacted to those initiated by the American side. According to Joseph Whelan (1979, p. 80), another authority on
Soviet negotiating behavior, this style of reacting became virtually an established practice. Confirming such proclivity, John Deane (1946, p. 8) also
wrote: "In every instance the proposal was originated by the British or the
Americans." According to another specialist on Soviet negotiating style,
Leon Sloss (Sloss & Davis, 1986, pp. 10, 38–39, 84), this is a characteristic
negotiating behavioral pattern, which has been observed in all major So-
viet-U.S. negotiations on arms control and disarmament, including SALT
I, SALT II, MBFR, START, and INF.

Why has there been a reluctance to take initiatives? The answer seems
to be that Russians have not been encouraged by their political systems to

take initiatives and actions. As long as they let the other side make the proposal to which they will react, Russians feel safe and above criticism, thereby avoiding undertaking any responsibility. In short, as a result of living for a long period in an authoritarian system under tsarist and communist dictatorships, many Russians have become *chinovniks* (bureaucrats), who avert risk-taking, volunteer nothing, and only follow orders from above (R. Smith, 1989, pp. 34–35; Bialer, 1986, p. 163). The characteristic uncertainty of the current transition period continues this condition.

An authoritarian system does not allow individual negotiators to make decisions without instruction from above. The best example of this was the Soviet period when Stalin was the only decision maker. All others, even the foreign minister, were simply errand boys without any rights or allowances. Deane (1951, p. 27) emphasized this point: "In negotiations with foreign nations, one may be sure that Soviet representatives come to the conference table without authority to make any departures from their instructions—only one man in the Soviet Union can make 'on the spot' decisions and he is Joe Stalin. The Molotovs, Vyshinskys, Gromykos and Maliks are little more than messengers." The same characteristics are evident in negotiations under a very different Russian leader—Boris Yeltsin—in dealing with the Chechen rebellion.

As long as they follow traditional customs and procedures, Russian diplomats are immune from taking responsibilities. Consequently, they are reluctant to take any bold initiatives, unless something special or urgent occurs. This hesitancy to take initiatives may be partly explained—according to Whelan (1979, p. 141)—by "the built-in ultra conservatism of a fear-ridden bureaucracy." Such a reactive posture naturally is not always beneficial for Russian diplomacy and negotiations. Owing to this unwillingness to take initiatives, Russia has often missed golden opportunities to achieve diplomatic or economic success. Despite this, Russians still prefer to let others make proposals first and then react to these proposals.

It may be true that, particularly during his early period of rule, Gorbachev took bold initiatives in foreign policy, particularly in the field of arms control and disarmament. As newly selected general secretary of the CPSU, he announced a number of unilateral proposals, including a freeze on further deployment of INF forces, a unilateral ban on underground nuclear testing and on testing of antisatellite weapons, concessions involving verification measures, and a proposal to cut Soviet and American arsenals of strategic weapons by roughly half (Genson, 1988, pp. 224–229). However, as already discussed, it appears that Gorbachev was strongly motivated to take such radical measures in foreign affairs by his goal to achieve his more important domestic objectives. He tried to use diplomacy to create benign international convictions that would enable him to succeed in his perestroika policy at home. Robert Legvold (1991, p. 712), professor at the Harriman Institute, Columbia University, pointed out: Gorbachev and in particular Edward Shevardnadze, his foreign minister, understood well "the intimate link between developments within the Soviet Union and in the world beyond." Gorbachev argued, according to Legvold: "What the Soviet Union can hope to accomplish abroad" cannot be separated from "what the world outside will permit the Soviet Union to accomplish at home." Legvold emphasized that "foreign policy is a function of the domestic order—its reflection, servant, and victim or beneficiary."

SECRETIVENESS

Secretiveness is inherent in negotiating. Negotiations cannot be conducted in a completely open and public fashion. However, Russian enthusiasm for secrecy is a notable pattern in their negotiating behavior. Russian suspicion of the external world and foreigners was rooted in a long tradition from pre-revolution days. Russians, whose land is not separated by ideal natural barriers such as oceans, high mountains, or large rivers, have to live in their almost "defenseless steppes," while regarding surrounding nations as a source of threat to their own security (Samelson, 1976, p. 24). Neighbors such as Mongols, Swedes, Poles, French, and Germans did in fact invade Russian territory, and a number of times the Russians were pushed into a corner of almost total defeat, saved only by the vast expanse of their country. The feeling of defenselessness, siege mentality, and xenophobia nurtured by Russia's geographical environment and historical experiences continued after the October Revolution. Intervention by Western powers, taking advantage of the confusion in the wake of the revolution and in the midst of the civil war, led to Stalin's policy of survival, of virtually completely closing the Soviet Union off from the outside world, which he considered hostile to Russia, and building up "socialism in one country" under encirclement by capitalist powers. Even after victory in World War II, Stalin's deep suspicion of the outside world kept the iron curtain of the Soviet Union closed, thus preventing Russians from contact with foreign counterparts.

This feature may stem from the more general difference between Russian and Western attitudes toward information. Russian secretiveness concerning information can operate in both ways: in some cases it may be advantageous to their negotiations while in other cases it may be disadvantageous. Negotiating requires give and take with regard to information as well as positions. Russian reluctance to supply information to their opponents leads, sooner or later, to a similar proclivity by their counterparts. Raymond Smith (1989, pp. 39, 41) was surprised, when he discovered that even during the most difficult days of World War II, Soviets placed the need to maintain secrecy above the need to obtain more effective help from the Allies. Stalin supplied a shopping list of lend-lease needs, but would not supply information to justify it. Russian reluctance to supply information, even to those who wish to give the country aid has continued after the ascent to power of Gorbachev and Yeltsin. In the post-Soviet period, G-7 members, including Japan, have continuously complained that the Russian failure to provide them with enough information has made their assistance difficult to fulfill.

Russians not only are reluctant to provide necessary information during negotiations, but may even try to supply false information. The distinction between the two Russian words, *lozh'* (lie) and *vran'e* (leg-pulling), is very subtle but important (R. Smith, 1989, p. 41). According to Ronald Hingley (1977, p. 95), *vran'e* is the more innocent of the two words, denoting the dissemination of an untruth indicative of a lively imagination. While lying is to be criticized, *vran'e* is to be taken as an obvious joke made for fun. A typical example of *vran'e* is the "Potemkin villages," which G. A. Potemkin erected in order to impress Catherine II, so that she could entertain a comforting illusion that her realm appeared more populated and prosperous than in fact it was. Everybody was aware of the fact that they were fake villages; nobody was supposed to say what they were. *Vran'e* may be considered as a kind of *pokazukha* (deceit for show), like the wisdom needed to survive in Russia's harsh natural and political environments. By resorting to *vran'e* and/or *pokazukha*, Russians hope to make negotiations advantageous for them. A Russian delegation may, for example, request to stop or postpone a negotiation by suddenly saying that its leader has become ill. In such a case, it would not be wise to accuse the Russians of feigning illness. Such an accusation would only reveal ignorance of Russian negotiating behavior.

Volte-Face

Russian negotiators do not mind suddenly changing their positions, even 180 degrees (Hingley, 1977, p. 46). They have shown an ability to switch overnight from one to the other extreme (R. Smith, 1989, p. 29). In view of what appeared to be an intransigent position only a few minutes ago, such a radical shift is hard to comprehend. What makes Russians suddenly shift position?

Firstly, as mentioned previously, Russians have tended to test the strength and determination of the other side at the negotiating table. Russians are not necessarily fundamentalist in their loyalty to beliefs, ideology, and principles. Rather, they adopt a flexible negotiating position, reacting to any change in the situation, particular "correlations of forces." Once they realize that they cannot realize their goals in the negotiation, they do not mind shifting positions. Secondly, Russians remain loyal to the instructions from the top political leaders at home. Russian diplomats are required to negotiate in accordance with instructions issued from Moscow. When the leaders at home alter their policies, Russian diplomats follow suit.

There is also a third reason for sudden dramatic shifts in negotiating position by Russians, the tendency to change position from one extreme to the other, skipping an intermediary position. According to the Russian philosopher Nicolas Berdyaev (1992, pp. 19–21), "the Russians are a people who are polarized to the highest degree: They are a conglomeration of contradictions. . . . The Russians have not been given to moderation and they have readily gone to extremes." Such mutually contradictory positions in Russian mentality can be seen in "humility and arrogance, slavery and revolt, freedom and collectivism, and nationalism and universalism."

There have been many attempts to account for the existence of such dichotomy or "dualism" through the geopolitical environment of Russia as a huge, vast, endless, and borderless land mass, or through the conflicting cultures of Europe and Asia (Tucker, 1963, pp. 69–70). Whatever the reason may be, if Russians decide to change their positions, they do not seem to mind shifting from one extreme to the other. As Bohlen (1978) noted, "the men of Moscow are never troubled about consistency and 'close their books at the end of every day.'" Another U.S. ambassador to the Soviet Union, Foy D. Kohler (1958, p. 910), wrote about his experience dealing with such sudden shifts of position during negotiation with Russians: "We kept negotiating for a long time with the Russians. Without much hope to accomplish any progress we were simply negotiating. Then one day, all of sudden, the Russian side informed us that they were ready to make an agreement with us in a few hours." Likewise, Hayter (1960, pp. 30–31) said that, due to their "total lack of inhibitions about consistency, the Russians do not hesitate to switch rapidly and easily from one standpoint to another." Lermontov (1994, p. 26), one of the greatest nineteenth-century Russian novelists, also refers in his masterpiece *A Hero of Our Times* to such "incredible flexibility" *(neimovernaia gibkost')* in the Russian mind and behavior. Professor Suzuki (1993, p. 163) of Kyushu University also remarked on the Russian habit and ability to make a very rapid swing, citing the Russian proverb, "a bear runs very fast."

One may wonder if a sudden shift in position implies compromise, in apparent contradiction to the previous point. In the Russian view, however, such a shift is regarded not as a compromise but rather as a tactical retreat. The distinction between compromise and retreat may appear to be negligible, but not necessarily so to the Russian way of thinking. Compromise is viewed as a shameful act. Retreat is also humiliating in the sense that it is tantamount to acceptance of the opponent's superior power position. However, retreat can also be justified as a legitimate temporary action because it is used as a tactic, ultimately aimed at achieving one's the final objectives (R. Smith, 1989, p. 31; Adomeit, 1982, p. 320).

There is much support in the literature for these characteristics of Russian negotiating behavior in the pre–Soviet as well as the Soviet period. Although there are few data from the post–Soviet period as yet, there is no indication of any changes either in behavior or in the reasons for it. Rare evidence from Russian negotiating behavior on sovereign territorial issues in Chechnya, Nagorno-Karabakh, and Moldova under Yeltsin and Chernomyrdin exhibit the same traits, however.

NEGOTIATING TACTICS

As mentioned at the start of this chapter, perceptions of negotiations, negotiating behavior, and negotiating tactics are inseparably connected with each other. Therefore, negotiating tactics may derive almost automatically from the perception of negotiations and negotiating behavior. However, negotiating tactics should not be regarded only as a logical extension of the former two. In the extreme case, any tactic may be employed freely so far as it is serves to accomplish one's goal, even when it does not accord well with, or even contradicts, the given concept of negotiations or negotiating behavior.

This can be applied to non–Russian people as well, which raises an important question: Do tactics exist that are used solely by Russians? Some consider that human beings are all more or less of the same nature (R. Smith, 1989, p. 49) and therefore, there can be no such thing as a unique form of human behavior. From this point of view, the answer to the above question would be negative: the capacity of human imagination is not unlimited, and such unique tactics cannot be invented. Even assuming that the Russians can invent new tactics, such tactics would soon be copied by other non-Russian people, and thus they would cease to be unique (Luce, 1979, p. 31).

However, even accepting this line of thought, the author of this chapter agrees with the view that "there are certain tactics and gambits for which Soviet/Russian negotiators seem to have a special fondness and which they use with a greater frequency than other tactics" (Wedge & Muromcew, 1965, p. 11). The argument is not that others do not use the same tactics, among others, but that observers have noted a Russian specialization in them. I will explain five tactics that Russians have appeared particularly to like and to use quite frequently, and that can be tested against post-Soviet practice as evidence becomes available.

EFFECTIVE USE OF TIME

One of the most successful Russian tactical techniques during the negotiating process is the efficient use of time (Craig, 1962, p. 122; Whelan, 1979, pp. 364–365, 483, 487–488; R. Smith, 1989, pp. 51–54). Observers sometimes wonder whether the Russian diplomats have a different concept of time from that prevailing among their Western counterparts (Sloss and Davis, 1986, p. 88; Dean, 1966, p. 44). According to Whelan (1979, p. 365), "[t]he Russians can sit through meeting after meeting, talking endlessly and repetitiously, hoping to wear down an adversary and win concessions through sheer fatigue and boredom on the other side." Why have Russians been good at manipulating time?

One reason is related to harsh natural conditions, including long and cold winters, which have contributed to the notion that patience and hardship are necessary to accomplish something. This concept of time nurtured among Russians was further reinforced by Marxist-Leninist doctrine. Marx and Lenin considered that time was on the socialists' side: History will ultimately see the victory of socialism, which was, in their view, the inevitable course of world development. Lenin (1964, Vol. 34, pp. 49–50) wrote that "gaining time means everything." Furthermore, in the Russian authoritarian political system, political leaders and negotiators have been freer from definite time constraints than their Western counterparts who have to negotiate against fixed timetables, such as tenure and other deadlines, to accomplish their goals by a certain date. In the West, political leaders and negotiators are often obsessed with a professional feeling of mission to "get the job done quickly and efficiently" (Ibid., p. 39). The Russian side tries to capitalize on this feeling of urgency, and use it to their own advantage in negotiations.

Russian tactics of time manipulation include stonewalling, repetition, and using time limits. One tactic that is played better by Russians than by most others is the waiting game. Only a few minutes before they board their return plane, Russians are said to make their final decision in negotiations. "The departure-time decision" is a technique that Russians employ in almost every negotiation, even in the post-Soviet period (Whelan, 1979, p. 571). Edward L. Rowny, one of the American veterans in arms control negotiations, reports that Russians do not give up their negotiating positions until the very last moment: "We thought that we had an agreement at 4:00 P.M.—until they [the Russians] raised a few more issues. We then had two more sessions at 8:00 P.M. and 10:00 P.M. Finally, at one minute to midnight, they agreed on the final points" (Sloss and Davis, 1986, p. 51).

AGREEMENT IN PRINCIPLE

Many Western diplomats who have had experience in negotiating with Russians point out the Russian tendency to rely on a technique of agreement "in principle" (Mosely, 1960, pp. 25–26; Deane, 1946, p. 20). Reaching an agreement "in principle" is regarded by Russians as the most important part of negotiations. Only then can details of the negotiations be worked out. In other words, the Russians prefer a deductive line of reasoning to an inductive one (R. Smith, 1989, pp. 54–57; Jönsson, 1979, pp. 50–51).

An agreement "in principle" is for Russians nothing but a promise, the interpretations of which depend on the existing circumstances or situation, so as to produce a favorable application to detail, a selective one, or, alternatively, none at all. Once having reached an agreement in principle, Russians tend to interpret it in such a way that enables them to formulate details that will be advantageous for them. Even granting that the "principle" is by definition general, abstract, and even vague, the Russian way of applying the principle is quite arbitrary and one-sided. Or else the principle becomes an end in itself. Arthur H. Dean (1966, pp. 465–467), head of the U.S. negotiation team in the U.S.-Soviet test ban and disarmament negotiations, confessed that, only after having bitter experiences more than once, he understood that there is an almost fundamental difference concerning the concept of agreement "in principle" between Westerners and Russians. For the former, an agreement "in principle" means that the agreement provides them with a guideline for formulating details. For the Russians, however, an agreement "in principle" will not necessarily be carried out in practice.

Rather, such an agreement represents simply a common point of view, at which remaining divergent viewpoints may converge if it suits either side to do so in the light of conditions existing at the time.

The Russian tactical negotiating technique that is closely related to an agreement in principle is a technique that U.S. diplomats call "cherry picking" (Rowny, 1980, p. 61; Sloss & Davis, 1986, p. 88). It is like choosing only the raisins out of a cake. The general agreement in negotiations can often be reached only in the form of package deals. Yet, Russians tend to pick out from these package deals only the parts they like, while ignoring any part they do not like. In short, they take what they consider for them to be acceptable and reject the rest. An example of "cherry picking" tactics can be seen in Gorbachev's policy regarding the 1956 Soviet-Japanese Joint Declaration. This declaration stipulated that the Soviet Union would transfer the Habomai isles and Shikotan Island to Japan upon the conclusion of a Soviet-Japanese peace treaty. During his official visit to Japan in April 1991, Gorbachev (1991, p. 94) divided, quite arbitrarily, the declaration into two parts: those parts that he considered to be still valid and those parts that he regarded as being no longer valid. Making this distinction clear, Gorbachev stated that his government would abide by only the former parts, but not by any of the latter parts: "We consider that in this document we should focus only on those parts which have become a historical reality, and which have accompanied international, legal, and physical results. On the other hand, we cannot simply resurrect those parts which have not hereafter taken place nor been materialized, and which history 'wiped out' from the scene."[2]

"Montage" tactics can be viewed as an extension of the technique of "cherry picking," albeit in a sort of reverse way (Suzuki, Itoga, et al., 1993, p. 180). This is a method to collect the best parts of various offers proposed by different negotiating partners, so as to integrate them into an ideal, but illusionary, offer. Russians either press their negotiating partners to propose such an offer to them, or they themselves pretend to be proposing such an ideal offer. In the latter case, once their partners accept such an offer, Russians undertake the task of gradually revising it, saying that it was simply an agreement "in principle," and thus naturally expected to be revised in the implementation process. In such a revision process, the proposal may sometimes be amended to such a degree that almost none of the original form remains.

DIVIDE AND RULE

Another tactical instrument that Russians apply in their negotiations is that of "divide and rule." This device was used as far back as the days of the

Roman empire. Mori Motonari, a feudal lord in Japan, taught his three sons the importance of uniting against one's enemies, using as an analogy the three arrows that are much harder to bend than only one or two. Lenin's motto was "split, split, and split again" *(Raskol, raskol, i eshche raskol)* (Drachkovitch, 1965, p. 64). Lenin (1964, Vol. 31, p. 55) thought that "the practical task of Communist policy is . . . to incite one [enemy power] against the other." He further elaborated on this, by saying: "The weaker side can win against the more powerful opponent . . . only if the former utilizes carefully, cautiously and skillfully the 'rift'—no matter how small it may be—between the enemies." Citing this teaching, V. Zorin's textbook for Soviet diplomats, *The Fundamentals for the Diplomatic Service* (1977, p. 76) advocated that this Leninist teaching should be followed by all Soviet diplomats, no matter where they may be assigned to work. Western negotiators dealing with their Russian counterparts have confirmed Russian diplomats' faithful acceptance of and efforts toward the realization of these teachings. For instance, Frederick Osborn (1951, p. 234), head of the U.S. negotiating team for atomic energy problems, stated: "The Soviet representatives were obviously instructed to try to split the other nations apart from each other."

In their fisheries negotiations with Japan, for example, Russians attempted to drive a wedge between the Japanese prime minister; Ministry of Foreign Affairs; and economic ministries, such as the Ministry of International Trade and Industry (MITI), Ministry of Finance, and Ministry of Agriculture, Forestry, and Fisheries, and to generate confrontation among them. It also tried to use differences in views and potential rivalries between the Japanese government and private business communities such as Keidairen (Association of Economic Organizations), between the Center (Tokyo) and prefectures (such as Hokkaido), and between cities in the same prefectures (such as the city of Nemuro, whose main interest is the reversion of the Northern Territories, versus the city of Wakkanai, whose interest lies more in fishing quotas) (Kimura, 1980, pp. 43–67).

A variant of the "divide and rule" tactic is to create an artificial competitor in the mind of negotiating counterparts, and generate competition. In an example of Russian foreign business trade negotiation techniques, Ale Flegon (1965, p. 97) cites the episode in which the Russians invited several Western companies dealing with the same commodities to come to Moscow at the same time and assigned each of them a room in the same hotel. The Western businessmen saw their competitors every morning and evening in the lobby, elevator, or restaurant of the hotel, and realized that they were not alone in the business negotiations with the Russians. They became anxious that they would lose a business opportunity with such severe competition, thereby playing into Russian hands.

LINKAGE

Linkage is another tactical instrument that Russians often exploit in negotiations. In contrast to "divide and rule," which is a tactic employed on parties, linkage (or coupling/decoupling) is a technique to unite or disengage issues of the dispute. The history of the linkage technique, like that of "divide and rule," is as old as the human race. It is conventional human wisdom to complement one's weakness on one issue or in one field with one's strength on other issues or in other fields. Then, what has been unique about the Russian type of linkage? The answer lies in their arbitrary use of linking. Russians formulate or disband a linkage very freely, depending upon their interests, but do not permit their opponents to do the same.

On the one hand, Russians have assumed the position that all fields of human activities are closely connected with each other. Emphasizing the value and need of "total diplomacy," they try to pursue a comprehensive, omnidirectional type of diplomacy. Russians never fail to argue, for instance, that between Russia and Japan it is necessary to establish mutually close, friendly, and cooperative relations in all fields. When Tokyo made an unpleasant claim such as the reversion of the Northern Territories or protest against the buildup of the Russian military forces in areas close to Japan, the Russians responded by imposing stricter controls on Japanese fishing, thereby applying linkage tactics between political and fishing issues. On the other hand, however, when they realized that the Japanese side was also attempting to apply similar linkage tactics, for instance, by reinforcing its weak diplomatic position with its stronger economic clout, the Russians insisted that Japan decouple these issues.

The Russians also argue that the development of economic relations between Russia and Japan will inevitably help improve the political atmosphere between the two countries, whereas, on the other hand, they oppose the use of Japanese economic power as a bargaining chip to achieve Tokyo's political objective. This Russian dislike of the Japanese tactics of the "inseparability of politics from economics" is another example of their tactical flexibility.

BAZAAR

The word "bazaar" has its origin in the Persian language, in which it means "market." It indicates a commercial transaction, which, without establishing in advance a fixed price or other business condition, aims instead at reaching a satisfactory price and other conditions through a bargaining process. It also indicates a technique of starting negotiations by demanding an exorbitant price or other demands so that, with the counterpart's acceptance of the offer and even with substantial concessions, one could still make a good profit.

The "bazaar" tactic is not one exclusively employed by Arab merchants in the Middle East. All nations use this technique in varying degrees. However, this technique, which tends to neglect long-term profit and instead aims at short-term benefits, cannot be popular in business transactions of a society where the long-range confidence in investments is highly respected. In Japan, for instance, the bazaar technique may be employed by a street vendor selling products to tourists, but never in high-class shops or department stores, where trust between the store and customers is highly valued and becomes a long-lasting relationship. In contrast, Russians, who, as previously pointed out, have a strong tendency to test the strength of their opponents, and who do not seem to worry about inconsistencies in their position, are fond of the bazaar technique (*New York Times,* January 27, 1981, p. 19).

Litvinov was well known as a diplomat who used the bazaar technique of business in the arena of international politics. Arthur Pope (1943, pp. 189–191, 493), the author of Litvinov's biography, wrote: "Litvinov knows very well when to make a fantastic proposal, when to give way, pretending to his opponents his possible concessions, and when to revert to the position close to his original one." The important point that Pope wishes to make is his conviction that "Litvinov has the typical Russian feeling for humanity as a whole." Litvinov's fondness for the "bazaar" tactic was emulated by Molotov and Gromyko (Craig, 1962, p. 366). Fred Ikle, a U.S. expert both in the theory of negotiations and in SALT I negotiations, in which the bazaar technique was frequently used by the Russian side, warned American negotiators of this strategy as a lesson for SALT II. If caution is not taken, Ikle has argued, the Soviet side will again make initial exorbitant demands and expect concessions from the United States as the price to be paid for the Russian withdrawing of their original demands (cited from Whelan, 1979, p. 494). Max Kampelman, head of the

U.S. delegation to the Conference on Security and Cooperation in Europe (CSCE) Review Conference held in Madrid in 1986, also reminded us of the fact that the Russians came "with inflated proposals that naturally had to be submitted to the most drastic surgery" (Sloss and Davis, 1986, p. 113).

As already noted, Russians have a tendency to make their concessions only at the very last stage of negotiations. The so-called *popolam* method, in which the Russians propose making a deal on a fifty-fifty basis, can be considered as a variant of the bazaar technique. In a negotiation, for instance, in which the price was originally $1,000, the United States may be tempted to make a concession of $200 at the initial stage. The Russians may then propose to the United States at this stage to adopt the *popolam* method. If the United States agrees to this, the United States would end up making a concession of $600, while Russia's concession would be only $400.

IN LIEU OF CONCLUSION

One of the questions that remains to be answered is whether Russian perceptions, behavior, and tactics stem from Russian—that is, cultural—rather than ideological grounds. In other words, are these traits relatively permanent or are they likely to pass with the passing of the Soviet system? The answers, unfortunately, must be tentative, and fall far short of providing a definite conclusion to this problem.

Firstly, it does not seem to be correct to consider Russian traditional culture and communist ideology as two diametrically opposing things. Generally speaking, any political, economic, or social ideas born abroad can only be transplanted to another culture when and where there are grounds to accept or absorb its ideas. Marxism was not an exception to this general rule, and it was in fact only able to penetrate into Russia because it fitted in with preexisting conditions there. To the extent that there is a difference between the two, a foreign idea must be adjusted to a certain degree to become harmonized with an indigenous culture, as was the case with Marxism, which was modified by Lenin and later by Stalin. As a result of this modification of Communist ideology into Leninism or Stalinism, it was not a very alien political and social ideology to Russian culture. Making a similar observation about the close correspondence between Russian traditional culture and communist ideology, Robert V. Daniels, of the University of Vermont (1988, p. 44), went so far as to say that "Russia has russified Communism more than Communism has communized Russia." Indeed, it can be argued that what was formerly regarded as communist ideological influences was in fact Russian national culture, although this is not to be taken to mean that all features of Soviet negotiating style can be traced back to Russian cultural roots alone.

There is also a technical problem. Since communist ideology and Russian indigenous political culture have been inseparably intertwined for more than seventy years, it is very difficult and perhaps even impossible to distinguish what is Russian from what is communist. Even in the heyday of the Soviet regime, the negotiating behavior of Russian politicians and diplomats was a mix or integrated amalgam of these two elements. In this regard, Russian politicians and diplomats are not different from their Japanese equivalents, for example, who are also a product of two cultures— the purely Japanese indigenous culture and Western diplomatic culture.

Finally, based upon my personal experiences, I have strong doubts about the argument that with the demise of the USSR Russian politicians and diplomats have ceased to be Soviet-type negotiators and converted to Western-type negotiators. Although I am neither a professional diplomat nor a businessman with experience in political or business negotiations with the Russians, as a researcher of Russia and a frequent visitor to Russia I have been keenly and carefully observing Russian behavioral patterns for more than thirty-five years. Most of my Russian friends and acquaintances are scholars or intellectuals who have been advocating reform in their political and economic system, namely, Russia's rapid transition to a democracy and market economy. However, ironically, despite their apparently strong advocacy for reform in Russia, their underlying perceptions and behavior do not seem to have changed much from Soviet days. For instance, although they talk a great deal about the need to conduct lively discussions in parliament, in practice, most of them end up stressing the need for guided democracy by a strong ruler *(krepkii khoziain)*. While almost all Russian intellectuals are knowledgeable about such economic concepts as profits, investment, and competition, many also show total ignorance about the actual mechanism of the free-competition system. Likewise, many Russians espouse the important role that negotiations play in solving conflicts, and yet do not have sufficient knowledge about how negotiations are actually conducted in the West. They do not yet have a full appreciation of basic conceptions and principles in negotiations, such as trust (Fukuyama, 1995, pp. 28, 356–357), give and take, compromise, fair dealing, reasonableness (Nicolson, 1963, p. 71), and the concept of *pacta sunt servanda* (contracts must be observed).

The question of permanence of observed attitudes and actions is one for which we have hypotheses but await evidence. There are not yet enough cases and data to enable analysts either to confirm the persistence of old patterns or to establish the existence of a new one, although there is sporadic evidence that established perceptions, behaviors and tactics have not yet been supplanted by those who would introduce new ones. The observed traits of the past then become hypotheses from the past to be tested against present practice as a guide to understanding future behavior. Although it is true that change is occurring, the important question for us is whether it is safer to overestimate or underestimate the scale and speed of their change. Personally, I am of a cautious opinion that, just as democracy and market economy must become a long-term rather than a short-term goal for Russia, the change in Russian negotiating will also be a long-term process, taking decades or even generations.

Notes

* This chapter first appeared in *International Negotiation,* Vol. 1, no. 3, 1996 (Kluwer Law International).
1. All the Russian-language materials on negotiations that the author of this chapter has obtained are as follow: Bogdanov, 1958; Ladyzhenskii & Blishchenko, 1962; Levin, 1962; Lebedev, 1963; Zorin, 1977; Kovalev, 1988; and Anderson [and] Shikhirev, 1994.
2. "Cherry picking" tactics by Gorbachev have been criticized by a Russian expert on Russo-Japanese relations. See Eremin, 1992.

References

Acheson, D. 1969. *Present at the Creation: My Years in the State Department.* New York: Norton.

Adomeit, H. 1982. *Soviet Risk-Taking and Crisis Behavior: A Theoretical and Empirical Analysis.* London: George Allen and Unwin.

Anderson, R., & Shikhirev, P. 1994. *Akuly i del'finy: Psikhologiia i etika rossiisko-amerikanskogo delovogo partnerstva.* Moscow: Delo Ltd.

Berdyaev, N. 1992. *The Russian Idea.* New York: Lindisfarne Press.

Binnendijk, H. 1987. *National Negotiating Styles.* Washington, DC: Foreign Service Institute, U.S. Department of State.

Bialer, S. 1986. *The Soviet Paradox: External Expansion, Internal Decline.* New York: Knopf.

Bogdanov, O. V. 1958. *Peregovory—osnova mirnogo uregulirovaniia mezhdunanodnykh problem.* Moscow: Znanie.

Bohlen, C. E. 1973. *Witness to History 1929–1969.* New York: Norton.

Bohlen, C. 1978. *Christian Science Monitor,* February 11.

Browder, R. P. 1953. *The Origins of Soviet-American Diplomacy.* Princeton: Princeton University Press.

Brady, L. P. 1991. *The Politics of Negotiation.* Chapel Hill: University of North Carolina Press.

Craig, G. A. 1961. "Totalitarian Approaches to Diplomatic Negotiation." In Sarkissian, *Studies in Diplomatic History and Historiography in Honour of G. P. Gooch.* London: Longmans.

Craig, G. A. 1962. "Techniques of Negotiation." In Lederer, *Russian Foreign Policy: Essays in Historical Perspective.* New Haven: Yale University Press.

Daniels, R. V. 1988. *Is Russia Reformable?* Boulder, CO: Westview.

Dean, A. H. 1966. *Test Ban and Disarmament: The Path of Negotiation.* New York: Harper and Row.

Deane, J. R. 1946. *The Strange Alliance: The Story of Our Efforts at Wartime Cooperation with Russia.* Bloomington: Indiana University Press.

Deane, J. R. 1951. "Negotiating on Military Assistance." In Dennett & Johnson, *Negotiating with the Russians.* Boston: World Peace Foundation.

Drachkovitch, M. M., eds. 1965. *Marxism in the Modern World.* Stanford: Stanford University Press.

Eremin, V. 1992. *Rossiia—Iaponiia: Territorial'naia problema: Poisk resheniia* (pp. 6–70). Moscow: Izdatel'stvo Respublika.

Faure, G. O., & Rubin, J. Z., eds. 1993. *Culture and Negotiation.* Newbury Park, CA: Sage.

Flegon, A., eds. 1965. *Soviet Foreign Trade Techniques: An Inside Guide to Soviet Foreign Trade.* London: Flegon.

Fukuyama, F. 1995. *Trust: The Social Virtues and the Creation of Prosperity.* New York: The Free Press.

Gorer, G., & Rickman, J. 1950. *The People of Great Russia.* New York: Cresset Press.

Gorbachev, M. 1991. *Vizit M. S. Gorbacheva v Iaponiiu (16 aprelia 1991 goda).* Moscow: Politizdat.

Hayter, W. 1960. *The Diplomacy of the Great Powers.* London: Harmish Hamilton.

Hingley, R. 1977. *The Russian Mind.* New York: Charles Scribner.

Israelian, V., & Lebedeva, M. 1991. "Peregovory—iskusstvo dlia vsekh." *Mezhdunarodnaia zhizn'* (November).

Jensen, L. 1988. *Bargaining for National Security: The Postwar Disarmament Negotiations.* Columbia: University of South Carolina.

Jönsson, C. 1979. *Soviet Bargaining Behavior: The Nuclear Test Ban Case.* New York: Columbia University Press.

Kimura, H. 1980. "Soviet and Japanese Negotiating Behavior: The Spring 1977 Fisheries Talks." *Orbis,* 24 (1).

Kohler, F. D. 1958. "Negotiation as an Effective Instrument of American Foreign Policy." *U.S. Department of State Bulletin,* 38, 910.

Kovalev, A. 1988. *Azbuka diplomatii,* 5th rev. and expanded ed. Moscow: Mezhdunarodnye otnosheniia.

Ladyzhenskii, A. M., & Blishchenko, I. P. 1962. *Mirnye sredstva razresheniia sporov mezhdu gosudarstvami.* Moscow: Gosudarstvennoe izdatel'stvo iuridicheskoi literatury.

Lebedev, V. Z., ed. 1963. *O sovremennoi sovetskoi diplomatii.* Moscow: Institut mezhdunarodnykh otnoshenii.

Legvold, R. 1991. "Soviet Learning in the 1980s." In Breslauer and Tetlock, *Learning in U.S. and Soviet Foreign Policy.* Boulder, CO: Westview.

Leites, N. 1953. *A Study of Bolshevism.* Glencoe, IL: The Free Press.

Lenin, V. I. 1964. *Polnoe sobranie sochinenii,* 5th ed. Moscow: Izdatel'stvo politicheskoi literatury.

Lermontov, M. I. 1994. *Geroi nashego vremeni.* Paris: Booking International.

Levin, D. B. 1962. *Diplomatiia: ee sushchnost', metody i formy.* Moscow: Izdatel'stvo sotsial' no-ekonomicheskoi literatury.

Luce, C. B. 1979. "How to Deal with the Russians: The Basis of Negotiation." *Air Force Magazine,* April.

Malia, M. 1994. *The Soviet Tragedy: A History of Socialism in Russia, 1917–1921.* New York: The Free Press.

Marshall, C. B. 1960. "The Problem of Incompatible Purposes." In Duchacek, *Conflict and Cooperation among Nations.* New York: Holt, Rinehart and Winston.

Mosely, P. E. 1960. *The Kremlin and World Politics: Studies in Soviet Policy and Action.* New York: Vintage.

Nicolson, H. 1946. *The Congress of Vienna: A Study in Allied Unity: 1812–1822.* New York: Harcourt, Brace.

Nicolson, H. 1963. *Diplomacy.* Oxford: Oxford University Press.

Osborn, F. J. 1951. "Negotiating on Atomic Energy, 1946–47." In Dennett & Johnson, *Negotiating with the Russians.*

Pope, A. U. 1943. *Maxim Litvinoff.* New York: Fischer.

Rowny, E. L. 1980. "Negotiating with the Soviets." *The Washington Quarterly,* Winter.

Samelson, L. J. 1976. *Soviet and Chinese Negotiating Behavior: The Western View.* Beverly Hills, CA: Sage.

Schlesinger, Jr., A. M. 1965. *A Thousand Days: John F. Kennedy in the White House.* Boston: Houghton Mifflin.

Shevchenko, A. N. 1985. *Breaking with Moscow.* New York: Knopf.

Sloss, L., & Davis, M. S., eds. 1986. *A Game for High Stakes: Lessons Learned in Negotiating with the Soviet Union.* Cambridge, MA: Ballinger.

Smith, R. F. 1989. *Negotiating with the Soviets.* Bloomington: Indiana University Press.

Smith, H. 1976. *The Russians.* New York: Quadrangle.

Suzuki, K., & Itoga, R. et al. 1993. *Chugoku, Roshiya Bizinesu no Jitsumu to Kosho Nouhau.* Tokyo: Gyosei.

Tucker, R. C. 1963. *The Soviet Political Mind: Studies in Stalinism and Post-Stalin Change.* New York: Praeger.

von Clausewitz, C. 1968. *On War.* London: Penguin Books.

Wadsworth, J. J. 1962. *The Price of Peace.* New York: Praeger.

Wedge, B., & Muromcew, C. 1965. "Psychological Factors in Soviet Disarmament Negotiation." *Journal of Conflict Resolution,* 9 (1).

Whelan, J. 1979. *Soviet Diplomacy and Negotiation Behavior: Emerging New Context for U.S. Diplomacy.* Special Studies Series on Foreign Affairs Issues, 1, Committee on Foreign Affairs, House of Representatives. Washington, DC: U.S. Government Printing Office.

Zartman, I. W., & Berman, M. 1982. *The Practical Negotiator.* New Haven: Yale University Press.

Zorin, V. A. 1977. *Osnovy diplomaticheskoi sluzhby.* Moscow: Mezhdunarodnye otnosheniia.

CHAPTER 4

JAPANESE, CHINESE, AND SOVIET/RUSSIAN NEGOTIATORS: AN ANALYTIC FRAMEWORK[*]

PETER BERTON

INTRODUCTION

The purpose of this chapter is to construct a framework of the concepts of negotiation, communication, and culture, and to introduce, in a comparative fashion, some of the basic characteristics of the negotiating behavior of the Japanese, the Chinese, and the Soviets (as well as the successor Russians). It also addresses the impact of culture and communication upon their negotiating behavior. Implicit in this endeavor are implications of these negotiating behaviors for American and other counterparts.

Although this study is based on a large number of primary and secondary works on the subject (including my own), it is obvious that a comprehensive coverage of the three concepts of negotiation, communication, and culture, and four national behavioral characteristics could easily fill twelve books. My aim, therefore, is much more modest: to present and develop some theoretical frameworks and illustrate, in a comparative fashion, the cases of Japan, China, and the Soviet Union/Russia.

Numerous books and articles have addressed the question of the relevance of culture to the negotiating process. This chapter offers the proposition that although language and communication patterns may be seen as a part of culture, it is useful to treat communication as a distinct, intermediary concept. Indeed, at the end of the twentieth century, communication, along with knowledge and information, is gradually driving our societies into a post-industrial phase, a revolutionary change not unlike the change from agrarian to industrial society. My second proposition is the importance of the comparative approach, and the selection of appropriate subjects for comparison.

COMPARATIVE APPROACH

In a television interview, the noted political scientist Seymour Martin Lipset made the statement that if you study only one country, then you cannot know any country, because to understand what is unique one must do comparative work. Having edited for almost fourteen years an international interdisciplinary journal, *Studies in Comparative Communism*,[1] I am, of course, keenly aware of the advantages of the comparative method, and that is what brings me to go beyond my study of the Japanese negotiating behavior (Berton, 1982, 1995, 1996, 1998).

SELECTION OF SUBJECTS

The choice of Japan, China, and the Soviet Union/Russia is dictated by the fact that I have been studying and teaching international relations in the Asia-Pacific region for over forty years, starting at a time when it was known as "International Relations in the Far East." Along with the United States, the countries chosen also happen to be the most important players in the region. We are, therefore, frequently involved in negotiations with these powers, as can often be seen on the front pages of our newspapers and on television news. Last, but not least, I have some familiarity with the languages concerned.

The Soviet Union was a bitter antagonist of the United States and its allies for the entire period of the Cold War. Communist China was involved in a hot war with the United States and its allies on the Korean peninsula, and both Communist superpowers carried on negotiations with the United States for decades on end. This gave rise to a number of books, pamphlets, and articles describing the difficulties encountered in dealing with representatives of these Communist countries. Negotiations with Japan gathered steam as the balance of payments turned sharply against the United States and the Japanese market remained partially inaccessible for American products and services.

The rapid expansion of trade and steady development of economic relations between the United States and the rest of the world has resulted in a phenomenal growth in face-to-face business negotiations with foreign businessmen. This has created a cottage industry of books explaining how to deal and negotiate with the Japanese and the Chinese, and after the demise of the Soviet Union on how to negotiate obstacles in the chaotic new Russian market. In the case of Japan, an ever growing number of books also tackled the allegedly superior Japanese business management techniques.

Because of the breakup of the Soviet Union and the creation of the Russian Federation as an independent state and successor to the Soviet Union, we have to deal with four powers, but five different cultures, and five political and social organizations. In selecting appropriate negotiation case studies, we can choose from among the United States' dealings with China, Japan, the Soviet Union, and Russia; China's negotiations with Japan, the Soviet Union, and Russia; and Japan's negotiating experience with the Soviet Union and Russia—a total of nine dyads.

SPECIALISTS VERSUS GENERALISTS

There has always been a tug of war between the generalists and the specialists. In the field of negotiation studies, there are those who stress the importance of general theory applicable to all negotiations, while others point to the importance of national differences.

These national differences start with the culture of a given nation, its social structure, communication patterns, and language. And although communism as we knew it during the Cold War is dead, the Leninist state has imposed certain characteristics on the practice of negotiations that have often been stronger than national characteristics.[2] Thus, dealing with the Chinese, we need to be reminded not only of Chinese cultural characteristics, but also of negotiating attributes of a Leninist state. Similarly, in dealing with present-day Russia, we should not forget that the senior policymakers were almost all Communist Party functionaries who grew up in a Leninist state culture.

The generalists (Zartman & Berman, 1982; Zartman, 1993), while conceding that culture does affect the perceptions and assumptions of negotiators, bring out two counterarguments. The first is that negotiation is a universal process, using a finite number of behavioral patterns. The second is that the plethora of international organizations have spawned an international diplomatic culture that socializes all diplomats into similar behavior.

VARIABLES OF THE NEGOTIATING PROCESS

To follow up on theoretical questions, the following six variables are, in my view, vital in the negotiation process: (1) distribution of power, (2) issues to be negotiated, (3) type of relationship between the negotiating parties,

(4) past record of negotiations, (5) venue of negotiations, and (6) personalities of the negotiators.

Power. Power is extremely important in negotiations, although even pre-
ponderance of power does not guarantee an overwhelmingly favorable outcome for the stronger party. Here, I would take exception to Gerald
Steibel's dictum that "Negotiation is a direct function of national strength"
(Steibel, 1972, p. 37). Some twenty-five years ago, a political analyst ven-
tured the thought that North Vietnam and Israel had much more influence
than their relative standing in the world's hierarchy of power. Nonetheless,
it is important to take into account who is the stronger party in any negotiations and by what margin. To show the importance of power relationship,
I have entitled my study of Japan's claim to the four northern islands occupied by the Soviet Union at the end of World War II, "Prospects for Soviet-
Japanese Relations: Legality, Morality, and Reality" (Berton, 1986), to
indicate that while the historical, legal, and moral arguments may be in
Japan's favor, the reality of Soviet power in 1985 vis-à-vis Japan precluded
a negotiated settlement of this territorial dispute in Japan's favor.

Issues. Issues to be negotiated need to be classified in terms of their importance. The first distinction can be along the lines of what I would call "high
politics" issues versus "low politics" issues. For example, national security, territory, and arms control clearly fall into the first category, while trade (except
commodities essential for national security), administrative matters, cultural
exchange, and environmental issues could be categorized as "low politics."

Type of relationship. The relationship between the two parties sets the tone
for the negotiating process. In my study of Sino-Soviet relations (Berton,
1985), I have developed a hierarchy of seven types of cooperative/con-
flictual relationships between states: (1) allies, (2) quasi-allies, (3) entente,
(4) equidistance, (5) détente, (6) cold war, and (7) hot war.

It is obvious that negotiations between the United States and Japan,
who are signatories to a security alliance, differ from those with states in
an adversarial relationship. In turn, adversarial relationships can range from
a shooting war to a cold war to a détente.

Past record of negotiations. Here it is useful to distinguish between the process
of reaching an agreement and the way the agreements were (or were not)
lived up to. The length of the relationship is likewise important, as it provides some measure of predictability of future behavior. And, finally, it is
important to know how many negotiations resulted in a satisfactory con-

clusion of an agreement, how many ended in a draw, and how many dead-locked and broke up.

The venue of negotiations. There is obviously home court advantage, in terms of proximity to higher policymakers, logistics, psychological atmosphere, and the like. But on occasion, a neutral site can have certain benefits.

Personalities of the negotiators. These matter a great deal in terms of their status, ability, knowledge, experience (including institutional memory), and psychological makeup.

PSYCHOANALYTIC AND PSYCHODYNAMIC APPROACH

Reference to personalities of the negotiators, and especially their psychological makeup, leads me to a discussion of the psychoanalytic and psychodynamic approach. The psychoanalytic approach was one of Daniel Bell's "Ten Theories" attempting to explain Russian behavior (Bell, 1958). Bell cited the work of the late Nathan Leites who applied psychoanalytic concepts to the study of Soviet behavior at the RAND Corporation. Psychological analysis usually addresses conscious conflicts, and the psychological insights are added to political, economic, social, and other dimensions. The psychoanalytic approach, on the other hand, taps into and stresses the unconscious motivation and intrapsychic conflicts of individuals and the collective group ideologies. Without trying to bog you down in psychoanalytic jargon, I will introduce three important psychoanalytic defense mechanisms vital to the process of negotiation, and show how they influence communication and negotiations in the international arena: (1) identification, (2) projection, and (3) projective identification.[3] These defense mechanisms are designed to protect the individual or group from danger (real or imagined). More specifically, these primitive defenses show how some individuals ascribe certain delusional fantasies to others, and how easily perceptions, reality testing, and judgment become obscured or distorted.

Identification. This process plays an important role in group psychology, for it explains why individuals who adhere to certain cultural mythic origins need to form an identification with a leader (or an idea or ideology) who concretizes the group's beliefs. The magnification of the group's "badness" is projected onto this messianic leader. All the badness lies in the outcast, the outsider as the "enemy," the invader into the group's harmony. In regressive groups, somewhere lies a Messiah who will save the group from calamity, including catastrophic change.

Projection. Here is a term many of us are familiar with. It is a one-way process whereby one imbues another person with certain qualities, attributes, or traits. Stemming from the infant's earliest primitive desires and fantasies, one projects painful and unresolved aspects of the self. For example, a president of a large corporation becomes in the eyes of the employees an idealized good parent, one who will meet their every need, become the caretaker, the nurturer, the provider; or make up for the shortcomings of a missing childhood. It is a one-way process because in this instance, the president does not identify with the projection or the group's fantasy and somehow manages to stay "on task." Similarly (as discussed later, under *amae*) one might speculate that the Japanese negotiators project onto the Americans the attributes of a stronger, elder brother/parent and expect "special" treatment. The Chinese, for example, having faced British aggression and forceful British negotiators in the nineteenth century, may now unconsciously project that image when negotiating with the Americans, the new hegemons.

Projective identification. This term refers to the two-way process whereby one projects an unconscious fantasy into the other and the other identifies with the projection (Klein, 1957). It is an unconscious form of communication designed to get rid of one's worst fears. This phenomenon is something of a role reversal, whereby one coerces the other to perform specific functions or to act in a certain way. The process puts into the other intolerable feelings, such as fear, undue responsibility, guilt, and shame. It is covert and often causes the recipient of the projection to experience confusion, enormous pressure, anxiety, chaos, envy, and many other unconscious feelings. For example, in negotiations members will remain unduly silent, forcing the others to unconsciously overreact and take on a caretaking role. Again, to come back to Japanese-American negotiations, it would become a two-way projective identification, if the Americans should accept the role the Japanese project onto them and respond according to Japanese expectations.

CULTURE

The sequence "Culture-Communication-Negotiation" implies that there is a direct connection between a given group's (or country's) culture and its communication patterns (including language). The latter, in turn, greatly affect the group's (or country's) negotiating behavior.

When one deals with questions of culture or national character or social group characteristics an important caveat is in order. One can always find cultural norms in one country that are also prominent, though to a lesser degree, in another country. One should also remember that some members of a given society (though a distinct minority) do not behave as the dominant majority. In other words, one can always find exceptions to the rule, and thus, broad-brush discussions of any society are by definition suggestive of general trends only.

What do we mean by culture? One can find well over a hundred definitions of culture in the social sciences, but let us offer here a few:

> Culture is a shared system of symbols, beliefs, attitudes, values, expectations, and norms for behavior (Bovee & Thill, 1992); or
>
> National culture is that component of our mental programming which we share with more of our compatriots as opposed to most other world citizens (Hofstede, 1989);[4] or
>
> Culture is a set of shared and enduring meanings, values, and beliefs that characterize national, ethnic, or other groups and orient their behavior (Faure & Rubin, 1993, p. 3); or
>
> [Culture is] an integrated system of basic assumptions, both normative and factual, about the nature of human beings and the social, physical, and metaphysical environment in which they exist (Cohen in Faure & Rubin, 1993, p. 24).

Still another definition of culture includes group prejudices.

Courtland Bovee and John Thill (1992), in discussing cultures and intercultural communications, note that cultures and subcultures vary in terms of (1) stability, (2) complexity, (3) composition, and (4) acceptance.

Stability. Conditions in the culture may be stable or may be changing slowly or rapidly. The transition from the Soviet Union to Russia, accompanied as it is by massive changes from command economy to market relations and from totalitarianism to democracy (an as yet undefined and evolving Russian brand), is bound to affect cultural mores. By way of contrast, Japan is a good example of a slowly changing culture. In the mid-1850s, after two and a half centuries of self-imposed isolation, the Japanese were forced to join the international community by Commodore Perry's black ships. But to minimize the shock to the system, the young leaders of the Meiji Restoration adopted the slogan of "Western Technology" and "Eastern Morals." They attempted to achieve not a symbiosis of the two worlds, but a careful grafting of useful "modern" innovation onto the fundamentals of Japanese culture. At the same time in China, this attempt failed, paradoxically because of the strength of Chinese tradition, whereas Japan as a country with a long record of cultural borrowings was always ready to adopt and adapt foreign ideas. Drastic cultural change in China had to await the revolution of 1911, ending centuries of Manchu rule, and especially the establishment of a Marxist-Leninist-Maoist "people's republic" in 1949. A slower, but nonetheless significant change is taking place in China right now when Leninist politics are asked to coexist with modified capitalist economics.

Complexity. Cultures vary in the accessibility of information. In the United States, information is contained in explicit codes, including words; whereas in Japan, a great deal of information is conveyed implicitly, through nonverbal communication, body language, physical context, and the like. Another way of looking at this phenomenon is the concept of *low-context* and *high-context* communication postulated by the anthropologist Edward Hall (1976, p. 79):

> A high-context (HC) communication or message is one in which most of the information is either in the physical context or internalized in the person, while very little is in the coded, explicit, transmitted part of the message. A low-context (LC) communication is just the opposite; i.e., the mass of the message is vested in the explicit code.

Hall (1976; Kohls, 1978) rank ordered cultures from low-context (explicit) to high-context (implicit): the most explicit was the Swiss-German, followed by the German, Scandinavian, United States, French, English, Italian, Spanish, Greek, Arab, Chinese, and lastly, the most implicit, Japanese. More on that later. Though the Russians were not a part of this project, they tend to be higher-context than the Americans, in that they would emphasize the context.

Composition. Some cultures are made up of many diverse and disparate subcultures; others tend to be more homogeneous. Japan is, of course, the prime example of the latter, whereas Russia is a good example of the former, with China falling somewhere in between.[5]

Acceptance. Cultures vary in their attitudes toward outsiders. Some are openly hostile or maintain a detached aloofness. Others are friendly and cooperative toward strangers. Again, Japan, as an insular society, is a classic example of the former, and the United States of the latter. China historically treated foreigners as uncultured barbarians. The Russians with their history of foreign invasions have naturally tended to look askance at foreigners. And lastly, at the present time, China and Russia, as Communist and post-Communist societies, display a great deal of suspicion toward foreigners.

JAPANESE CULTURE

Let us begin to discuss some sociocultural characteristics of Japan, China, and Russia, and their effect upon their respective negotiating styles. Starting with Japan (Berton, 1995, 1996),[6] one should first mention *Nihonkyo* (Japanism), a term used by the social critic Yamamoto Shichihei.[7] This is a kind of tribalism that so thoroughly permeates all aspects of Japanese life and personality that its followers are not even conscious of their adherence to its doctrine. The doctrine of Nihonkyo is a simple, indefinable system of concepts characterized by the worship of tradition, which is essential in the Japanese personality. The concept of Nihonkyo fits nicely with Robert Christopher's (1983) contention that "the Japanese people as a whole have only one absolutely immutable goal—to ensure the survival and maximum well-being of the tribe."

Next, we should mention that in Japan *group* orientation, rather than individualism, is paramount (Nakane, 1970).[8] This leads to a strong group identity and "we-they" mentality. As for group dynamism, hierarchical structure is prevalent, as it was in Confucian China. Significantly, Japanese language and speech patterns provide ample proof of hierarchical social relationships. For example, the Japanese make the distinction between giving to or receiving from a person of higher or lower rank or status in society in relationship to the speaker, and the Japanese (and in this case also the Chinese) have separate words for older and younger brothers or sisters. Within this hierarchical society, values and relationships that seem to predominate (perhaps because of the insularity, crowded environment, and homogeneity of the population) are "harmony" *(wa)*, "civil formality" *(tatemae)*, and dependency *(amae)*.

The last concept was articulated in the mid–1950s by the eminent psychoanalyst Dr. Doi Takeo (Doi, 1973). He proposed that *amae* was a key concept for understanding Japanese personality structure. To feel *amae* is "to depend and presume upon another's benevolence." It is the feelings that all normal infants have toward the mother: dependence, the desire to be passively loved, the unwillingness to be separated from the warm mother-child circle and cast into a world of objective "reality." Put another way, *amae* is a dependency need that manifests itself in a longing to merge with others. This longing can be fulfilled under normal conditions in infancy, but it cannot be easily satisfied as one grows up. Yet the need for *amae* continues, and it is argued that this search for *amae* beyond infancy manifests itself in a variety of social conventions and characteristics.

Dr. Doi followed his *amae* research with a book-length study (Doi, 1986) of *tatemae* and *honne* (appearance and reality). Dr. Doi also ties *tatemae* to group harmony *(wa)*.

> *Tatemae* is a certain formal principle which is palatable to everybody concerned so that the *harmony* of a group is guaranteed, while *honne* is the feelings or opinions which they privately hold regarding the matter (Doi, 1986, p. 159) (emphasis added).

A less charitable American specialist on Japanese negotiating behavior (March, 1988) called it "patient dissembling," "disdain for frankness," and "a refined tendency to call things by other names."

Amae, wa and *tatemae* lead to other characteristics, namely politeness, indirectness, avoidance of conflict, the use of intermediaries, silent pauses in conversation, and the ambiguity of the Japanese language—all of them very important for the negotiating process.

Twenty years after his articulation of the importance of *amae,* Dr. Doi linked it to the Japanese patterns of communication (Doi, 1973a). He posited that "all interpersonal communications in Japanese society have the emotional undertone of *amae,*" and that many short breaks in Japanese conversation can be explained as feeling out one another and assessing the situation. He concluded that "what is most important for Japanese is to reassure themselves on every occasion of a mutuality based upon *amae.*" Dr. Doi also talked about the ambiguity of the Japanese language, and how little the Japanese communicate in international conferences. The ambiguity of the Japanese language is legendary. Lack of precision is, of course, wonderful for poetry, when a thought can trail off into nothingness, but it is not desirable for legal contracts. Is that one of the reasons why the Japanese prefer oral agreements to formal contracts? Let me quote again Dr. Doi (1973a, p. 183):

> Japanese communication is usually quite loose in logical connections. You can go on talking for hours, even gracefully, without coming to the point. That is why it is sometimes extremely difficult to render a Japanese speech or article into English.

Finally, we should mention that the eminent anthropologist Ruth Benedict, in her famous book on the Japanese character, *The Chrysanthemum and the Sword* (1946),[9] classified Japan as a "shame culture," in contrast to Western "guilt cultures." She concluded that the Japanese have a dual nature, at once aesthetic and aggressive. Michael Blaker (1977) also sees duality in Japanese domestic ideals of conflict resolution: (1) harmonious cooperation or harmonious unity, and (2) the warrior ethic. While Blaker was writing about diplomatic encounters, Japanese businesses often socialize their new employees in a boot camp atmosphere, and competition in international trade is treated as trade wars. No wonder, then, that American businessmen see their Japanese counterparts' behavior as a continuation of the samurai spirit. See, for example, the publication in English of the famous work, *The Book of Five Rings [Gorin no Sho]* by a seventeenth-century masterless samurai Miyamoto Musashi (Miyamoto, 1982), with the subtitle *The Real Art of Japanese Management* and *A Guide to Winning Strategy;* or David Rogers' (1984) *Fighting to Win: Samurai Techniques for Your Work and Life.*

RUSSIAN CULTURE

Dual nature—although is this case passive and violent—is likewise ascribed by anthropologists to Russia. Although some Russian historians have noted dualities in Russian character, the British anthropologist Geoffrey Gorer (Gorer & Rickman, 1962) has related the long periods in Russian history of calm and fatalistic acceptance of oppression punctured by short violent rebellions and upheavals to the manner in which Russian infants are brought up. The swaddling of infants is the metaphor of behavior. The Russian baby is swaddled in such a way that for long stretches of time he is completely denied freedom of motion and he learns to accept this unquestionably. But when the infant is unswaddled, he begins to express his frustration in violent movements.

In the case of communist and post-communist societies (China and Russia), however, there is another duality involving the tension between the society's historical traditions and the imposed Marxist dogma and Leninist practice. In shorthand fashion, one used to ask, "Are the Soviets *Russian* communists, or Russian *communists?* Alexander Solzhenitsyn, as a loyal Slavophile, sees present-day Russia's problems solely in terms of its recent disastrous three-quarter-century experience with communism. Western observers, on the other hand, see much continuity between tsarist authoritarian pathologies and aggressive foreign policy and its Soviet successor state. Many see Josef Stalin's ruthlessness and industrialization as a continuation of Ivan the Terrible and Peter the Great's Europeanization or modernization.[10]

Invasions of Russia through the ages, from the Mongols to Hitler (what Leon Sloss and Scott Davis [1987] call "the burden of a painful history") have created in the Russian psyche deep feelings of insecurity, inferiority (covered up by assertions of superiority), and extreme suspiciousness. Hence, Russian and Soviet negotiators have insisted on being treated as representatives of a superpower, on equal terms with the United States.

CHINESE CULTURE

The same dichotomy between Russia's tsarist history and its recent communist experiment is, of course, still present in China. And the continuity of tsarist authoritarianism, degenerating into Stalinist totalitarianism, is true *mutatis mutandis* of China. It has been often observed that traditional China was a "Government of Men" instead of a "Government of Laws." Lucian Pye, an authority on Chinese politics, in discussing cultural differences between China and the United States, makes a related point that "Chinese culture traditionally shuns legal considerations and instead stresses ethical and moralist principles, where Americans are thought to be highly legalistic" (Pye, 1992, p. 23). At the same time, it should be noted that in spite of elections and parliaments, communist-Leninist states, such as China and the Soviet Union, are (or were) in the Western sense, lawless societies.

When one watched the first revolutionary Chinese leaders, such as Mao Tse-tung and Chou En-lai, it was clear that in spite of being Marxist-Leninists, they were also imbued with the Middle Kingdom spirit—proud of the millennia of China's history and its central ("Center of the Universe") role in East Asia. But along with pride, their generation of Chinese were also keenly aware of the one hundred years of humiliation that befell China after the disastrous Opium War with Britain in the mid-nineteenth century. Since Hong Kong was lost at that time, one can understand the feelings of present-day Chinese leaders as they regained sovereignty over that British colonial outpost in the summer of 1997.

Thus, Chinese culture and history combined with Marxist-Leninist mores is what influences the Chinese negotiator.

THE CULTURE OF LENINIST STATES

At its height, the international communist movement consisted of a dozen ruling states and almost a hundred nonruling communist parties around the world. In the early 1950s, the Soviet Union was the unquestioned leader, but less than a decade later communist China went its own way, and the international communist movement splintered along the Moscow-Peking poles, with some independents, like Yugoslavia and a few communist parties in the Free World, attempting to maintain distance between the two communist superstates. The ruling communist states (officially they called themselves socialist on the way to communism) shared many characteristics, the chief among them being the fact that they were ruled by Leninist parties that controlled almost every political, economic, social, and cultural institution. These parties had a monopoly of power and control over all communications: personal, print, and broadcasting. As mentioned earlier, present-day Chinese and Russian senior policymakers are (or were) Communist Party functionaries who were socialized in a Leninist state culture.

It should also be noted that in spite of the Marxist dogma about the primacy of economics, in reality, politics is all-pervasive in all Leninist societies. Thus, misunderstandings arise among Western negotiators who believe that politics, economics, and social relations occupy separate realms, and fail to realize the all-pervasive impact of politics on all aspects of life in Leninist party states.

CLAIMS OF CULTURAL UNIQUENESS AND EXCEPTIONALISM

Claims of cultural uniqueness are not unique. The Japanese persistently talk about the uniqueness of their culture, and in the heyday of their militarism and imperialism, they proclaimed the doctrine of *Hakko Ichiu,* "the four corners of the world under one [Japanese] roof." The Chinese have claimed cultural superiority for millennia. Though the Jews consider themselves "The Chosen People," they have competition from the British and also from the Japanese (one sect actually believed that the Japanese are the Ten Lost Tribes). The French proudly promote their "mission civilisatrice." The Russians point to the impenetrable Russian soul and the fact that certain Russian words and phrases defy translation into foreign languages. In addition to uniqueness, the Russians have also been imbued with messianism. In tsarist times, the slogan was that "Moscow is the Third Rome [after Rome and Constantinople] and there shall never be a fourth one." The fact that Russia was the first country in the world to have established a Marxist-Leninist regime seems only to have contributed to the Russian sense of uniqueness and mission. Last, but not least, the Americans have claimed "Manifest Destiny" and "exceptionalism" for their history and mission.[11]

Proclaimers of uniqueness or cultural superiority, however, can be divided into two groups: some peoples have quiet confidence and accept their cultural superiority as an article of faith, while others are not quite sure. This is particularly true of Japan, an island nation that has produced a magnificent culture and that both prides itself on its uniqueness and is somewhat unsure of these claims. Otherwise, why would there be so many books and articles on the Japanese character *(Nihonjin ron)?*[12] The Russians, another talented people, proclaim their superiority and at the same time exhibit doubts about it; why must they insist that almost everything in the world was invented by them?[13] The French seem to be firm believers in the superiority of French language and culture. Likewise the Chinese.

Why should there be such a difference between "unique" countries? My feeling is that "soft" believers, such as the Japanese and the Russians, have been cultural borrowers. In addition, both peoples exhibit a sense of vulnerability: Russia has been periodically invaded and Japan is poor in natural resources. Does this have an effect on the way the Russians and the Japanese negotiate compared to the Chinese, the French, and the Anglo-Saxons? I believe there is a difference in that the Chinese, for example, have a vision, while the Japanese get bogged down in obsessive details. The Russians are by nature suspicious, while the Japanese are terribly afraid of losing face and also tend to panic toward the end of negotiations (see Negotiations, p. 115–116).

Henry Kissinger (1994, p. 142) perceptively compares Russian and American exceptionalism in a way that seems partially to corroborate my theory:

> The openness of each country's frontiers was among the few common features of American and Russian exceptionalism. America's sense of uniqueness was based on the concept of liberty; Russia's sprang from the experience of common suffering. Everyone was eligible to share in America's values; Russia's were available only to the Russian nation, to the exclusion of most of its non-Russian subjects. America's exceptionalism led it to isolationism alternating with occasional moral crusades; Russia's evoked a sense of mission which often led to military adventures.

DECISION-MAKING PROCESS

It is essential for negotiators to know their opposite number's decision-making process. In totalitarian countries most major decisions were made either by a strong top leader like Josef Stalin or Mao Tse-tung, or by a small, self-perpetuating oligarchy, whether the Politburo, or on important national security occasions, a smaller subcommittee of the Politburo. In present-day Russia, the final decision is made by President Boris Yeltsin himself, or in consultation with a small coterie, often members of the extra-constitutional Security Council.

Japan is a special case of a society that eschews strong leadership. One strong leader, the early postwar prime minister Yoshida Shigeru, was pejoratively called *Wanman* ("One Man") Yoshida. Normally, the country is run by consensus emanating from below, and some political scientists have opined that there is no power at the center. Interestingly, the director general of the International Research Center for Japanese Studies, the noted Jungian analyst Dr. Kawai Hayao (Kawai, 1985), in his analysis of Japanese mythology, suggested over a decade ago that in contrast to the Western "Central Power Ruled Model," Japan can be characterized as a "Hollow Center Balanced Model."[14]

As a result, the locus of decision making in Japan (whether in politics or in business) is not at the top, but in the middle. It is in upper-middle officialdom or management that different options are threshed out, leading to a consensus decision that is then sent up the chain of command where approval is generally pro forma. This process of decision making by consensus is called *ringi kessai,* after the document *ringisho,* which is stamped with the seal of each person who is on the list. The advantage of this process is that everyone who affixes his seal shares in the responsibility for the decision. This process of consultation is akin to binding the roots of a tree before transplantation and is called *nemawashi* (literally, "tying the roots"). Building a consensus is, of necessity, a slow process, and this affects any changes or concessions that might be offered during negotiations.

MAN VERSUS ENVIRONMENT

Many Japanese observers take it to be virtually axiomatic that there is a basic incompatibility between American and Japanese negotiators. The noted Japanese political scientist Mushakoji Kinhide (Mushakoji, in Japanese, 1967; in English, 1976) believes that this basic incompatibility derives from a fundamental philosophical difference in views about the relationship between humans and their environment. He juxtaposes the American *erabi* style and the Japanese *awase* style. The American style (choosing, can-do, or "manipulative") is grounded in the belief that "man can freely manipulate his environment for his own purposes." The Japanese style ("adaptive"), on the other hand, "rejects the idea that man can manipulate the environment." I would even go further and state that a Japanese not only adjusts to the environment; he becomes at one with it—a form of symbiotic harmony. From this Japanese attitude follow appeals to past obligation and requests for present favor (see discussions of *amae* dependency elsewhere in this chapter). Japanese acceptance of the environment in my view stems from vulnerabilities caused by frequent natural disasters in a land of poor resources.

Inasmuch as Marxism-Leninism is an ideology of progress, overcoming nature's obstacles and adapting nature to the requirements of a modern society is an article of faith among communists. Many of the numerous five-year plans in both the Soviet Union and communist China included ambitious, "largest in the world" schemes to harness hydroelectric power (the latest being China's current ecologically precarious plan to dam the Yangtze River) and otherwise manipulate nature (building canals between river systems, reversing the flow of rivers, creating massive irrigation projects, and the like).

In traditional Chinese view, Man could be in harmony with Nature. The Chinese needed water for irrigation, and from time to time had to control floods. The principle here was that if you wanted to transform Nature, you had better work with Nature. There was no need for Man to adjust to Nature in the manner of the Japanese. The Russians, by contrast, were in an inferior position toward Nature, as they had to live in harsh climatic conditions in their vast land.

COMMUNICATION

At the outset, a few brief comments on communication might be useful.[15] First, communication is a *symbolic* activity, and therefore it includes nonverbal displays (described later), as well as objects, such as the flag. Second, communication is a *process* involving encoding (so that thoughts, feelings, emotions, or attitudes are in a form recognizable by others) and decoding (perceiving and interpreting incoming messages and stimuli from the environment). Third, communication is *transactional* (interactive), meaning that the people with whom we communicate have an impact on us and we have an impact on them. Fourth, communication takes place at varying *levels of awareness* (both consciously and unconsciously; see Psychoanalytic and Psychodynamic Approach, p. xxx). Incidentally, we are more aware of our behavior with people from other cultures than with our own people, but at the same time we have to interpret the behavior of negotiators from other cultures. Fifth, *intention* is not a necessary condition for communication, for as Watzlawick, Beavin, and

Jackson have postulated: "one cannot *not* communicate" (Watzlawick et al., 1967, p. 49). (In negotiations, one constantly communicates, even before the first verbal exchanges.) Sixth, every communication has two dimensions: a *content* (*what* is said) dimension, and a *relationship* (*how* it is said) dimension. The relationship dimension is usually encoded and decoded unconsciously. The content dimension is usually encoded verbally, while the relationship dimension tends to be encoded nonverbally, and therefore vitally important to the negotiating process. I would also add that in psychoanalytic terminology one distinguishes *manifest* content (what is actually said) from *latent* content (what is thought but not communicated, or what remains in the unconscious), while the *affect* shows how the message is communicated.

COMMUNICATION CHANNELS

One of the most striking distinctions among communication patterns is the role and quantity of nonverbal communication. One can distinguish the following five channels of communication that carry as much as or more information than verbal exchange alone.[16] And, of course, each culture uses these channels in its own unique way.

Occulesics. This refers to the use or avoidance of eye-to-eye contact during conversation. Americans, for example, are more dependent on direct eye contact as a sign of active listening, and often sincerity. They may feel that without eye contact they are "out of contact" with the other person. In other cultures, staring at the other person may be an act of impoliteness, or even challenge that can lead to unpleasant consequences.

Hepatics. Hepatics relates to the degree, if any, of touch (or tactile contact) in the process of communication. When Europeans and Americans meet, they usually shake hands; Latin Americans may embrace; others may kiss or touch cheeks (one, two, or three times); while still others, like the Japanese, simply bow (how deeply depends on the social standing of the parties), avoiding physical contact altogether.

Kinesics. This term is related to the movement of hands, head, torso, etc. to amplify messages, both verbal and nonverbal, or on occasion even to deliver contradictory signals. For example, the Japanese constantly nod during conversation, signifying the fact that they heard the message, but not necessarily expressing agreement. This has confused countless foreign counterparts in negotiations, as has the Japanese practice of answering a negative question with a "yes" and perhaps a nod, but which signifies a "no" in terms of substance. For example:

"You are not an American?"

"Yes, I am not."

Proxemics. Proxemics addresses personal space or "comfort zone" in the act of communication. While in some cultures getting close to the other party's face may signify sincerity, in ours it is considered an invasion of our "private" space, and may trigger a public negative response.

Chronemics. This term refers to the timing of verbal exchange, "turn taking," pauses, silences, and interruptions during conversation. Eastern people generally are quite comfortable with silences, and do not feel obligated to "take turns," while Westerners (especially Americans) expect "turn taking," feel uncomfortable when the other party does not respond, and proceed with their presentation, occasionally feeling the need to make unnecessary concessions.

TIME

The previous section focused on the dimension of time, which in itself is a complicated topic. Time can be seen as structure and as a form of communication. Time can be used as a tactic to manipulate negotiations. Time is associated with such attributes as polychronic, monochronic, synchronic, and diachronic. Timing is, of course, also of critical importance, whether in planning when to commence negotiation, when to hang tough, and when to offer concessions and bring negotiations to a close.

The anthropologist Edward Hall (Hall & Hall, 1987) stresses the distinction between monochronic (M) time and polychronic (P) time as of particular importance in analyzing the success or failure of negotiations. Most cultures operate on polychronic time, which is characterized by the simultaneous occurrence of many things and by a great involvement with people. For example, there is more emphasis on completing human transactions than on holding to schedules. By contrast, to be on monochronic time means to pay attention to and focus on only one thing at a time. Hall indicates that the United States, Germany, Switzerland, and Scandinavia are dominated by "the iron hand of M-time." In these societies there is a prevalence of structured time, strict adherence to schedules, and the notion that time is tangible: it can be "spent," "saved," "wasted," or "lost" (Ibid., p. 16ff.). No wonder that in the United States particularly, it is widely believed that "time is money" (a concept that is alien to polychronic people, whether they are Latin, Asian, or Russian). It seems to me that perhaps Max Weber's notion of the relationship between the Protestant ethic and the development of capitalism has something to do with monochronic societies' attitude toward time. Hall goes on to indicate that monochronic people follow rules of privacy, while polychronics are more concerned with close relationships; further, the former are accustomed to short-term relationships, while the latter have a strong tendency to build lifetime relationships.

All three cultures discussed in this chapter—Japan, China, and Russia—are clearly polychronic. The Japanese do not value or understand privacy, partly because they live in such close quarters; there are few inside walls in a traditional Japanese house, mostly sliding doors. In fact, there is no concept of privacy in Japan and no corresponding word for it in the Japanese language. When they need to use the term, the Japanese resort to saying or writing "puraiwashi," (their polysyllabic version of "privacy"). Nonetheless, the Japanese have sufficiently absorbed the international business system, that they do stick to schedules, and are in that sense monochronic. The Russian Bolsheviks invented the famous five-year plans (later adopted as economic policy by the Chinese communists), which also shows that these two societies have amalgamated certain characteristics of the monochronic system.

Closely associated with time are the concepts of tempo and rhythm. In negotiations, if one side for cultural reasons proceeds at a faster pace than the other, we might say that they are not "in synch," which is shorthand for not being synchronic.

Time can actually be used as a weapon by all three of our subjects, which is effective strategy in dealing with monochronic people who make short-range plans and often disclose their busy schedule to their negotiating counterparts, with the result that the former can become easy prey of delaying tactics (more later in the section on Negotiation, pp. 115–116).

NONVERBAL COMMUNICATION

To a certain extent, all humans communicate both verbally and nonverbally. But being a homogeneous society in crowded circumstances, the Japanese more than others have learned to communicate with each other in shorthand fashion and even without words. Such nonverbal communication is known in Japan as *haragei* (the art of communicating through your body—literally "stomach" or what we in the West call gut feelings). Here is how a Japanese author (Matsumoto in McCreary, 1986, p. 58) describes *haragei:* (1) be euphemistic, eschewing logic or reason; (2) keep the message vague and ambiguous; (3) be empathetic; (4) don't publicly disagree; (5) don't be legalistic; (6) play it artistically and wholeheartedly; (7) don't attract attention; (8) don't come on strong; (9) don't seek the truth; (10) don't tell the truth; (11) let language talk and be silent.

Significantly, when the Japanese negotiate with the Chinese, they claim that the two peoples are *Dobun doshu* (same script and same kind), referring to the common use of Chinese characters and the sharing of racial characteristics. Hence, when communicating the two can understand each other without words.

LET SILENCE TALK AND LANGUAGE BE SILENT

As Matsumoto Michihiro phrases it, silence is the most important "component" of nonverbal communication. In terms of talkativeness—the other extreme of silence—the Americans are clearly at one end of the spectrum and the Japanese on the other, with the Chinese somewhere in between. In fact, some inexperienced American businessmen mistook Japanese silence as a rejection of their offers, and proceeded to lower their price. Silence can be a pause in conversation, or speech can be a break between silences. According to Raymond Smith (1989), who had extensive experience in negotiating with the Soviets, Americans emphasize content and slight context. They share facts but guard emotions, focusing on words. The Soviets do the opposite: they guard facts and focus on pauses.

POLITENESS/RUDENESS

In terms of the negotiators' attitudes, there is a huge distinction between the Japanese on the one hand, and Chinese and Soviets on the other, as if they were at opposite poles. The Japanese negotiators are invariably polite, and will do everything to keep the negotiations civil. (We are not talking here about wartime experiences. In early 1942, General Yamashita Tomoyuki asked for the unconditional surrender of British forces in Singapore, with a simple demand: "Yes ka, No ka?")

At the height of the Cold War, a Chinese negotiator habitually called his American counterpart "a capitalist crook, rapist, thief, robber of widows, stealer of pennies from the eyes of the dead, mongrel of uncertain origin," charged President Dwight Eisenhower and Secretary of State John Foster Dulles with murder, and ended his tirade by pronouncing that the American diplomat "had blood on his hands and was a murderer lying in the gutter with filthy garbage" (Steibel, 1972, p. 29).[17]

The Soviet negotiators, in stark contrast to the Japanese, used rudeness as a tool to put the other side on the defensive. As for present-day Russian negotiators, we should remember that most of the diplomats not only were socialized under the Soviet regime but also grew up in a society where elementary norms of civility were lacking.

NEGOTIATION

The Negotiation Process

Broadly speaking, the negotiation process can be divided into the pre-negotiation stage, the negotiation itself, and the post-negotiation stage. The negotiation stage can be, in turn, divided into three phases: the first phase of assessment, the second or middle phase of bargaining and concession-making, and the third and final phase of closure.

General Characteristics and Approaches

As a broad generalization, it might be worth mentioning that several authors have commented that Chinese negotiators are closer to Western negotiators than they are to Japanese negotiators, and that Professor Kimura Hiroshi (Kimura, 1980) has concluded that neither the Japanese nor the Russians have as yet adopted the Western notion of negotiation.

In approaching negotiations the Chinese, Japanese, and Russians all seem to be more serious, tight, and skeptical than the Americans. The Chinese, the Japanese, and the old Soviets also seem to be more single-minded and disciplined than the American negotiators, although it is probable that the post-Soviet Russians may be less so, especially in the business sphere. Group dependence again seems to separate the Americans from the Chinese, Japanese, and Soviets/Russians. The Japanese negotiator is extremely fearful of losing face. The Soviet/Russian negotiator is suspicious, if not paranoid, looking over his shoulder as if somebody is out to cheat him. This sense of insecurity, while understandable in the light of Russian history, does not facilitate a businesslike and congenial negotiating atmosphere.

PRE-NEGOTIATION STAGE

The pre-negotiation stage includes a commitment to negotiation and the arrangement of a conference. Here each side defines the problem and develops negotiation strategies, including how to arrange the venue, agenda, and rules in one's favor. Each side may also engage in a pre-conference propaganda campaign (as was almost de rigueur in the case of communist negotiators) or in threatening behavior. Here the Chinese strategy of "Kill the chicken to scare the monkey"—take action against a weak antagonist to warn the stronger ones—comes to mind. For example, when the Dutch government sold some weapons to Taiwan, the Chinese government on the mainland took drastic action against the Dutch, to warn the major arms suppliers like the United States or France. Chinese propaganda campaigns may also include proclamations of a "nonnegotiable principle."

All three negotiating teams (Chinese, Japanese, and Soviet/Russian) engage in a lot of preparatory work, with the Japanese being the most methodical. Collection of information for its own sake is a characteristic of the Japanese, dating back to the self-imposed seclusion in the seventeenth century, if not earlier when Japan was culturally dependent upon China. In fact, some observers have commented that the Japanese general trading companies *(sogo shosha)* could compete with the CIA and other major intelligence organizations in the quantity of information in their files. This abundance of information probably redounds to the benefit of the Japanese negotiators in trade and other economic matters.

Venue and Agenda/Rules

It is obvious that controlling the venue of negotiations and the agenda (and accompanying rules) provides great advantages. The Japanese on the whole do not actively and persistently seek these advantages. To a certain extent they are protected by a tradition of international rotation schedules. For example, the Group of Seven (G-7) annual summits follow a strict rotation schedule, though Japan was not selected for the first several conference sites. By contrast, the communist negotiators would not only go to great lengths to assure themselves the advantages that come from controlling the venue and agenda, but would engage in lengthy negotiations to control such details of the negotiating process as the shape of the table (North Vietnamese versus Henry Kissinger in Paris in the early 1970s). One high-ranking American negotiator went so far as to state that in the Soviet view (and by extension other communists') form is substance. The Americans on occasion give up even negotiating about the venue, as happened during Kissinger's preliminary negotiations with Chou En-lai in 1971. One wonders why the American president Richard Nixon had to travel to Peking in February 1972, emulating the historical role of barbarians paying tribute to the Son of Heaven, and not insisting on a neutral site?

NEGOTIATION'S FIRST PHASE: ASSESSMENT

The first phase of actual negotiations is a period of assessment, of getting to know and sizing up the opposite number, of making the opening moves, and of developing possible scenarios toward reaching a satisfactory conclusion.

Getting to Know the Opposite Number

Of the three cases presented in this chapter, the Soviet negotiators seemed to have cared the least in terms of getting to know their opposite numbers. In fact, we might say that one of their favorite tactics was the use of invective, not the best way to win friends and influence people. During the Cold War period (and especially during and after the "hot war" on the Korean peninsula), the Chinese diplomats also engaged in virtuosic ad hominem attacks. But during more normal times, the Chinese are bent on cultivating relations with their opposite numbers for a specific purpose of later using "old friends" to extract concessions. (In the Chinese tradition "friendship" implies obligations.) This practice is so pervasive that Lucian Pye (1992), Richard Solomon (1985, 1987, 1999), and Alfred Wilhelm (1994), who wrote extensively on negotiating with the Chinese, specifically warn American negotiators not to fall into this trap.

Another element in this practice is the Chinese concept of *guanxi*, a kind of special relationship, with undertones of dependency. This, of course, brings memories of Japanese *amae* dependency (discussed in greater detail later), but also of Japanese obligations and reciprocals of *on, gimu,* and *giri,* articulated by Ruth Benedict (1946). Japanese negotiators are very sensitive to Chinese overtures for special relationship and usually resist them. On the other hand, Japanese negotiators will generally invest a good deal of time to build a trustworthy relationship before they would venture to talk business.

Opening Moves

In opening diplomatic negotiations, it is customary to make a *tour d'horizon,* a kind of grand survey of the world situation. During the Communist period, Soviet negotiators usually engaged in haranguing the capitalist and imperialist systems. As for the Chinese and Japanese, the former are far more attuned to a broad, overall approach than the latter, who tend to focus on the issues at hand. No wonder, then, that Henry Kissinger praised Chou En-lai's broad vision, while Charles De Gaulle likened a visiting Japanese prime minister to a transistor salesman. It is only fair to add that

President George Bush once appeared in Tokyo with the presidents of the American Big Three automakers, putting himself in the position of an automobile salesman.

A common characteristic of both Communist Chinese and Soviet negotiators is the insistence on developing an "agreement in principle," which can later be used as a weapon or an argument against specific proposals by the other side.

Expectations of *Amae* Dependency

Ambassador Kitamura Hiroshi (Kitamura, 1971) was the first Japanese diplomat to note that *amae* psychology has played a very important role in Japanese-American relations. He argues that the Japanese feel that because the United States is more powerful than Japan, it should—to a certain extent—indulge them: "The unbalanced relationship between Japan and the United States is . . . highly conducive to initiating an *amae* psychology." And when the American behavior in negotiations did not gratify or satisfy the Japanese desire for *amae,* this would in turn produce frustration and hostile attitudes on the part of the Japanese.

But did Japanese perceptions of and attitudes toward the United States change as the power relationship between the two countries changed over time? And was there, therefore, a corresponding decline in *amae* expectations? In a recent article, Ambassador Kitamura (1994) sadly notes that despite considerable rise in status, the Japanese still seem to harbor feelings of *amae* toward America, perhaps in a different guise. Yet no signs have emerged that Japan was getting to a position where she could *dispense* some *amae* to the United States. Unhappily, I think that Japan is essentially comfortable *receiving amae.* One should mention, however, that many younger Japanese diplomats do not have feelings of *amae* toward their American counterparts and furthermore are aware that *amae* does not work with the Americans.[18]

Of course, *amae* feelings are not unique to Japanese diplomacy. One can argue that in the Anglo-American English-speaking so-called special relationship, the British expect special treatment *(amae?)* from the United States. Soviet and now Russian diplomats have used the arguments that geographically Russia lacks natural defenses and that the country has been constantly invaded throughout its history (by the Mongols, the Swedes, the Poles, Napoleon, the Allies after World War I, and by Hitler). They conveniently fail to mention that the Soviet Union invaded half a dozen Central and East European countries and colonized the three Baltic states during or in the aftermath of World War II. The Soviet/Russian diplomats also seek sympathy by invoking the twenty-eight million sacrificed in that great conflict. And now the Russians plead underdevelopment and difficulties in their transition from command to market economy. The Chinese use similar arguments that economically developed "rich" countries should show more understanding and be prepared to make concessions to "developing" countries like China, as well as provide help in facilitating China's entry into international economic organizations.

NEGOTIATION'S SECOND OR MIDDLE PHASE: BARGAINING AND CONCESSION-MAKING

This is the main part of the negotiating process, and many of the characteristics of different cultural groups are exhibited here in their fullest. But before bargaining begins, the two sides must present their opening positions, and there is often a dance to decide who initiates the first step. The Chinese are particularly adept at withholding their opening bid until the other side has committed itself to its opening position. In Peking, for example, the Chinese would invite the other side, as *guests* to start, while in Washington they would expect the *hosts* to show their cards.

In the middle phase, the Soviets have used threats and other pressure tactics, such as propaganda campaigns addressed at world opinion; the Chinese attempt to shame and play adversaries against each other; and the Japanese will typically dig in and keep repeating their position. Parties may play the "good cop, bad cop" routine, demand recesses or intermediaries, and test the patience of their counterparts. While the Japanese have generally outlasted Western negotiators by slowing down tactics, they have been no match for the Chinese, who would on occasion simply stonewall (Ogura, 1979).

NEGOTIATION'S THIRD PHASE: CLOSURE OR END GAME

The end of the negotiating process may involve a decision to break off negotiations, put them on hold, or come to some sort of a conclusion. The latter may involve last-minute activities, including:

Eleventh-Hour Concessions
Both Chinese and Japanese negotiators often wait until the last minute before offering meaningful concessions to the other side. Michael Blaker has used the phrase "Probe, Push, and Panic" (1973) to describe Japanese tactics. (He added "Postpone" in his chapter in this volume.) In a June

1996 television interview with U.S. Trade Representative Charlene
Barshefsky (Barshefsky, 1996), Paul Solman, economics reporter for the
Public Broadcasting Service (PBS) *NewsHour* with Jim Lehrer, asked if
negotiations with China are "always this kind of a cat-and-mouse game:
we have to threaten sanctions, go down to the last minute?" Barshefsky
replied that "This is an unfortunate cycle, but it seems the only cycle that
the Chinese have responded to with respect to implementation of trade
agreements." Asked if this was also the case with the Japanese, the Trade
Representative replied that this was not the case in every agreement with
the Japanese. But in the case of China, she confirmed that if you look at
the history with China, all agreements came about after months and
months of education, consultation, and negotiations, but only at the end
of the day after sanctions have been threatened. This is a pernicious cycle,
but not one that the United States has created, and it is one to which the
Chinese seem to respond.

POST-NEGOTIATION STAGE: IMPLEMENTATION OF AGREEMENTS AND REOPENING OF POST-AGREEMENT NEGOTIATIONS

The Soviet record is mixed: they have scrupulously and faithfully adhered
to payments schedules (realizing that loss of credit would dry up future
sources), while at the same time cheating on agreements involving national-security matters. (The controversial Krasnoyarsk radar station built
in contravention of an agreement with the United States to limit ABM
systems to Moscow is one such example.) The present Russian record in
adhering to commercial agreements is not very good, corner-cutting
being the order of the day. The Japanese, very much lacking in strong principles and believing in situational ethics, are likely to attempt to renegoti-
ate agreements if the circumstances have drastically changed. In
negotiating with the Chinese, Americans have found out that no matter
what agreement is reached, it may be subject to review and objection by
some higher-up not directly participating in the negotiating process. The
Chinese also have the unsavory reputation of bringing up new demands
after the conclusion of negotiations.

CONCLUSIONS

This chapter stresses the importance of the impact of different national
communication patterns upon the process and outcome of negotiations as

a distinct, intermediary influence, apart from the cultural traits that condition the actions of the decision makers and actors in the process of negotiation. In this regard, I have emphasized the importance of nonverbal communication and different channels of such communication (occulesics, hepatics, kinesics, proxemics, and chronemics). In addition, I have stressed the advantages of the comparative method, whether in the analysis of culture, communication patterns, or the negotiating process. In comparing cultures, I have found that it is not enough to examine elements of Japanese, Chinese, and Russian cultures, and I have added a category of "The Culture of Leninist States." After all, since Russia experienced three-quarters of a century and China half a century of all-pervasive control exercised by Leninist parties, in effect they were or are Leninist party-states. Likewise, it is highly desirable not to limit analysis to the conscious motives of the negotiating actors and their superiors, but to delve into the unconscious mechanisms operant in group psychology and in individual defense mechanisms. Included in this psychoanalytic domain are specific notions of identification, projection, and projective identification. The psychoanalytic and psychodynamic approach can significantly enrich our analysis of the entire negotiation process, beginning with the pre-negotiation stage and ending with the post-negotiation stage and problems associated with the implementation of the agreements.

Of the different cultures, communication patterns, and negotiation styles discussed in this chapter, the Japanese seem to be the one closest to being unique. In fact, Professor John Graham, a contributor to this volume and a student of comparative negotiating behavior in two dozen cultures, once remarked that if Americans are at one end of the spectrum, the Japanese are surely at the other end.[19] The empirical study (cited earlier) rank ordering communication patterns in accordance with their high context/low context also found the Japanese at the very end of the spectrum, with the United States toward the other end, though not at the extreme end. Other comparative studies have found Chinese negotiators to be closer to Western counterparts than to the Japanese, and neither Japanese nor Russian negotiators seem to have adopted the Western notions of negotiation.

Claims of cultural uniqueness are not unique. Many peoples claim uniqueness or cultural superiority, including the Chinese, Japanese, Russians, French, and the Anglo-Saxons, to name a few. But these peoples can be divided into two groups: those who accept their cultural superiority as an article of faith, and those who are not quite sure. I put the Japanese and the Russians in the second category because both peoples have been cultural borrowers and seem to exhibit a sense of insecurity and vulnerability.

I argue that, as a result, there are differences in negotiating styles between the first and second groups. The negotiators from the first group seem to have more confidence and a broader vision, while those in the second group harbor more suspicion and are afraid to lose face.

In terms of culture stability, again Japan takes the top honors, with both China and Russia showing signs of transition: China trying to accommodate a Leninist political system with an evolving modified market economic system, and Russia jettisoning both the totalitarian political system and the command economic system. Whatever the final destination of these changes in both China and Russia, the cultural milieu is bound to undergo changes.

In describing cultures, many authors have stressed the dualities and contradictory attributes, whether the aesthetic/aggressive nature of the Japanese, or the passive/violent nature of the Russians. Equally important, it seems to me, is to emphasize the effects of the communist experiment with all its pernicious impact on Russian and Chinese societies. These societies today show that while some of the Communist policies reinforced prerevolutionary trends, others created discontinuities with the past. It would take a post-Communist period of some length for some kind of a synthesis to emerge, to borrow Marxist/Hegelian terminology. In the meantime, the Chinese or Russian negotiator is bound to exhibit a dual character.

The Japanese explicit and implicit pleadings of *amae* dependency have related parallels in Russia and China, where arguments are made during negotiations to evoke sympathies. In Russia, this usually takes the form of reminding the negotiating partners that Russia was always forced to fight off invaders and pleading human suffering and almost thirty million casualties in World War II. In China, this can take the form of cajoling and manipulating "old friends," persons with prior experience in China or prior dealings with the Chinese, as well as pleading underdevelopment to obtain preferential treatment.

It is hoped that this effort to present conceptual frameworks for the study of culture, communication, and negotiation, illustrated by selective examples from the national characteristics of Japan, China, and the Soviet Union/Russia, would provide deeper insights into these complex subjects.

NOTES

* This chapter is dedicated to the memory of my mentor, Professor Philip E. Mosely, former Director of the Russian (now Harriman) Institute, Colum-

bia University, who himself wrote the first significant account of Soviet negotiating techniques (Mosely, 1951).

I wish to thank Paul Langer for reading a preliminary draft of this chapter and offering many helpful criticisms, and Joan Lachkar for helping me formulate psychoanalytic and psychodynamic perspectives. Needless to say, all responsibility remains mine alone.

1. Now, for obvious reasons renamed *Communist and Post-Communist Studies.*

2. When I heard the most senior South Korean negotiator describe his dealings with his North Korean counterparts, I was reminded of the generic "Communist" negotiators. And the South Korean statesman was unable to identify specific "Korean" characteristics of the North Korean negotiating team.

3. Here I follow the definitions of Dr. Joan Lachkar (1992).

4. Geert Hofstede delineates five dimensions of culture: (1) power distance; (2) collectivism vs. individualism; (3) femininity vs. masculinity; (4) uncertainty avoidance; and (5) long-term orientation.

5. John Graham of the School of Management at the University of California at Irvine (and a contributor to this volume) in his study of comparative negotiation styles distinguishes between northern and southern Chinese. There are, of course, also numerous national minorities in China, such as Tibetans, Mongols, Uighurs, and Kazakhs.

6. This section on Japan's culture follows closely the section on "Japanese Cultural Characteristics" in my previous work on Japanese negotiating behavior (Berton, 1996).

7. Japanese names are given in Japanese style, surname first, followed by the given name.

It is common knowledge that Yamamoto wrote the book on the Japanese and the Jews using the pseudonym of Isaiah BenDasan, so that it would appear that the book (BenDasan, 1972) had been written by a Sephardi Jew long resident in Japan.

8. It should be noted, however, that not all scholars accept the model of Japan as a harmonious and group-oriented society. See Befu, 1980.

9. In a recent study of Ruth Benedict's archives, Pauline Kent (1994) discovered that the original Report 25, which was later expanded into the famous book, *The Chrysanthemum and the Sword,* does not include, to any significant extent, discussions of Japan as a "shame culture." Curiously, the subsequent addition of the "shame culture" concept became the dominant theme of Benedict's book.

10. A third duality was the difference between Russia's European and Asian policies. In the West, Imperial Russia often behaved in the context of the Concert of Europe. The Asiatic Department, responsible for Russian policy toward the Ottoman Empire, the Balkans, and the Far East, often acted independently and aggressively (Kissinger, 1994).

Post-Soviet Russia has experienced a split between the "Atlanticists" and the "Eurasianists" (Kimura, 1996a). This arises from the duality of Russia as a state facing both Europe and Asia, and symbolized by the two-headed eagle in the tsarist coat of arms.

Another useful way of tackling the Russian cultural dimension is to present a set of American and Russian mutual stereotypes, and both positive and negative images of each other collected by Robert Anderson and Petr Shikhirev (Anderson & Shikhirev, 1994, pp. 99 and 108).

Russian Stereotype of Americans: people like us, who are more successful and who can teach us about market relations and democracy.

American Stereotype of Russians: bunglers, mafiosi, nouveau riche, and troublemakers.

Russian Positive Images of Americans: Energy, practicality, efficiency, organization, responsibility, easy to get along, ability to seek compromises.

Russian Negative Images of Americans: Stinginess, poor knowledge of Russia and Russian culture (especially language), limited outlook, paternalistic attitude toward Russian partners, suspiciousness and distrust.

American Positive Images of Russians: High intellectual potential and education, inventiveness and imagination, desire to learn, dependability in friendly relations, warmth, sociability.

American Negative Images of Russians: Disorganization (lack of discipline), low level of business culture, quickness to take offense, confusing personal and business relations, daydreaming ("on cloud nine"), promises are not thought through, inclination toward dependency, weak initiative.

11. The latest book on the subject is by Seymour Martin Lipset, *American Exceptionalism: A Double-edged Sword* (1996).

12. Some fifteen years ago the Nomura Research Institute compiled a list of 700 titles published since 1945. See Befu, 1980.

    For an original position that the Japanese society cannot be explained using concepts of Western social science, see Hamaguchi Esyun's "A Contextual Model of the Japanese: Toward a Methodological Innovation in Japan Studies" (Hamaguchi, 1985).

13. One of the foremost contenders for Russia's presidency, General Aleksandr Lebed, boasted on television that Russia was a great country, citing as evidence his claim that 84 [or 86; I don't recall the exact figure] percent of all discoveries and inventions were made by the Russians, and then stolen and claimed by others.

14. See also van Wolferen, 1989. Some writers have referred to the Japanese political system as an onion: you peel and peel, and in the end there is nothing at the core.

15. Here I borrow from Gudykunst and Kim, 1984.

16. The following discussion is based on a handout prepared by Dr. Bruce La Brack of the University of the Pacific, distributed at the panel on "Communicating Across Cultures" at the Twelfth Worldwide Conference of People to People International, Newport Beach, California, September 25–29, 1996.

17. Such degree of gratuitous insults may have been motivated by the Chinese negotiator's desire to establish his bona fides as genuinely anti-American and anti-imperialist for consumption back home.

18. Ambassador Edamura Sumio made this point during his comments on my paper, "The Psychological Dimensions of Japanese Negotiating Behavior," at the Kyoto Conference on Japanese Studies, October 1994 (Berton, 1996).

19. Professor John Graham's comments on my paper (Berton, 1995) at a special meeting of the Southern California Japan Seminar at the UCLA Faculty Center, February 11, 1995.

REFERENCES AND SELECTED BIBLIOGRAPHY

Anderson, R., & Shikhirev, P. 1994. *"Akuly" i "del'finy": Psikhologiia i etika rossiisko-amerikanskogo delovogo partnerstva* ["Sharks" and "Dolphins": The Psychology and Ethics of Russian-American Business Partnership]. Moscow: Delo.

Axtell, R. E. 1991. *Gestures: The DO's and TABOOs of Body Language Around the World.* New York: Wiley.

Barshefsky, C. 1996. U.S. Trade Representative, television interview with Paul Solman, *NewsHour with Jim Lehrer,* June 21.

Befu, H. 1980. "A Critique of the Group Model of Japanese Society." *Social Analysis,* No. 5/6, 29–43.

Bell, D. 1958. "Ten Theories in Search of Reality: The Prediction of Soviet Behavior in the Social Sciences." *World Politics,* 10 (3), 327–365.

Bendahmane, D. B., & McDonald, Jr., J. W. 1987. *International Negotiation: Art and Science—Report of a Conference on International Negotiation, June 9–10, 1983.* N.p.: U.S. Department of State, Foreign Service Institute, Center for the Study of Foreign Affairs.

BenDasan, I. 1972. *The Japanese and the Jews.* New York: Weatherhill. Translation of *Nihonjin to Yudayajin.* Tokyo: Yamamoto Shoten, 1970.

Benedict, R. 1946. *The Chrysanthemum and the Sword: Patterns of Japanese Culture.* Boston: Houghton-Mifflin.

Berton, P. 1982. "The Soviet and Japanese Communist Parties: Policies, Tactics, Negotiating Behavior." *Studies in Comparative Communism,* 15 (3), 266–287.

Berton, P. 1985. "A Turn in Sino-Soviet Relations?" In Hsiung, *Beyond China's Independent Foreign Policy: Challenge for the U.S. and Its Asian Allies* (pp. 24–54). New York: Praeger.

Berton, P. 1986. "Prospects for Soviet-Japanese Relations—Legality, Morality, and Reality: An American Perspective." In *Kokusai Shinpojiumu '85—International*

Symposium '85. Tenki ni tatsu Kokusai Josei to Nisso Kankei—Japan-Soviet Relations in a Changing Global Context Hokoku [Report] (pp. 65–69 & 331–354). Tokyo: Kokusai Shinpojiumu '85 Soshiki Iinkai. In Japanese and English.

Berton, P. 1995. "Understanding Japanese Negotiating Behavior." *ISOP Intercom* (University of California, Los Angeles, International Studies and Overseas Programs), 18 (2), 1–8.

Berton, P. 1996. "The Psychological Dimensions of Japanese Negotiating Behavior." In *Kyoto Conference on Japanese Studies, 1994* (pp. I-273 - I-284). Kyoto: International Research Center for Japanese Studies, The Japan Foundation, Vol. I. See also discussions of the paper by Dr. Takeo Doi, St. Luke's International Hospital and Ambassador Sumio Edamura, Ministry of Foreign Affairs, in same volume, pp. I-285 - I-292.

Berton, P. 1998. "How Unique is Japanese Negotiating Behavior?" *Nichibunken Japan Review: Bulletin of the International Research Center for Japanese Studies* (Kyoto), 10, 151–161.

Bettinghaus, E. P., & Cody, M. J. 1987. *Persuasive Communication,* 4th ed. New York: Holt, Rinehart and Winston.

Blackman, C. 1997. *Negotiating China: Case Studies and Strategies.* St. Leonards, NSW, Australia: Allen & Unwin.

Blaker, M. 1973. "Probe, Push, and Panic: The Japanese Tactical Style in International Negotiations." In Scalapino, *The Foreign Policy of Modern Japan* (pp. 55–101). Berkeley: University of California Press.

Blaker, M. 1977. *Japanese International Negotiating Style.* New York: Columbia University Press.

Blaker, M. 1993. "Evaluating Japan's Diplomatic Performance." In Curtis, *Japan's Foreign Policy after the Cold War: Coping with Change* (pp. 1–42). Armonk, NY and London: M. E. Sharpe.

Blaker, M. 1999. "Japan Negotiates with the United States on Rice: 'No, No, a Thousand Times, No!'" Ch. 2 in this volume.

Booher, D. 1994. *Communicate With Confidence!: How To Say It Right the First Time and Every Time.* New York: McGraw-Hill.

Bovee, C. L., & Thill, J. V. 1992. *Business Communication Today,* 3rd ed. New York: McGraw-Hill.

Brady, L. P. 1991. *The Politics of Negotiation: America's Dealings with Allies, Adversaries, and Friends.* Chapel Hill: University of North Carolina Press.

Casse, P. 1992. *The One-Hour Negotiator.* Oxford: Butterworth-Heinemann.

Chang, J. J. 1991. "Negotiation of the 17 August 1982 U.S.-PRC Arms Communiqué: Beijing's Negotiating Tactics." *China Quarterly,* 125, 33–54.

Christopher, R. C. 1976. *The Japanese Patterns of Behavior.* Honolulu: University of Hawaii Press.

Christopher, R. C. 1983. *The Japanese Mind: The Goliath Explained.* New York: Linden Press/Simon & Schuster.

Cohen, H. 1982. *You Can Negotiate Anything.* New York: Bantam Books.

Cohen, R. 1991. *Negotiating Across Cultures: Communication Obstacles in International Diplomacy.* Washington, DC: United States Institute of Peace Press.

Cohen, R. 1993. "An Advocate's View," Ch. 3 in Part I, "International Negotiation: Does Culture Make a Difference?" In Faure & Rubin, *Culture and Negotiation: The Resolution of Water Disputes* (pp. 22–37). Newbury Park, CA: Sage.

Cohen, R. 1997. *Negotiating Across Cultures: International Communication in an Interdependent World,* rev. ed. Washington, DC: United States Institute of Peace Press.

Condon, J. C., & Saito, M., eds. 1974. *Intercultural Encounters with Japan: Communication—Contact and Conflict.* Tokyo: Simul Press.

Craig, G. A. 1962. "Techniques of Negotiation." In Lederer, *Russian Foreign Policy: Essays in Historical Perspective* (pp. 351–373). New Haven: Yale University Press.

Dellerman, F. J. 1979. "Soviet Negotiating Techniques in Arms Control Negotiations with the United States." Unpublished Ph.D. dissertation, International Relations, University of Southern California, August, 2 vols.

De Pauw, J. W. 1981. *U.S.-Chinese Trade Negotiations.* New York: Praeger.

Destler, I. M., Sato, H., Clapp, P., & Fukui, H. 1976. *Managing an Alliance: The Politics of U.S.-Japanese Relations,* esp. Ch. 4, "Misperceptions across the Pacific," largely written by Professor Sato, pp. 89–124. Washington, DC: Brookings Institution.

Doi, L. T. 1962. "Amae: A Key Concept for Understanding Japanese Personality Structure." In Smith & Beardsley, *Japanese Culture: Its Development and Characteristics* (pp. 132–139). New York: Wenner-Gren Foundation for Anthropological Research.

Doi, T. 1973. *The Anatomy of Dependence.* Tokyo: Kodansha.

Doi, T. 1973. "The Japanese Patterns of Communication and the Concept of Amae." *The Quarterly Journal of Speech,* 59 (2), 180–185.

Doi, T. 1986. *The Anatomy of Self: The Individual versus Society.* Tokyo: Kodansha. Translation of *Omote to Ura.*

Druckman, D., ed. 1977. *Negotiations: Social-Psychological Perspectives.* Beverly Hills, CA: Sage.

Druckman, D., et al. 1973. *Human Factors in International Negotiations.* Beverly Hills, CA: Sage.

Evenko, L. I., Graham, J. L., & Rajan, M. N. 1990. *An Empirical Study of Marketing Negotiations in the Soviet Union* (Report 90–121). Cambridge, MA: Marketing Science Institute.

Faure, G. O. 1995. "Nonverbal Negotiation in China: Cycling in Beijing." *Negotiation Journal,* 11 (1), 11–17.

Faure, G. O., & Rubin, J. Z., eds. 1993. *Culture and Negotiation: The Resolution of Water Disputes.* Newbury Park, CA: Sage.

Fisher, G. 1979. *The Cross-Cultural Dimension in International Negotiation.* N.p.: U.S. Department of State, Foreign Service Institute, Center for the Study of Foreign Affairs.

Fisher, G. 1980. *International Negotiation: A Cross-Cultural Perspective.* Yarmouth, ME: Intercultural Press.

Fisher, G. 1988. *Mindsets.* Yarmouth, ME: Intercultural Press.

Fisher, R., & Ury, W. 1981. *Getting to YES: Negotiating Agreement without Giving In.* Boston: Houghton Mifflin.

Foster, D. A. 1992. *Bargaining Across Borders: How to Negotiate Business Successfully Anywhere in the World.* New York: McGraw-Hill.

Friedheim, R. L. 1999. "Explaining Japan's Failure in the International Whaling Negotiations." Ch. 6 in this volume.

Fuller, G. 1991. *The Negotiator's Handbook.* Englewood Cliffs, NJ: Prentice-Hall.

Goldman, A. 1988. *For Japanese Only: Intercultural Communication with Americans.* Tokyo: The Japan Times.

Gorer, G., & Rickman, J. 1962. *The People of Great Russia: A Psychological Study.* New York: Norton.

Gould, J. W. 1986. "Intercultural Business Communication." In Sigband & Bell, *Communication for Management and Business* (pp. 67–93). Glenview, IL: Scott, Foresman.

Graham, J. L. 1993. "The Japanese Negotiation Style: Characteristics of a Distinct Approach." *Negotiation Journal,* 9 (2), 123–140.

Graham, J. L., & Sano, Y. 1984. *Smart Bargaining: Doing Business with the Japanese,* esp. Ch. 3, "The Japanese Negotiation Style," pp. 17–32. Cambridge, MA: Ballinger.

Gudykunst, W. B., & Kim, Y. Y. 1984. *Communicating With Strangers: An Approach to Intercultural Communication.* New York: Random House.

Gulliver, P. H. 1979. *Disputes and Negotiations: A Cross-Cultural Perspective.* New York: Academic Press.

Hall, E. T. 1966. *The Hidden Dimension.* Garden City, NY: Doubleday.

Hall, E. T. 1973. *The Silent Language.* New York: Anchor Press.

Hall, E. T. 1976. *Beyond Culture.* New York: Anchor Press.

Hall, E. T., & Hall, M. R. 1987. *Hidden Differences—Doing Business with the Japanese.* See the Vocabulary of Human Relationships, p. 61, and Glossary, pp. 157–160. Garden City, NY: Anchor Press/Doubleday.

Hamaguchi, E. 1985. "A Contextual Model of the Japanese: Toward a Methodological Innovation in Japan Studies." *The Journal of Japanese Studies,* 11 (2), 289–321.

Hecht, J. L., ed. 1991. *Rubles and Dollars: Strategies for Doing Business in the Soviet Union.* New York: Harper Business.

Hofstede, G. 1989. "Cultural Predictors of National Negotiation Styles." In Mautner-Markhof, *Processes of International Negotiations* (pp. 193–201). Boulder, CO: Westview.

Hofstede, G. 1991. *Cultures and Organizations: Software of the Mind.* Berkshire, England: McGraw-Hill.

Iga, M. 1986. *The Thorn in the Chrysanthemum: Suicide and Economic Success in Modern Japan.* Berkeley: University of California Press.

Ikle, F. C. 1964. *How Nations Negotiate.* New York: Harper & Row.

Imai, M. 1975. *Never Take Yes for an Answer: An Inside Look at Japanese Business.* Tokyo: Simul Press.

Imai, M. 1981. *16 Ways to Avoid Saying No: An Invitation to Experience Japanese Management from the Inside.* Tokyo: Nihon Keizai Shimbun.

Joy, C. T. 1955. *How Communists Negotiate.* New York: Macmillan.

Kawai, H. 1985. "The Japanese Mind as Reflected in Their Mythology." *Psychologia* (Kyoto), 28 (2), 71–76.

Kennan, G. F. 1967. *Memoirs, 1925–1950.* New York: Little, Brown.

Kent, P. 1994. "Ruth Benedict's Original Wartime Study of the Japanese." *International Journal of Japanese Sociology,* 3, 81–97.

Kimura, H. 1980. "Soviet and Japanese Negotiation Behavior: The Spring 1977 Fisheries Talks." *Orbis,* 24 (1), 43–67.

Kimura, H. 1996a. "The Russian Decision-Making Process Toward Japan." *Japan Review,* 7, 61–81.

Kimura, H. 1996b. "The Russian Way of Negotiating." *International Negotiation,* 1, 365–389; and Ch. 3 in this volume.

Kissinger, H. 1994. *Diplomacy.* New York: Simon & Schuster.

Kitamura, H. 1971. *Psychological Dimensions of U.S.-Japanese Relations.* Cambridge: Harvard University, Center for International Affairs, Occasional Papers in International Affairs, No. 28.

Kitamura, H. 1994. "Psychological Factors in Friction Between Japan and America." *Japan Review of International Affairs,* 8 (3), 203–220.

Klein, M. 1957. *Envy and Gratitude.* New York: Basic Books.

Kohls, L. R. 1978. "Basic Concepts and Models of Intercultural Communication." In Prosser, *USIA Intercultural Communication Course: 1977 Proceedings.* Washington, DC: United States Information Agency.

Kreisberg, P. H. 1994. "China's Negotiating Behaviour." In Robinson & Shambaugh, *Chinese Foreign Policy: Theory and Practice* (pp. 453–477). Oxford: Clarendon Press.

Lachkar, J. 1992. *The Narcissistic/Borderline Couple: A Psychoanalytic Perspective on Marital Treatment.* New York: Brunner/Mazel Publishers.

Lakos, A. 1989. *International Negotiations: Soviet Diplomacy and Negotiating Behavior, A Bibliography.* Monticello, IL: Vance Bibliographies, February.

Lall, A. 1966. *Modern International Negotiation: Principles and Practice.* New York: Columbia University Press.

Lall, A. 1968. *How Communist China Negotiates.* New York: Columbia University Press.

Leites, N. 1953. *A Study of Bolshevism.* Glencoe, IL: The Free Press. A shorter version under the title *The Operational Code of the Politburo* appeared in 1951.

Lipset, S. M. 1996. *American Exceptionalism: A Double-Edged Sword.* New York: Norton.

Lustig, M. W., & Koester, J. 1993. *Intercultural Competence: Interpersonal Communication Across Cultures.* New York: Harper Collins.

Macleod, R. 1988. *China, Inc.: How To Do Business with the Chinese.* Toronto: Bantam Books.

March, R. M. 1982. "Business Negotiation as Cross-Cultural Communication: The Japanese-Western Case." *Cross Currents,* 9 (1), 55–65.

March, R. M. 1988. *The Japanese Negotiator: Subtlety and Strategy Beyond Western Logic.* Tokyo and New York: Kodansha International.

Matsumoto, M. 1984. *The Unspoken Way: Haragei: Silence in Japanese Business and Society.* Tokyo: Kodansha.

McCreary, D. R. 1986. *Japanese-U.S. Business Negotiations: A Cross-Cultural Study.* New York: Praeger.

Miyamoto, M. 1982. *The Book of Five Rings (Gorin no Sho): The Real Art of Japanese Management—A Guide to Winning Strategy.* New York: Bantam Books.

Miyamoto, M. 1994. *Straightjacket Society: An Insider's Irreverent View of Bureaucratic Japan.* Tokyo: Kodansha International.

Moran, R. T. 1985. *Getting Your Yen's Worth.* Houston, TX: Gulf Publishing Company.

Mosely, P. E. 1951. "Some Soviet Techniques of Negotiation." In Dennett & Johnson, *Negotiating with the Russians* (pp. 271–303). Boston: World Peace Foundation.

Moser, L. 1986. "Cross-Cultural Dimensions: U.S.-Japan." In Bendahmane & Moser, *Toward a Better Understanding: U.S.-Japan Relations* (pp. 21–34). N.p.: U.S. Department of State, Foreign Service Institute, Center for the Study of Foreign Affairs.

Moser, L. 1986. "Negotiating Style: Americans and Japanese." In Bendahmane & Moser, *Toward a Better Understanding* (pp. 43–51).

Mushakoji, K. 1967. *Kokusai seiji to Nihon* [International Politics and Japan]. Tokyo: Tokyo University Press.

Mushakoji, K. 1976. "The Cultural Premises of Japanese Diplomacy." In Japan Center for International Exchange, *The Silent Power: Japan's Identity and World Role* (pp. 35–49). Tokyo: Simul Press.

Nakane, C. 1970. *Japan: A Vertical Society.* Tokyo: University of Tokyo Press.

Nakanishi, M., & Johnson, K. M. 1993. "Implications of Self-Disclosure on Conversational Logics, Perceived Communication Competence, and Social Attraction: A Comparison of Japanese and American Cultures." In Wiseman & Koester, *Intercultural Communication Competence.*

National Foreign Assessment Center. 1979. *Soviet Strategy and Tactics in Economic and Commercial Negotiations with the United States: A Research Paper.* Washington, DC: Central Intelligence Agency, June (ER 79–10276).

"Negotiating with the Soviets: Goals, Style, and Method: A Roundtable Discussion." *Foreign Service Journal,* November 1985, 24–27.

Neustupny, J. V. 1987. *Communicating with the Japanese.* Tokyo: The Japan Times.

Nierenberg, G. I. 1981. *The Art of Negotiating.* New York: Simon & Schuster.

Noble, G. W. 1992. *Flying Apart: Japanese-American Negotiations over the FSX Fighter Plane.* Berkeley: University of California, Institute of International Studies.

Ogura, K. 1979. "How the 'Inscrutables' Negotiate with the 'Inscrutables': Chinese Negotiating Tactics vis-à-vis the Japanese." *China Quarterly,* No. 79, 529–552.

Ogura, K., n.d., 1983? *Trade Conflict: A View From Japan,* esp. Ch. 3, "The Socio-Psychological Framework of U.S.-Japan Relations," pp. 19–27, and Ch. 5, "Japanese Cultural Traits and U.S.-Japan Economic Friction," pp. 35–39. Washington, DC: Japan Economic Institute. See also K. Ogura, "The Sociopsychological Structure Surrounding U.S.-Japan Economic Relations." *The Wheel Extended,* April-June, 1983. Different version of Ch. 3 of the preceding work.

Ogura, K. 1985. "Nikkan Kokko Nijushunen wo kangaeru 10—Nikkan Gaiko Kosho ni okeru 'Tatemae to Honne': Keizai Kyoryoku Kosho ni okeru 'Purojekuto shugi' wo megutte" [Reflecting on the Twentieth Anniversary of the Restoration of Diplomatic Relations Between Japan and South Korea, No. 10—"Tatemae and Honne" in Diplomatic Negotiations Between Japan and South Korea: "Projectism" in Economic Cooperation Negotiations]. *Gendai Koria* [Contemporary Korea], November, 24–29.

Ogura, K. 1992. "Nichi-Bei Keizai Kosho Mitsu no Otoshi Ana" [The Three Pitfalls in Japan-U.S. Economic Negotiations]. *Sekai Keizai Hyoron* [World Economy Review], November, 40–44.

Onda, H. 1987. *Koshosha to shite no Sorenjin* [The Soviets as Negotiators]. Tokyo: Kyoikusha.

Ozawa, S. 1990. *Naze Nihonjin wa Kokusai Kosho ni Yowai no ka: Nihonjin no Shippai* [Why Are Japanese Weak in International Negotiations: The Failure of the Japanese]. Tokyo: Riyonsha.

Peabody, D. 1985. *National Characteristics.* Cambridge: Cambridge University Press.

Poortinga, Y. H., & Hendriks, E. C. 1988. "Culture as a Factor in International Negotiations: A Proposed Research Project from a Psychological Perspective." In Mautner-Markhof, *Processes of International Negotiations* (pp. 203–212).

Prosser, M. H. 1978. *The Cultural Dialogue: An Introduction to Intercultural Communication.* Boston: Houghton Mifflin.

Pye, L. W. 1992. *Chinese Negotiating Style: Commercial Approaches and Cultural Principles.* New York: Quorum Books. Revised edition of *Chinese Commercial Negotiating Style* (1982). Cambridge, MA: Oelgeschlager, Gunn & Hain. A Rand study (R-2837-AF).

Rajan, M. N., & Graham, J. L. 1991. "Nobody's Grandfather Was a Merchant: Understanding the Soviet Commercial Negotiation Process and Style." *California Management Review,* Spring, 40–57.

Rogers, D. J. 1984. *Fighting to Win: Samurai Techniques for Your Work and Life.* Garden City, NY: Doubleday.

Rowny, E. L. 1992. *It Takes One to Tango.* Washington, DC: Brassey's.

Rubin, J. Z., & Brown, B. R. 1975. *The Social Psychology of Bargaining and Negotiation.* New York: Academic Press.

Samelson, L. J. 1976. *Soviet and Chinese Negotiating Behavior: The Western View.* Beverly Hills, CA: Sage.

Samovar, L. A., & Porter, R. E., eds. 1994. *Intercultural Communication: A Reader,* 7th ed. Belmont, CA: Wadsworth.

Sawyer, J., & Guetzkow, H. 1965. "Bargaining and Negotiation in International Relations." In Kelman, *International Behavior: A Social-Psychological Analysis* (pp. 464–520). New York: Holt, Rinehart and Winston.

Schecter, J. L. 1998. *Russian Negotiating Behavior: Continuity and Transition.* Washington, DC: United States Institute of Peace Press.

Sloss, L., & Davis, M. S., eds. 1986. *A Game for High Stakes: Lessons Learned in Negotiating with the Soviet Union.* Cambridge, MA: Ballinger.

Sloss, L., & Davis, M. S. 1987. "The Soviet Union: The Pursuit of Power and Influence through Negotiation." In Binnendijk, *National Negotiating Styles* (pp. 17–43). N.p.: U.S. Department of State, Foreign Service Institute, Center for the Study of Foreign Affairs.

Smith, R. F. 1989. *Negotiating with the Soviets.* Bloomington: Indiana University Press.

Solomon, R. H. 1985. *Chinese Political Negotiating Behavior: A Briefing Analysis.* Santa Monica: The Rand Corporation (R–3295).

Solomon, R. H. 1987. "China: Friendship and Obligation in Chinese Negotiating Style." In Binnendijk, *National Negotiating Styles* (pp. 1–16).

Solomon, R. H. 1999. *Chinese Negotiating Behavior: Pursuing Interests through "Old Friends."* Washington, DC: United States Institute of Peace Press.

Spector, B. I. 1978. "Negotiation as a Psychological Process." In Zartman, *The Negotiation Process: Theories and Applications* (pp. 55–66). Beverly Hills, CA: Sage.

Steibel, G. L. 1972. *How Can We Negotiate with the Communists?* New York: National Strategy Information Center.

Subcommittee on National Security and International Operations, Committee on Government Operations, United States Senate (Comp.). 1969. *Peking's Approach to Negotiation: Selected Writings.* Washington, DC: U.S. Government Printing Office.

Subcommittee on National Security and International Operations, Committee on Government Operations, United States Senate (Comp.). 1969. *The Soviet Approach to Negotiation: Selected Writings.* Washington, DC: U.S. Government Printing Office.

Subcommittee on National Security and International Operations, Committee on Government Operations, United States Senate (Comp.). 1970. *Negotiation and Statecraft: A Selection of Readings.* Washington, DC: U.S. Government Printing Office.

Thayer, N. B., & Weiss, S. E. 1987. "Japan: The Changing Logic of a Former Minor Power." In Binnendijk, *National Negotiating Styles* (pp. 45–74).

Tourevski, M., & Morgan, E. 1993. *Cutting the Red Tape: How Western Companies Can Profit in the New Russia.* New York: The Free Press.

Tung, R. L. 1984. *Business Negotiations with the Japanese.* Lexington, MA: Heath/Lexington Books.

Ueda, K. 1974. "Sixteen Ways to Avoid Saying 'No' in Japan." In Condon & Saito, *Intercultural Encounters with Japan* (pp. 185–192).

van Wolferen, K. 1989. *The Enigma of Japanese Power: People and Politics in a Stateless Nation.* New York: Knopf.

van Zandt, H. F. 1970. "How to Negotiate in Japan." *Harvard Business Review,* November-December, 45–56.

Warschaw, T. A. 1980. *Winning by Negotiation.* New York: McGraw-Hill.

Watzlawick, P. et al. 1967. *Pragmatics of Human Communication: A Study of Interactional Patterns, Pathologies, and Paradoxes.* New York: Norton.

Wilhelm, A. D., Jr. 1994. *The Chinese at the Negotiating Table: Style and Characteristics.* Washington, DC: National Defense University Press.

Wiseman, R. L., & Koester, J., eds. 1993. *Intercultural Communication Competence* (International and Intercultural Communication Annual, Vol. XVII). Newbury Park, CA: Sage.

Yamamoto, S. 1979. *Nihon shihon-shugi no seishin* [Capitalistic Spirit in Japan]. Tokyo: Kobunsha.

Young, K. T. 1968. *Negotiating with the Chinese Communists: The United States Experience, 1953–1967.* New York: McGraw-Hill.

Zartman, I. W., ed. 1978. *The Negotiation Process: Theories and Applications.* Beverly Hills, CA: Sage.

Zartman, I. W. 1993. "A Skeptic's View," Ch. 2 in Part I, "International Negotiation: Does Culture Make a Difference?" pp. 17–21. In Faure & Rubin, *Culture and Negotiation.*

Zartman, I. W., & Berman, M. R. 1982. *The Practical Negotiator.* New Haven: Yale University Press.

Zhao, Q. 1993. *Japanese Policymaking: The Politics Behind Politics—Informal Mechanisms and the Making of China Policy.* Westport, CT: Praeger.

Zimmerman, M. 1985. *How To Do Business with the Japanese.* New York: Random House.

PART II

STRUCTURE AND PROCESS

CHAPTER 5

INTERNATIONAL COMMERCIAL NEGOTIATIONS: A FOCUS ON JAPAN

JOHN L. GRAHAM

Trade between Japan and the United States will continue to be crucial to world peace and prosperity well beyond the turn of the millennium. While creative and friendly governmental relations will help provide a positive background for commercial cooperation across the Pacific, the thousands of business people who conduct the day-to-day business transactions between companies in the two countries are the fundamental ingredients of the bilateral relationship. These thousands of managers, executives, and entrepreneurs in both Japan and the United States are the focus of this study.

The evidence that Japanese and American negotiation styles and behaviors differ is legion. With my own colleagues I have tried to identify the main areas of difference using interviews, field observations, and laboratory simulations, the last including questionnaires and videotaping (Graham, 1993). Most of the work done on international negotiation styles, including my own, has been comparative in nature, involving *intra*cultural negotiation settings. A few people have begun to address the issue of *inter*cultural negotiations in a systematic way (for example, Francis, 1991; and Adler & Graham, 1989), but really we know very little about how people behave when bargaining with foreigners.

Some of my most recent work has involved testing a model of the determinants of negotiation outcomes in fourteen countries, including Japan and the United States (Graham, Mintu & Rodgers, 1994; Graham &

Mintu-Wimsatt, 1997). The model "works" reasonably well, but often differently across the several countries. In all fourteen cases data collected in intracultural negotiations were used for the empirical tests. In the current study we have had forty-two Japanese and forty-two American business people participate in an intercultural negotiation simulation. Data were collected from "both sides of the table" and are used to test the theoretical model developed earlier. We can then compare the new intercultural results directly with those intracultural results reported previously toward building a better understanding of what happens when differing negotiation styles mix.

The remainder of the chapter is divided into five parts. First, based on the literature a few predictions are made regarding differences between intercultural and intracultural settings. Next, the theoretical model is briefly described and hypotheses stated. The methods of the study are described in the third section. Results are reported in the fourth. The chapter is concluded with a discussion and interpretation of the findings.

THE LITERATURE ON INTERNATIONAL NEGOTIATIONS

In their seminal article regarding international negotiation behaviors, Sawyer and Guetzkow were among the first to posit that negotiators' behaviors and outcomes can be influenced by situational constraints, such as, intercultural negotiations versus intracultural negotiations: "The face-to-face conduct of negotiations may be influenced by behavioral discrepancies when persons of different cultural backgrounds are brought together" (1965, p. 502).

Support for their supposition has come from a broad array of disciplines. The intercultural communication and psychology literature suggests that people behave differently with members of their own culture than with members of foreign cultures. Research in non-business contexts has demonstrated that when individuals interact with people from different cultures, the differences between them become salient (Bouchner & Ohsako, 1977). Moreover, when people in interpersonal situations confront these actual differences, they tend to exaggerate them (Sherif & Hovland, 1961; Vassiliou et al., 1972).

Mishler (1965) reports that in international exchanges: "The greater the cultural differences, the more likely barriers to communication and misunderstandings become." Some researchers have even questioned whether "managers from significantly different cultures such as Japan and the

United States can ever completely understand each other " (Peterson & Shimada, 1978). Studies in the following five research areas are particularly relevant.

INTERPERSONAL ORIENTATION

Most of the literature summarized in later sections suggests that negotiators will adjust their behavior from one situation to another. However, Rubin and Brown (1975) imply that people with a low interpersonal orientation (IO) will behave consistently across intra- and intercultural situations. They suggest that a high-IO person is "responsive to the interpersonal aspects of his relationship with others. He is both interested in, and reactive to, variation in the other's behavior." Alternatively, a low IO is "characterized, first and foremost, by a nonresponsiveness to the interpersonal aspects of his relationship with the other. . . ." (Rubin & Brown, 1975, pp. 158–159).

Thus, one might conclude that some people will behave in the same way no matter who is on the other side of the negotiation table—someone from the same culture or someone from a different culture. Graham and Herberger (1983) carry this idea one step further when they suggest that American negotiators naturally tend to be low IOs:

> *I am what I am.* Few Americans take pride in changing their minds, even in difficult circumstances. Certainly John Wayne's character and behavior were constant and predictable. He treated everyone and every situation with his action-oriented, forthright style. He could never be accused of being a chameleon (p. 166).

So an explanation for ethnocentricity and obstinacy at the international negotiation table is offered. However, most of the rest of the pertinent literature argues that behavior changes will occur across the two settings, and for a variety of reasons.

NEGOTIATOR SIMILARITY

The present study provides an excellent opportunity to test Evans's (1963) "similarity hypothesis." Evans's ideas—"the more similar the parties in a dyad are, the more likely a favorable outcome, a sale"—have stimulated a series of studies investigating relationships between similarity and a variety of negotiation outcomes. Weitz (1979), in his excellent critical review of this stream of research, concludes that support for Evans's similarity hypotheses is weak, and in some cases, flawed by confounds. However, the previous work provides an important background for the issues to be considered here.

McGuire (1968) cites a "considerable body of evidence" and posits the mechanism underlying the influence of similarity:

> Presumably the receiver, to the extent that he perceives the source to be like himself in diverse characteristics, assumes that they also share common needs and goals. The receiver might therefore conclude that what the source is urging is good for "our kind of people," and thus change his attitude accordingly (p. 187).

Evans (1963), Davis and Silk (1972), and Bagozzi (1978) all discuss at some length the relationship among similarity, attraction, and outcomes. Implied in Evans's work is a causal relation among the three constructs, with attraction mediating: similarity → attraction → outcomes. Thus, negotiators in same culture dyads might be expected to be more attracted to partners and achieve higher negotiation outcomes—profits and satisfaction.

COMMUNICATION PROBLEMS

Closely related to the issue of negotiator similarity are intercultural communication problems. Everyone writing in the area of international negotiations reports substantial communication problems at the negotiation table that often lead to undesirable outcomes for one or both parties (cf., Sawyer & Guetzkow, 1965; or Rubin & Brown, 1975). Condon's (1974) views are most insightful—he classifies intercultural communication problems into four categories:

1. Language and language behavior;
2. Nonverbal behavior;
3. Values; and
4. Patterns of thought.

Condon adds that these categories might be considered in order of ascending perplexity. That is, misunderstandings at the level of language are often obvious and most easily corrected. Misunderstandings at the lower levels are seldom obvious to the participants in an interaction.

Empirical support for Condon's views is broad. Pertinent is an article by Graham and Andrews (1987), which describes in depth how communication problems, at all four levels, result in undesirable outcomes for Americans negotiating with Japanese business people. It follows then that negotiation outcomes will be less favorable in intercultural negotiations because communication problems are much more likely to occur.

RECIPROCITY AND INTERACTIONAL SYNCHRONY

A series of studies by social psychologists and sociolinguists suggests that negotiators in a dyad tend to imitate one another's behaviors and balance individual negotiation outcomes. Gouldner (1960) explains that a "reciprocity norm" establishes a stable set of mutual rewards that guides interactions such as negotiations. Putnam and Jones (1982) report that reciprocity is more evident in integrative message patterns than in distributive strategies. Walton and McKersie (1965), Rubin and Brown (1975), and Pruitt (1981) all describe a tendency of negotiators to match one another's bargaining strategies.

Even deeper than Gouldner's reciprocity norm are the unconscious influences of concepts of interactional synchrony and emotional contagion. Condon (1968) and others have reported that a speaker's body movements are coordinated with one another and coordinated with the articulation of speech. Hatfield, Cacioppo, and Rapson (1994) describe in great detail the evidence that humans naturally mimic those with whom they interact.

Therefore, based on these concepts of reciprocity, synchrony, and emotional contagion negotiators in intercultural interactions might be expected to adapt their usual intracultural behaviors to more closely reflect those of their foreign counterparts. Likewise, outcomes of intercultural negotiations may reflect a compromise between results typical of the differing intracultural styles.

ACCULTURATION THEORY

Acculturation theory suggests what might happen at the point of culture contact. That is, what will result from the mix of negotiation and communication styles?

Acculturation theory is a "mature" paradigm in anthropology. It received the most attention during the 1930s and 1940s. This attention was primarily a response to problems with native peoples in the Americas and problems of British colonial rule. The questions were: To what extent can indigenous peoples be assimilated into "advanced" cultures, and how might this process of assimilation be facilitated? The most widely accepted definition of acculturation is that of Redfield, Linton, and Herskovits (1936): "Acculturation comprehends those phenomena which result when groups of individuals having different cultures come into continuous first-hand contact, with subsequent changes in the original cultural patterns of either or both groups" (p. 55).

The difference between the acculturation paradigm and more recent social-psychological models is the units of analysis. Acculturation theory has really been applied in a macro sense, the units of analysis being entire cultures. The units of analysis in social psychology have been the individual or, at most, small groups.

Acculturation theory fits the specific situation of intercultural negotiations very well. Acculturation theory is particularly useful if process measures are selected as the dependent variable. That is, what factors will determine which parties will adopt which negotiation and communication styles, given that these styles are culture specific?

Certainly, the most obvious example is language. What language will be spoken during intercultural negotiations? Will one party adopt the language of the other party? The circumstance of Japanese and American intercultural negotiations is interesting. Most often, English is the language spoken during the negotiations between Japanese and Americans. Part of the explanation is that the Japanese possess greater linguistic abilities than Americans. Japanese schools teach and emphasize English. However, in the long term, the most important explanation is the power differential, both economic and military. The Japanese emphasis on learning English can be attributed in large part to the American occupation following World War II. Additionally, until recent times, Japan has been economically dependent on the United States. However, there are exceptions. For example, it is common practice for high-level Japanese executives to use interpreters, even though they may speak and understand English. Here the use of interpreters is expressive of the person's power. Further, with the increasing economic interdependence of recent years, changes are taking place. Japanese businessmen now complain about Americans' ignorance of Japanese business customs.

All the theories suggest generally that behavior will be different in cross-cultural negotiations. Adler and Graham (1989) have provided information on how Japanese and Americans adjust their behavior during cross-cultural negotiations. The current study is an extension of that work wherein a model of negotiation processes is tested using cross-cultural interactions as the context.

The Negotiation Model

The theoretical model depicted in figure 1 is identical to that tested in Graham, Mintu, and Rodgers (1994) and Graham and Mintu-Wimsatt (1997). Because their conceptual development is complete, we will only summarize it here.

Figure 1:
Model of Negotiations

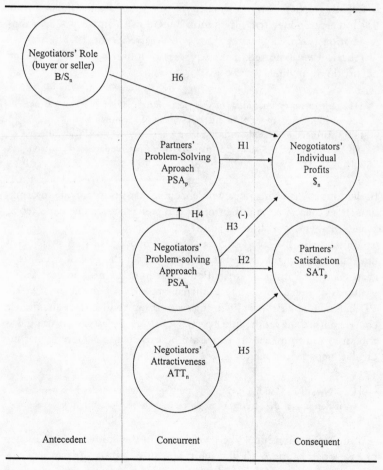

Two dependent constructs are used in the study: (1) individual profits attained by bargainers in a negotiation simulation; and (2) satisfaction of their partners, measured using a post-exercise questionnaire.

The first independent variable considered is a problem-solving approach (PSA). A PSA involves first an emphasis on asking questions and getting information from clients about their needs and preferences. Second, once the other's requirements and circumstances are fully understood, the negotiator then accommodates the product or service offering to the client's needs. The focus is on cooperation and an integrative approach, wherein the needs of both parties are discussed and eventually satisfied. Despite a variety of labels used for the PSA concept (for instance, cooperative orientation by Rubin & Brown, 1973; or representation bargaining strategies by Angelmar & Stern, 1978), most researchers have reported a positive relationship between PSA and negotiation outcomes.

H1.   Negotiators' individual profits are positively affected when partners use strategies that are more oriented toward problem-solving.

H2.   Partners' expressed satisfaction with agreements is positively affected when negotiators use strategies that are more oriented toward problem-solving.

In the former case, bargainers who encourage targets to provide information about themselves and their needs and preferences can be expected to achieve higher negotiation outcomes.

Walton and McKersie (1965) suggest the opposite of PSA strategies is distributive or individualistic bargaining strategies, the goal of which is to change a target's attitudes, attributions, or actions. Promises and threats are examples of distributive or instrumental appeals (cf., Angelmar & Stern, 1978). Rubin and Brown (1975) suggest that distributive strategies induce concession-making by the other party. Consequently, bargainers using distributive or instrumental strategies can be expected to achieve higher individual negotiation outcomes, or

H3.   Negotiators' individual profits are negatively affected when negotiators use strategies that are more oriented toward problem-solving.

Another relationship to be investigated in this study is the influence of a negotiator's approach (behaviors and attitudes) on the partner's negotiation approach. Rubin and Brown (1975) suggest the importance of adjusting one's bargaining tactics based upon impressions of opponents. Pruitt (1983) and Walton and McKersie (1965) are among several researchers who describe a tendency of negotiators to imitate or match one another's bargaining strategies. Although empirical support for these latter propositions is limited at best, the following hypothesis is suggested:

H4.   Negotiators' use of strategies that are oriented toward problem-solving positively influences partners to use strategies that are oriented toward problem-solving.

The reader will appreciate the importance of the structural relations presented in figure 1 and the necessity of the partial least squares analysis. For example, as conceived, the relationships represented in hypotheses 3 and 4 should suppress the relationship represented by hypotheses 1 (cf., Bagozzi, 1980). That is, the correlation coefficients may actually be understating the true relationship. A structural equations approach will help to sort out which relations are the most meaningful within the complex model proposed.

Another important concurrent construct is attractiveness of the negotiator (here we do not consider physical attractiveness, but rather ask questions about interest and comfort levels between negotiators). Graham (1986) has shown target attractiveness to influence the source's satisfaction positively in a negotiation simulation. Rubin and Brown (1975), in their review of the negotiation literature, conclude that, generally, interpersonal attraction enhances bargaining outcomes. Therefore, to the extent that a person receives social rewards from a relationship with an attractive other, that person will be more satisfied with the relationship (or the negotiation agreement).

H5.   Partners' satisfaction is positively affected by negotiators' attractiveness.

The final relationship represented in figure 1 is between the role of the negotiator (the buyer or seller) and individual profits. Status and role (cf. Rubin & Brown, 1975) have been found to influence negotiations. In associated studies, Graham et al. (1994) have found that in some countries buyers tend to achieve higher profits than sellers.

H6.   Buyers achieve higher individual profits than do sellers.

METHODOLOGY

Participants

Forty-two American and forty-two Japanese business people participated in this study. All had been members of executive education programs or graduate business courses and had an average of greater than eight years business experience. On average, the participants were over thirty years of age, and at least 45 percent of their work involved contact with people outside their respective firms. Table 1 reports the demographic character-istics and the corresponding means and standard deviations of the variables of interest.

NEGOTIATION SIMULATION

The negotiation simulation, developed by Kelley (1966) and used by Clopton (1984) involves bargaining for the prices of three commodities. Each bargainer receives an instruction sheet, including a price list with as-sociated profit for each price level. Participants are allowed fifteen minutes to read the instructions and plan their bargaining strategies. Though sim-ple enough to be learned quickly, the simulation usually provides enough complexity for a half hour of interaction. Within the one-hour time limit, bargainers use face-to-face, free communication. No explicit rewards (such as grades or money) were associated with performance or participation in the simulation. Several other negotiation and bargaining simulations were considered. Kelley's game was selected primarily because it best simulates the essential elements of actual commercial negotiations observed in pre-liminary field research, including multiple issues (that is, integrative and distributive) and the potential for a variety of negotiation strategies, in-cluding logrolling and cooperation (Pruitt 1983).

DATA-COLLECTION INSTRUMENTS

After the bargaining session, each individual completed a questionnaire. To ensure equivalence, the Japanese translation of the simulation instructions and questionnaire were back-translated into English by different transla-tors, and then the original and back-translated versions were compared and discrepancies resolved.

We considered two negotiation outcome variables. Negotiators' indi-vidual profits ($\$_n$) were derived directly from the agreed-upon bargaining

Table 1 Group Characteristics and Descriptive Statistics, means (s.d.)

	Japanese Negotiators		American Negotiators	
	Intracultural ($n = 44$)	Intercultural ($n = 42$)	Intercultural ($n = 42$)	Intracultural ($n = 160$)
Age	36.8 (5.1)	30.4 (4.0)	33.2 (9.0)	32.8 (9.5)
Years of work experience	13.1 (5.5)	8.4 (8.3)	9.8 (8.6)	9.6 (8.1)
Percentage of work involving contact with people outside firm	51.8 (19.9)	57.9 (25.7)	46.3 (32.3)	51.7 (30.3)
Individual profits ($)	47.9 (7.7)	43.2 (11.6)	48.5 (9.7)	44.9 (11.1)
Satisfaction (SAT), $\alpha_J = .82$, $\alpha_A = .86$	3.8[a] (0.9)	14.4 (3.1)	16.3 (2.9)	14.6 (3.2)
Problem-solving approach (PSA), $\alpha_J = .63$, $\alpha_A = .83$	10.3 (2.2)	10.4 (1.8)	9.8 (3.0)	9.6 (2.6)
Negotiator attractiveness (ATT), $\alpha_J = .77$, $\alpha_A = .73$	12.0 (2.0)	12.6 (2.0)	12.4 (2.5)	11.9 (2.3)

[a] single item measure

solutions. Partners' satisfaction (SAT_p) with the negotiation was measured using a single item included on the post-simulation questionnaire.

Process-related measures also were derived from post-exercise questionnaires. Participants rated their own PSA bargaining strategies. Finally, partners rated the interpersonal attractiveness (ATT_n) of their respective negotiators.

DATA ANALYSIS

The measurement problem was attacked first by calculating Cronbach α reliability coefficients (α is a measure of the intercorrelation of the separate items in each scale, that is, a measure of the internal consistency of multiple item measures) as suggested in Davis, Douglas, and Silk (1981). (See table 1.) For the Japanese the three-item PSA scale performed only marginally regarding absolute a scores and the comparative criterion outlined by Davis, Douglas, and Silk (1981) (in other words, scores should be greater than .65 and overlap with 90 percent confidence intervals of the original scale, in this case English).

Loading pattern coefficients (estimates of the coincidence of the separate items in a single measure) and parameter estimates were calculated for each cultural group using partial least squares (PLS). Then the statistical significance of the parameter estimates was determined using a maximum-likelihood estimation technique (Joreskog & Sorbom, 1981), with the PLS latent variable correlation matrix as input, to calculate the t-value for each parameter estimate. The significance levels present some evidence that relationships do exist, in fact, as opposed to the hypothesis that they are the results of a spurious arrangement (Fornell & Robinson, 1983).

Using PLS as the analysis approach is appropriate for three reasons. First, using PLS, parameters can be estimated independent of sample size. Given that sample size varies for our four groups from 160 to 42, PLS seems more appropriate for parameter comparisons across groups than LISREL (a less flexible structural equations program) by itself. Second, PLS avoids parameter estimation biases inherent in regression analysis (Fornell, Rhee & Yi, 1991) and some of the restrictive assumptions underlying LIS-REL (Fornell & Bookstein, 1982). Third, and perhaps most important, PLS provides the most flexibility regarding measurement of the constructs. That is, in both correlation and regression analyses, additive scales must be used as measures of the PSA and ATT constructs. LISREL can be used with either additive scales or with a reflective indicator measurement approach wherein each item is modeled as on of a set of multiple indicators of an unobservable construct. Using LISREL, the internal consistency of the measures (the degree of correlation between the separate items) can be determined simultaneously with parameter estimation.

PLS allows not only for additive scales and reflective indicators but also for a formative indicator measurement approach. In a formative indicator model, individual items are viewed as representing multiple causes of the constructs. This is an important distinction, as Fornell and Bookstein (1982, p. 441) describe:

> [U]nobserved constructs can be viewed either as underlying factors or as indices produced by the observable variables. That is, the observed indicators can be treated as reflective or formative. Reflective indicators are typical of classical test theory and factor analysis models; they are invoked in an attempt to account for observed variances or covariances. Formative indicators, in contrast, are not designed to account for observed variables; they are used to minimize residuals in the structural relationship.

RESULTS

In table 2 are reported the findings of the study. Columns II and III include the results from the analyses of the intercultural data collected for the current study and columns I and IV include results reported in previous papers (Graham, Mintu, & Rodgers, 1994; Graham & Mintu-Wimsatt, 1997).

Hypothesis 1 was supported only for the American intracultural negotiations (column IV). Negotiation partner's problem-solving-oriented strategies appear to have had no effect on negotiator's profits in the other three circumstances.

Hypothesis 2 was weakly supported for the American intracultural negotiations (column IV). In the other circumstances a negotiator's taking a problem-solving approach appeared to have had little effect on partner's satisfaction.

Hypothesis 3 was not supported for any of the circumstances. Indeed, contrary to the stated hypothesis, when Japanese negotiators used more problem-solving-oriented strategies they achieved higher individual profits.

Both hypotheses 4 and 5 were supported across all circumstances. Negotiation partners tended to reciprocate negotiator's problem-solving strategies. Negotiator's interpersonal attractiveness was found to strongly influence partner's satisfaction levels.

Table 2 Results, PLS Parameter Estimates (using formative indicators)

	Japanese Negotiators		American Negotiators	
	I. Intracultural[a] (n = 44)	II. Intercultural (n = 42)	III. Intercultural (n = 42)	IV. Intracultural (n = 160)
H1, $PSA_p \rightarrow \$_n$	-.09	.18	.06	.28**
H2, $PSA_n \rightarrow SAT_p$	-.07	.24	.16	.14*
H3, $PSA_n \rightarrow \$_n$	-.15	.31**	.04	-.01
H4, $PSA_n \rightarrow PSA_p$	.36**	.52**	.26*	.29**
H5, $ATT_n \rightarrow SAT_p$	.39**	.52**	.67**	.39**
H6, $B/S_n \rightarrow \$_n$	.43**	.16	.08	.19**
$R^2 - \$_n$	.27**	.24**	.01	.10**
$R^2 - SAT_p$	.16**	.32**	.50**	.18**

[a] measures of SAT using a single item
* $p < 0.10$
** $p < 0.05$

Hypothesis 6 was supported only for the intracultural negotiations. Role of the negotiator (buyer or seller) appears to have made no difference in negotiator's profits in intercultural negotiations.

The hypothesized model explained substantial portions of the variation in negotiation outcomes for the Japanese bargainers in the intercultural negotiations—individual profits equaled 24 percent and partner satisfaction equaled 32 percent. The model explained little with regard to American profits in the intercultural negotiations, except half of the variation in partner's satisfaction (50 percent).

POST HOC ANALYSES

Given the surprisingly poor performance of the model in explaining American profit levels in the intercultural negotiations, other potential causal factors were considered. In particular, the post-negotiation questionnaire included a measure of extroversion/introversion (Eysenk's six-item scale, 1958), which proved to be salient in previous analyses (for example, Graham, 1985). Americans who were more introverted based upon the Eysenk scale achieved significantly higher individual profits when negotiating with Japanese ($r = -.36$; $p < .05$). Extroversion/introversion was unrelated to individual profits in the other three circumstances.

DISCUSSION

Reciprocity and imitation seem to be operating in all circumstances. Although communication theory suggests that intercultural misunderstandings will cause all kinds of problems in negotiations, bargainers in both cultures appear to be able to size up (either consciously or unconsciously) the strategies of their negotiation partners and adjust their own behavior accordingly. The concepts of interactional synchrony and emotional contagion seem to be supported in our study.

The effects of interpersonal attractiveness appear to be a cultural universal, at least across the intracultural negotiation settings in the fourteen cultures reported in Graham et al. (1994) and Graham and Mintu-Wimsatt (1997), and the two intercultural settings examined here. Indeed, interpersonal attraction seems to be an even more important determinant of overall satisfaction in Japanese/American intercultural negotiations than in the respective intracultural negotiations. It is also of interest to note that Japanese negotiators who were more extroverted (Eysenk's scale, 1958) were more interpersonally attractive to their American counterparts in the intercultural negotiations ($r = .35; p < .05$).

For the Japanese negotiating with Americans, things appears to be different in two major respects (compare columns I and II in table 2). First, when Japanese work together, role is the most important issue—buyers achieve higher profits than sellers. This key relationship disappears in the intercultural negotiations. Indeed, in the intercultural negotiations, PSA strategies take on a new importance for the Japanese. The Japanese taking a problem-solving approach achieved higher individual profits, while there is no such relationship between the constructs in the intracultural data. Sharing information seems to be a key factor in their negotiations with Americans.

Things are also different for the Americans when they bargain with Japanese (compare columns III and IV). The importance of role is also dampened in the intercultural interactions, but it was never such an important factor in negotiations between Americans anyway. More important, the influence of the Japanese partner's PSA strategies has no effect on the American's individual profits. Reciprocity still seems to be at work, but the informativeness of the Japanese partner appears to be of little direct economic benefit. Rather, the Americans who keep their mouths shut, the introverted ones, seem to achieve higher profits when working with Japanese.

CONCLUSIONS

Clearly in this chapter we are just scratching the surface of a wonderfully rich and interesting kind of human behavior—face-to-face international negotiations. Cultural differences seem to be key. A variety of other methods will be useful in the continuing study of the topic—game theory, experiments, field interviews and observations, and videotaping of simulated negotiations. Contributions can be made using a variety of perspectives—business, sociology, psychology, anthropology, communications theory, and sociolinguistics. Former U.S. ambassador to Japan James Hodgson has described culture as the "thicket" that must be traversed on the way to fruitful Japanese-American cooperation. His metaphor implies the hard work necessary for all of us to gain mutual international understanding.

REFERENCES

Adler, N. J., & Graham, J. L. 1989. "Cross-Cultural Interaction: The International Comparison Fallacy." *Journal of International Business Studies,* Fall, 515–537.

Angelmar, R., & Stern, L. 1978. "Development of a Content Analytic System for Analysis of Bargaining Communication." *Journal of Marketing Research*, 15, 93–102.

Bagozzi, R. P. 1978. "Marketing as Exchange: A Theory of Transaction in the Market Place." *American Behavioral Scientist*, March-April, 535–556.

Bagozzi, R. P. 1980. *Causal Models in Marketing*. New York: John Wiley and Sons.

Bouchner, S., & Ohsako, T. 1977. "Ethnic Role Salience in Racially Homogenous and Heterogenous Societies." *Journal of Cross-Cultural Psychology*, 8, 477–492.

Clopton, S. 1984. "Seller and Buyer Firm Factors Affecting Buyers' Negotiation Behavior and Outcomes." *Journal of Marketing Research*, 21, 39–53.

Condon, J. C. 1974. "Perspective for the Conference." In Condon & Saito, *Intercultural Encounters with Japan*. Tokyo: Simul Press.

Condon, W. S. 1968. *Linguistic-Kinesic Research and Dance Therapy A.D.T.A. Convention Proceedings*.

Davis, H. L., & Silk, A. J. 1972. "Interaction and Influence Processes in Personal Selling." *Sloan Management Review*, Winter, 59–76.

Davis, H., Douglas, S., & Silk, A. 1981. "Measurement Reliability: A Hidden Threat to Cross-National Marketing Research?" *Journal of Marketing*, 45, 98–109.

Evans, F. B. 1963. "Selling as a Dyadic Relationship—A New Approach." *American Behavioral Scientist*, 6 (May), 76–79.

Fornell, C., & Bookstein, F. 1982. "Two Structural Equation Models: LISREL and PLS Applied to Consumer Exit Theory." *Journal of Marketing Research*, 19, 440–52.

Fornell, C., & Robinson, W. 1983. "Industrial Organization and Consumer Satisfaction/Dissatisfaction." *Journal of Consumer Research*, 9, 403–412.

Fornell, C., Rhee, B-D, & Yi, Y. 1991. *Marketing Letters*, 2, 309–320.

Francis, J. N. 1991. "When in Rome? The Effects of Cultural Adaptation on Intercultural Business Negotiations." *Journal International Business Studies*, third quarter, 403–428.

Gouldner, A. W. 1960. "The Norm of Reciprocity: A Preliminary Statement." *American Sociological Review*, 25 (September), 161–179.

Graham, J. L., & Herberger, R. A. 1983. "Negotiators Abroad—Don't Shoot from the Hip." *Harvard Business Review*, July-August, 160–168.

Graham, J. L. 1986. "The Problem-Solving Approach to Negotiations in Industrial Marketing." *Journal of Business Research*, 14, 549–566.

Graham, J. L., & Andrews, D. 1987. "A Holistic Analysis of Cross-Cultural Business Negotiations." *Journal of Business Communications*, 24 (4), 63–77.

Graham, J. L. 1993. "The Japanese Negotiation Style: Characteristics of a Distinct Approach." *Negotiation Journal*, 9 (2), 123–140.

Graham, J. L., Mintu, A. T., & Rodgers, W. 1994. "Explorations of Negotiation Behaviors in Ten Foreign Countries Using a Model Developed in the United States." *Management Science*, 40 (1), 72–95.

Graham, J. L., & Mintu-Wimsatt, A. 1997. "Culture's Influence on Business Negotiations in Four Countries." *Group Decision and Negotiation*, 6, 483–502.

Hatfield, E., Cacioppo, J. T., & Rapson, R. L. 1994. *Emotional Contagion*. Cambridge: Cambridge University Press.

Joreskog, K., & Sorbom, D. 1981. *LISREL V: Analysis of Structural Linear Relationships by Maximum Likelihood and Least Squares Methods*. Chicago: National Educational Resources.

Kelley, H. 1966. "A Classroom Study of Dilemmas in Interpersonal Negotiations." In Archibald, *Strategic Interaction and Conflict: Original Papers and Discussion*. Berkeley, CA: Institute of International Studies.

McGuire, W. J. 1968. "The Nature of Attitudes and Attitude Change." In Gardner & Aronson, *The Handbook of Social Psychology*. Reading, MA: Addison-Wesley.

Mishler, A. L. 1965. "Personal Contact in International Exchanges." In Kelman, *International Behavior: A Social-Psychological Analysis* (pp. 550–561). New York: Holt, Rinehart and Winston.

Peterson, R. B., & Shimada, J. Y. 1978. "Sources of Management Problems in Japanese-American Joint Ventures." *Academy of Management Review*, 3, 796–805.

Pruitt, D. G. 1981. *Negotiation Behavior*. New York: Academic Press.

Pruitt, D. G. 1983. "Achieving Integrative Agreement." In Bazerman & Lewicki, *Negotiating in Organizations*. Beverly Hills, CA: Sage.

Putnam, L. L., & Jones, T. S. 1982. "Reciprocity in Negotiations: An Analysis of Bargaining Interaction." *Communication Monographs*, 49 (September), 171–191.

Redfield, R., Linton, R., & Herskovits, M. 1936. "Memorandum on the Study of Acculturation." *American Anthropologist*, 38, 54–60.

Rubin, J. Z., & Brown, B. R. 1975. *The Social Psychology of Bargaining and Negotiation*. New York: Academic Press.

Sawyer, J., & Guetzkow, H. 1965. "Bargaining and Negotiation in International Relations." In Kelman, *International Behavior: A Social-Psychological Analysis* (pp. 464–520).

Sherif, M., & Hovland, C. I. 1961. *Social Judgement: Assimilation and Contrast Effects in Communication and Attitude Change*. New Haven: Yale University Press.

Vassiliou, V., Triandis, C. H., Vassiliou, G., & McGuire, H. 1980. "Interpersonal Contact and Stereotyping." In Triandis, *The Analysis of Subjective Culture* (pp. 89–115). New York: Wiley.

Walton, R. E., & McKersie, R. B. 1965. *A Behavioral Theory of Labor Negotiations*. New York: McGraw-Hill.

Weitz, B. 1981. "A Critical Review of Personal Selling Research: The Need for Contingency Approaches." In Albaum & Churchill, Jr., *Critical Issues in Sales Management: State of the Art and Future Research Needs*. Eugene: University of Oregon.

CHAPTER 6

EXPLAINING JAPAN'S FAILURE IN THE INTERNATIONAL WHALING NEGOTIATIONS[*]

ROBERT L. FRIEDHEIM

INTRODUCTION

The behavior of Japanese negotiators in the yearly meetings of the International Whaling Commission (IWC) is difficult for an outsider to understand. To some, it is inexplicable in that Japanese representatives seemed to follow strategy and tactics that were most likely to produce an outcome that would be unsatisfactory to her negotiators, and perhaps to her interests. Japanese representatives did not seem to engage in bargaining practices typical of multilateral negotiations. Perhaps as a consequence, Japan suffered a stinging defeat at the forty-sixth session held in Puerto Vallarta, Mexico, in May 1994. A sanctuary for whales in the Southern Ocean received a requisite three-fourths vote, no quota was provided for Japanese whalers in the North Pacific, and no special arrangements were made for what Japan claimed were highly dependent coastal artisanal whalers.

Although Japanese delegates "learned" from their experience and their efforts at promoting their case for the restoration of whaling were more spirited at the Forty-seventh Meeting in Dublin, Ireland, in spring 1995, the situation remains essentially the same as is was at the end of the forty-sixth session—a sanctuary still in place, no quota for Japanese commercial whalers, no quota for Japanese artisanal whalers, and the motives of Japanese scientists questioned because, it was claimed, the scientists engaged in lethal research and their scientific take was a cover for a commercial operation. Japan had to be satisfied with the fact that a resolution their delegation submitted requesting examination of the legality of "matters relating to a sanctuary" (as recommended by the Working Group on a Southern Ocean Sanctuary convened at Norfolk Island) was tabled, but not defeated (IWC, 1995).

These measures were but the latest defeats for Japan on the issue of the right of Japanese whalers to take whales on the high seas. At future meetings of the IWC, Japan will be confronted with three choices: (1) attempt to alter the outcome within the organization (continue to negotiate); (2) take extreme measures and try to restore her whaling rights outside of the IWC (defect); or (3) accept defeat (Ikle, 1964, pp. 59–75). Since most developed states strongly oppose resumption of whaling, perhaps no clever tactics would have fundamentally altered the general outcome.[1] Still, it seems to this observer that ineffective Japanese bargaining behavior contributed to Japan's defeat. Why did Japan behave the way she did in the 1980s and 1990s in the International Whaling Commission negotiations? How can Japanese behavior be explained? Social scientists may turn to our cumulative knowledge and our theories to help us understand. Three approaches stand out:

RATIONAL CHOICE

Many analysts of international negotiations still believe that agents of a collectivity choose goals (preferences) calculated to maximize the interests they represent, assess the alternatives and the consequences that would flow from each alternative, and choose tactics most likely to produce an optimal realization of their goals (March, 1994, pp. 2–5). In the bargaining arena they make offers, issue threats, and attempt to reach agreement with other parties that are "Pareto optimal" (a situation in which they can be made better off while those on the other side of the negotiating table are made no worse off). If, despite their best tactical efforts, they cannot arrange an outcome better than the status quo ante, they opt out of the negotiation since their best alternative is the status quo (Raiffa, 1982). Is the history of Japan's participation in the IWC best explained by such a conceptual framework?

CULTURAL MOLDING—"THE JAPANESE WAY"

Whatever its merits, a pure rational-choice approach has its limitations. It cannot explain the outcomes in many important negotiations. In fact, some critics charge, such models, however useful they are *prescriptively,* are not very useful *descriptively* in assessing the outcome of most "real world" negotiations (Banzerman & Neale, 1991, p. 109). They claim that to understand how real people behave in a negotiating setting one must assess how their personalities and cultures contribute to their behavior. In dealing with Japan and the IWC, we will put aside the question of personality[2] but we will look at the input of culture and values in helping to mold Japanese behavior. While all negotiators reflect their cultural roots, some scholars have asserted that Japanese bargaining behavior is especially distinctive and culture driven (Nakane, 1973; Doi, 1973). One scholar who has looked carefully at Japanese bargaining behavior in multilateral negotiating settings, albeit before World War II, saw a pattern of behavior that was based upon "deeply rooted cultural habits" (Blaker, 1977, p. 226). Similar "cultural habits" appeared in the IWC negotiations, as we shall see. But is culture a necessary and sufficient explanation of the outcome?[3]

CONSTRAINTS ON NEGOTIATORS

Recently, a number of scholars have emphasized the importance of structure in the outcome of decisions made in the public, especially international, arena. This school of thought emphasizes the pattern of constraints under which a diplomat must operate, and how they influence behavior. The major constraints are caused by the structure of the domestic system that he/she represents. Japanese negotiators in the IWC, these scholars would emphasize, were influenced by the constraints imposed by their bureaucratically dominated political system. Perhaps we should look to "bureaucratic politics" to explain why inappropriate tactics were used in the IWC (Allison, 1971; Halperin, 1974). Japan's delegates were simply not free to choose what might have worked best.

More recently, international bargaining has been conceptualized as a two-level game (Putnam, 1988). In this framework, the negotiator bargains at two levels—domestic and international—and the output of the former heavily impacts the latter. Bargaining at the domestic level narrows the "win set" at the international level because the foreign-policy negotiator must always be concerned with the necessity of ratifying (in the broadest sense, this means accepting and implementing the outcome, not just legal ratification) a joint or international decision at the domestic level. The domestic level includes more than the interplay in the bureaucracy while a negotiator's instructions are being devised. It may also include the direct participation at the international level of transgovernmental connections (a faction of one government interacting directly with a faction of another government), transnational connections (the public of one state acting in concert with the public of another), and cross-level connections (a government official from one government interacting directly with the public of another state) (Knopf, 1993).

This chapter will explore all three of these theories of foreign-policy decision making and their links with international bargaining, and will attempt to apply them to Japan's efforts to find an acceptable solution to the problem of whaling in the twentieth century. First, the nature of the substantive bargaining problem will be explicated. Japan's bargaining response to these problems in the IWC will then be explored. The three theories will then be examined and "fitted" to the actual bargaining patterns found. Finally, we will assess the usefulness of these methods to understanding Japan's bargaining behavior at the IWC and Japan's bargaining in general, as well as negotiation theory.

I should note that the author believes that Japan's diplomatic failure in the IWC matters beyond being a test-bed for international-relations theorizing. First, the issue matters to Japan. She has been isolated on this issue. Her values have been attacked, and she must find a way of dealing with the issue because it is important to her sense of self-worth and place in the world. Second, the issue matters to us all as we contemplate the rapidly evolving post - Cold War international system and the role that Japan will be expected to play, particularly through multilateral fora. Were the results of Japan's efforts an anomaly and therefore likely to be restricted to this special issue, or does it tell us something about Japan's ability to play a major role in the bargaining necessary to achieve a stable world system? Third, the problem matters to those interested in resolving international problems with a high emotional and ideological content. Is what happened in the last ten years of IWC negotiations an example of an international politics with a high symbolic content in which little or no tolerance was shown to "reasonable" proposals that violated a new "ethic" . . . and might this be repeated in other fora? Fourth, the issue matters to those concerned with the environment. In some respect the attempt to end whaling raised critical questions about the nature of sustainability, a principle of environmental management enshrined in The Rio Declaration and Agenda 21, laboriously worked out in 1992 at the Rio Conference on Environment and Development as the appropriate standard for environmental management (United Nations, 1992).

THE PROBLEM: JAPAN IN THE INTERNATIONAL WHALING COMMISSION

HOW WE GOT TO WHERE WE ARE

The history of whaling is a record of extraordinarily rapacious behavior. Little concern was shown for the survival of the largest mammals this world has known. European and American whalers from the sixteenth to the twentieth centuries hunted one species after another to the point of extinction, usually switching to smaller species when the larger animals were so decimated that hunting them was no longer commercially viable. Whalers of bowhead, sperm, humpback, and gray whales targeted large, slow animals that usually floated when killed (Gambell, n.d., p. 1). Whale oil was the major source of lighting fuel before Colonel Edwin Drake discovered oil in Pennsylvania in 1859. Demand was high. In addition, whales were commercially valuable in the gilded age for their bones, which were turned into stays in women's corsets. In sum, whales were a source of wealth. They were common property resources, available to any claimant with the capability to hunt them in the oceans of the world.

Japan joined the high seas hunt after the Meiji Restoration (1868) removed the prohibition on leaving the islands of Japan. Japanese whalers were mostly interested in hunting whales for food. (One of the principal reasons for the "opening" of Japan by Admiral Perry and his "Black Fleet" was Japanese authorities' treatment of stranded American whalers [Borton, 1955, p. 13].)

Millennia before the major states of the world developed distant-water whaling fleets, peoples in many areas of the world used whales and other cetaceans for food. Often these were communities of "aboriginal" peoples, especially the Inuit people of the far north in Canada, Greenland, Russia, and the United States. Even in cases where these fisherfolk did not fit the aboriginal label—in the Faroe Islands, northern Norway, Iceland, Japan, and some Caribbean Islands such as St.Vincent and Bequia—they were artisanal or small-type exploiters. They usually lived in remote locations, and even today operate at or near subsistence and have rarely overexploited cetaceans. Whaling is not merely a significant contribution to their livelihood, but is integral to their culture. The right of Inuit whaler to continue to take whales, although often under attack, is protected under the IWC treaty. Small-type whalers have no such protection.

Whaling needed little regulation when the technical capabilities of the whalers was low. The hunter's desire to take every animal spotted was counterbalanced by limits in hunting equipment, navigation equipment, vessel speed, and ability to process animals into useful products. But that changed with the advent of steam-powered vessels and the 1884 invention by the Norwegians of an explosive grenade harpoon fired from a cannon mounted on a fast-catcher vessel. When floating factory ships were developed, shore processing stations were no longer needed for hunting in remote regions. As Dr. Ray Gambell, IWC secretary, noted, this made fast-swimming species such as the blue, fin, and sei into targets for the whalers and helped spread the hunt into the Antarctic (Gambell, n.d.). It was inevitable that by the 1930s serious overharvesting would occur, so serious that the concerned states were willing to enter into an international convention to regulate whaling.

The first "modern" effort at managing whales was found in a 1931 convention. It was characteristic of early attempts to manage common property resources. It was an attempt between the interested parties to regulate the taking of whales without trying to solve the open-entry problem. That is, there was little incentive for a number of parties to cooperate to not overexploit a resource if one or more present or new fisherman could come in and take what they pleased. Those who would accept restrictions while others did not were "suckers." For example, Japan, which began whaling in Antarctica in 1934, refused to adhere to the 1931 (and successor 1937) conventions. This made the signatories "suckers" and Japan (and Germany) "free-riders." Japanese whaling was at its prewar peak in 1941, with 2,972 crewman employed on 6 factory ships and 45 catcher vessels. The signatories used a "species" approach, attempting to regulate by restricting hunting to baleen whales only. It also regulated by other "biological" standards. The convention established "seasons," exempted the taking of females accompanied by calves or other immature whales, and established size limits for some of the whales to be taken. It required the collection of statistics so that regulation could be put on a more "scientific" basis. The signatories tried to use an international convention to solve not so much an overharvesting, but an overproduction problem. It was clear that the predominant influencers of attempts to regulate whaling during the 1930s were the industry managers. Little or no infrastructure at the international level was created that could carry the load of managing the necessary rules.

The 1931 agreement proved to be inadequate to the task of managing whaling. It was extended by a 1937 agreement signed by nine whaling states (including the previously noncooperating Germany) that

1. prohibited taking of right and gray whales;
2. set size limits for blue, humpback, and sperm whales;
3. restricted the Antarctic season to three months;
4. closed factory ship operations in most of the world oceans north of forty degrees south latitude; and
5. tried its hand at enforcement by asking each signatory to place a government inspector on whaling vessels flying its flag.

It used similar management devices as its predecessor to manage whaling. These measures were supplemented by a protocol signed in 1938 that banned the taking of humpback whales, and created a whale sanctuary in the Pacific sector of Antarctic waters (Protocol 1938).

Although a significant portion of the major whaling fleets was sunk during World War II, the resumption of whaling was anticipated in a 1944 agreement promoted by the Whaling Committee of the International Council for the Exploration of the Sea. An overall quota—a measure that had eluded earlier negotiators—was worked out at approximately two-thirds of the prewar catch. However, it was to be measured in a new unit, the notorious Blue Whale Unit (BWU). Since most whalers from Allied states were still interested in whale oil and the largest whales produced the most oil, the total catch quota was measured in "blue whale" equivalents. That is, one blue whale equaled 2 fin or 2.5 humpbacks, or 6 sei whales. The impact should have been predictable—every whaling nation rushed to take as much of the BWUs as they could. There was soon more competition from Japan, which was interested mostly in providing scarce protein to feed its war-raved population. Over objections of other states, the Supreme Commander for the Allied Powers allowed Japan to resume Antarctic whaling on a "temporary" basis in 1946–47. Japan returned to Antarctic whaling in full force. By 1965, Japanese whalers were taking nearly 27,000 whales a year. Until 1963, the Japanese consumed more whale meat than any other type of meat (Friedheim & Akaha, 1989, p. 129). Russia was also a major whaling state after World War II largely for the same reasons as Japan—whales were high-quality protein, and the cost, compared with the equivalent protein from land sources, was low. To this day we do not know how many whales Russian whalers took before they dropped out of pelagic whaling. The numbers are likely to be very large, but during the monopoly of power of the Communist Party over the Soviet Union, the totals were deliberately underreported to the IWC.[4]

The International Whaling Commission was established in 1946. It has not enjoyed a reputation as an effective organization, either in terms of its own stated goal of insuring "an optimal level of whale stocks" (ICRW 1946, Preamble) or in terms of other "nonconsumptive" goals, such as preservation of the great whales. Indeed, "it seems that the whole history of the IWC has filled whale scientists and conservationists with despair" (Freeman, 1990, p. 107). Often it is characterized as having been established too late to prevent the decline of the larger species, often using inappropriate standards for its conservation measures (such as "Blue Whale Units"), or merely being the captive of the whaling states because of its constitutional defects. Until the 1980s, it seemed to be powerless to stop what some called the "whaling Olympics." Critics concede that the situation got somewhat better after a "new management procedure" was put in place (in 1975), and some of those critics were even more favorable to the organization after a moratorium was put in place (in 1982) (Gambell, n.d.). But on the whole the IWC has been a weak and relatively ineffective organization throughout its history. A research group of Norwegian and American analysts, dividing its history into three phases, judged that in the first phase (1946 to mid-1960s) effectiveness of the organization was low, in the middle phase (mid-1960s to the end of the 1970s) it was medium as a result of the new management procedure, and in the most recent phase (mid-1970s to 1991) it was low again (Wettestad & Andresen, 1991, p. 55). Since most of the analysts are citizens of states at interest, their conclusions are open to attack. Nevertheless, they tried to make their judgments based upon specific criteria that tried to measure "integrative potential," and therefore they present a judgment that should not be dismissed out of hand.

The tasks assigned to the IWC were difficult to accomplish on both technical and political grounds. Data were unavailable to conduct management on grounds that were scientifically valid. Moreover, the foxes had to be set to guard the henhouse. No one else was available. The highly competitive stakeholders were trying to engender voluntary cooperation among themselves in a situation in which they hoped they could continue whaling and not reduce their take below the catch tonnage considered economically viable for their fleets. Each hoped the other "fox" could be induced to reduce its take. Usually what occurred was that each did reduce take, but since no one wanted to be a "sucker," not enough to restore the stocks to some notion of an "appropriate" level. The IWC was never empowered (except negatively, through the moratorium, the closing of areas, etc.) to allocate the resource and reduce the hunter's incentive to take every animal he encountered. The IWC could not make an authoritative determination that State A's hunters had the right to take X animals and State B's hunters had the right to Y animals. In short, the IWC had serious constitutional defects.

The International Convention for the Regulation of Whaling (ICRW) was negotiated in Washington in 1946. The United States, the major physically intact developed state, was just beginning to recognize its responsibilities for postwar leadership and its obligation to assist the reconstruction of its devastated friends and former foes. While the United States was still a whaling state, the age of the Yankee whaler was over. Before too long it would be a non-whaling state, as would many of the other European states. Nevertheless, the ICRW was negotiated by most of its parties to protect their whaling interests. Their status changed over the years, and much of the evolution of IWC policy can be explained by the fact that many of the major players no longer had significant commercial whaling interests to protect.

ICRW was constructed along the lines of earlier attempts at whaling regulation. The purpose of the agreement was to "ensure proper and effective conservation and development of whale stocks" and "thus make possible the orderly development of the whaling industry" (ICRW 1946, Preamble). To that end, the convention established the IWC. The commission was composed of one member from each of the contracting parties. Each contracting party had one vote. Decisions were to be taken by simple majority of members voting, but important substantive decisions required a positive three-fourths majority (ICRW 1946, Article III [2]).

Member states could "defect." If a state notified the commission that it objected to a policy decision (technically an amendment to the schedule), that policy decision would not be effective with respect to that government unless or until it withdrew the objection (ICRW 1946, Article V [3]). Member states also could issue permits to conduct scientific whaling, and allow the whalers to "process" or use commercially the whales taken as long as the scientific data derived was transmitted to an international data archive (ICRW, 1946, Article VIII). Compliance with the agreement was self-enforcing. Each contracting government was supposed to ensure the application of the treaty to its citizens (ICRW 1946, Article IX). The commission was authorized to create a secretariat (which was always kept small) and establish subordinate bodies (most importantly a Technical Committee and Scientific Committee). The commission was authorized to perform studies and collect statistical data (ICRW 1946, Article IV). It was also expected to cooperate with member governments and international agencies.

The major policy tool of the IWC is found in an attached document, a "schedule" through which the commission could regulate whaling by, among other measures, specifying

1. protected and unprotected species;
2. open and closed seasons;
3. open and closed waters (including sanctuaries);
4. size limits for each species;
5. time, methods, and intensity of whaling; and
6. gear restrictions (ICRW 1946, Article V [1]).

These measures were to be employed "for the conservation, development and optimal utilization of whale resources" and are supposed to be based on scientific findings (ICRW 1946, Article V [2]). While the commission could ban all whaling, or whaling in a particular region, the agreement *did not* give the commission the right to restrict the number or nationality of factory ships or allocate specific quotas (ICRW, 1946, Article V [2]). Its ability to limit entry was constrained. It could not allocate or determine *who* should get *what*. Like five of the eight fisheries commissions created after World War II, it could not divide the catch and eliminate the incentive for a whaling company (and its sponsoring state) to take as much of an overall quota as possible (Friedheim, 1972, pp. 242–251).

During its early years, the dominant influence on the IWC was industry managers who affected the national policy of the whaling states and often participated in the IWC Technical Committee as representatives or observers (Peterson, 1992, p. 160). The yearly catch limit (16,000 BWUs) established by the IWC, while lower than the overall yearly prewar catch (30,000 BWUs), was woefully inadequate for maintaining many species and stocks at a sustainable level. While the postwar limits were set after study by cetologists, the state of the science was such that they were largely guessing at what might be a viable yield.

In 1961 a new attempt was made to make whaling management more scientific. A committee of three (and later four) population dynamicists was formed to assess baleen whale stocks using more mathematically sophisticated tools than available earlier.[5] Drastic reductions in take were recommended. These recommendations were resisted by the active whaling states until 1965, and even then the whalers were given three years to adjust their catch downward to below the sustainable yield. Blue Whale Units were not eliminated until 1972, and observers reporting to the commission were not authorized until 1972.

The difficulties in gaining consensus among whalers; their state protectors; cetologists; and the increasingly assertive conservationists, preservationists, and animal-rights activists did not go unnoticed. In 1972 a resolution of the Stockholm Conference on the Human Environment called for a ten-year moratorium on commercial whaling, partially in response to the inability of the IWC to manage in a sustainable manner (Caldwell, 1990, pp. 21–93). In 1974 the IWC responded with a "New Management Procedure" that went into effect in 1975. It purported to reorient management with a different conceptual approach. Management of whaling was to be on the basis of Maximum Sustainable Yield (MSY). (Crutchfield & Pontecorvo, 1969; Christy & Scott, 1965; Scott, 1955, pp. 116–124) In theory, if the original stock size could be calculated, it should be possible to take whales when they are at 50 to 60 percent of their original abundance. This rate of predation should be sustainable over time, presuming the stocks to be exploited can be brought back to the acceptable percentage of their original numbers. Stocks that fell 10 percent below MSY were to be exempt from exploitation and treated as *Protection Stocks*. Stocks at 10 to 20 percent above MSY could be exploited, but not heavily, so that they too could recover. They were to be treated as *Sustained Management Stocks*. Stocks more than 20 percent above MSY were viewed sufficiently abundant to be taken at a higher rate. They were to be treated as *Initial Management Stocks*.

Unfortunately, the scheme proved unworkable. Data were difficult to acquire. The method was probably flawed scientifically, and it did not take the economics of the industry into account. The evident failings of the MSY scheme finally induced 25 of 32 members of the IWC at its 1982 meeting to vote for a moratorium on commercial whaling that was to take effect in 1985–86 and be reviewed by 1990. During that period the quota was reduced to zero, and the Scientific Committee was to embark upon a comprehensive assessment of whale stocks and the development of a new management procedure to replace maximum sustainable yield. It was arduous work, and there was little consensus within the concerned community of cetologists. Indeed, after much study, five different schemes were proposed. The third on the list, the C Procedure (named after its developer, Dr. Justin Cooke) was finally recommended by the Scientific Committee in 1991 for implementation as a key component of the Revised Management Plan. But it was turned back in the spring 1991 plenary session in favor of the maintenance of the commercial moratorium. Strenuous efforts were made to adopt the Revised Management Procedure in the subsequent four (Forty-fourth through Forty-seventh) meetings of the IWC, but they were all turned back in favor of the maintenance of the moratorium, and in the forty-sixth session, a southern ocean sanctuary was created. In response, Iceland gave notice of its withdrawal from the commission, and announced it wanted to set up a regional marine mammal commission for the North Atlantic (Government of Iceland, 1991). The commission reached a crisis.

Although deeply disturbed by the trends, Japan has not exercised her right to withdraw from the organization, but Shima Kazuo, then Japan's commissioner, indicated that such a move was under consideration.[6] At first, Japan indicated that it would not accept the moratorium and it entered an objection. But Japan withdrew its objection under heavy pressure from the United States. In the 1980s and 1990s, Japan had a major dilemma in deciding upon a strategy for dealing with the problem of restoring a right to whaling that would be recognized by the world community. It could drop out as Iceland did, and act unilaterally or in concert with like-minded states, but (as I will show) there were important negative incentives. Japan also could "opt out." But it tried that and could not stand the diplomatic pressure. It was reduced to two lines of conduct. First, it could stay in the organization, help reform its weaknesses, and expect that "reasonable" delegates from other states would then accept the lifting of the total moratorium, or hope that anti-whaling sentiment would abate in other developed states perhaps because of government change. Second, it could pursue limited "workarounds" or mitigating efforts to a total ban on whaling. In fact, Japan pursued both courses of action simultaneously. Three "mitigations" included avoidance, exceptions, and substitution.

Avoidance of the impact of a total ban was possible by purchasing whale meat that was either caught legally in a non-signatory country's waters or was "poached" by "pirate" whaling vessels such as the *Sierra*. Japan has been accused of such conduct.[7] Exceptions to the total ban were also possible under the Whaling Commission Convention. The United States has successfully requested a quota of bowhead whales for Alaskan Inuit whaling villages. Japan has requested and been refused a permit that would have authorized "small-type coastal whaling." A more controversial form of exception is the provision in the ICRW that allows "scientific whaling." Iceland, Norway, and Japan exercised their rights under that provision. All are under vehement attack from anti-whaling forces. As Greenpeace put it, "scientific whaling is almost universally regarded as nothing more than commercial whaling under a different name." While meat of the whales killed has been sold commercially to help pay expenses of the expeditions, Japan, for one, denies that scientific whaling expeditions even recover their costs.[8] Moreover, they state that high-quality investigatory work has been done to support the effort to put a new management plan on scientific basis. Finally, it has been possible to substitute high-seas whaling for whaling within a state's 200 mile economic zone with permission and possibly participation of the coastal state. It is also possible to shift the fishing effort to other gear, such as drift nets (Johnston, 1990, pp. 5–39), or to other species, such as small cetaceans.

WHY WE ARE WHERE WE ARE TODAY

The IWC's agenda at yearly meetings is notable for continuity of issues. But there are certain key points where a jump shift has taken place. Such a jump shift took place with the adoption of the moratorium in 1982. From that time forth, the IWC has been a very different bargaining arena than previously. Did Japan's representatives see and understand the radical nature of the shift?

The most obvious change was a shift in the working majority. A majority of IWC member states formed to oppose the resumption of commercial whaling—a powerful coalition that can command the votes of three-quarters of the delegations on important issues. At times, its opponents complained that the majority was packed or padded by the votes of small states who were "bought off" by anti-whaling governments or nongovernment organizations. (For example, it was whispered that a small Caribbean state that adopted an anti-whaling stance at the Forty-Sixth Meeting in Puerto Vallarta paid off its membership financial arrears with a suitcase full of cash in order to have its voting rights restored. Where they got the cash is officially still unknown. But even if true, their vote did not tip the scales at the meeting.) The coalition is large, united, and apparently stable over the long run, barring domestic political change. Perhaps sufficient bargaining pressure could force it to make incremental changes in its positions, but it is unlikely that its basic core commitment—to end commercial whaling—can be reversed.

Why did an anti-whaling coalition form? One clear answer is because the interests of most of the major states of the world have shifted. They no longer participate in whaling; they no longer expect whaling to be an important, or even measurable, contribution to their economic well-being; therefore they have no domestic reason to foster whaling. In fact, the economic argument for them has shifted to the nonconsumption side. Many have whale-watching industries that gross million of dollars. They have an incentive to keep whales alive in the wild.

The consequences of most developed states' disinterest and disapproval in retaining a right to whale have been critically important to Japan. Whatever goodwill Japan has created in relationships with other states does not carry over to the whaling issue. With no major pro-whaling interest groups or pressure groups to make a bi- or multilevel game within these countries competitive, the foreign offices of the major developed states have no incentive to try to resist the ardent push of the anti-whaling forces for instructions that would call for the elimination of commercial whaling. The cynical might consider the whaling issue a "throwaway" for most developed governments. That is, whatever analytical or scientific understanding of the whaling issue a developed state government official might have personally, he/she can throw it away and concede to the anti-whaling, animal-rights segment of the strong environmental forces that have arisen in recent years, without losing political capital. He/she does not have to worry about enormous financial capital outlays to *do* something about the problem, as he/she must for global change, acid rain, or other transboundary problems.

Not only have interests changed in most developed states, but so have the perceptions of their citizens. Environmental awareness has become a major concern of public life. Driving this changed set of perceptions are many ardent, committed direct-action environmental groups. On issues they deem salient, they are adamant and intolerant. They lobby to change the positions of governments on both domestic and international policies. They do not trust governments, or governments alone, to "do the right thing," and take direct action with their own governments, non-governmental organizations, other governments, corporations, and individual citizens of other states. They operate on a transnational basis, and some even have a noticeable presence in Japan.[9]

Whaling is a favored issue of such groups. To them, the very idea of "consuming" an "intelligent" (Klinowska, 1989, pp. 19–20) creature is considered not merely poor resource-management policy but morally repugnant. As one anti-whaling leader put it, "as a matter of principle, we are deeply opposed to commercial whaling and believe it is no longer justifiable. We believe the time has come for the IWC, serving the will and conscience of the international community, to recognize that the killing for profit of the global resource of whales is no longer acceptable in evolving world public opinion" (IWC, 1994a). They view themselves as moral arbiters (Bramwell, 1990) and are willing to take virtually any action to reach their goal—including direct participation in the meetings of the IWC, issuing anti-whaling statements whatever their technical or scientific veracity in all possible fora, blocking whaling vessels in port and on the hunt, and various other acts of "guerrilla theater." It has gotten to the point where Japan, Iceland, and Norway refuse to provide information to the IWC about the registration of whaling vessels "following acts of terrorism directed against whaling vessels" (IWC, 1991a).

At the least, these groups have become a serious impediment to the orderly conduct of business at IWC meetings. At the worst, they have poisoned the atmosphere of the meetings, making any serious negotiations virtually impossible because of their physical harassment of delegates from states defending whaling, etc. At the 1990 meeting of the IWC, only 29 states with voting rights were represented while representatives of 68 nongovernmental organizations wandered the meeting hall floor, committee rooms, and delegation lounges. We could debate whether these groups are "Arcadian environmentalists" (Lewis, 1992, pp. 253–256) or millenarians, but the indisputable fact is their presence in the whaling question is felt strongly, and directly.

THE REAL BARGAINING GAME BEING PLAYED TODAY IN THE IWC

There should be no illusion over the real "game" being played today in the IWC. The majority wishes *to end whaling,* certainly commercial whaling. It expects to accomplish this by preventing reform of past whaling practices and the implement of the Revised Management Plan. Without these reforms, the moratorium cannot be lifted. Its tactics include delay, forcing the commitment of time and effort to side issues, and proposing an alternative scheme.

Delay is a very effective tactic. Opponents of whaling are well aware of how weak are the remnants of commercial whaling fleets in Japan and Norway, the only two states threatening to continue "commercial" whaling. In Japan, there is virtually no working fleet, and few whalers with recent experience. Economically, whaling as a potential commercial enterprise is very questionable without government subsidies. The whaling fleet in Norway is stronger because it is active, but its catching efforts are confined to a localized region. The anti-whalers hope that with delay, the enterprises will go bankrupt, the whalers get too old to put to sea, and the vessels and equipment will rot at the pier. After tying up the effort at reform for years they hope that no "rational" government will view whaling as having sufficient economic promise to be worth reviving.

There are many ways to delay action in the IWC. Opponents of the resumption of whaling seem to have found most of them. Nothing that has been done to implement the Revised Management Procedure is good enough. Consequently, no reform provisions have been put to a vote, and as long as there is a possibility that commercial whaling might resume, none will be. And so the game goes on—the algorithm to underlie new quota must be "tested" before it can be implemented. A Revised Management "Scheme" must be developed and perfected before the Revised Management Procedure can be put to a vote. Recommendations of the Scientific Committee are ignored. Norway's proposal to create an inspection and observation program required under the "scheme" is not put to a vote because it is "a useful starting point . . . but not nearly comprehensive enough" (IWC, 1994b, p. 1). The effect of the moratorium on whale stocks must be tested before the moratorium is lifted. The impact of global warming must be tested on the whale stocks, etc.[10]

The question of humane killing is a perfect diversionary issue. No one who claims to be civilized could object to a consideration of ways to reduce the suffering of a fellow mammal. It is a real issue, but it allows for endless hours to be spent on obfuscation. When Japan raised the question of humane killing of all wild animals and not just whales, its pleas to widen the discussion so that the "moral" values of all states and not just Japan would be debated were swept away. Workshops and discussions on this issue consumed virtually whole annual meetings, such as the forty-forth session. Expanding the agenda to other related, but not directly relevant issues such as small cetaceans was also a successful diversionary tactic.

While many of the opponents justify their tactics as being appropriate to the moral obligation to end the immoral practice of whaling, they border on cultural imperialism, racism, and Japan "bashing." Tolerance of any other way of life, any other sets of beliefs that could include use of whales is so repugnant that any tactic is justified. Anything to embarrass the opponent is permissible. The sessions of the IWC in recent years are tactically brutal, and any assessment of bargaining in this arena must take this into account.

THE OSTENSIBLE BARGAINING GAME—IMPLEMENTATION OF THE REVISED MANAGEMENT PLAN

In the last several annual meetings of the IWC, delegations have gone through the motions of dealing with the key issue on the agenda—developing those measures and plans that would allow for the implementation of the Revised Management Plan. As we noted, the real plan is that by going through the motions, the opponents of implementation hope to kill any changes in the management system for whales that would allow the resumption of whaling. Going through the motions means ignoring or denigrating any real work that might provide ammunition to pro-whaling forces. This includes scientific advice. As a result, the chairman of the Scientific Committee, Dr. Phillip Hammond, resigned in disgust when he recognized how cavalierly the work of the Scientific Committee was treated. In his letter of resignation (May 26, 1993), he noted "what is the point of having a Scientific Committee if its unanimous recommendations on a matter of primary importance are treated with such contempt."

Reform measures are on the agenda, and they have to be duly considered. The algorithm for determining sustainability had to be reduced from fifteen rival proposals to one. The Revised Management Procedure was seemingly moved forward. But it had to be tested. That was added to the agenda. The Australian delegation, however, in the Forty-fourth Meeting introduced the idea that a New Management "Scheme" must be considered and implemented before the New Management Procedure can be voted upon (IWC, 1992a, p. 1). All aspects of the scheme, such as inspections, had to be settled before action on the plan could be considered. By the fiftieth or latest meeting all aspects have still not been considered and therefore the procedure cannot be implemented. Obviously since every detail has not been settled the moratorium cannot be lifted.

In the meantime, since Japan and Norway have pressed the issue of reform, and as technical issue after technical issue is settled, delay may not work forever. In the last four sessions, the anti-whaling forces have turned in a different direction to end commercial whaling, in at least one of the most important whale regions of the world—the Southern Ocean. At the Forty-fourth Meeting, France introduced the idea of creating a whaling sanctuary in the Southern Ocean (IWC, 1992b, p. 29). Naturally, within a sanctuary all whaling would be banned. Its effects would be reviewed every ten years. In its original formulation it would cover 13 million square miles and reach up to 40 degrees south latitude. The item was referred for study and recommendations to a workshop to be held on Norfolk Island. This measure would make the end of the moratorium virtually meaningless.

The experts gathered at Norfolk Island recommended that the idea receive more study, including legal study. But that did not stop sanctuary supporters. Since the expert group did not say the sanctuary was an unacceptable idea, they pressed for a vote on the issue.

Supporters had to work to gain a three-quarters majority. The original geographic boundaries of the sanctuary overlapped the two hundred Exclusive Economic Zones (EEZs) of Argentina and Chile. While there is no scientific justification for excluding Argentina's and Chile's EEZs, in order to gain the requisite majority, there was sufficient political justification. Therefore supporters proposed that the sanctuary's boundary dip below the economic zones of the two Latin American states (IWC, 1992c). Japan, Norway, and several Caribbean states tried to remove from the sanctuary protection the only whale species that was likely to be exploited in the foreseeable future—the minke whale—but that effort failed. The sanctuary proposal was put to the vote and passed with 23 yeas, 1 nay, and 5 abstentions. Japan, of course, was the one negative vote. Even Norway abandoned Japan, absenting itself from the vote rather than abstaining, so that it would not have to put itself on record (IWC, 1994e).

Japan suffered other humiliating blows. A long-term effort had been to provide relief for small Japanese coastal communities by winning recognition for a special status for small-type coastal whaling. While Japan's arguments were convincing to an impressive cadre of social scientists, they fell largely on deaf ears in the IWC debates. One objection was that, while small-type coastal whaling may be small, it is still commercial and someone is making a profit from the killing of intelligent creatures. To counter this argument, Japan developed a new action plan for community-based whaling (CBW). In the plan, the distribution of whale meat would be arranged by local governments and the profit removed from distribution (IWC, 1994f). But the new CBW arrangements also were turned down.

JAPAN'S DILEMMA

Japan suffered virtually complete diplomatic defeat in recent IWC meetings. It is difficult to see how the situation could be worse. The moratorium remains in place, with new obstacles constantly being placed in the way of reforms that would allow the Revised Management Plan be implemented. A sanctuary has been created in the Southern Ocean. Japan received no interim North Pacific quotas. Japan's plan for community-based whaling is not likely to be taken seriously, and no relief is in sight for small-type coastal whalers. Japan's scientific whaling, which includes lethal methods, is viewed as a disguised commercial operation and is subject to constant diplomatic harassment by opposing governments and, in the field, from Greenpeace. Japan has few and not very powerful friends on the whaling issue.

Japan must decide on a course of action. All three of the choices mentioned in the introduction look unpromising. Japan could return to a future session in the hope of continuing to bargain to change the position of the majority to allow for "reasonable" takes of whales in coastal waters, the North Pacific, and the Antarctic. But I see nothing that Japan could offer that would make the opponents of whaling generally more amenable to Japan's wishes. Japan could accept partial defeat, trade off whaling in the Southern Ocean, and hope to bargain to restore some rights to coastal, or perhaps even to North Pacific minke whaling. Japan could also surrender completely, end all whaling, be restored to good graces in the IWC, and be regarded with favor by the world environmental community. This would be at a very low price to its overall economic well-being, but at a very high price to its values and sense of self-worth.

Japan could defect by remaining in the IWC but defy the policies approved by the majority or it could drop out and act either unilaterally or in concert with like-minded states. Norway has defied the IWC, thus far seemingly successfully. The Norwegians authorized the resumption of minke whaling in the North Atlantic under an objection they lodged in 1985. However, they are under heavy pressure to drop their hunt. The Japanese might reinstitute their own objection under Article V (3) of the ICRW and resume whaling. Japan might stay in the IWC but increase purchases of "illegal" whale meat or cheat by taking more whales in its scientific expeditions than it reports. Obviously these measures would prove highly unpopular with the majority of IWC members (IWC, 1994g).

Japan might drop out and resume whaling unilaterally or form or join a rival organization. Iceland dropped out, as did Canada much earlier. A North Atlantic Marine Mammal Commission was formed in 1992 by the Faroe Islands, Greenland, Iceland, and Norway that might act not as a supplemental but as a rival organization to the IWC and control the take of marine mammals in its region. Thus far, it has not. Such a move was rumored to be under consideration, as was the rumor that Japan might join the organization. A rival organization might be useful for those objecting to the behavior of the majority in the IWC because it would provide some legal protection for its members—all are enjoined by Articles 65 and 118 of the 1982 Convention on the Law of the Sea to work through appropriate international organizations to conserve and manage marine mammals. Or, the Japanese might be forced to defect completely by denouncing what they might view as the capricious, unscientific, value-laden, anti-Japanese, and racist policies of the IWC and withdraw after one year's notice under Article XI of the ICRW. But the price might be substantial.

The chief ingredient of that price will be the attitude of the United States. The United States has been the principal enforcer of whaling and other international environmental regimes, such as the Convention on International Trade in Endangered Species (CITES). Domestic law requires that the United States use its domestic jurisdiction to impose punishments upon states violating what it claims are their obligations under international environmental treaties. An amendment, the so-called Packwood Amendment to the basic U.S. fisheries law (the Magnuson Act) requires that an offending state lose its right to fish in the U.S. 200-mile EEZ. Another amendment—the Pelly Amendment—forces U.S. authorities to deny an offending state the right to export seafood to the United States. The Packwood Amendment is no current threat since, for other reasons, all foreign fishing in the U.S. 200-mile EEZ has been terminated. But the

Pelly Amendment is a serious deterrent, since there is a multimillion dollar trade between the United States and Japan in fisheries products. But beyond the specific dollars involved, such an action could well trigger a trade war. There are already so many unresolved trade issues between the United States and Japan that all concerned with harmonization of relations between the two countries feel very uncomfortable. Whaling could add a nasty element of cultural misunderstanding, aid "Japan-bashers," entangle Japan and the United States in General Agreement on Tariffs and Trade (GATT) and successor World Trade Organization (WTO) proceedings, and escalate mistrust to a point where U.S.-Japan relations will be very difficult to untangle. Moreover, enforcement of penalties against states that defy what the environmental community perceives as their environmental treaty obligations is quite popular with a substantial proportion of the U.S. Congress. Often senior officials on both sides hope to avoid making the situation worse by enforcing the Pelly Amendment, but whenever a U.S. administration tries to avoid or delay certification of a state, environmentalists sue in the courts to ensure enforcement.

FITTING THE THEORY TO THE BEHAVIOR

JAPAN'S BARGAINING BEHAVIOR IN THE IWC

Individuals and groups who interact with each other develop predictable patterns of behavior. The following attributes of Japan's interactions with others in the IWC seem to be characteristic of Japan's approach to protecting her whaling interests within the IWC:

MODERATION OR REASONABLENESS

Given the original premise upon which Japan's position is based, the positions that Japan espoused at the IWC were moderate and reasonable. Consequently, Japan felt there was nothing to negotiate. Japan's stance was not a negotiating stance, but a problem-solving stance.

If the underlying problem in the IWC was failure to prevent the overharvesting of whales because of flawed procedures, then the task at hand was to reform those procedures so that the hunt could be made sustainable. This was the heart of Japan's position. Her negotiators worked toward and cooperated with others on the necessary research to develop criteria to be applied in a Revised Management Plan. They also were willing to develop humane killing methods and declare whale species as Sustained Management Stocks and as Protection Stocks that were even more stringently regulated.[11]

Japan was even willing to use the sanctuary idea, as long as it did not include a very abundant species that research showed could sustain a limited take. Since sufficient progress had been made on these issues to feel confident that, in the foreseeable future, the "Whaling Olympics" would not recur, Japan demanded the restoration of all her whaling rights. Even in specific demands, Japan was moderate. Since the 1982 moratorium, researchers estimated 785,000 minke whales in the Southern Ocean. A take of 2,000 per year, requested by Japan, would not effect the stock's sustainability, nor would a quota of 50 in the North Pacific and special status for small-type whalers threaten the survival of those whale stocks.

Unfortunately for Japan, participants had to be convinced of the underlying premises of Japan's position to be convinced of Japan's "reasonableness." From the perspective of one branch of the environmental movement, Japan was the leading advocate of "sustainability." Sustainability, its supporters claim, includes the right of human beings to exploit nature and nature's creatures, but draws the line on exploitation if the survival of a species is threatened. In espousing sustainability, Japan's representatives couldn't see why she was under vehement attack. After all, one of the most important problems of the late twentieth century is finding mechanisms acceptable to most if not all states that will prevent the overexploitation of resources in global commons such as the ocean (Friedheim, 1993). This is a position that should be applauded by environmentalists, not derided. But while some environmentalists recognize the importance of solving the problem of exploitation of common property resources, there has been a shift in values in many developed states. For some opponents, the whale is a special, intelligent creature that should be exempt from human predation. Others do not care about human standards, but support every effort to save every living creature from human exploitation, whatever the consequence to humankind. To them, there is a reason for their unreasonableness. The new "ethic" has created a formidable opponent, as we shall see.

Could a mutually acceptable solution, or one in which both sides could be made better off, be worked out between these two positions? It was a bargaining situation in that it was a dynamic event with parties, values, outcomes, and movement (Zartman, 1976, p. 8). Consequently, difficult as the situation was for Japan, it required a bargaining stance. Japan did not adopt a bargaining stance. Japan's reservation price—the minimum she would find acceptable—and her maximum preferred position seem virtually indistinguishable (Raiffa, 1982, pp. 46–47). Though Japan has been involved in this negotiation every year in modern times, there are no obvious signs she has thought seriously about her best alternative to a negotiated agreement (BATNA) (Fisher & Ury, 1981). Japan's position is a problem-solving approach. A problem exists. Barriers to solving the problems are identified, and solutions worked out. At the final stage all that needs be done is implement the correct solutions. Japan's stance is very close to a "Boulware" strategy: begin with what you deem a fair opening offer and hold firm.[12]

Persistence as a Strategy

Japan's general bargaining position in the IWC was to hold firm to her demands, show patience as detailed issues were worked out, and expect to outlast the opposition by sheer persistence. This was aided by the size of Japan's delegation—usually over fifty—and the continuity of her leadership. Shima headed the Japanese delegation from 1987 to 1995. If Japan kept at the effort to get the imperfections of the management regime cured, surely when all delegates saw that the management system was technically perfected, they would see that Japanese whaling would not be a danger to the sustainability of the whale stocks, and they would eventually accede to Japan's request to restore whaling rights. Discipline and fortitude were needed. Others must be persuaded of the correctness of Japan's position, or outlasted.[13]

Others have noted a tendency among Japanese negotiators to value commitment and resolve (ketsui) and to believe that, if Japan shows resolve, opposing negotiators will take their demands seriously (Blaker, 1977, p. 174). This tendency was evident in the behavior of the Japanese delegation. A will to win was clearly shown. This reinforced and was intertwined with the belief in the substantive correctness of their position. Surely, if they showed patience, others would see that Japan was not making extravagant demands, that Japan's position represented a reasonable solution to the problem.

Some say that in negotiations Americans are impatient and too quick to make unnecessary concessions in order to conclude a negotiation expeditiously. But although many of the representatives of the NGOs that harassed Japan in the IWC were American, they and their allies in developed-state delegations were a different breed than "normal" developed state negotiators. They were committed to a new "ethic," their sense of commitment quasi-religious. From their perspective, they were morally correct and they were not going to compromise, and certainly not concede to the idea that any whaling, much less full-scale whaling, might resume. But since their behavior was at times so extreme, it is hard to believe that Japanese delegates took them as serious persons however vociferous their participation. Surely, governments of the major states would see that their delegates had been led astray by people who represented fringe elements of their societies. They would come to their senses and reverse "irrational decisions" (IWC, 1994a, p. 2).

Underestimating an opponent is a major error. The anti-whaling forces have captured major state delegations, and that may not change. They are very, very persistent. In addition to being certain that they control the outcome on major issues, they constantly attempt to widen the agenda of the commission. The tactical effect is to create many fronts on which a state like Japan must fight. They raise new issues all the time, including bringing small cetaceans such as porpoises under the jurisdiction of the commission. Small cetaceans are not mentioned in the 1946 List of Nomenclature but, as the United States delegate put it, the IWC should now "broaden the debate to all cetaceans subject to commercial operations" (IWC, 1991b). They demand new information on scientific work, more studies, detailed reports on whale strandings, examinations of the records of the hunts of indigenous people, etc. They insist that the situation be re-reviewed in the light of new threats, such as global change. They demand that states report information normally considered matters of domestic jurisdiction (IWC, 1991c). In short, they keep their opponents busy answering queries and defending themselves against charges of sloppy technical work or moral insensitivity.

PASSIVITY

The concomitant behavioral pattern associated with a "tough it out" strategy is seeming passivity. Japan rarely initiated new proposals, new or different ideas, or activities in the IWC. It was not until the forty-sixth session that Japan's delegates mounted any counterattack. Even then, when Japan tried to propose a new initiative, it was in an area where her delegates felt comfortable—research to promote conservation of large baleen whales in the Southern Ocean (IWC, 1994h).

Japanese delegates rarely strongly criticized the proposals of others or issued threats or warnings. As discussed earlier, when Japan was put on the defensive by the activist majority, her defense was stolid and not creative.

The task was difficult and circumstances adverse, but one might have put
forth new proposals that, for example, might repackage a basic position in
a different way to require response from an opponent. Diversionary tactics are also useful. But ultimately, if Japan is to escape from the IWC with
something of value, she must make proposals that represent attempts at
compromise or that, as Lax and Sebenius phrased it, "create value" (Lax &
Sebenius, 1986, pp. 88–116). If not, Japan must depend upon others to res-
cue her (a hope for *amae?*).[14] To be effective, Japan must also respond positively to her critics with plans or proposals that indicate that Japan has
taken seriously the concerns of her opponents, "has considered the structure of the other side's values and opportunities. . . ." (Keeney & Raiffa,
1991, p. 134). For example, many environmentalists worry that if a commercial market continues to exist for whale products, it will be impossible to prevent unauthorized or illegal whaling. If Japan's demands for
restoration of commercial whaling are to be seriously entertained, Japan
must show that she will vigorously participate in all efforts to end illegal
whaling. But this is but one of many substantive avenues that have been
left unexplored.

It is difficult to predict whether a more creative attempt to "create
value" would have succeeded, but passivity only seemed to incite further
attacks. It created a belief that Japan was intransigent and unyielding; that
Japan *wanted* to restore unrestricted whaling at any price; that others must
always be suspicious of Japan's motives; that Japan is supporting an immoral
activity. These beliefs may border on racism and anti-Japanese feelings, and
some of them go over the border into outright racism. In turn, Japanese
participants and observers feel that their motives and behaviors are misun-
derstood, and that there is a war of "meat"-based cultures against a "fish"
culture. These feelings have poisoned the atmosphere (Sumi, 1989). One
key element needed for a positive-sum outcome is trust. It is in very short
supply in the IWC, making it problematic as to whether there can be a
positive-sum outcome, instead of an imposed outcome.

Japan seemed always to be waiting for the other shoe to drop, or prepar-
ing to fight off the next assault in an environment where the other shoe
will drop. If Japan does not surrender, the next assault, whether petty and
harassing or more critical and strategic, *will* occur.

GO IT ALONE

Over the years of IWC meetings, Japan has rarely sought allies. Until the
Forty-sixth Meeting, Japan has essentially tried to achieve her aims alone.

IWC meetings are a multilateral bargaining arena, and those who try to go it alone put themselves at a grave disadvantage. The structure of the situation calls for coalitional behavior. If there are three parties to a bargaining situation, the possibility of two-against-one always exists. Consequently any proponent of a position should always seek collaborators.

Japan was slow in seeking like-minded friends, and consequently has been isolated in the IWC. Some of this is a natural concomitant of her substantive interests. Japan is the only state currently seeking to whale legally in the Southern Ocean, and therefore has no natural allies on this issue. But on questions of the right of a state to engage in whaling in its own geographic region as long as the stocks are not threatened, and the right of its highly dependent artisanal whalers to continue to whale to maintain their lifestyle and their values, allies *were* available. To be sure, they were mostly small, economically weak states, but an effective coalition built among them could have forced the opponents of whaling to pay a higher price in seeking to find common value. In fact, when there was a hint in the Japanese press that Japan might have tied economic aid to Caribbean states to supporting Japan's positions in the IWC, anti-whaling forces protested vigorously.

Japan began actively to seek out allies only in the forty-sixth session. By that time a bandwagon effect had occurred, and her enemies had built a solid coalition against her (Lax & Sebenius, 1986). A and B agreed, and brought over C who also agreed, and D who did not want to be left off of the winning side joined up. A or B also were owed some favors by E, so E cooperated, and so on. In a sequence of actions over the 1980s and 1990s, the anti-whaling coalition, calling themselves the "like-minded states," put Japan in a position where her bargaining alternatives were limited and her choices painful.

LEGALISM

In arguing her case, Japan relied heavily upon the notion that her case was legally correct. But in doing so, she missed the major point—the IWC is not a court but a negotiating arena. Even if Japan's interpretation of the ICRW is legally correct, it is at best a useful bargaining point in debate. It is an inadequate anchor for anything but a "claiming strategy" in negotiation. That is, it sets up a situation in which Japan "claims" rights and expects others to grant them, and in turn, provides those on the other side of the table with little or no "value" in return.

Japanese delegates argue that actions in recent years have turned the rules of the whaling regime on their head and are illegal: the majority has illegally transformed the IWC into something that violates the explicit language of the 1946 agreement. In particular, the ICRW preamble calls for members to help preserve whale stocks so that "sustain[ed] exploitation" should be possible. The IWC was established as a conservation organization. Its basic mandate is predicated on controlled consumption, not total preservation of whales. Moreover, "proper conservation of whale stocks ... [should] ... make possible the orderly development of the whaling industry" (ICRW, Preamble). The heart of the IWC's work should be amending the schedule. But in recent years, amendments have been blocked. The organization has taken action via resolutions, which can be made under Article VI. But these are mere "recommendations," without binding force. Yet the United States, through its domestic actions, attempts to give them binding force, and for all practical purposes they have binding force.

These are powerful arguments. Assuming that the founders' original intent forever freezes the notion of permissible behavior, or at least limits the scope of permissible change, then Japan's position could be seen as correct. The majority argues that they act in the spirit of the original agreement, but that no original agreement can account for changing circumstances, and that what they are doing falls under the notion of "progressive development." They are merely updating the actions of the organization to deal with the problems of the times. There is nothing in the ICRW or, for example, Agenda 21 that prohibits setting a stricter standard.[15] Naturally, in the process of "updating" the agreement, the majority has substantially expanded the mandate of the organization.

At this point, there is no certainty as to a decision or recommendation that a mediatory or judicial international body might make. There is even less certainty as to how the member states of the IWC would implement a ruling favorable to Japan. The final outcome might be no better than Mexico's fate when she brought the tuna controversy to a GATT panel, won, and then was forced to suspend any further action in order not to get the issue brought into the NAFTA debate. The diplomatic and economic weight of the United States prevailed.

Japan's emphasis on legal rights in the negotiation indicates that she feels deprived of substantive and procedural justice (Zartman, 1976, pp. 38–41). Japan's representatives feel a sense of outrage. But keeping resentments boiling rather than looking for creative ways out of their dilemma probably will not help. It also avoids the question of whether acting more appropriately in multilateral bargaining before the situation got so bad might have obviated the worst case. Japan's low state came about, if only partially, because of inadequate tactics.

TACTICAL POVERTY

Some may blame extenuating circumstances for Japan's IWC delegation's failing to come up with creative tactics. Substantial numbers of her delegates have scientific backgrounds, and such behavior is alien to their positivist instincts and training. But most other delegations are also staffed largely by persons with a scientific background, and they have become competent "political" scientists who can maneuver very effectively in a multilateral arena. This cannot explain why Japan did so poorly in IWC negotiations.

It is clear that many of the actions a delegation must take to function successfully in a multilateral setting were distasteful to the Japanese delegation. For the most part, they shied away from the rough and tumble of operating in an arena where tactics do matter, where the logic of one's position will not automatically persuade. Since I am not a specialist in Japanese political behavior I should not make judgments as to why this is so, but merely note that from observation, it is so. However, others have commented on the Japanese propensity for risk minimization and conflict avoidance (Blaker, 1977b, pp. 98–99). I have recounted many of the actions necessary to success of which Japan's delegates did not avail themselves until Japan had been defeated on virtually all issues she cared about. Japan did not participate vigorously in debate to defend her own positions and attack others. Japan did not attempt to join, much less lead, a group of "like-minded" states that could have extracted a price for its cooperation. Japan did not try to manipulate the rules of procedure for her benefit but had to respond to the manipulations of others. Japan almost always reacted, almost never anticipated. But Japan was always scrupulous; she did not leak information to the press before providing it officially to IWC members (IWC, 1994d). As far as I know, meetings of Japan and her possible friends did not take place between IWC sessions to map strategy and tactics. Japan was not vigorous in making friendly amendments to documents of "like-minded" states and hostile amendments to documents submitted by opposing states until she tried to get minke whales exempted from the Southern Ocean Sanctuary. There is no record of Japan's encouraging a contact or compromise group meeting at or between IWC sessions, or seeking an "honest broker." These are common devices used in other multilateral negotiations to reduce conflict and promote agreement.

As of this writing, there is no indication that Japan has considered the development of a package that includes a tradeoff. In such a tradeoff, typically a party to a negotiation indicates willingness to accept a less satisfactory outcome on an issue of lesser importance or salience for a more

satisfactory outcome on an issue of greater salience. But that requires
that within the country, government, and delegation there must be
agreement on what is of greater and lesser salience. I doubt if Japan has
made such a determination. At a certain point in the history of a negotiation, the calculation of salience is influenced more by the notion of
what can be saved rather than by that thing's intrinsic value. As shown
earlier, Japan has no allies on Southern Ocean whaling, but should have
on regional and small-scale whaling. Will she sacrifice the former for the
latter? Is she ready to salvage what she can, or continue to defend all at
a high price?

Finally, the behavior of Japan's delegation does not indicate that there
was a good general understanding of international negotiations or its sub-
set, multilateral negotiations (Friedheim, 1993, pp. 41–69, 310–359). As I.
William Zartman (Zartman & Berman, 1982, p. 9) has shown, the typical
international negotiation goes through identifiable phases. During the
early or diagnostic phase, it becomes evident how the participants are
framing the issue. What is being sought is a "formula" or "common definition of the conflict in terms amenable to a solution." In a bilateral negotiation, that common definition must be shared by both parties or
defection will result. But in a multilateral negotiation, while unanimity is
desirable, it may not been essential. Decision can come about if the decision rules allow for some form of majority rule. In the early 1990s the end
of commercial whaling was the formula notion around which a majority
was forming. While defection was still possible (it was a true negotiation),
the opportunities available to those delegations in a small minority were
not overturning the formula of the large majority, but mitigating it, or perhaps undermining it. The final phase of a typical international negotiation
requires a refinement of the details. During this phase, a clever "loser" can
do many things to help his situation. That is where we are today. Is Japan
prepared to do this?

FITTING OBSERVATIONS TO THEORIES

None of the three theoretical approaches—rational choice; a special, culturally derived "Japanese Way"; or the constraints under which Japanese
delegates operate—provides a satisfactory explanation of Japan's bargaining
behavior in the IWC. However, all three do provide partial explanations,
and each can contribute something useful toward understanding of that
behavior. Let us touch briefly on each.

RATIONAL DECISION MAKING

If what is sought and the relationship of one's interests to what is sought is the core of rational decision, then a rational approach can illuminate a portion of Japan's behavior.[16] Japanese delegates clearly understood that their purpose was to advance Japan's interests. More abstractly, they "would prefer more primary goods than less" (Rawls, 1971, p. 142). Japan's delegates certainly exercised a rational choice in terms of the ends pursued. They, like virtually all other decision makers, exhibited bounded or limited rationality: They did not necessarily consider all their options, nor did they pursue their ends sequentially, and did not consider all of the consequences of their alternatives, but under the now widely accepted conditions of bounded rationality, they were rational (March, 1994, pp. 8–9). However, it is questionable whether Japanese delegates were rational in the means they chose to use to pursue their ends (von Winterfeldt & Edwards, 1986, p. 2).

In an effort to understand the problems of developing a positive-sum outcome in the IWC, I conducted an experiment using a decision analytic technique called Multi-Attribute Utility Technology (MAUT). Instead of trying to capture all of the ongoing political activity in the organization, I assumed that the members had become serious about a thorough reform of the organization and were willing to engage in a constitutional type of negotiation to form a "new" IWC. This allowed me to model the potential behavior of participating states over some key issues—both substantive and procedural—in the IWC debates.

To perform a MAUT it is necessary to (1) identify the objectives of a decision and the functions the decision is intended to perform, (2) identify the stakeholders, (3) elicit value dimensions or attributes from stakeholders, (4) assess the relative importance of each value as found in the previous step, (5) ascertain single-attribute utilities or payoffs, (6) aggregate the payoffs with measures of importance, and (7) perform a sensitivity analysis (Edwards & Newman, 1982). The results of these preliminary steps can be expressed in matrix form.

I tested Japan and several other states as stakeholders. For each, their value dimensions were elicited on the issues at hand (and not all of their values in the abstract). A partial list of these included contribution of whaling to GNP, contribution of whaling to local or regional economies, moral values, ecosystem concerns, aboriginal rights, management costs, national jurisdiction concerns, international obligation, and leadership. The other side of the matrix was composed of the substantive and procedural issues, such as a new constitutional statement of IWC purpose, principle of sustainability, entry control measures, geographic jurisdiction, special rights for small-type coastal whalers and aboriginal peoples, killing rules, enforcement measures, and scientific whaling, as well as membership rules, voting rules, op-out provisions, and others. I wrote three scenarios to test possible national approaches. The first was a non-consumption regime; the second a limited coastal consumption regime; and the third a restored but controlled pelagic whaling regime.

In the classic use of such models, an analyst usually attempts to elicit the values of the actual decision makers. I had no resources to do so and I doubt if many delegations would have allowed it. Instead, as a second best, I used American students to "place sit" or stand in for the real-world decision makers.

The experiment worked well and provided answers that seemed intuitively correct, including for Japan. This gave me confidence that in terms of substantive rationality, Japanese negotiators were rational. My students playing Japanese decision makers not only chose the outcomes that could be expected of Japanese decision makers, but reflected Japanese utilities (or payoffs) in a fashion that was convincing: a pelagic whaling regime was worth substantially more than a coastal whaling regime, and a non-consumptive regime was almost valueless.

The model provided a good test of rationality concerning ends, but not for the process of matching means to ends. It focused on making substantive decisions, not executing the decisions. International bargaining is a process in which decisions made in preparation for bargaining must be executed. The previous section of this chapter shows failures to match means to ends, failures that have so far led to a non-positive-sum outcome. Unfortunately there is not a very good connection between decision analytic methods and methods used to analyze that ubiquitous form of behavior we call bargaining. At best, then, rational choice theory provides only a partial explanation of Japan's behavior.

THE "JAPANESE WAY," OR CULTURE AS THE KEY EXPLANATORY VARIABLE

I believe Japan's behavior is distinctive, that patterns could be seen. But that does not mean that I have discovered the wellspring of Japanese behavior.[17] Have those patterns been caused by "set codes that are culturally determined" (Zartman, 1976, p. 483)? And, if they are culturally determined, are Japanese negotiators fated to repeat those patterns over and over again?

On the first question, since my observations were similar to other scholars', especially Blaker's, I believe that the most likely explanation is found in culture. But what are the attributes of the culture that are causally related to particular patterns discerned? Being only marginally acquainted with the literature on Japanese behavior, I leave it to specialists to comment on whether what I observed was "typically" Japanese and to explain what in Japanese culture conditioned its representatives to act as they did.

Nevertheless, from the point of view of instrumental rationality, I believe that whatever "caused" Japanese bargaining efforts in the IWC, a good portion of it was dysfunctional. It lowered rather than increased the probability of some degree of success in meeting Japan's objectives and finding a positive-sum outcome. But must Japan go on repeating such behavior? Bargaining is a process that involves learning, which involves adaptation. Japan has been successful in adapting in many other realms. Japanese negotiators can improve their success rate if they examine their actions with an open mind and not mistrust "countercultural learning because it goes against the grain" (Zartman, 1976, p. 483).

CONSTRAINTS

Japanese negotiators in the IWC were, I believe, constrained in their range of tactical options by the instructions they received. Of course, all diplomats, except in very ad hoc situations, have instructions they must obey. But the substance of the constraints and the manner in which they will effect bargaining outcomes differ from state to state. In Japan's case, instead of culture molding outcome, one might argue that structure molds outcome so that, for example, the slow pace of Japanese decision making is not an artifact of the culture but of a bureaucratically dominated political system (Curtis, 1988, p. 247). This is one of the systemic structural features of Japan that could explain why Japan behaved as she did in the IWC. The instructions were written within a bureaucratically dominated system with a close alliance between the bureaucracy, big business, and the ruling political party. It is run by a conservative coalition. It is characterized by state-run capitalism with an important role for the Ministry of International Trade and Industry (MITI) and an overrepresentation of rural areas and small towns in the Diet. It is a consensus-based system that pays a high transaction cost for reaching agreement. Consequently, it makes decisions slowly, and they are hard to change. While this is probably too sweeping a set of generalizations (perhaps even a caricature, especially in the light of increasing pluralism) (Fukui, 1977, pp. 22–59), if one posits constraints as the principle causal factor, these attributes could explain the deep causes of Japan's tactical failure in the IWC.

I believe there is merit to this approach,[18] but I am not a Japan politics specialist. I hope this report can be the basis of further work by a scholar with the skills and resources to read the Japanese press in depth, assess Japanese public opinion, interview senior officials in the relevant bureaucratic agencies, and look at leadership patterns on the issue. I must rely upon my acquaintance with participants in IWC matters, Japanese and American ocean officials, and social science theory. My evidence is anecdotal. Most of it is related directly to the Japanese delegation or the bureaucracies it deals with; thus, it is long on information about these organizations and short on public opinion, Diet politics, and interest groups. It is therefore difficult to demonstrate the usefulness of the two-level game approach to the problem.

There are signs of increasing Japanese pluralism on the whaling issue—the growth of anti-whaling environmental groups in Japan, the increase in the economic value of whale-watching (Okata Journal, 1992)—but there seems to be very little dissent concerning the *goals* of Japanese bargaining in the IWC. Restoration of the right of Japan to resume whaling albeit under controlled conditions was desired by the public and leaders of most major institutions. In other words, there were few overlapping cleavages in Japanese society on the issue that would have made it difficult for delegation members to present the strongest case for a restoration of commercial and small-type whaling (Axelrod, 1969, pp. 158–163). There was dissensus, according to insiders, on the question of how far Japan should go *tactically* and how Japan's position on whaling might effect the *interests* of other groups in the political system and their bureaucratic sponsors.

One key issue best explained by the constraint argument is why Japan has stayed in the negotiations, even under the most adverse circumstances. It is difficult to conceive of any worse outcome—no reopening of commercial Southern Ocean whaling; a sanctuary in the Southern Ocean; no regional quota; no special status for artisanal whalers; the delegation outvoted on every substantive and procedural issue, subjected to vicious personal attacks, scorned in the world's newspapers, and possibly subject to sanctions by the United States! It is in the interest of the Japanese delegates, the Fisheries Agency, and the Institute for Cetacean Research (which conducts much of Japan's whale research) to take strong counteraction, or even defect from the negotiations, and this has been clear for many years. Matters were only going to get worse for Japan. But the delegation did not take stronger action—probably because it could not.

Until the forty-seventh session, the Japanese delegation to the IWC was headed by Shima, deputy director of the Fisheries Agency. He is an experienced and articulate bureaucrat and negotiator who has headed the delegation for seven years. Having been the focus of the anger and unseemly behavior of anti-whaling groups, he has a personal incentive for Japan to take stronger measures, and perhaps even withdraw from the IWC. His agency has to worry about precedents being set in the IWC. There are already rumors that any new constraints on whaling that Japan might be forced to accept might also be applied to other marine hunting (fishing) activities, in particular, tuna fishing (*Asahi*, 1993). The Institute for Cetacean Research, also maligned by anti-environmentalists on every conceivable ground, including science, likewise has little incentive to stay in the negotiations.

While a Fisheries Agency bureaucrat heads the delegation, it is staffed by bureaucrats from other agencies. Many delegates were drawn from the Ministry of Foreign Affairs (MOF), which has a strong interest in seeing that the IWC negotiation does not get out of control and impinge upon other issues of importance to Japan. Anecdotal evidence also points to the strong hand of MITI. Their interest also was to see that whaling did not get entangled with ongoing trade negotiations that Japan has been conducting with the United States and others. Since whaling is an infinitesimal contributor to Japan's GNP, and there are substitutes for whale-derived protein, MITI wanted to be very sure that a U.S. trade sanction was not invoked, since it might lead to a round of retaliations. Matters could unravel very quickly if that were to happen, and the trade problems between the United States and Japan might be exacerbated.

Since there was a consensus that Japan's goals were worthy goals but no consensus on how to achieve those goals, Japan's delegates were forced to stay in the negotiation to the bitter end. Although the outcome was predictable several years ago, no action was taken to prevent the worst from happening. Japan is now faced with deciding whether it can continue to whale under IWC auspices, or at all. However difficult it will be to form a new consensus within Japanese society and government regarding whaling, it is now imperative.

If one believes in rational choice, Japan has two options—withdraw or surrender. If it chooses the first, Japan should proclaim its adherence to "sustainability" as a rival principle to "non-consumption," withdraw from the IWC, and seek allies to establish a rival organization(s) to give their legal claims legitimacy. This judgment should be based upon an assessment of the fact that the rules of the game are stacked against them, that they can no longer adapt to this framework, and that they cannot manipulate the system to their advantage. If the price is judged to be too high, Japan can exercise Ikle's other option—it can openly surrender and find substitutes for whale meat. This course would create heavy psychological, but trivial material costs.

On the other hand, if one believes that Japan is most likely to behave in ways that meet cultural expectations, there is another scenario for the future of Japan's relationship to the IWC. Japan could remain a member, attend every meeting and claim adherence to the sustainability principle, convince itself that with persistence some day the majority will come to their senses, continue to take a small number of whales under the right to conduct scientific whaling but not otherwise "cheat" on the moratorium, and never admit defeat. By never admitting defeat, by continuing to fight even under adverse circumstances, Japan can convince itself that it will ultimately be victorious. For all practical purposes, Japan will appear to be continuing to negotiate, but in reality will have surrendered. This may be the least-cost alternative for Japan, but if faced with a similar set of circumstances, most other governments would find it a bitter pill to swallow. Will Japan?

NOTES

* An earlier version of this chapter was published as "Moderation in the Pursuit of Justice: Explaining Japan's Failure in the International Whaling Negotiations," *Ocean Development and International Law,* 27 (1996), pp. 349–378.

1. And, perhaps no clever tactics will be needed to create a favorable outcome if the governments leading the anti-whaling effort change their position because of changes at the electoral polls.

2. This is because of the author's lack of competence in this type of research.

3. For other analyses of the cultural input to negotiation see: Cohen, 1991, 1997; Hofstede, 1989; and Poortinga & Hendricks, 1989.

4. The logs of Russian whalers are currently being reanalyzed in order to estimate the Russian take. The effort is being paid for by the United States. *United States Opening Statement* (IWC/46/OSUSA); *Resolution on the Unreliability of Past Whaling Data* (IWC/46/60); and Table 4 (IWC/46/8a) and *Intersessional Meeting of the Working Group on a Sanctuary in the Southern Ocean* (p. 3), 46th Meeting of the IWC (IWC/46/19).

5. They were Dr. D. G. Chapman (USA), Mr. K. R. Allen (New Zealand), Mr. S. J. Holt (FAO), and Dr. J. Gulland (UK).

6. "It is my urgent task now to recommend to my Government as soon as I return to Tokyo that the hitherto cooperation to IWC by Japan come under a

critical review. . . ." *Closing Statement by the Commissioner for Japan,* 46th Meeting of the IWC (IWC/46/67).

7. In 1993, an environmental organization—Earthtrust—commissioned two scientists to perform DNA tests on samples of whale tissue purchased in retail markets in Japan to determine their origin. In addition to minke whale meat from the Southern Ocean, fin whales, and sei whale meat was discovered in some samples. These could only have been obtained illegally. "DNA Testing . . . ," 1994; Baker & Palumbi, 1994.

8. It is claimed that the total expenses for the 1987–88 expedition was 1.7 billion yen. Another 350 billion yen was provided as a subsidy by the Japanese government, and 1.3 billion yen was recovered from the sale of whale meat, leaving a shortfall of 50 million yen, which had to be raised by public donations. "A Disguised Commercial Operation?" 1989.

9. For example, see the report on an anti-whaling petition and hunger strike by Kamejima, 1993.

10. Dr. Justin Cooke, developer of algorithm "C," demonstrated the fallacy in this argument: "If environmental effects are severe then even reducing catches to zero would do little to mitigate them." "Simulation trials of the RMP Catch Algorithm in the presence of adverse external influences of whale populations," 46th Meeting of the IWC (SC/46/Mg 12).

11. While I believe that Japan's position was reasonable, I also believe that Japanese planning for the resumption of whaling is inadequate. While it is very likely that in the first stage of a resumption of commercial whaling, Japan's announced maximum catch would not threaten sustainability, Japanese authorities have failed to answer two key questions. First, if Japan resumes whaling and others do not, why should Japan enjoy a monopoly of a commonly owned resource? This requires legal, political, and economic analysis. For example, Japan might pay into a fund to compensate the world's owners in order to exercise its monopoly. Second, and more likely, if Japan's resumption of whaling is an economic success and attracts others to re-enter the whaling industry, are the existing rules of the IWC sufficient to prevent the resumption of the "whaling Olympics"? What type of management scheme beyond what is already proposed would be needed? This must be thought through before the moratorium can be lifted.

12. This term is named after Lemuel Boulware, former vice-president of General Electric Company. He would make an offer in wage negotiations he viewed as fair to both sides and then not budge from his position (Raiffa, 1982).

13. This position is also reflected in the Japanese press. Below is a portion of an editorial in the *Mainichi Daily News,* May 31, 1994, p. 2: "The IWC is a disappointment to us, but we should continue our membership in the organization and keep advancing our views as we see fit. We have no need to compromise on the universal principle of sustained use of wildlife compati-

ble with the environment. Sooner or later, rational people will understand our position."

14. Unfortunately, there are very few potential rescuers or those who might understand Japan's motives. Cf. Doi, 1973.

15. The basis of the majority's legal case can be found in Resolution 19.63 of the International Union for the Conservation of Nature: "EMPHASIZING that nothing in Agenda 21 restricts the right of a State, or competent international organization, to prohibit, limit or regulate the use of marine mammals more strictly than is required for sustainable use, within areas under its jurisdiction or control. . . ." *Report of the IUCN General Assembly,* January17–26, 1994.

16. Cf., "we proceed from the premise that Japanese political actors rationally maximize subject to institutional constraints" (Ramseyer & Rosenbluth, 1993).

17. A number of American specialists on Japanese politics believe that there has been an overemphasis on the uniqueness of Japanese culture and the use of culture as an explanation of Japanese political behavior. On the other hand, diplomats, and those who prepare materials to train diplomats, are more willing to accept culture as an explanatory variable. See the contrasting views in Curtis, 1988, p. 247; and Fisher, 1980, pp. 32–36.

18. Because of my acquaintanceship with a number of Japan's delegates, it is difficult for me not to believe that they were seriously constrained. They are capable, articulate, and worldly persons who understood the issues and politics within the IWC but could not act upon their insights.

REFERENCES

"A Disguised Commercial Operation?—The Costs of Scientific Whaling" (1989). *Science and Technology in Japan,* 8 (31).

Agenda 21, RIO Declaration on Environment and Development, and Statement of Forest Principles. 1992. New York: United Nations.

Akimichi, T., Asquith, P. J., Befu, H., Bestor, T. C., Braund, S. R., Freeman, M. M. R., Hardachre, H., Iwasaki, M., Kalland, A., Manderson, L., Moeran, B. D., & Takahashi, J. 1988. *Small-type Coastal Whaling in Japan.* Edmonton, Alberta: Boreal Institute of Northern Studies.

Allison, G. 1971. *The Essence of Decision: Explaining the Cuban Missile Crisis.* Boston: Little, Brown.

Asahi. 1993. March 12, p. 3.

Axelrod, R. 1969. *Conflict of Interest: A Theory of Divergent Goals with Applications to Politics.* Chicago: Markham.

Baker, C. S., & Palumbi, S. R. 1994. "Which Whales Are Hunted? A Molecular Genetic Approach to Monitoring Whaling." *Science,* 265, 1538–1539.

Banzerman, M. H., & Neale, M. A. 1991. "Negotiator Rationality and Negotiator Cognition: The Interactive Roles of Prescriptive and Descriptive Research." In Young, *Negotiation Analysis* (pp. 109–130). Ann Arbor: University of Michigan Press.

Barstow, R. 1990. *1990 Noordwijk IWC Meeting Marks Historic Turning Point for Cetaceans: A Summary Report And Analysis.* Weathersfield, CT: Cetacean Society International.

Blaker, M. 1977. *Japanese International Negotiating Style.* New York: Columbia University Press.

Blaker, M. 1977. "Probe, Push and Panic: The Japanese Tactical Style in International Negotiations." In Scalapino, *The Foreign Policy of Modern Japan.* Berkeley and Los Angeles: University of California Press.

Borton, H. 1955. *Japan's Modern Century.* New York: Roland.

Bramwell, A. 1990. *Ecology in the 20th Century: A History.* New Haven: Yale University Press.

Caldwell, L. K. 1990. *International Environmental Policy: Emergence and Dimensions.* Durham: Duke University Press.

Christy, Jr., F. T., & Scott, A. D. 1965. *The Common Wealth in Ocean Fisheries.* Baltimore: Johns Hopkins University Press.

Cohen, R. 1991. *Negotiating Across Cultures.* Washington, DC: U.S. Institute of Peace Press. Rev. ed., 1997.

Crutchfield, J., & Pontecorvo, G. 1969. *The Pacific Salmon Fisheries: A Study in Irrational Conservation.* Baltimore: Johns Hopkins University Press.

Curtis, G. L. 1988. *The Japanese Way of Politics.* New York: Columbia University Press.

"DNA Testing Emerges From Courtroom to Detect Whales Killed Unlawfully." 1994. *Wall Street Journal,* August 9.

Doi, T. 1973. *The Anatomy of Dependence.* Tokyo: Kodansha.

Editorial. 1994. *Mainichi Daily News,* May 31, p. 2.

Edwards, W., & Newman, J. R. 1982. *Multiattribute Evaluation.* Beverly Hills, CA: Sage.

Fisher, G. 1980. *International Negotiation: A Cross-Cultural Perspective.* Yarmouth, ME: Intercultural Press.

Fisher, R., & Ury, W. 1981. *Getting To Yes: Negotiating Agreement without Giving In.* Boston: Houghton Mifflin.

Freeman, M. M. R. 1990. "A Commentary on Political Issues with Regard to Contemporary Whaling." *North Atlantic Studies,* 2 (1–2), 106–116.

Freeman, M. M. R. 1993. "The International Whaling Commission, Small-Type Whaling, and Coming to Terms with Subsistence." *Human Organization,* 52 (3), 143–151.

Friedheim, R. L. 1972. "International Organizations and the Uses of the Ocean." In Jordan, *Multinational Cooperation* (pp. 223–281). New York: Oxford University Press.

Friedheim, R. L. 1993. *Negotiating the New Ocean Regime.* Columbia: University of South Carolina Press.

Friedheim, R. L., & Akaha, T. 1989. "Antarctic Resources and International Law: Japan, the United States, and the Future of Antarctica." *Ecology Law Quarterly,* 16 (1), 119–154.

Fukui, H. 1977. "Studies in Policymaking: A Review of the Literature." In Pempel, *Policymaking in Contemporary Japan* (pp. 22–59). Ithaca: Cornell University Press.

Gambell, R. n.d. "The Management of Whales and Whaling." Manuscript.

Government of Iceland, Ministry of Foreign Affairs. 1991. "Government of Iceland Announces Withdrawal from International Whaling Commission." Press Release.

Halperin, M. 1974. *Bureaucratic Politics and Foreign Policy.* Washington: Brookings Institution.

Hofstede, G. 1989. "Cultural Predictors of National Negotiating Style." In Mautner-Markhof, *Processes of International Negotiation* (pp. 193–202). Boulder, CO: Westview.

Ikle, F. 1964. *How Nations Negotiate.* New York: Harper & Row.

Institute of Cetacean Research. 1990. *Japanese Research on Antarctic Whales Resources.* Tokyo.

Institute of Cetacean Research. 1989. *The Research on Whales Stocks in the Antarctic: The Results of the Preliminary Study in 1987/88.* Tokyo.

International Convention for the Regulation of Whaling, signed at Washington, on December 2, 1946. 1953. *United Nations Treaty Series,* 161, 74.

IWC. 1994. *Closing Statement by the Commissioner for Japan* (IWC/46/67). Forty-Sixth Meeting.

IWC. 1992. *Government of Chile: "Establishment of a Sanctuary in the Southern Ocean"* (IWC/46/34). Forty-Sixth Meeting.

IWC. 1992. *Government of France: "A Southern Ocean Whale Sanctuary"* (IWC/44/19). Chairman's Report on the Forty-Fourth Meeting.

IWC. 1994. *Intersessional Meeting of the Working Group on a Sanctuary in the Southern Ocean* (IWC/46/19). Forty-Sixth Meeting.

IWC. 1994. *Joint Opening Statement by the Observers for ICC and IWGIA.* Forty-Sixth Meeting.

IWC. 1994. *Kazuo Shima: "Closing Statement by the Commissioner for Japan"* (IWC/46/67). Forty-Sixth Meeting.

IWC. 1994. *The Present Practice of the Secretariat Concerning the Commission's Documents and Reports* (IWC/46/14). Forty-Sixth Meeting.

IWC. 1994. *Proposed Consideration for Sanctuary in the Southern Ocean* (IWC/46/35/ Rev. 1). Forty-Sixth Meeting.

IWC. 1991. *Report of the Aboriginal Subsistence Whaling Sub-Committee* (IWC/43/13). Forty-Third Meeting.

IWC. 1991. *Report of the Humane Killing Working Group* (IWC/43/ item 10b). Forty-Third Meeting.

IWC. 1991. *Report of the Technical Committee* (IWC/43/5). Forty-Third Meeting.

IWC. 1991. *Report of the Technical Committee* (IWC/43/5, Plenary Item 9). Forty-Third Meeting.

IWC. 1992. *Report of the Working Group on Revision of the Schedule* (IWC/44/14). Forty-Fourth Meeting.

IWC. 1994. *Report of the Working Group on Supervision and Control* (IWC/46/65). Forty-Sixth Meeting.

IWC. 1994. *Resolution on International Trade in Whale Meat and Products* (IWC/46/61). Forty-Sixth Meeting.

IWC. 1995. *Resolution on Legal Matters Relating to the Adoption of the Southern Ocean Sanctuary* (IWC/47/45). Forty-Seventh Meeting.

IWC. 1994. *Resolution on Promotion of Research Related to Conservation of Large Baleen Whales in the Southern Ocean* (IWC/46/58). Forty-Sixth Meeting.

IWC. 1994. *Resolution on the Unreliability of Past Whaling Data* (IWC/46/60). Forty-Sixth Meeting.

IWC. 1994. *Robbins Barstow: Cetacean Society International Opening Statement* (IWC/46/OS/CSI). Forty-Sixth Meeting.

IWC. 1994. *Simulation Trials of the RMP Catch Algorithm in the Presence of Adverse External Influences on Whale Populations* (IWC/46/MG12). Forty-Sixth Meeting.

IWC. 1994. *United States Opening Statement* (IWC/46/OSUSA). Forty-Sixth Meeting.

Johnston, D. M. 1990. The Driftnet Problem in the Pacific Ocean: Legal Considerations and Diplomatic Options. *Ocean Development and International Law,* 18, 215–39.

Kalland, A., & Moeran, B. 1990. *Endangered Culture: Japanese Whaling in Cultural Perspective.* Copenhagen: Nordic Institute of Asian Studies.

Kamejima, Y. 1993. *The Japan Times,* May 13, p. 4.

Keeney, R., & Raiffa, H. 1991. "Structuring and Analyzing Values for Multiple-Issue Negotiations." In Young, *Negotiation Analysis.*

Klinowska, M. 1989. "How Brainy Are Cetaceans?" *Oceanus,* 32 (1).

Knopf, J. W. 1993. "Beyond Two-Level Games: Domestic-International Interaction in the Intermediate Range Nuclear Forces Negotiations." *International Organization,* 47, 599–628.

Lax, D. A., & Sebenius, J. 1986. *The Manager as Negotiator: Bargaining for Cooperation and Competitive Gain.* New York: The Free Press.

Lewis, M. W. 1992. *Green Delusions: An Environmental Critique of Radical Environmentalism.* Durham: Duke University Press.

March, J. G. 1994. *A Primer on Decision-Making: How Decisions Happen.* New York: The Free Press.

Nagasaki, F. 1990. "The Case for Scientific Whaling." *Nature,* 344, 62–63.

Nakane, C. 1973. *Japanese Society.* Harmonsworth, UK: Penguin Books.

"Okata Journal: The Whale: Food for Soul or Stomach." 1992. *The New York Times,* April 6, p. A4.

Peterson, M. J. 1992. "Whalers, Cetologists, Environmentalists and the International Management of Whaling." *International Organization, 46* (1), 147–186.

Poortinga, Y. H., & Hendricks, E. C. 1989. "Culture as a Factor in International Negotiations: A Proposed Research Project from a Psychological Perspective." In Mautner-Markhof, *Processes of International Negotiation* (pp. 203–212).

Protocol Amending the International Whaling Agreement, June 24, 1938. 1938. 53 Stat. 1794, 196 L.N.T.S. 131.

Putnam, R. D. 1988. "Diplomacy and Domestic Politics: The Logic of Two-Level Games." *International Organization, 41*, 427–460.

Raiffa, H. 1982. *The Art and Science of Negotiation.* Cambridge: Harvard University Press.

Ramseyer, J. M., & Rosenbluth, F. M. 1993. *Japan's Political Marketplace.* Cambridge: Harvard University Press.

Rawls, J. 1971. *A Theory of Justice.* Cambridge: Belnap Press of Harvard University Press.

Scott, A. D. 1955. "The Fishery: The Objective of Sole Ownership." *Journal of Political Economy, 63*, 116–124.

Small-Type Coastal Whaling in Japan: Report of an International Workshop. 1988. Occasional Publication Number 27, Japan Social Science Association of Canada Fund to Promote International Education Exchange and Boreal Institute for Northern Studies.

Sumi, K. 1989. "The 'Whale War' Between Japan and the United States: Problems and Prospects." *Denver Journal of International Law,* 17 (2), 317–372.

von Winterfeldt, D., & Edwards, W. 1986. *Decision Analysis and Behavioral Research.* Cambridge: Cambridge University Press.

Wettestad, J., & Andresen, S. 1991. "The Effectiveness of International Resource Cooperation: Some Preliminary Findings." *International Challenges,* 11 (3).

Whales. 1991. Greenpeace International via Greenbase, September 18.

Young, O. R., Freeman, M. M. R., Osherenko, G., Andersen, R. R., Caulfield, R. A., Friedheim, R. L., Langdon, S. J., Ris, M., & Usher, P. 1994. "Subsistence, Sustainability and Sea Mammals: Reconstructing the International Whaling Regime." *Ocean and Coastal Management,* 23, 117–127.

Zartman, I. W. 1976. *The 50% Solution.* Garden City: Anchor Books.

Zartman, I. W., & Berman, M. R. 1982. *The Practical Negotiator.* New Haven: Yale University Press.

CHAPTER 7

INSTITUTIONS MATTER: NEGOTIATING THE EUROPEAN UNION

FRANK R. PFETSCH

INTRODUCTION

Negotiation analysis mostly concentrates on face-to-face constellations between two or more negotiators who's emotions, competencies, visions, leadership, skills, personal styles, strategies, etc. determine the outcome of the negotiation process. Notwithstanding the importance of such factors, we want to concentrate in this chapter on the environmental factors that also determine the negotiation process; such structure-related factors are institutions in the broad sense of the term, comprising assemblies, norms, rules, values, ideologies, cultures, symmetric or asymmetric constellations, etc., hence all those factors that influence a negotiator's action besides personal qualities.

The model of analysis (which I will describe later) in its simple form concentrates on the relationship between the actor and his environment; the outcome, then, depends on the particular shape this relationship takes; more specifically, the outcome differs according to the different institutional settings.

Our empirical domain is the regime that has become the European Union (EU), with its communitarian and its intergovernmental institutions. The main hypothesis is that these two institutional patterns lead to different outcomes. In choosing the EU, we concentrate on its various bodies of decision making as the institutional core of negotiations.

Negotiations and decision making[1] are central to pluralistic and representative democracies in a wide range of political bodies. Decisions in the political sense of the term are, in general, made by small groups for a greater community (Pfetsch, 1995b). In assemblies that function as organs of representation, decisions are reached through negotiation, voting, or balloting; the negotiation process leads to decisions but not all decisions are reached by negotiation. By studying the negotiation process we study at the same time one of the two or three decision-making processes. Their arena consists of various levels of private and public organizations, among political institutions such as the different organs of the European Community. By choosing EU institutions we restrict ourselves to elected political elites, selected administrators, and representatives of private organizations. The public is itself not present but is represented, and is the subject of the various outcomes of negotiation and decision-making processes. The legitimacy of the EU institutions is questioned with decreasing acceptance rates by the electorate in various member countries. By this the elite institutions are challenged and have to respond during their discussions at the 1996 Intergovernmental Conference (IGC) for the reform of the EU.

In describing our empirical field, the European Union (EU) with its predecessor organizations, we proceed from the general to the specific.

In general the EU, with its supranational institutions (the Council, the Commission, the Parliament, the Court), represents, compared to other international organizations, the most integrated form of international cooperation; other international organizations are intergovernmental by nature. The community institutions of the EU can make binding decisions with majority voting, and they can sanction deviations from these decisions. In other international arenas, only the Security Council of the UN, together with the International Court of Justice, is invested with these powers.

But the EU, with its European Council and its Council of Ministers, is at the same time an intergovernmental organism; thus the Community was from its beginning "a two-track enterprise" (Pfetsch, 1994, p. 120). With the 1992 treaty of the European Union these two methods of cooperation have become more differentiated: The so-called first pillar, which is mainly the single common market, is characterized by collective governance where the community institutions play an ever more important role. The second (Common Foreign and Security Policy, CFSP) and third (Justice and Home Affairs, JHA) pillars are intergovernmental by nature; thus they are characterized by cooperation among and concertation with the individual governments as main actors.

The European Union has been characterized as a "intergovernmental bargaining system" (Scharpf, 1993, p. 13) and negotiation is seen as the "predominant policy mode" (H. & W. Wallace, 1996, p. 32). Such a system embraces a multitude of heterogeneous actors with different policy styles and lobbying practices, bound together in overlapping networks, engaged in shifting coalitions, moving within and across the different levels of the EU system (Kohler-Koch, 1994). Negotiation theories normally underline the positive effects of cooperation: actors are bound together in view of a common goal, can learn about the differences of interest, and can steer intentionally their cooperation. With some reservations,[2] these positive effects of negotiations can be demonstrated. Negotiations within the EU are facilitated by the existence of a supranational institutional framework that creates stable communications through repetitive games with the same players, facilitates the information flow, improves decision making through the existence of stable procedures that make expectations more calculable, promotes the community spirit, and stabilizes the implementation of decisions, and, if necessary, sanctions deviations. It is this communitarian institutional framework that allows such positive effects. In the center of this institutional network are assemblies in which negotiations take place. They can take the form of committees, ad-hoc expert meetings, ministerial meetings, meetings of the commissioners, reunions of parliamentary bodies, conventions of the heads of executives, etc. The "comitology" functions as a key instrument of negotiation and mediation.

Research on the conditions and explanations of the negotiation and decision-making process has focused on a multitude of factors, concepts, and approaches. The history of political thought has concentrated on external determinations of decisions, such as the materialistic determinism in Marx' tradition, or on internal conditioning, such as Schmitt's occasional "Dezionismus," Saint-Simon's positivism, Schelsky's concept of technical necessity (Sachgesetzlichkeit), Sorel's collective spontaneity, or Max Weber's poietic subjectivism. These mostly antidemocratic positions do not match the reality of decision making in the real world of representative democracies. Instead we have to deal with multi-issue, multilayered and often multicultural processes of interaction between actor(s) and environment(s) (Müller, 1973, p. 48).

Here, we focus on an important part of the possible forms of "decision-making and solution-finding" (Welsh, 1973), that is collective decision making in the EU bodies since they are the most common decision-making institutions in representative democracies (Taylor, 1975, p. 417). Giovanni Sartori (1984, p. 93) has defined assemblies as durable and institutionalized small groups of three to thirty members. They are in direct interaction and produce decisions continuously rather than occasionally. The assemblies we are studying in the EU context mostly fit this definition. Thus, we take as the empirical base of negotiation processes the communitarian and the intergovernmental organs of the EU—the Council of Ministers and the European Council together with the national bodies of the EU member states as the main intergovernmental institutions, and the European Commission, the European Court of Justice, and the European Parliament as the main communitarian bodies.

This chapter identifies the determinants of the complex group processes within the European Union, and explains the relations between decision production through negotiations and its conditions and consequences. What does negotiation and decision-making theory tell us about the policies of the EU, and in what way does it help to understand and explain the very specific political process of the EU? Are there any differences in the negotiation process between the community method of collective governance and the intergovernmental method of cooperation between governments? This last question is in the center of our inquiry.

Analysis of decision processes in assemblies has become a multidisciplinary enterprise. We draw from the findings of social psychology, sociology of organizations, political science, economics, and mathematics, among others. We proceed with interrelated hypotheses that are tested in various contexts and that can reproduce the horizon of an integrative decision theory as an outcome of negotiations.

From a theoretical point of view, assembly negotiations function as a pool of different interests of their members that should eventually lead to a common policy. A wide spectrum of voluntary or coercive procedures and techniques can lead to the aggregation of individual preferences for a collective decision: economically, through market forces (bargaining and exchange), or politically, through consensus-producing processes (negotiating and voting). Power resources and their application play an important part in a process with multiple preferences.

Assembly decisions are usually not reached by a single act. They are the result of complex processes and structures involving a multitude of persons and opinions. Preexisting fixed interests rarely initiate these processes according to a utility function. Instead, opinions and structured decisions are formulated during a dynamic trial-and-error process prior to the voting. It is in negotiations as a part of "preparatory" diplomacy or problem-counseling that the issue area is defined and decisions

Figure 1. Model of Analysis

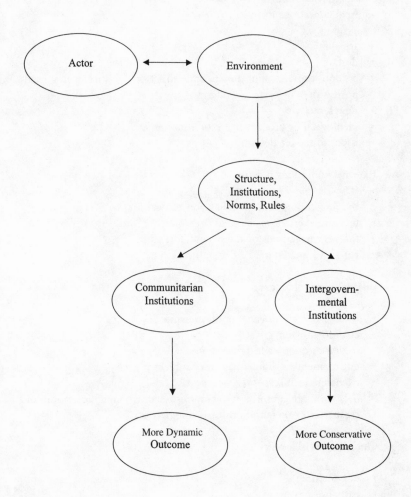

are prepared. The meeting in the lobby, the walk in the woods, the round of golf, the dinner reception, and others are situations in which influence is manifest and approximation attempts are made or even solutions found. Formally, the decision process takes place in a given framework, in which the decision makers pursue their interests. They have instruments at hand that cause costs, risks, or benefits. Internal and external conditions, instruments, targets, costs/benefit considerations, and outcomes are five basic variables of a decision process.

Internal conditions include

- size;
- duration;
- composition (organizational differentiation, political party composition);
- representativity;
- ideological or programmatic orientation; and
- issues to be decided on.

External conditions include

- binding and nonbinding character of decisions,
- pressure exerted on the negotiators,
- future expectations of action, and, foremost,
- rules and procedures of decision making.

Instruments include

- use of power, influence, and leadership;
- coalition-forming;
- setting of quotas and proportions;
- enlargement or differentiation of subject matters;
- exchange or linkage;
- delay through submission to committees or through ratification; and
- escape into generalizations or ideologization.

Outcome variables include

- nondecisions,
- partial decisions,
- radical decisions,
- ambiguous decisions,
- majority decisions,
- stable decisions,
- conservative or progressive decisions, and
- future-oriented decisions.

These variables of our analytical model are linked-together hypotheses that are empirically tested with case studies from different empirical domains and illustrating examples. In such a way we strive to develop middle-range theories that help to explain the negotiation processes.

The underlying premises are twofold; on the one hand, more integration of European states leads to greater peace in the war-prone arena of Europe and, on the other hand, establishing a federal pattern of this regional system is the best way to secure diversity within unity. Hence, the often quoted success story for which the EU stands can be measured by these two finalities. Other measures of success, however, must equally be considered, such as people's welfare, democratic participation, human rights, environmental protection, quality of life, etc.

FRAMEWORK

We distinguish between internal and external conditions of negotiations in assemblies, and between factors that can be influenced by actors and those that cannot. Whereas the former distinction is in the center of the agent-structure debate, the latter refers to the distinction between objective and subjective factors of the negotiation process. Internal conditions are related to the assembly itself, and the external determinants stem from a broader set of norms derived from the political community as a whole. Preexisting conditions or conditions that cannot be altered by the actors immediately determine the structure of the negotiation bodies. On each of these aspects we establish hypotheses that we later test with regard to the European Union.

STRUCTURES AND CONDITIONS

We start studying the internal and external conditions of the negotiation process in groups.

THE INTERNAL STRUCTURE OF ASSEMBLIES

As to the internal structure, there are a number of variables determining the structure of assemblies, such as size, duration, composition (organizational differentiation, political party composition), representativity, ideological or programmatic orientation, and issues to be decided.

The Size of Assemblies

The size of an assembly effects its structure as a working unit. From organizational theory and empirical observations we can establish a number of hypotheses:

HYPOTHESIS I: The bigger the assembly, the more it becomes organizationally differentiated (committees, subcommittees).

A day-to-day observation can illustrate this hypothesis. By inviting people for dinner and sitting around a table one can observe that conversation among all the guests is possible as long as there are not more than about eight guests (see Olson, 1971, pp. 52–55). If there are more than ten to fifteen (Pfetsch, 1987) then the discussion takes place among three or four sitting near each other.

We can test this hypothesis (see Thomas & Fink, 1963) by studying the different EU assemblies as the EC grew from 6 to 9, 9 to 12, and finally 12 to 15 members. The more the Community expanded in scope and membership the more it became heterogeneous and the more negotiations were bounded by the circumspection of many participants (H. Wallace, 1985, p. 33).

The plans of some governments at the 1996 Intergovernmental Conference (IGC) to reduce the number of commissioners and strengthen the presidency of the council is one strategy to overcome further differentiation and, as a consequence, inefficiency.

With increasing numbers of actors there is also the chance that more issues are put on the EC agenda as compared to a national agenda (Cobb & Elder, 1983). In other words, each enlargement brought new dimensions and areas of activity (see Granell, 1995, p. 137). The first enlargement brought in a more democratic perspective and a new world dimension with its transatlantic relations. With the second enlargement new social and cohesive orientations were brought to bear with Latin American links. The third wave of enlargement emphasized environmental and social aspects, and opened an outlook to Third World countries as well as Eastern nations with expectations for the fourth round of enlargements. These expansions enlarged the policy issues, and, as noted by Peters, "the presence of alternatives is an important characteristic of agenda-setting in the EC" (Peters, 1994, p. 18). The more there are issues considered to be important, the more there is a necessity to find an organizational frame in the form of a Directorate General (DG), committee, or other group. Thus the committees of the European Parliament reflect the DGs in the commission.

HYPOTHESIS II: The smaller the assembly, the higher the ballot's value or weight for each individual under unchanged voting procedures.

This hypothesis states only a numerical calculation: if there are only two voters then the weight of each is one-half. If there are ten voters the weight of each is only one-tenth. The smaller the unit of decision making, the more the preferences of the participants count (see Tullock, 1971).

The search for securing equal representation and keeping the assemblies small is evident in the construction of various EU organs. Qualified majority voting, as well as the introduction of the rotation system in the Council of Ministers, follows on these lines. The troika solution enlarges the mandate of each country in the political process. Because of the fear by the bigger states of losing control of the decision-making bodies, the provision was introduced that one of the bigger countries must be represented, and arguments were put forward in the IGC to restrain the scope and the authority of the community arenas. On the other hand, because of the fear of losing equal rights and weights, the smaller countries are against any concentration of officeholders in EU organs.

HYPOTHESIS III: The higher the number of participants, the higher the costs of producing consensus (internal costs), and the less are the disadvantages for the individual voter (external risks).

The first statement refers to more or less organizational circumstances: the more participants there are, the more time is needed to produce consensus and, consequently, the more costly is the production process of results. Internal costs comprise such costs as bargaining and influence costs, implementation and monitoring costs, information costs, etc. (Cornett & Caporaso, 1994, p. 226). As to the external risks (Sartori, 1984, p. 85) there is a tendency that results produced by a small group of insiders leaving out important politicians and people who are affected by the decisions taken are not accepted and, consequently, do not last long (see Buchanan & Tullock, 1962, p. 45). Amendments are the result of such restricted decision-making processes.

With more actors coming in, as in the enlargement of the EC/EU, the more diverting interests are being pursued. Each country brings in its own interests and wants them to be pursued. With an increase in number an assembly becomes more heterogeneous and the windows of opportunities for agreements become narrower (H. & W. Wallace, 1996, p. 33). Hence, with unanimity in important policy fields, the time needed to achieve consensus increases. It can be said that the amount of time spent on discussions of issues increases with the increase of member countries in the EU.

Disadvantages for an individual actor would arise if he were victim of a "tyranny of the majority" (Alexis de Tocqueville). This, however, rarely happens because of the voting rules expressed in the treaty and the voting practice in EU organs. As a rule, decisions are taken on a consensus basis even in cases where majority voting would be possible. It is part of the community spirit not to vote down a country by pushing through a decision with the majority rule.

Duration

HYPOTHESIS IV: The less time is available, the easier it is in a system of majority voting for leading majorities to win.

Decisions made under time pressure have a tendency to be pushed through by the majority party, which does not take into account minority positions. The dictate of the majority prevails even if there is the political will to include minority positions. On the contrary, if there is no time limit, the parties can seek consensus on a broader scale.

In the EU this hypothesis can only be tested in a selected number of policy fields, since unanimity is still required in the domain of high politics. As mentioned above even with majority voting the consensus principle is dominant in EU organs. It has to be seen if this hypothesis remains true in the future, when more majority voting will be possible and where the advantage is with bigger countries that possess more weight in the council; in principle, no decision can be made by smaller countries without the consent of bigger ones. Also, as a principle and more in theory than in practice, there should be no discrimination against any one group—be it rich or poor, northern or southern, central or peripheral, agrarian or industrial, etc.

Composition

HYPOTHESIS V: Subgroups within an assembly can, by forming coalitions with others, reach a majority position and minimize the influence of an existing majority. Minorities can also benefit from a situation in which two or more majority groups of equal size with opposing views counterbalance their weight and have to rely on the support of smaller parties.

Under certain conditions minorities get their chance. According to our hypothesis, small groups have either no influence at all or some influence taking into account their relative weight (see Moscovici et al., 1969; Allan, 1984). This can be the result of the behavior of the majority groups towards each other. If the bigger countries cannot agree on a particular issue, the smaller ones get their chance by joining one side. Various winning coalitions can be calculated according to the weighted votes in the constituency with majority voting (see Brams et al., 1994, p. 100) and vote trading (Riker & Brams, 1973/74).

Coalition-forming in EU organs is an ongoing process and does not show a stable pattern. There are various coalitions possible depending on the issue. As a political rule, without the endorsement of Germany and France no major development can go ahead (Lodge, 1991, p. 7). Even the German-French tandem recently deviated from its unity on agricultural policy. A good example of using differences among parties within an assembly was the tactic applied by the U.S. government toward the EU during the negotiations in the Uruguay round (Landau, 1996). The U.S. negotiator succeeded in splitting the German-French tandem and forming an alliance with Germany to get its position through.

Representativity
HYPOTHESIS VI: Decisions are more likely to be stable when an assembly is highly representative, consensual, and unpressured to decide. The follow-up costs are usually lower.

This hypothesis states the other side of the coin formulated in hypotheses III and IV. If an assembly is representative and time is available to discuss extensively, then it can include the major actors with their interests. Consequently, the outcome of such negotiations is highly legitimized (Marin, 1983, p. 205) and has a tendency to last longer. One of the unique principles of the EU is that it tries to create a homogenous pattern of policy representation (Pfetsch, 1995a, p. 189). The small countries should be able to have their say as much as the poorer and the peripheral countries. By equilibrating these various differences and diversities, the EU is attractive also to minor states in terms of power. Otherwise it could not be understood why smaller countries, such as the Benelux states, are among the champions of European integration.

So far the decisions initiated by the commission and taken by the council are fairly stable in the sense that a high proportion of them are implemented in the member countries; they last long since equal representation is the dominant principle in EU organisms. Even decisions made with time restraints like those on agricultural policy or the budget show fairly stable results.

Ideological and Programmatic Orientation
HYPOTHESIS VII: The ideological and/or programmatic proximity of organized member groups reduces the spectrum of controversial alternatives and leads to coalitions. This produces a high consensual potential as a prerequisite for solutions.

Ideology can aggregate diverse interests and can serve as a unifier in the decision-making process. In parliamentary systems governments are formed on the basis of "natural allies" procuring maximum payoffs for the participating parties (Dodd, 1976, p. 38). This empirically tested relationship rarely holds in the case of EU parties since they do not possess that coherence observable within national constituencies. Nevertheless, some alliances may be formed on the basis of ideological vicinities.

Party alignments do not play a decisive role in the council or commission or even in the European Parliament. In national constituencies parties provide a mechanism for coordination of policies across levels of government or across institutions. Fragmentation is, among others, the result of the fact that neither the European Council nor the Council of Ministers possess party affiliations as a coordinating instrument. Political parties within the European Parliament are aggregations of national parties; they lack the unity required for a more coherent policy. On the executive side the European Council and the Council of Ministers are intergovernmental entities separately responsible to their national constituencies. What brings them together is a common interest in the European project and the advantages that they can expect from it in terms of national policy-making. As for the executive and legislative bodies of the EU it is argued that the styles and cultures of the commissioners are as important as specific calculations about national advantages that might result (Peters, 1994). Here, the professional styles and the political cultures of the various countries may play a role. It is said that within the Brussels apparatus the French administrative traditions dominate because French is used more commonly than other languages. Externally, however, English is the more commonly used language.

Ideology is, therefore, not an important factor. More important factors of consensus-building are the common will to build Europe, the visions on the Union's finalities (which induce certain institutional patterns), the will to secure a country's interest in a specific matter, a common economic interest in bigger markets (large-scale production), and the pressure from outside by globalization processes.

Issues

HYPOTHESIS VIII: A greater amount of material and conflicting issues facilitates compromises and the settlement of controversial issues. Multi-issues facilitate compromises.

In general, economic goods are accessible to division, diversification, and differentiation. Quantity and quality, price-cost relations, time and space, and other factors are opportunities for give-and-take, for package deals, and for substitutive and/or compensatory deals (see Sebenius, 1991).

Even in case of indivisible goods—goods "that cannot be split physically into parts, and concerns that cannot be compromised on" (Albin, 1991, p. 47)—there exist a number of compensatory and functional strategies to overcome a deadlock in negotiations. Additional issues can be added, resource expansion can facilitate solutions. An example is the deal among the Twelve about the site of the central bank for the European Union. In the decision about the central bank (which is now in Frankfurt) other European institutions, such as the European Environmental Agency (Copenhagen), Europol (The Hague), and European Drugs Agency (London), were included and by that other countries got their share.

A compromise is facilitated by dealing with divisible goods. This is so because, among other reasons, such goods are accessible to a give-and-take and are not highly value loaded. But even in the case of indivisibility and non-negotiable interests, such as value-loaded goods with symbolic meaning, there are ways of compromising through exchange and functional strategies. Cecilia Albin has shown that even in the case of the most sensitive good, the city of Jerusalem, a solution could be found by differentiating according to functions the city has and these can be shared by Jews and Arabs (Albin, 1991, pp. 45–76).

Since most economic issues are multi-issue by nature, compromises can be reached even in such fields as agriculture. The Single European Act was presented by Jacques Delors "in large bunches." Other new items on the agenda had appeared during the biannual meetings of the heads of the executives since each host of such meetings wanted to have major initiatives adopted by his colleagues. It is stated that one of the unique features of the EU is its openness towards a variety of issues and competing policies, a variety that seems to be bigger than on national agendas (Peters, 1994, pp. 11, 12).

This diversity of issues is promoted by the various commissioners. Each one has personal ambitions. Commissioners can use activism for reviving their political careers either on the national or on the European stage (Peters, 1994, p. 14). The fragmentation of the commission gives room for such maneuvers since the borders of the DGs are not always clearly defined. Thus environmental policy falls in the competence of DG XI and the Quasi-Nongovernmental Organization (Euro-Quango) of the European Environmental Agency. But other DGs have their say in this policy field—the DG XVI for regional affairs, for example. The absence of adequate coordination mechanisms known in national governments, such as party alignments or inter-ministerial bodies, leads on the one hand to more openness for policy initiatives, and on the other to difficulties in forming a coherent governmental policy. This lack of an "adolescent bu-reaucracy" (Mazey & Richardson, 1993) allows an advocate of an attrac-tive issue not only to have the issue considered, but also to have it considered in a particular format by a receptive DG.

It is not only by differentiation of issues that negotiations are facilitated, but also by a characteristic of the EU. With the increase in numbers of par-ticipants in EU organs, the number of issues increases as well. There are more issues to be negotiated than in national constituencies, hence there is an increase in negotiable issues at hand.

EXTERNAL CONDITIONS

Conditions external to the actor determine the negotiation process. We understand by this the binding and nonbinding character of decisions, the pressure exerted on the negotiators, future expectations of action, and, foremost, the rules and procedures of decision making.

Binding and Nonbinding Decisions
HYPOTHESIS IX: Binding decisions affect the content (substance) and rules of the decision process. The more binding decisions are, the more they tend to be pragmatic and bundled; nonbinding decisions are more radical and emphasize extreme positions.

The nonbinding nature of decisions leaves the decision maker with less responsibility as to the implementation of the decisions taken. Therefore, radical positions can serve as a means to integrate parties on a common platform vis-à-vis an adversary (Rothstein, 1979). Binding decisions force the parties to look out for positions that allow their implementation in a later stage. Decisions made by the Council of Ministers in Brussels can serve as examples of the effect of binding decisions; the voting in the Gen-eral Assembly of the UN as examples of the consequences of radical posi-tions. The binding nature of decisions is the distinguishing feature of the EU compared to other international organizations. Since EU "regulations" are binding in their totality, "directives" in their goals and "decisions" in in-dividual cases, pragmatism prevails and radical positions do not get a chance. Only if a member government wants to avoid a decision might it use a radical proposal and then veto it.

The Degree of Pressure on Decision Makers
HYPOTHESIS X: External or internal pressure on the negotiators to pro-duce results can either facilitate compromises or harden positions.

Last-minute decisions can result from the pressure given by a strict timetable. The manipulation of the timetable—for example stopping the clock, as shown during negotiations on agrarian policy or in the recent GATT negotiations—is the last resort to reach an agreement in time. This time pressure can be healthy because it forces the parties to come to an agreement; without such pressure it is possible that no resolution would be reached. External pressure can, however, cause the negotiating parties to react negatively. External pressure can also serve as an alibi for a policy.

In the EU arena decisions often have to be made at a certain point in time. In debates on agricultural issues or on the budget, time pressure secures to a great extent the making of decisions. Pressure on the decision-makers comes also from external pressure groups that, as a consequence, may block a consensual decision in EU assemblies. Dominant basic values and overarching general priorities can compensate such for pressure; this may lead to second-best solutions for individual countries.

Future Scope of Action

HYPOTHESIS XI: The numeric voting power does not always dominate in a system of majority voting. Besides pure voting power other considerations of the political environment may determine the voting behavior as well, such as future expectations (obligations towards an external/foreign power, future coalitions, maneuverability of future governments, estimates on future voting behavior, etc.).

Future expectations play an important role in EU decision making. The securing of support for future actions has often been a consideration for a compromise in a present action. The prospect of preventing military quarrels among European countries in the future was an important unifier and has so far determined the will of European, especially French and German, politicians to develop interdependent structures. Also, the vision of the future can guide negotiators in their actions. A driving force for the development of the European Community has always been the will to achieve an integrated ensemble of states. In addition the often quoted "shadow of the future" (Axelrod, 1984) is a way acquainting negotiators with each other, and thus, by forming an esprit de corps, decisions are made by customary arrangements.

Rules of Decision Making

HYPOTHESIS XII: In assemblies of high basic consensus, majority rule in decision making is a common practice. In highly heterogeneous assemblies, unanimous decision making is preferred. The necessity to decide unanimously (even unwillingly) increases with the heterogeneity of the assembly.

Unanimity as a decision rule gives each member of an assembly a veto position and, by this, preserves the member's interests. Majority vote to the contrary gives an assembly the right to reach decisions against members. Therefore, if an assembly accepts majority vote, this is a sign of greater consensus and a basic common denominator. In the EC discussions in the 1960s the six members were not yet prepared to accept qualified majority vote in the Council of Ministers; the Luxembourg compromise (1966) indicated a lack of basic understanding. The same unwillingness can be observed in the Security Council in the UN. The consensus–minus–one formula that was introduced later on can be seen as one step to enable decision making in cases against the member's own concern. Also, in multilateral fora no-votes count as abstention but consensus prevails. The same holds for the compromise found in 1997 at the Amsterdam conference of the EU with the "constructive abstention" formula, which means that a motion can pass even if one member country abstains in the Council of Ministers.

The importance of this hypothesis is shown in the discussion to proceed from unanimity to the majority voting in the EU Council. The reluctance by some of the member states to introduce majority voting on issues of high politics shows that these countries are not yet prepared to give up their veto position; this is at the same time a cause and a sign of heterogeneity in the EU.

HYPOTHESIS XIII: The internal costs of the negotiation process rise when decision-making rules approach unanimity; the external costs will decrease.

The rule of unanimity demands more time and effort to produce outcomes than majority voting. The year-long negotiations in the different GATT rounds or the SALT negotiations show the difficulties in reaching agreements under conditions of unanimity. The GATT agreements lasted for the agreed-upon period; the SALT I and II agreements were finalized only after revisions and modifications.

Countries which favor majority voting do so—among other reasons—in order to secure effectiveness and efficiency. In some instances a quick reaction is necessary especially in situations of crisis.

HYPOTHESIS XIV: The rule of unanimity supports outcomes that are oriented to the status quo, because a redistribution of the (unchanged) decision issue would disadvantage at least one party.

The difficulties in reaching consensus by all participants often reduce the field of alternatives to the smallest possible common denominator. The risk of change is usually higher than it is for keeping the status quo and, therefore, parties can either avoid decisions or propose blue sky formulas (Bachrach & Baratz, 1963; Fraenkel, 1968, p. 66). Therefore, the tendency to produce conservative decisions prevails, if everybody has to agree and nobody loses against his own will. Likewise, the UN Security Council rarely made decisions against a member state when it was involved in a given crisis.

Usually, in the field of high politics the status quo is preserved, and, by that, vital interests are guaranteed and disadvantages to one of the member states avoided.

INSTRUMENTS

The use of material and immaterial resources is of strategic importance to the purpose and assertion of interests. These resources cannot be seen apart from the above discussed structural conditions. Instruments of decision making and techniques to influence decisions are:

- use of power, influence, and leadership capacity;
- increase of consensual potential through coalitions;
- setting of quotas and proportions;
- enlargement or differentiation of subject matters;
- exchange or linkage;
- delay through submission to committees or ratification; and
- escape into generalizations or ideologization.

POWER, INFLUENCE, AND LEADERSHIP

Hypothesis XV: Power and influence based on resources can determine the outcome of negotiations in favor of their user. Unequal distributions of power cause struggles among the different groups and are energy consuming.

Power and influence of individuals or groups in an assembly are based on internal and external sources. Members of representative political assemblies rely on their power-base (the voters), who determine the extent of their representation. The clientele of an assembly member is an outer limiting factor to his "weight," since not only the backing of his voters but also economic, ideological, and reputational resources are important.

Among the four sources of power identified by Crozier that are in the hands of organizations, two can be described as outer sources: control of the environment and control of the information and communication channels. Inner sources are competence and the handling of organizational rules (Crozier & Friedberg, 1979, p. 50). The specific office and person are the subjects of power from internal sources. Instruments based on power resources may consist of pressure (threats, promises, blackmailing, deception) from an external power or from a decision maker with an extremely strong power base that is exerted on a weaker partner or adversary. Such pressure—which also can be used by a weaker party perhaps with less success—can either force a solution or impede the decision making.

Robert Michels (1989, p. 46) was among the first who tried to identify the sources of leadership in organizations. He differentiated technical-administrative, psychological, and intellectual sources. The perceived antagonism between elite and masses served as a base to the iron law of oligarchy. Michels's explanatory model describes certainly just one extreme position of an assembly's organization, that is one of extreme size that favors the stabilization of the leadership position. Socio-psychological experiments have shown that groups are not necessarily more prone to make decisions than individuals. To the contrary, in order to activate a group the courage to take risks must come from a "born leader" (Irle, 1971). During conferences and meetings one must not underestimate the authority given to the negotiator (discussion leader, president of parliament, chairman of the conference); he can influence the agenda and the outcome of a conference by formal and informal diplomacy, informative traveling before the conference, opening speeches, scheduling, convening of the conference, deciding on the order of speakers, using the media, drafting the final declaration and further use of the procedural and organizational rules (Raven, 1965, pp. 371–382; Kaufmann, 1968, pp. 50, 76–79, 83–101). The target to bring the conference to a conclusive end demands a refined diplomacy vis-à-vis the group members.

These techniques are used extensively by the presidents of the EU. Every government holding the presidency invests a lot into the half-year term for its own prestige and the initiation and implementation of political interests and visions. Also, a skillful and strong president of the European Commission can considerably influence the development of the Union. Strong figures like Hallstein and Delors have left their traces, whereas others acted more within the council. Hence, the role of individual politicians, with their skill, knowledge, visions, endurance, health conditions, and other qualities, can certainly be important to the decision-making process. In the approaches of rational choice the actor is considered as a rational maximizer of his or her utility. The reality of decision making in EU organs with a multiplicity of actors and solutions does not correspond to that preconceived rational utility acting. "Preferences are unstable and uncertain and the decision that something needs to be done often creates the preferences rather than vice versa" (Peters, 1994, p. 20).

Each assembly has the task to produce results, that is decisions. It is as evident as necessary that this needs energy. This energy can be consumed by internal struggle so that nothing is left for external problem-solving and decision making. A more equal distribution of power and influence and, thus, a more balanced situation becomes possible when, for example, the chairman and the host country are named by a rotation system or when the host country is a neutral state. In this case the dominance of one state and its representatives cannot originate from organizational or local advantages.

Deviancies in the numeric size of one party and the subsequent effects on decisions can also be explained with the talent and the persuasive power of politicians. Decisions can be influenced not only by the authority of an office, but also by the authority of an individual.

The EU member states possess different national resources, such as size, population, economic capability, and military strength. But it is one of the characteristics of the community to secure equal representation in the different decision-making organisms. This is done by weighing votes, by rotation in offices, by equal representation in EU organisms, and other means. Whether this principle will last in the future is an open question.

COALITION-BUILDING

Coalitions are built in order to provide a payoff to each of the participants. Every participant will expect a share of the payoffs at least proportional to the amount of resources contributed to a coalition (Gamson, 1961, p. 376). Also, it is possible that a party as a lastcomer or new-comer can get more depending on that party's role in the coalition (see Riker & Brams, 1973/74). The bigger the payoff, the better. In the case of the EU this proportionality of gains and costs is not put into practice. There are net payers and net beneficiaries. The community spirit tries to equalize differences in wealth.

For a certain period of time agreements among coalition partners can stabilize majority decisions. Such institutionalized coalition governments are common in many parliamentary democracies. Specific agreements on certain matters, like exchange deals or personal questions, are reached through linkages. In the case of the EU, again, there is—with very few exceptions—no such thing as a stable coalition pattern. Nevertheless Helen Wallace has shown that the French-German tandem played a decisive role in the promotion of the Single European Act. On various occasions the relatively stable France-Germany coalition contrasted with relatively short-lived coalitions between France and Belgium. On the whole the interesting thing about coalition-building is the observation that there is not one decisive criterion for such a get-together. Neither ideological alignments among Social Democrats or Christian Democrats, nor cultural affinities (such as among Anglo-Saxons or Latin countries), nor common historical experiences (such as former war alliances) alone determine the formation of coalitions in the EU. There are rather ad hoc alliances such as among the free-trade UK, Benelux, Denmark, and Germany as against the protectionist France, Italy, and Greece; or among the environmental Germany, the Netherlands, and Denmark (together with the three new EU states) against the anti-environmental Greece, Italy, Spain, Portugal, Ireland, and Belgium (Sbragia, 1996, p. 238). Other, more permanent coalitions arise from the global view on Europe's finality. There are, on the one hand, countries favoring a closer European Union with a more federal outlook (Germany, the Benelux, Spain, Austria, and to a lesser degree, Italy) and, on the other hand, countries favoring looser intergovernmental approaches (the UK, Denmark, and to a lesser degree, France and Greece). A third category can be added, consisting of countries with a supranational outlook (Finland, Greece, Sweden, Ireland, Portugal, and to a lesser degree, France, Spain, Italy, and Denmark). The differences determine to a large degree their proposals for the institutional reform of the EU.

SETTING QUOTAS AND PROPORTIONS

At least theoretically, institutionalized or informal forms of representation allow a proportional participation of the most important political and social forces (Lehmbruch, 1967, p. 7; Nordlinger, 1972, pp. 22–24). The weighting of the votes in the European Council secures some sort of proportional representation of the member countries. In some cases the setting of quota and proportions can lead to stable decisions (Hypothesis VI)—though with limited success, because of the tensions among heterogeneous groups, or because the quota did not include all or favored some groups.

The idea of proportional representation finds its expression in a variety of forms in all EU institutions. The representation of all member states is reflected in the number of Parliament seats that are approximately proportional to the size of the population; all member states are represented in the commission (the bigger countries have two seats), and the weighing of votes is introduced in the council in cases of qualified majority voting. In addition all countries have one representative in the Court of Justice, and the interest groups of the member countries are represented in the Social and Economic Committee. The Committee of Regions consists of representatives of states (Länder), regions, provinces, or municipalities proportional to the size of the member countries. These modes of participation with proportional representation protect possible minority positions but, by way of a veto in cases of unanimity voting or of fixed proportions for individual countries, create a bias in favor of the smaller countries.

Another form of quotas consists in fixing a certain quantity or quality to commercial goods in the foreign trade. The agreement reached in mid-1996 by the EU culture ministers on a system of quotas on television productions is an example of that sort. The nonbinding character and the exemption of new services of the accord reflects a compromise between the French-led supporters of tougher quotas and quota opponents led by Britain and Germany.

ENLARGEMENT OR DIFFERENTIATION OF THE SUBJECT MATTER

The enlargement of the subject matter to be decided through addition or exchange can lead to consensual solutions (Hypothesis VIII). In the same way, parts of a package deal can be excluded or declared nonconsensual (see Rules of Decision Making). An example is the argument of "vital interests" in the EC's Luxembourg Compromise of 1966. Another common way to differentiate an unspecified item, like oil or wages, is to split it up in parts (oil: quantity, quality, kind) or add specifics (wages: additional wage costs). Thus, a conclusion can be reached, like price fixing or wage increases (see Rothstein, 1979; Pfetsch, 1987, pp. 269–270).

EXCHANGE OR LINKAGE

Further means to promote acceptable settlements of opposing interests are exchange and linkage (see Hypothesis VIII and Issues). In the United States, log-rolling is an exchange technique by which specific singular interests, otherwise not acceptable to a majority, are linked (see Breyer, 1981). An older strategy of conflict regulation is the coupling of two matters and/or offices; this was a tradition in the multi-ethnic Habsbourg empire; in today's Republic of Austria it was possible to exchange the Foreign Ministry post against the increase in milk prices. In the Federal Republic of Germany, the NATO double-track resolution can be seen as a rather peculiar variant of a supposed coupling.

The linkage techniques are rather common in EU negotiations. Weber and Wiesmeth (1991) show how issue linkage can enhance cooperation using examples from the European Community, the Common Agricultural Policy, and the European Monetary System. The agreement of one particular country to a proposal from others can be linked to compensations in other fields. The peripheral countries, such as Ireland, Portugal, and Greece, are especially likely to link their pro-European engagements to their share of the structural or cohesion funds. Another example is the negotiation of the single market in which vertical measures for particular products were linked to horizontal measures, such as the right of establishment (see H. Wallace & A. R. Young, in H. & W. Wallace, 1996, p. 150).

DELAY

In the process of decision making there is always the danger of missing the target, of driving into a dead end or encountering a tension-loaded atmosphere. In these cases a transfer to committees is often necessary to cool down the temper, win time, or update information. Another means of breaking a deadlock is a reference to further regulating and executing laws. This often happens during negotiations of constitutional drafts or rules that will need further specifications in the future. This strategy could mean a way out of a deadlock when there exists an unwillingness to decide.

Delays in the Community are often results of a not (yet) existing consensus in a particular policy field. For example, when Jacques Delors took office as president of the European Commission he visited all the capitals of the member-states in order to find out possible fields of action. As a result he postponed foreign and security policies and concentrated on the Economic and Monetary Union as well as on financial issues (Delors Plan I and II). The setting of a timetable is another form of delaying political programs. A time schedule, on the one hand, half-binds the actors; on the other hand, it gives opportunities to revise and modify policy plans according to changing conditions. Thus the schedule for the Currency Union, with its requirements and conditions for the transition phases, provides open delays or noncompliance. Something similar happened in the 1970s when the Werner plan, which foresaw the realization of a Monetary Union already for the '70s and '80s, was not put into practice.

ESCAPE INTO GENERALIZATIONS OR IDEOLOGIZATION

The escape into non-binding generalizations or radical ideologization is one form of avoiding a decision on a specific and concrete item (see Binding and Nonbinding Decisions). The item can be disguised behind ideological phrasing (sometimes called political or "blue-sky" propositions); seen from the actor's position, the advantage of ideological catch words is their wide-range appeal to everyone without mentioning a specific item. In this way, problematic redistributions are avoided and a heterogeneous assembly can continue to operate and demonstrate its unity to the outside.

COSTS AND BENEFITS

Decision-making processes produce costs that increase with the size of the assembly, though the external risks may diminish accordingly (Hypothesis III). The procedural and organizational rules, too, may influence an assembly's running costs and/or additional costs later on. Internally, unanimous decision making is cost intensive, but it is low in additional costs afterwards. Majority decision making is less cost intensive in producing decisions, but may cause higher costs with regard to external risks (Hypothesis XIII). Another feature of the size of assemblies is the respective value of each vote. The value will decrease when the number of members increases (Hypothesis II).

In the case of the EU it has been said that negotiations cannot be understood in the light of rational-choice approaches (Keck, 1995; Schneider, 1994; Allan, 1984). Neither can fixed preferences nor rational cost-benefit calculations be the basis of the establishment of procedures and EU institutions. Rather a more holistic approach, such as the social communication theory, seems to be appropriate to understand and explain negotiation processes in the EU and with its outside world (see Habermas, 1981; Müller, 1994).

OUTCOMES

After having dealt with the independent variables—the conditions and the instruments of the decision-making process in assemblies—we are now dealing with the dependent variable—the outcome of the decision-making process. We will be dealing with the objectives, the assembly performance, and the outcomes of assembly processes. Outcome variables are non-decisions, partial decisions, radical decisions, ambiguous decisions, stable decisions, conservative or progressive decisions, and future-oriented decisions.

The analysis of decision processes has revealed a multitude of dependencies between the independent variables of "framework" and "means" on the one hand, and the dependent variables of "value of decisions" and "costs" on the other hand. Different parts of the framework may influence each other, or, depending on the subject matter, means and framework are exchangeable. Dependent and independent variables may also have reversible relations. A theory of decision making with a wider range cannot indicate the goals or, in general, the performance of assemblies in any material way, but only specify their formal aspects. The assemblies that are analyzed here all have the common feature of coming from different positions and wanting to produce a common policy; assemblies that are convened only to discuss or clarify certain points of view are not included. Structural conditions and the use of means can support or hamper the following assembly performances.

NON-DECISIONS

The non-decision on a material item can be one of the results of a decision-making process. A decision on non-decision can be produced by a very heterogeneous group with highly dissenting interests, or it can be used as a strategy to avoid unfavorable results. Both considerations played a role during the period of the French boycott of community meetings which became known as the policy of the empty chair in the 1960s. Or a veto against a proposal can express a general opposition on the part of one country as in the present case of Great Britain as a revenge for the sanctions on the export of British beef. The potential for consensual solutions increases with the ideological or programmatic proximity of the different groups (Hypothesis VII) or with larger packages, that is with more subject matter to decide on. Internal or external pressure can accelerate or delay a decision (Hypotheses X and XI). Compromises become more likely when the groups estimate that a matter in the future (such as participation in a coalition government or campaigning) is more important than an actual topic (Hypothesis XI). The level of consensus is an equally important aspect of decisions on regulations for elections and voting. A high basic consensus facilitates majority decisions; divergent interests favor unanimous decision (Hypothesis XII).

Deadlocks in the decision process can be broken by delay or adjourn-
ment. One way to defer a matter is to transfer it to committee. In committees experts can produce and handle more information.

Thus one important technique of political actors is to create non-decisions when decisions might be inimical to their interests. Such a technique is secured by the principle of unanimity in the various
policy-making bodies of the EU—foremost on issues of high politics. The
Community gives many examples of this strategy, such as the numerous
plans, proposals, and reports produced by special committees for the further development of the Community. Most of them became obsolete
shortly after their publication like the Fouchet Plans in the 1960s; others
became concrete policies like the Werner or the Delors Plans. Also, social
programs are very unpopular with a substantial number of influential EU
members, and whenever they are put on the agenda they run the risk of
being cut back or even cut out.

PARTIAL DECISIONS

A solution can cover the entire subject matter or just parts of it (partial decision). Broad decisions can be reached through enlargement and differentiation (Hypothesis VIII) or exchange and linkage. Partial decisions can
symbolize the lowest common denominator in cases of sharp differences
in opinions among member governments. Scharpf (1988) holds that in the
EU as well as in federal systems, countervailing forces among actors at the
various levels of decision making create a so-called decision-trap
(Entscheidungsfalle). This implies an inability to move to more progressive
visions and a tendency to stick with conservative solutions. Peters (1994)
argues that the opposite could be true. Because of its openness—and I
would like to add because of its elite structure—the EU can channel demands from social groups more easily than national governments can. "The
fragmentation of the institutions and the multiple points of access permit
policy entrepreneurs within the EC to have the system consider a wide
range of options" (Peters, 1994, p. 24).

RADICAL RESOLUTIONS

A nonbinding general statement, that is a nonbinding radicalization or
ideologization, can also be the answer when highly heterogeneous
groups struggle to reach binding material decisions (Hypothesis IX).
Pragmatic solutions are common when the assembly is forced to reach a

binding solution. The particular structure of the EU does not allow radical solutions but rather pragmatic ones (see Representativity).

AMBIGUOUS DECISIONS

Decision-making processes may also produce a choice of options when there is no need for binding decisions (ambiguous decision). The result will be realistic and pragmatic recommendations (Hypothesis IX) unless this situation leads to empty phrases, irresponsible demands or overgeneralizations. Compromises are also ambiguous decisions, since they account for both sides and can, thus, be interpreted in different ways. The diverting interests of EU actors in policy matters can in some instances only be brought together by this form of decision formula. It could be the minimum consensual platform for otherwise diverting interests.

MAJORITY DECISIONS AND COMPROMISE

An outcome either reflects just the numeric majority or it includes minority positions. Majority positions are successfully implemented when the majority is not forced to compromise; minorities have their chance to influence the decision process when the majority party is split or a big party has no absolute majority and needs a small party as its coalition partner (Hypothesis V).

A fairly large assembly under time pressure favors the majority positions compared to smaller assemblies without time pressure (Hypothesis IV). According to the EU-community law the majority rule must be applied on specified issues, especially on the common market and on not-so-common fields like foreign and security policies. In reality, however, even in these fields a consensual approach is preferred to majority voting.

STABLE AND UNSTABLE DECISIONS

Decisions either become stable in time or must be revised, rejected, or modified. The stability of decisions depends on a great number of factors. Decisions tend to be stable when they have been reached without time or power pressure (Hypothesis IV), with a high consensus (Hypothesis VI), on the basis of unanimous decision making (Hypothesis XIII and XIV), or with respect to the further scope of action (Hypothesis XI). Representativity alone, such as with fixed quota, does not suffice, unless there is a high consensual potential, such as through ideological or programmatic proximity among the organized members (Hypothesis VII and Setting of Quota and Proportions). Those coalition governments with a barely sufficient majority have shown themselves to be relatively stable. In the EU the practice of voting follows a pattern of consensus and is not a "tyranny of the majority." This is caused by the expectation of other, more stable decisions in the future.

CONSERVATIVE OR PROGRESSIVE DECISIONS

Decisions reached in a group process are aimed either at the preservation of the status quo or at initiating change. Unanimous decision making favors status quo - oriented decisions (Hypothesis XIV); majority decision making is more flexible and holds more options for change. Thus such countries as Germany, the Benelux states, Italy, Greece, Portugal, and Spain, which are willing to deepen or/and widen the EU, favor qualified majority voting in the council in the field of foreign and security policies (as well as in other policy fields such as those of justice and home affairs). Those countries reluctant or even refraining from the integration process, such as the UK, Denmark, and Ireland, want to keep unanimity voting. Thus, the preservation of a veto position can prevent necessary changes and stabilize the status quo.

However, in EU assemblies both types of outcomes are possible, and the result depends, of course, not only on the rules of the game. Political will is the decisive factor and where there is will there is a way, which could result in a change of the rules. A majority of governments like the British and the Danish want to preserve national competencies as much as possible. Others expect a federal European state and are, therefore, prepared to concede more competencies to a third-level organization such as the EU.

FUTURE-ORIENTED DECISIONS

Last, but not least, solutions of a decision-making process can refer to a future matter or a current topic. Negotiations among coalition partners over future government participation or electoral campaigns require the will to compromise (Hypothesis XI). Instead of short-term gains the agents may prefer a long-term benefit. Gains in the long run may engage short-term costs.

Many decisions in EU organisms can be seen in this perspective. It could be that actors agree with one another in the present to ensure consent in future negotiations. It could also be that the vision of a future Europe directs the actions of its members.

CONCLUSIONS

At the beginning of this chapter we asked questions about the specific nature of EU negotiation processes and how processes influence outcome. The emphasis was mainly on two very important aspects of EU policy, namely, the representativity of the member countries in the various bodies, and the efficiency and effectiveness in producing outcomes. These two aspects are connected to the two additional issues, namely, the deepening and the widening of the EU.

Our analysis has shown that there are, on the one hand, general theoretical statements covering the negotiation processes as a whole and, on the other hand, very specific characteristics of each of the EU assemblies.

With regard to more general observations, we mentioned some of the unifying forces that keep diversities, fragmentations, and segmentations together. The community spirit, community institutions, leadership of the commissioners, will to construct Europe and intensify and widen the political arenas in terms of policy fields and members—all these driving forces have so far influenced negotiations in EU bodies that, most of the time, have led to consensus and have worked through ups and downs toward further integration.

With regard to the specifics of the negotiation and decision-making processes in the various EU bodies, some of the differences must be mentioned. Since the assemblies vary in size (15 members in the council and 16 in the Court of Justice), modes of representation, structure and voting procedures, and otherwise, we can hardly draw general conclusions that describe and/or explain outcomes. However, as to our initial question about differences between negotiations within the community institutions and the intergovernmental organs of the EU, we can draw some conclusions since they are structured differently. Assemblies that practice the community method show more evolution than intergovernmental assemblies. This may be because qualified majority voting allows more dynamics and because the process can be geared more effectively by the supranational organisms. Intergovernmental cooperation with unanimity voting has the tendency to preserve the status quo. Also, economic goods can be negotiated more easily with multiple techniques than issues of high politics with more national values. Whereas the former type of negotiation mainly deals with interest conflicts, the latter deals with value conflicts. Hence, we can explain the different outcomes of negotiations in the community and the intergovernmental bodies with their different structural and procedural conditions. Community institutions have a tendency to produce change, intergovernmental bodies to produce more conservative outcomes. Hence, institutions matter and different institutions matter differently.

NOTES

1. In this contribution we use the terms *negotiation* and *decision making* interchangeably. The term *decision making* is a broader term in that it covers the outcomes of the negotiation process and, in addition, decisions brought about through voting and balloting. The outcome of negotiations are decisions, but not all decisions are achieved through negotiations. The terms *negotiation process* and *decision-making process* can be used synonymously.
2. In some cases, selfbinding of actors can complicate understanding; see Genschel & Plümper, 1996.

REFERENCES

Albin, C. 1991. "Negotiating Indivisible Goods: The Case of Jerusalem." *The Jerusalem Journal of International Relations,* 13 (1), 45–76.
Allan, P. 1984. "Comment négocier en situation de faibless?" *Annuaire suisse de science politique,* 24, 223–237.
Axelrod, R. 1984. *The Evolution of Cooperation.* New York: Basic Books.
Axelrod, R. 1985. "Achieving Cooperation under Anarchy." In Axelrod & Keohane, *World Politics,* 38 (1).
Bachrach, P., & Baratz, M. S. 1963. "Decisions and Non-Decisions: An Analytical Framework." *American Political Science Review,* 62 (3), 632–642.
Brams, S. J., Doherty, A. E., & Weidner, M. L. 1994. "Game Theory." In Zartman, *International Multilateral Negotiation* (pp. 95–112).
Buchanan, J., & Tullock, G., eds. 1965. *The Calculus of Consent.* Ann Arbor: University of Michigan Press.
Cobb, R. W., & Elder, C. D. 1983. *Participation in American Politics.* Baltimore: Johns Hopkins University Press.
Cornett, L., & Caporaso, J. A. 1994. "And Still It Moves! State Interests and Forces in the European Community." In Rosenau & Czempiel, *Governance without Government* (pp. 219–249).
Crozier, M., & Friedberg, E. 1979. *Macht und Organisation.* Königstein: Athenäum.
Dodd, L. C. (1976). *Coalitions in Parliamentary Government.* Princeton: Princeton University Press.
Fraenkel, E. 1968. *Abschied von Weimar: Zur Soziologie der Klassenjustiz und Aufsätze zur Verfassungskrise 1931–32.* Darmstadt: Wissenschaftliche Buchgesellschaft.
Gamson, W. A. 1961. "A Theory of Coalition Formation." *American Sociological Review,* 26 (3), 373–382.

Genschel, P., & Plümper, T. 1996. "Kommunikation und Kooperation in der internationalen Bankenregulierung." Max-Planck-Institut für Gesellschatsforschung, February. Manuscript. (Conference of the Deutsche Vereinigung für Politische Wissenschaft, Sektion Internationale Beziehungen in Arnoldshain).

Granell, F. 1995. "EU Negotiations with Austria, Finland, Norway and Sweden." *Journal of Common Market Studies,* 33 (1).

Habermas, J. 1981. *Theorie des kommunikativen Handelns.* Frankfurt: Suhrkamp.

Hadwen, J. G., & Kaufmann, J. 1962. *How United Nations Decisions Are Made.* Leyden: Sythoff; New York: Oceana Publications.

Irle, M. 1971. *Macht und Entscheidungen in Organisationen.* Frankfurt/M: Akademische Verlagsgesellschaft.

Kaufmann, J. 1968. *Conference Diplomacy.* New York: Oceana Publications.

Keck, O. 1993. "The New Institutionalism and the Inter-Paradigm-Debate." In Pfetsch. *International Relations and Pan-Europe: Theoretical Approaches and Empirical Findings* (pp. 35–62). Münster: Lit.

Keck, O. 1995. "Rationales kommunikatives Handeln in den internationalen Beziehungen." *Zeitschrift für internationale Beziehungen,* 2 (1), 5–48.

Kohler-Koch, B. 1994. *The Evolution of Organized Interests in the EC: Driving Forces, Co-Evolution or New Type of Governance?* Berlin: Paper presented at the XVIth World Congress of the International Political Science Association.

Kremenyuk, V. A., ed. 1991. *International Negotiation.* Oxford: Jossey-Bass.

Landau, A. 1990. *Les négociations économiques internationales: strategies et pouvoir.* Brussels: Bruylant.

Lehmbruch, G. 1967. *Proporzdemokratie.* Tübingen: Siebeck.

Marin, B. 1983. "Organizing Interests by Interest Organizations." *International Political Science Review,* 4 (2), 197–216.

Mazey, S., & Richardson, J. 1993. "Transference of Power, Decision Rules, and Rules of the Game." *Lobbying in the European Community.* Oxford: Oxford University Press.

Michels, R. 1989. *Zur Soziologie des Parteiwesens in der modernen Demokratie.* Stuttgart: Kröner.

Moscovici, S., Lage, E., & Naffrechoux, M. 1969. "Influence of a Consistent Minority on the Responses of a Majority in a Color Perception Task." *Sociometry,* 32, 365–379.

Müller, H. 1994. "Internationale Beziehungen als kommunikatives Handeln." *Zeitschrift für internationale Beziehungen,* 1, 15–44.

Müller, N. 1973. *Strategiemodelle.* Opladen: Westdeutscher Verlag.

Nordlinger, E. A. 1972. *Conflict Regulation in Divided Societies.* Cambridge: Center for International Affairs, Harvard University.

Olson, M. 1971. *The Logic of Collective Action: Public Goods and the Theory of Groups.* Cambridge: Harvard University Press.

Peters, G. B. 1994. "Agenda-Setting in the European Community." *Journal of European Public Policy,* 1 (1), 9–26.

Pfetsch, F. R. 1987. "Politische Theorie der Entscheidung in Gremien." *Journal für Sozialforschung*, 27 (3/4), 253–275.

Pfetsch, F. R. 1994. "Tensions in Sovereignty: Foreign Policies of EC Members Compared." In Carlsnaes & Smith, *European Foreign Policy, the EC and Changing Perspectives in Europe.* London: Sage.

Pfetsch, F. R. 1995a. "The Development of European Institutions." In European Union/Southern African Development Community, *Seminar on the Regional Integration Process* (pp. 187–205), Brussels and Paris, June 12–15. Cean: n. p.

Pfetsch, F. R. 1995b. *Erkenntnis und Politik.* Darmstadt: Wissenschaftliche Buchgesellschaft.

Raven, B. H. 1965. "Social Influence and Power." In Steiner & Fishbein, *Current Studies in Social Psychology.*

Riker, W. H., & Brams, S. I. 1973/74. "The Paradox of Vote-Trading." *American Political Science Review,* 67, 1235–1247; 68, 1687–1692.

Rosenau, J., & Czempiel, E.-O., eds. 1994. *Governance without Government.* Cambridge: Cambridge University Press.

Rothstein, R. L. 1979. *Global Bargaining: UNCTAD and the Quest for a New International Economic Order.* Princeton: Princeton University Press.

Rubin, J. Z., & Swap, W. C. 1994. "Small Group Theory: Forming Consensus Through Group Processes." In Zartman, *International Multilateral Negotiation* (pp. 132–147).

Sartori, G. 1984. "Selbstzerstörung der Demokratie? Mehrheitsentscheidungen und Entscheidungen von Gremien." In Guggenberger & Offe, *An den Grenzen der Mehrheitsdemokratie* (pp. 83–107). Opladen: Westdeutscher Verlag.

Sbragia, A. M. 1992. *Europolitics: Institutions and Policymaking in the "New" European Community.* Washington, DC: Brookings Institution.

Sbragia, A. M. 1996. "Environmental Policy: The 'Push-Pull' of Policy-Making." In H. & W. Wallace, *Policy-Making in the European Community* (pp. 235–255).

Scharpf, F. W. 1988. "The Joint Decision Trap: Lessons from German Federalism and European Integration." *Public Administration,* 66, 239–268.

Scharpf, F. W. 1993. *Games in Hierarchies and Networks.* Frankfurt: Campus.

Sebenius, J. K. 1991. "Negotiation Analysis." In Kremenyuk, *International Negotiation.*

Steiner, I. D., & Fishbein, M., eds. 1965. *Current Studies in Social Psychology.* New York: Holt, Rinehart and Winston.

Taylor, M. 1975. "The Theory of Collective Choice." In Greenstein & Polsby, *Handbook of Political Science* (pp. 413–481), Vol. 3. Reading, MA: Addison-Wesley.

Thomas, E. J., & Fink, L. F. 1963. "Effects of Group Size." *Psychological Bulletin,* 60 (4), 371–384.

Tullock, G. 1971. "Federalism: Problems of Scale." *Public Choice,* 6.

Wallace, H. 1985. "Negotiations and Coalition Formation in the European Community." *Government and Opposition,* 4, 453–472.

Wallace, H., & Wallace, W. 1996. *Policy-Making in the European Community.* Oxford: Oxford University Press.

222   FRANK R. PFETSCH

Weber, S., & Wiesmeth, H. 1991. "Issue Linkage in the European Community." *Journal of Common Market Studies,* 22 (3), 255–267.

Welsh, W. A. 1973. *Studying Politics.* New York and London: Praeger.

Wessels, W. 1992. "Staat und (westeuropäische) Integration. Die Fusionsthese." In Kreile, *Die Integration Europas* (pp. 36–61). Opladen: Westdeutscher Verlag.

Zartman, I. W., ed. 1978. *The Negotiation Process: Theories and Applications.* Beverly Hills, CA: Sage.

Zartman, I. W., ed. 1994. *International Multilateral Negotiation: Approaches to the Management of Complexity.* San Francisco: Jossey-Bass.

CHAPTER 8

LEADERSHIP IN MULTILATERAL NEGOTIATIONS: CRISIS OR TRANSITION?

GUNNAR SJÖSTEDT

INTRODUCTION

Since World War II multilateral negotiation has represented a main instrument to build, and to sustain, international regimes. A traditional, common assessment in the literature has been that the success of regime-building has been conditioned by the leadership of the United States (Kindleberger, 1973). According to this view Washington has started most of the significant multilateral negotiations shaping international regimes concerning military as well as nonmilitary matters. American policymakers and diplomats have repeatedly led such talks to a successful outcome. American political power has been a prerequisite for the effective implementation of numerous international agreements. Therefore, an alarming observation is that in recent years the U.S. role as the natural leader in many multilateral negotiations has become increasingly questioned, even by the American political elite itself. Both the willingness and the capacity of Washington to steer negotiations towards a constructive agreement has allegedly diminished, perhaps to a dangerously low level (Keohane, 1980).

Since the arrival of the Reagan administration in Washington in the early 1980s the U.S. attitude towards multilateral institutions has grown increasingly critical. The U.S. government has become more and more concerned with short-term benefits. Recall that at the close of World War II the United States was willing to make substantial sacrifices of short-term gains in order to establish organizations such as the International Monetary Fund (IMF) or the General Agreement on Tariffs and Trade (GATT) (Bordo, 1992).[1] Over time Washington has grown less willing to make costly political or economic investments in order to develop international collective goods like reliable rules of the game for economic exchange. One manifestation of an increasingly national policy-orientation in Washington has been the withdrawal of the United States from UN institutions such as UNESCO (Imber, 1979; Secretary of State, 1990). Other evidence includes the notable change of U.S. diplomatic behavior from offensive leadership to a more defensive posture in important multilateral processes of negotiation (Imber, 1989; Ahnlid, 1996; Hart, 1995). One task of this study is to assess the significance of this development to international political processes in building, or sustaining, international regimes.

Two cases will be particularly examined: the last multilateral negotiations under the aegis of GATT—the Uruguay Round—and the continuing talks on climate change. In both cases a successful, or lacking, American leadership strongly influenced the process. The Uruguay Round (1986–1994) started in a fashion that immediately recalled earlier negotiations in GATT. The negotiations were essentially initiated by the United States. Likewise, Washington performed a major part in setting the agenda and directing the negotiations towards an outcome that would reinforce the international free-trade regime in line with its inherent norms and principles. However, when the Uruguay negotiations reached their scheduled endgame around 1989, the U.S. role in the process had changed dramatically. Instead of acting as a determined leader, the United States now performed more like a *process braker* (Sjöstedt, 1993; Zartman, 1994). Typically, a "braker" is not willing to accrue the full political costs of stopping a negotiation by leaving it or by refusing to accept a final agreement representing costly commitments. Instead, typical braker tactics include delaying the process or warding off costly elements meant to be included in a final agreement. The issue of financial services offers a good example (Key, 1997). In the early stages of the Uruguay Round, Washington had worked hard to have financial services covered by the free-trade stipulations of GATT *(diffuse reciprocity)*. In the endgame, the United States had, in contrast, become virtually isolated in its insistence on *fair* trade rules *(specific reciprocity),* a position that was clearly in contradiction with the fundamental GATT principle of *nondiscrimination* (Ahnlid, 1996). The considerable influence of the United States was necessary to conclude the Uruguay Round, but also prevented the free-trade regime in its original sense from being reinforced in an entirely consistent way. The main explanation seems to be that the United States transformed its role of *leader* into that of *braker*.

Also, in the global negotiations on climate warming, the United States has performed more like a *braker* than as a *leader*. Although the United States made some concessions in Kyoto in 1997, its long-term, consistent strategy in the climate talks has been to avoid costly commitments in the form of reduced emissions of greenhouse gases. The official argument for the U.S. *braker* stance has been that existing scientific knowledge about climate warming and its consequences remains insufficient to motivate the extremely costly measures that are required to reduce greenhouse gas concentrations in the atmosphere to a satisfactory level. According to Washington, a more rational strategy would be to await the development of more cost-effective technology designed to cope with the climate problem (Hart, 1995; Michel, 1996).

Faltering U.S. leadership in contemporary multilateral negotiations has not come as a complete surprise. By the 1970s a debate had developed concerning the problem of *hegemonic stability,* a notion that the preservation of an open—liberal—world economy required that it was continuously defended by a dominant Great Power (Kindleberger, 1973). The oil crisis of 1973 was a stark indication that American dominance of the world economic/political system was threatened. One sign was the considerable concessions that American oil companies, the Seven Sisters, had been forced to make to the governments of oil-producing countries in the early 1970s. Academic assessments of selected indicators seemed to confirm that U.S. issue-specific power in such areas as trade, investment, and energy was indeed diminishing (Keohane & Nye, 1977; Krasner, 1991). At the same time there were no indications that the European Union (EU), Japan, or any other nation would replace the United States as a hegemon in these issue areas in the foreseeable future. Indeed, the theory of collective goods predicts that cooperation between a small number of Great Powers—such as the United States, the EU, and Japan—*cannot* easily substitute for the leadership provided by a single hegemon (Olson, 1965).

These circumstances seem to forewarn that the gradual decline of U.S. hegemony in the economic-political sphere represents a mounting threat to international, liberal regimes. The gist of the argument states that the persuasion of a hegemon is required to make a sufficiently great number of governments forego short-term gains in order to attain more important long-term benefits generated by global regimes. Only a hegemon would be willing to accrue the costs necessary for the effective policing of liberal regimes (Gilpin, 1987; Lake, 1988; Baldwin, 1993).

If the above proposition about a changing international power distribution is correct, the prospect for future global cooperation and regime operation in areas such as trade, finance, monetary affairs, and the environment is now growing increasingly grim. Regime implementation in individual countries will deteriorate. It will become more and more difficult to reach instrumental agreements in multilateral negotiations. The main question addressed in this chapter is, hence, whether there are any realistic remedies for the suggested problems of leadership in multilateral talks. A particularly significant question is whether any individual state or seemingly powerful group of nations, such as the European Union, would be able to take over leadership responsibilities from the United States.

The analytical approach employed in this chapter may be referred to as *role analysis*, which opens new avenues for leadership assessment. A traditional study of hegemonic stability pertains to *the systems level of analysis* and has primarily been concerned with *structural power*. The dynamics of interstate negotiation is not explicitly considered in that kind of study. The focus is set on the compliance to international treaties and the crucial "ranger" mission of the hegemon (Chayes & Chayes, 1993; Victor, 1998). Leadership in negotiated regime-building remains a more neglected topic (Young, 1994). One exception is the conceptual analysis by Arild Underdal in one of the few theory-oriented books dealing with multilateral negotiation; *International Multilateral Negotiation. Approaches to the Management of Complexity,* edited by William Zartman (1994). The Underdal article draws particularly from organization literature. It introduces a useful theoretical outlook on multilateral leadership. Underdal proposes a demand-supply perspective that emphasizes the interaction between *leader* and *follower* in the dynamics of leadership. A distinction is made between different modes of leadership, such as *coercive* and *instrumental*. "While coercion basically comes down to imposing one actor's preferences on some other(s) or preventing others from doing so to others, instrumental leadership is essentially a matter of finding means to achieve common goals" (Underdal, 1994, p. 187). Finally, Underdal's theoretical framework indicates valuable approaches for the identification of the positive conditions for leadership.

The Underdal approach provides a useful point of departure for the present study although it needs extension and further elaboration in order to better clarify the key question addressed: *What is required by a state—or an international organization—striving to perform a leadership role in a multilateral negotiation?* The method chosen departs from a conception of leadership as a *role* that a particular country or organization can—or cannot—perform in a given negotiation. *Role* is understood as *a recurrent pattern of behavior of states or organizations participating in a negotiation, which can be attributed a distinct meaning in the process.* For example, a state or organization may perform the role of *mediator.* In this case the "recurrent pattern of behavior" would represent the intervention of a third party in a conflict. The "distinct meaning" is the intention to narrow the gap between the positions of two or more contending parties.

The *primary objective* of this study is to clarify what is typical for "the recurrent pattern of behavior" associated with *the performance of a leadership role* in multilateral negotiation. The Uruguay Round and the global negotiations on climate change will serve as empirical reference cases.

LEADERSHIP IN MULTILATERAL NEGOTIATION: A FRAMEWORK OF ANALYSIS

Arild Underdal defines international *leadership* as an "asymmetrical relation of influence in which one actor guides or directs the behavior of others toward a certain goal over a certain period of time" (Underdal, 1994, p. 178 and note 1). Manifest leadership may express itself in various ways, as indicated by Underdal's crucial distinction between differing *modes of leadership.* Hence, on some occasions leadership may manifest itself as sanctions or other forms of coercive power. In other situations leadership corresponds to cooperative and constructive interparty communication and perhaps tactical concessions in order to promote mutual trust. However, effective leadership in operation always means that the performance of targeted actors engaged in the negotiation are in the long term guided in the direction of a final, instrumental agreement shaped in line with the intentions of the leader.

Although the basic meaning of Underdal's definition of leadership is quite clear, it has to be specified to serve as a criterion for the identification of *patterns of behavior* indicating a leadership role. Sometimes the performance of a leadership role is highly visible, for example because it is exhibited in a formal organizational structure, which has been set up to support a multilateral negotiation. Thus, in the European Union the commission has been given the prerogative to initiate decision making in the EU institutions (Gould & Kolb, 1964). Other international secretariats have competencies that are weaker than but similar to those possessed by the European Commission, for example, the executive bodies of the IMF and the World Bank (Krueger, 1997).

Multilateral negotiations are usually conducted within a system of formal negotiation bodies. Chairs are typically given a leadership role, which sometimes is purely procedural but on other occasions may be quite important also from a substantive point of view. A major task of the chair is to organize the work of the respective conference or committee and then to steer debate and committee work. The competence and skill of the chair may sometimes represent the difference between success and failure in a negotiating body. The leadership of the chair, or of other conference officers (such as rapporteurs), may vary considerably with respect to form as well as to sources of authority. In this regard Lance Antrim has made a useful distinction between *inspirational, procedural,* and *substantive* leadership (Antrim, 1994).

Leadership roles in multilateral negotiations are, however, not necessarily codified. Indeed, critical consultations often take place in informal groups entirely outside the formal organization of the multilateral negotiation (Winham, 1986). Leadership actions have one thing in common regardless of their form: *They all represent, or generate, the influence of one actor on others.* However, influence is not necessarily leadership. All nations taking active part in a multilateral negotiation are striving to influence its outcome as far as they can, and some are successful, at least to some extent. For most countries this influence is, however, strongly limited. Small and weak states are typically forced to focus on one issue, or maybe only a few, of particular concern to them. For example, in the GATT rounds many poor, developing countries focused on the Negotiating Group on Tropical Products and were able to generate a certain amount of influence in this particular context. At the same time these states have remained relatively peripheral parties in GATT rounds as a whole because tropical products have always represented an insignificant element of the general agenda (Hudec, 1988; Winham, 1986). Leaders in negotiations like the Uruguay Round need to have a capacity to significantly influence developments in all, or at least many, negotiation groups.

Thus, *influence* is a prerequisite but not a sufficient condition for a leadership role in multilateral talks between governments. In order to produce leadership, influence has to meet a number of qualifying conditions:[2]

1. *Cause of influential action.* Leadership is based on calculated actions aimed to drive the process of negotiation in a certain desired direction.
2. *Scope of leadership.* A strong leader should be able to guide the whole negotiation from initiation to agreement, or at least influ-

ence its main developments. Genuine leadership requires a considerable amount of overall process control.

3. *Purpose of influential action.* According to Underdal, "the leader exercise[s] . . . positive influence, guiding rather than vetoing collective action. Thus, leadership is associated with the collective pursuit of some common good or joint purpose" (Underdal, 1994, p. 178). Leadership actions by states or organization tend to pave the way for a final agreement. States that are able to halt a negotiation certainly display significant, international power, but they do not perform a leadership role.[3]

The role of leadership is manifested by deliberate actions carried out by states or organizations that have an intended, beneficial process impact that is widespread. Such actions may be framed in different ways depending, for example, on the influencing method chosen by the actor performing as a leader (coercion or instrumental cooperation, for example). The prevailing external conditions also matter. In this regard *the character of the negotiation process itself* is of particular significance. As pointed out by William Zartman (1994), the essence of multiparty negotiation is the "management of complexity," which pertains to issues as well as to the number of actors involved. A multilateral process may be broken up into a number of consecutive stages recurring in virtually every negotiation, each of which is characterized by a particular kind of state interaction. *Agenda-setting* begins with the initiation of the process; parties are summoned to the negotiation table for the task of coping with a certain problem or problem area. Thereafter, agenda-setting specifies what topics are going to be negotiated, how these issues are going to be framed and approached in the negotiation, and what objectives are going to be pursued. *Formula* refers to the choice of a general approach to problem-solving and agreement. *Detail* means bargaining over specific and limited issues, usually within the constraints of the formula. Finally, *termination* brings the whole process to an end with the conclusion of a final agreement (Zartman & Berman, 1982; Hampson with Hart, 1995, pp. 25–28).

Process stages presumably represent different conditions for state diplomacy in general, as well as for leadership action in particular. For example, agenda-setting in multilateral negotiations is typically characterized by information gathering, problem analysis, and extensive communication between negotiation parties. In contrast, negotiation on detail is likely to occur in a relatively highly structured environment, in which parties focus on specified issues and exchange detailed concessions. Therefore, leadership analysis has to take the current process stage into consideration as an important element of the structure of a multilateral negotiation.

SUMMARY CASE DESCRIPTIONS

The Uruguay Round and the negotiations on climate change are both illustrative as well as problematic when seen in a leadership perspective. Both processes are genuinely multilateral, as each of them involves at least 150 different actors (states as well as international organizations). The complexity of the agenda represents an important challenge for countries striving for leadership. Both cases contain elements of successful leadership as well as examples of leadership failure. Accordingly, these two examples of multilateral talks should represent prolific references for an exploratory analysis of the mechanics of, as well as the conditions for, an effective leadership role.

MULTILATERAL TRADE NEGOTIATION IN GATT: THE URUGUAY ROUND

The Uruguay Round was formally opened at a ministerial meeting in Punta del Este outside Montevideo in September 1986 under the auspices of GATT.[4] This event had been preceded by several years of pre-negotiations initiated by the United States. The agenda of the Uruguay Round was to a considerable degree conditioned by the outcome of earlier multilateral trade negotiations in GATT, and especially the Tokyo Round (1973–1979) (Winham, 1986). A main issue of the pre-negotiations was if a new GATT negotiation was really necessary at the current time. Another principal question was whether the upcoming trade negotiations should deal with a number of "new" trade issues that had hitherto *not* been covered by GATT talks: trade in services, intellectual property rights, and foreign direct investments (United Nations Centre on Transnational Corporations, 1990). A large group of developing countries opposed this proposal. Subtle compromises were needed to solve these problems. For example, for all practical purposes *trade in services* became part of the agenda but was formally kept outside of the GATT context. The work program also included traditional GATT issues, tariffs, and nontariff barriers to trade. The organization set up to handle the negotiation consisted of about fifteen negotiation groups and two decision-making councils for horizontal issues, one of which was particularly concerned with services. About two years were dedicated to issue clarification and technical problem-solving before substantive talks got under way. The general objective for the negotiation was to increase international market access on equal, competitive terms by reducing various kinds of tariff and nontariff barriers to trade. During the process the GATT Secretariat gave substantial collective technical support to negotiation parties. Negotiations could not be terminated in 1990 as scheduled in the formal work plan. The ministerial meeting in Brussels intended to conclude the trade talks failed to settle some of the key issues. Binding liberalization commitments with regard to agricultural goods and services represented two of the most difficult areas. After Brussels followed four years of protracted negotiation characterized by relative stalemate. A principal reason why a settlement was eventually reached was probably that a failure of the Uruguay Round would have threatened the credibility of the whole GATT regime. Issue complexity helped delay a successful end to the Uruguay negotiations. However, the main stumbling blocs were of a political nature. The North–South conflict of interest was a constant undercurrent of the process. The dispute between the United States and the EU over a large part of the agenda was crucial. As long as Brussels and Washington could not settle their differences it was impossible to conclude the Uruguay Round with a constructive agreement. The transformation of GATT into WTO—the World Trade Organization—represented a sort of general face-saving device that facilitated the conclusion of the Uruguay Round.

THE CASE OF CLIMATE CHANGE NEGOTIATIONS

Negotiations on climate change originated from alarming reports from the international scientific community.[5] The major climate change research project, which was launched by the United Nations Environmental Program (UNEP) in the mid-1970s, represented an early beginning of the pre-negotiations (Michel, 1996, p. 5). Another initial step forward was the 1979 First World Climate Conference organized by UNEP in collaboration with the World Meteorological Organization (WMO). Analytical work communicated by the International Council of Scientific Unions (ICSU) was also important in the processes gradually putting climate change on the international agenda (Ibid.). A Scientific Committee on the Problems of the Environment, set up jointly by ICSU, UNEP, and WMO indicated an increasingly sharper focus on climate change. The final Document of the Villach conference organized by the Scientific Committee requested a global convention addressing climate change (Ibid., p. 6).

When more organized international consultations on climate change got under way they unfolded on three different tracks: the Intergovernmental

Panel on Climate Change (IPCC), the Intergovernmental Negotiating Committee for a Framework Convention for Climate Change (INC), and the United Nations Conference on Environment and Development (UNCED). UNEP and WMO jointly created IPCC in 1988. Organized in three committees, the IPCC was to analyze the climate problem as such; to identify its social, economic, and other consequences; and to assess appropriate responses. Particularly, the science report produced by the world scientific community had a great impact and paved the way for the creation of INC, which was established by the UN General Assembly in December 1990 (Resolution 45/212). INC was a more traditional negotiation body than IPCC, as participating nations were represented more conventionally by diplomats and experts from the capitals. The task given to INC was to negotiate a convention on climate change to be finally accepted at the UNCED summit meeting in Rio de Janeiro in June 1992. Climate warming was part of the agenda of UNCED, but was not really negotiated in this context. However, through the comparatively transparent UNCED process, climate warming, as well as other environmental problems, were highlighted in the eyes of large elements of the general public. The attention given to climate change in the media as well as in a great number of nongovernmental organizations put some pressure on negotiators in INC.

The framework agreement for climate change did not contain binding commitments. It served as a platform for continued negotiation on climate warming by identifying the elements of a future climate convention. After the Rio meeting in 1992 climate talks remained protracted for several years. Some progress was made at the first formal meeting of the parties to the framework agreement in Berlin 1995, which designed a concrete plan for the reduction of greenhouse gases. In Kyoto in December 1997 the parties to the framework agreement for the first time succeeded in reaching a binding agreement stipulating the reduction of CO_2 emissions. This accord has sometimes been interpreted as a breakthrough in the global climate talks. The degree of success may, however, easily become overvalued as the concessions made by the United States and other countries that had blocked the road towards an agreement were relatively modest.

LEADERSHIP ACTIVITIES IN THE CASE STUDY NEGOTIATIONS: AN EXPLORATORY INVENTORY

Useful methods of influence in a multilateral negotiation are likely to differ across *process stages*. Hence, the relative capacity of a country to perform a *leadership role* may likewise differ from one process stage to another. A critical element of a capacity for effective leadership may be the capability of easily changing leadership methods and style as the negotiation process unfolds. Leadership studies should, therefore, be comprehensive and ideally include the entire negotiation process. However, this study employs a somewhat simplified version of this approach. The two cases of multilateral negotiation used as reference cases will be looked into through three *windows of analysis,* each of which pertains to a separate process stage. The first window focuses on *agenda-setting,* including "initiation." The second and third windows pertains to *negotiation for formula* and *endgame bargaining,* respectively. The endgame includes negotiation on detail.[7]

First Window of Analysis: Agenda-Setting

In the Uruguay Round the United States played a crucial leadership role with regard to *initiation* and *agenda-setting.* Like in earlier GATT rounds an important element of initiation diplomacy consisted of consultations led by Washington within an initially small but gradually growing group of key trading nations (Croome, 1995). Hence, U.S. initiation diplomacy first concentrated on talks with the EU and Japan, and thereafter involved other significant trading nations, such as Canada, before discussions became fully multilateralized. This early phase of agenda-setting terminated in 1984–85 with a general call for participation in a preparatory committee set up to organize the planned ministerial meeting in Punta del Este. The invitation was directed to the members of the GATT regime, both contracting parties and observers.[8]

The process of *coalition-building* with like-minded countries supporting a new GATT round was substantially bolstered with the help of technical argumentation concerning the need to reinforce the international trade regime. Knowledge and current information about the status of the trading system to carry this diplomatic argumentation was stocked in the highly competent ministries and central agencies shaping the American trade policy. However, coalition-building was also dependent on the production and dissemination of *new* consensual knowledge, particularly related to the so-called new trade issues: services trade as well as trade-related intellectual property rights and direct investments. Economic-scientific knowledge (or acknowledged theory) was needed to demonstrate, first, that the new issues had a genuine character of international trade and, second, how they could be integrated into the GATT legal framework.

Thus, one important element of U.S. leadership targeting like-minded countries, primarily the members of the Organization for Economic Co-operation and Development (OECD), was to *initiate and coordinate knowledge-building and issue analysis regarding relevant trade matters* in these nations. The OECD as such had an important role to perform in this connection, particularly in early agenda-setting. When pre-negotiations for the Uruguay Round started, the large "dissident" coalition of developing countries successfully opposed addressing the so-called new trade issues in the GATT framework, including the Secretariat. Therefore, OECD represented an important instrument for coordination and exchange of information regarding the new trade issues amongst industrialized countries that facilitated U.S. leadership tactics. The objectives and working methods of OECD pushed its issue analysis in the general direction favored by American strategists.

Another important element of U.S. leadership strategy in agenda-setting was an effort to break down the loose "dissident" coalition of developing countries resisting the introduction of the new trade issues. Bilateral diplomacy outside the GATT context had an important part to play in this regard. However, once an organizational structure was established to support the pre-negotiations for the Uruguay Round this institution became an important arena for the struggle between those countries that favored a new GATT round and the "dissidents" that did not. The new trade issues were at the forefront of this confrontation. Led by Brazil and India the dissidents used judicial argumentation based on references to the GATT treaty to demonstrate that the new issues did not fit into the trade regime. The United States had a leading role in producing and disseminating *new* economic-scientific knowledge supporting the opposite position.

The establishment of the Preparatory Committee paving the way for Punta del Este was a clear sign that the "dissidents" were not strong enough to veto, or defer, a new GATT round. Nevertheless, the results of Punta del Este also demonstrated that the "dissidents" had real political clout as special procedural and institutional arrangements had to be invented for the new issues.[9] The talks on these topics had to be kept separate from the negotiations on goods in special negotiating bodies that were formally not part of the GATT system. This was a considerable concession to the "dissidents" in the procedural power game of the Uruguay Round.

The crucial U.S. leadership continued also after Punta del Este although under slightly new and more favorable conditions. Once the formal decision had been taken to start the Uruguay Round, negotiations were transferred to Geneva and for all practical purposes also to GATT. Then the option for the "dissident" group was significantly curtailed to employ legal arguments to hinder progress in the talks on the issues. Negotiations were soon conducted within an elaborate network of formal institutions including specialized Negotiation Groups for all issue areas, including the "new trade issues" that were formally negotiated *outside* GATT.

The contributions of committee chairpersons and the GATT Secretariat to the process of agenda-setting clearly facilitated the negotiation process. For example, the chairperson established a work program and a schedule for his—or her—committee and watched over its implementation. The GATT Secretariat recorded the discussions held at committee sessions, provided necessary background information to the committee work process and recurrently summarized the positions taken by individual negotiating parties. However, although this influence evidently was quite significant *it did not represent genuine leadership* as it was ultimately controlled by negotiating parties. Hence, the GATT Secretariat was not permitted to take any initiative of its own. The support provided by the Secretariat was commissioned by negotiating parties. Committee chairpersons may appear to have had more leeway than Secretariat officials but in reality their political room of maneuver was also very narrow. Everything a chairperson did to influence the negotiation process needed approval by negotiating parties, which provided the real leadership to the Uruguay Round.

The direction to agenda-setting and issue clarification was primarily given in the interaction of negotiation parties participating in the Uruguay Round. Government contributions to the negotiation was essentially of two different types: submission of prepared papers and oral statements "at the table." The interventions made by individual participants varied considerably depending on issue, countries involved, or external conditions. However, altogether state submissions constituted a certain pattern. The work in the Negotiation Groups was driven by proposals put forward by a few leading countries, and particularly the EU and the United States. The submissions of these countries framed agenda-setting discussions. Other countries made proposals that added information, clarified arguments, or suggested compromise solutions to conflicts of interest regarding minor issues. However, all these interventions were ultimately motivated and constrained by the submissions made by the Great Powers.

The creation, dissemination, and employment of science-based consensual knowledge was also of critical importance in the initiation of *the global negotiations on climate change.* The role and significance of the scientific community was, however, quite different than it had been in the Uruguay

Round. There theory-oriented academic economists had contributed to facilitate the definition of the new issues (services, intellectual-property rights, and trade-related investments) as trade but under the strict control of national governments. In sharp contrast, the climate negotiations had been initiated and driven by elements of the international scientific community supported by a few international organizations.

At first the climate talks were highly fragmented and unfolded in several settings. These discussions can be traced back to 1957–58, which was the International Geophysical Year (Michel, 1996, p. 2). The climate issue was on the agenda of the 1972 UN conference on the Human Environment but did not generate any particular political action. However, the UN Environmental Program (UNEP)—a result of the Stockholm conference—immediately became engaged in the problem of climate change. One manifestation of this interest was the research programs related to climate change and the First World Climate Conference in 1979 organized jointly with the World Meteorological Organization (WMO).

Together with the International Council of Scientific Unions (ICSU), UNEP and WMO provided important elements of leadership to the early, and still informal, pre-negotiations on climate change. Considerable resources were allocated to research on the causes and consequences of climate warming. The interested organizations supplied instruments for the coordination of research and, hence, contributed to focusing the international consultations. The UNEP and WMO represented an interface for the communication between the research community and policymakers at both the national and the international level. The Scientific Committee on the Problems on the Environment, sponsored by ICSU, UNEP, and WMO, was a concrete manifestation of the organizational support to the scientific community.

At the end of the 1980s national governments had become heavily involved in international climate talks. The purpose was typically to highlight the seriousness of the climate problem and to assess its causes and effects. One important accomplishment was the establishment in 1988 of Intergovernmental Panel on Climate Change (IPCC), which organized, formalized, and multilateralized international consultations on climate change. The work of IPCC mobilized political support for the climate issue in other negotiation bodies.

A special feature of IPCC was that its work process was *not* effectively controlled by national governments. The IPCC's scientific assessment was authoritative because it had been produced by an interdisciplinary layer of the competent world scientific community. By confirming that climate warming is a real problem with the help of scientific models and facts IPCC produced a strong motivation for international negotiation. The analysis of the models used in IPCC largely determined the agenda for the anticipated negotiations. Furthermore, IPCC offered a clear focus for the negotiations; provided carefully developed negotiation concepts (such as greenhouse gases or sinks); and indicated a negotiation approach: the reduction of emissions of identified greenhouse gases. Agenda-setting had functioned as a learning process with scientists as "teachers" and policy-makers as "pupils."

SECOND WINDOW OF ANALYSIS: FORMULA NEGOTIATIONS

A classic feature of the GATT rounds was *formula negotiation* on linear—over-the-board—reductions of tariffs on goods. An explicit formula was needed to manage a fundamental and problematic negotiation problem: how to coordinate and multilateralize the results of bilateral tariff talks regarding a particular issue. The formula determined a collective objective, such as average 50 percent tariff cuts. Such a linear tariff formula had been tried out unsuccessfully in the so-called Dillon Round in 1960, was developed and applied in the Kennedy Round (1964–67), and was further elaborated and refined in the Tokyo Round (1973–79). When the linear tariff formula was introduced into the Uruguay negotiation it was accepted with little negotiation, and this only concerned details. In contrast, formula negotiations became politically difficult and technically complex in several other issue areas, especially those concerning trade in agricultural goods and the so-called new trade issues (services, intellectual property rights, and trade-related investments). In most issue areas formula negotiations in the Uruguay Round involved several, or even many, countries, and sometimes also a few international organizations. For example, a model used to compare and aggregate different types of subsidy, which had originally been developed in the OECD, represented an important input into the formula discussions in the agricultural area. In several important issue areas, for example agriculture and services trade, different formulas were competing with one another. Usually, the EU and the United States confronted each other in these strategic talks. For example, in the early agenda-setting negotiations on services trade the United States still strove for unconditional liberalization, such as the elimination of government regulations effecting trade flows. The EU approach was to distinguish between trade-effecting regulations that were legitimate and those that were not when the GATT regime was used as a criterion.

The pattern of state interaction unfolding in the formula negotiations in the Uruguay Round was similar to that in agenda-setting. Committee chairpersons continued to organize negotiation work and to lead diplomatic discussion "at the table." Secretariat support in the form of circulated protocols from formal meetings and recurrently revised negotiated texts were seemingly indispensable. Country submissions produced new ideas for technical problem-solving and clarified the political, controversial issues as well as party positions. However, in the formula negotiations the main moving force in the Uruguay process continued to be the exchange of major proposals tabled by a few Great Powers. The interaction between the EU and the United States was especially important in this regard. However, other actors like Japan and Canada also contributed to frame the formula negotiation. The identity of leading actors varied somewhat across issue areas and included individual states as well as coalitions of nations. For example, in the agricultural sector the coalition of free-traders called the Cairns group belonged to the small number of actors contributing to drive the process.[10]

The Framework Agreement for Climate Change of 1992 may be regarded as an official, negotiated formula for continued negotiations on the climate issue. The governments particularly concerned with climate warming had wanted to reach an agreement in Rio de Janeiro including binding commitments by developed countries to begin reducing the emission of greenhouse gases. When it was clear that this objective would remain unattainable at the UNCED conference in Rio the Framework Agreement was developed to serve another long-term objective: to establish viable guidelines for continued international talks.

The Framework Agreement was negotiated between 102 countries at five sessions of INC, taking place between February 1991 and May 1992. The principal actors of the process were national delegations, representatives of the ad-hoc INC Secretariat, and elected conference officers (chairs of the conference and of working groups). The diplomatic interaction in the INC process had certain characteristics similar to those manifested in the Uruguay Round. With the large part of the procedural questions settled at the first INC session (in Chantilly, Virginia, February 4 through 14, 1991), delegations started to present precise proposals for a negotiation formula at the second session of INC. It has been reported that 16 delegations contributed formal proposals to this debate on formula. Three main approaches dominated this debate and gave direction to the negotiation process. The EU argued for specific commitments to stabilize CO_2 emissions. Japan offered a plan for "pledge and review." The idea was that each particular state should make an individual pledge to reduce CO_2 emissions to a certain degree during a certain period of time. A UK-U.S. paper was tabled with a proposal for a "phased comprehensive approach" including a formula for a tradeoff between measures concerning emissions and sinks, respectively. India, supported by other developing countries, activated the issue of financial compensation for the reduction of emissions.

Only the proposals by the EU and Japan were truly comprehensive with an offensive direction. India was in reality concerned with detail under the assumption that developed countries would be able to reach an accord. The British intention with the text tabled jointly by London and Washington was evidently to induce the United States to make a minimum commitment concerning emission control. Neither the EU nor Japan was able to mobilize sufficient influence to lead the overall process of climate talks. Particularly, they could not change the U.S. recalcitrance regarding emissions of greenhouse gases.

At the last session of INC in New York in the spring of 1992, elected conference officers seemingly provided the necessary tactical leadership to finalize bargaining on the final text, the draft Framework Agreement. An extended Bureau was set up, consisting of conference and working group chairs as well as a few selected delegations. At an extraordinary intersessional meeting in Paris the extended Bureau managed to find a way to eliminate most of the remaining sticking points. A critical element was that the chair of INC—with great difficulty—was able to produce general approval for a new U.S.-British comprehensive text including a minimal commitment for emission control. The acceptance of this text paved the way for the Framework Agreement that was eventually celebrated in Rio de Janeiro.

The INC process dealing with formula was seemingly significantly influenced by external forces. For example, both developed and developing countries strove to build up a common position with the help of activities outside the formal negotiation process, for example in OECD, in the context of the economic summits, or at conferences organized ad hoc. However, the crucial influence came from IPCC, which from the start of INC had provided the skeleton of a formula and hence partly reduced formula negotiation in INC to negotiation on detail.

THIRD WINDOW OF ANALYSIS: ENDGAME NEGOTIATION

As in most multilateral talks, negotiation on detail in the Uruguay Round may be characterized as "editing diplomacy." Bargaining became focused on draft texts pertaining to the various topics dealt with in the negotiation groups but also on a final text embracing the entire result of the Uruguay Round. In most interventions spokespersons for individual states, or for a coalition of governments, wanted to secure a special interest by proposing, or supporting, a particular formulation pertaining to a specific element of the draft text. However, in some sensitive areas such as agriculture, discussion of details partly concealed conflicts of interest between the Great Powers that had been resolved in the formula negotiation. The direct dialogue between the economic Great Powers (EU, Japan, and the United States) concerning politically important questions was to a large extent handled outside the formal Uruguay Round institutions.

Within the formal institutions the bargaining process was closely monitored by the chairs of negotiation bodies and continuously supported by the GATT Secretariat. For instance, the Secretariat summarized discussions, supplied requested background information, and continuously updated the texts to include the achievements attained in the bargaining process. Negotiation groups reported to the major negotiation bodies, called councils, which had a responsibility to package and integrate the results emerging in the various issue areas. Without Secretariat support or planned and carefully organized formal meetings, bargaining on detail would have been very hard to conclude in the multilateral trade talks of the Uruguay Round. Nevertheless, formal management and technical support of bargaining on detail did not represent sufficient leadership to bring the Uruguay negotiations to a complete end at the Brussels ministerial meeting in December 1990.

Led by the GATT Secretariat and its director-general consultations resumed in early 1991 in spite of bad prospects for success. Contracting parties condoned this initiative. An outright failure of a GATT round was believed to seriously threaten the stability of the entire trading system. Thus, the GATT Secretariat provided the necessary leadership to keep the Uruguay Round on the rails after the Brussels meeting. At this point no single country, or coalition of states, was able or willing to shoulder leadership responsibility. The conclusion of negotiations on detail was blocked by serious political contention between important countries. For example, several important developing countries remained opposed to the plan of bringing the so-called new trade issues into the GATT regime. The main political difficulty was, however, the discord between the United States and EU with regard to agriculture, as well as other significant issues. In contrast to previous multilateral trade negotiations (such as the Tokyo Round, 1973–79) the EU-U.S. contention did not eventually generate decisive direction to the negotiation as the two parties were unable to reach an agreement on several significant issues.

In the area of *climate change* the Framework Agreement of 1992 included a formula that negotiating parties could use as a joint frame of reference in future regime-building talks. This agreement described the problem area and indicated a solution: emission reduction and possibly sink enhancement. The formula was acknowledged, repeated, and reinforced at the meeting with the Parties to the Framework Convention in Berlin in 1995. The next step in the negotiation, resolutely moving the process towards bargaining on detail, was to specify commitments (quantities, time schedules) regarding the reduction of CO_2 emissions into the atmosphere. Such initial commitments were made in Kyoto in December 1997.

From a technical point of view the step from formula to detail in the climate talks was in many ways uncomplicated and straightforward. This was due to the way in which the formula had been produced, using careful scientific work at the international level combined with organized communication amongst policymakers in key countries with the help of scientific networks ("epistemic communities"). The IPCC had a key role in this connection and provided leadership to the climate negotiation that was based on a rational and scientific analysis of key issues.

MANIFESTATIONS OF MULTILATERAL LEADERSHIP: A SUMMARY ASSESSMENT FROM THE URUGUAY ROUND AND THE CLIMATE TALKS

Both the Uruguay Round and the climate negotiations had a great number of formal participants. Taking into consideration that the climate talks unfolded in IPCC, INC, and UNCED, the number of representatives of nations and organizations was probably several thousand. However, most of these actors had but a peripheral role.[11] For example, most of the 30 or so international organizations that were invited to the Uruguay Round were observers or participants that only made an occasional statement. Many nations in both the Uruguay and the climate negotiations were *followers, observers,* or simply *nominal participants.* The dynamics of the process of negotiation can in both cases be derived from the interaction of some 30 to 40 actors, both states and organizations. It may be argued that together all these central actors shouldered a sort of collective leadership role. Such an interpretation would, however, be too diffuse from an analytical point of view. In order to sharpen the analysis it is necessary to identify specific *patterns of performance* that in various ways manifest a leadership role; coalition-building, comprehensive issue presentation, identification of joint interests, process management, and process control.

Coalition-Building

It may argued that the essence of leadership in a multilateral negotiation is activities leading to the formation of coalitions. The process includes a number of major decision points. Choices have to made on principal issues, such as whether negotiations should be started at all, what issues should be covered, what framework should be used for analysis and problem-solving, and whether or not a draft for final agreement is acceptable. A major leadership function of a multilateral process is to create and sustain a sufficiently strong coalition in favor of propositions that move the negotiation forward or bring it to a successful end. One example is lobbying in order to secure a majority—or consensus—for a particular proposition. Another principal task of a grand coalition is to take responsibility for the whole process. One illustration is the Groupe de la Paix, which was created by a number of Middle Powers towards the end of the Uruguay Round when the conflict of interests between the United States and the EU threatened to paralyze negotiations.

Comprehensive Issue Presentation

Like many other contemporary negotiations the Uruguay Round and the climate talks were characterized by a high degree of complexity. One reason was the sheer number of issues, actors, and interests involved in the process. Other explanations pertained to the intricacy and technical difficulty of the issues at hand, uncertainty with regard to crucial causal relationships, and lack of relevant knowledge on the part of many countries. Hence, before serious pre-negotiations had begun with regard to climate warming the awareness of this problem was very low in many countries. Concerning some issue areas the situation was quite similar in the Uruguay Round. For example, when U.S. representatives argued for the inclusion of trade-related intellectual property rights into the agenda during the early pre-negotiation few governments were aware of their own national problems regarding "pirate goods" and related subjects. Hence, a crucial leadership task is to inform negotiation parties, or prospective participants, about the issues and their general significance. Once a formal organization has been established for the negotiation, standard operating procedures may be employed to disseminate knowledge/information about the issues. A much more demanding, and crucial, task is to offer a comprehensive issue presentation at the beginning of the negotiation when governments and other actors have to be convinced about the need to start new talks. Such an information offensive requires intensive communication between *sender* and *receiver*, as well as a capacity of the *sender* to fully understand the information needs of the *receiver* and respond to them effectively.

IDENTIFICATION OF JOINT INTERESTS

In order to influence other countries significantly *comprehensive issue presentation* often needs to be combined with a description of the joint interests served, or the collective goods, that would be the result of a successful multilateral negotiation on the proposed agenda. In the case of the Uruguay Round the determination of joint interests was typically made in terms of the allegedly generally valid doctrine—or theory—of free trade. However, for many countries an abstract presentation of the expected benefits of free trade did not automatically provide satisfactory motives for the participation in a new round of negotiation. Convincing argumentation presupposed a certain knowledge and understanding of the position and political difficulties of the particular country concerned. Again this required a fairly intensive communication with flexible possibilities for constructive feedback from targeted countries.

PROCESS MANAGEMENT

Multilateral talks on complex and technically difficult topics like international trade or climate warming require a fairly developed institutional framework to become manageable for negotiating parties. Furthermore, negotiations require organizational support of various kinds, such as secretarial assistance for negotiation groups to provide necessary documentation or to supply records from meetings. Thus, to some extent *process management* may be provided by the institutional machinery set up to assist a particular negotiation. However, it can also be anticipated that such a formal organization of process management would be rather rigid without a capacity to respond flexibly and creatively to specified queries of individual countries.

PROCESS CONTROL

The development of a multilateral process concerning the negotiation of complex, politically controversial issues will inevitably be steered by its own inherent logic, at least to some extent. For example, the intricacy of issues will require extensive room and resources for issue clarification and technical problem-solving. An established formula may be a prerequisite for conclusive negotiations on detail. The participation of a multitude of countries with differing interests and capabilities is likely to create a need for some sort of formal negotiation institutions, including a plan of work and a timetable. The chairs of negotiation groups and other bodies provide a certain leadership by organizing negotiation in line with the agreed plan of work. The chair may also influence process development in a positive way by organizing informal meetings on tricky issues with particularly interested parties. The skill of the chair may sometimes determine whether a particular meeting, or a full work period for a negotiating group, may be concluded successfully or not. However, ultimately the elected formal officers of negotiation bodies are dependent on the political will of negotiating parties to work out an agreement or to establish a consensus regarding a proposal. Formal chairs should be regarded as facilitators of a negotiation rather than genuine leaders. They can clarify sticking points, define common ground between opposing parties, and indicate compromise solutions to conflicts of interest. But chairs are in no position to put pressure on parties to make them accept a proposal. Neither can they bring radically new proposals into the process but are constrained by parameters and restrictions that negotiating parties have established. Therefore, ultimately critical process control in multilateral negotiations can only be exercised by one or more of the parties themselves taking on a leadership role. The typical method of this kind of leadership bringing "political energy" into the process is that a nation presents comprehensive proposals concerning the issue(s) currently at stake that frame the exchanges of parties and give them direction. Such leading papers typically generate submissions tabled by other parties, which may include additional suggestions, general comments, expressions of support, or counterproposals. A variety of issues may be at stake, including an understanding of the problem at hand, a conceptual framework for issue analysis, or a plan for the exchange of offers and requests.

ENDGAME DOMINANCE

In a multilateral process the endgame tends to develop a character of crisis management. Typically a number of minor issues remain unsolved when the negotiation approaches its prescribed termination date. Some of these topics may, however, represent highly politically sensitive matters, which are of such a nature that they can only be solved at the very end of the negotiation process. In GATT several of these problematic endgame topics have concerned the conflict of interest between the economic Great Powers, especially the EU and the United States. An unresolved issue concerning the EU and the United States will block a final agreement in GATT/WTO. At the same time the bilateral dialogue between the United States and the EU will represent a strong political impact determining when and how the multilateral process is to be terminated.

CONDITIONS FOR A LEADERSHIP ROLE

The ultimate question addressed in this study is whether the leadership of *one single, hegemonic state* is necessary to reach a meaningful agreement in a complex multilateral negotiation. The assessment of the cases, the Uruguay Round and the climate negotiations, does not offer any obvious answers to this query. It is clear that in both cases the process suffered because it lacked leadership and because the United States played a braker role during a considerable part of the negotiations. As a result, both the Uruguay and the climate negotiations remained deadlocked for long periods of time. Nevertheless, neither process ended in failure. The fact that the firm commitments to reduce emissions of greenhouse gases remain modest even after the Kyoto negotiations of 1997 does not preclude progress in the future. Successful environmental negotiations, for example concerning ozone depletion or acid rain in Europe, have developed in a similar way. First some sort of framework agreement was established, which later served as a frame of reference for successful, stepwise bargaining on emission reduction. The Marrakesh Agreement terminating the Uruguay Round was very difficult to reach but once established it was heralded as the most far-reaching extension of the international trade regime after the establishment of GATT. Obviously, some political forces must have guided the two case negotiations towards a successful conclusion.

This analysis of the Uruguay Round and the climate negotiations indicates that leadership in a multilateral process is based on roughly five *sub-roles,* or patterns of performance: coalition-building, comprehensive issue presentation, determination of joint/common interests, process management, and process control, trade and coercion (see figure 1).

To some extent, the sub-roles may be substitutes for one another at a given point in time. For example, a Great Power may choose to put pressure (coercion) on a number of other countries sequentially instead of

Figure 1. Manifestations of and Conditions for a Leadership Role in Multilateral Negotiation

LEADERSHIP		POWER BASE	
PATTERNS OF PERFORMANCE	COMPETENCE/ RESOURCES	BACKGROUND FACTORS	
Coalition-building	DIPLOMATIC COMPETENCE		
Comprehensive issue presentation	ADMINISTRA-TIVE RESOURCES		
Determination of joint/common interests	PRECEDURAL PREROGATIVES	ISSUE-SPECIFIC POWER	STATUS
Process management			
	SUPERIOR KNOWLEDGE		
Process control			

relying on cooperation (for example, trying to demonstrate the collective/joint gains associated with a given proposal at a meeting of a negotiating committee). However, the sub-roles also respond to complementary needs emerging in a negotiation. Such needs may, in turn, be associated with a particular phase of the process in the sense that it is there where they emerge. For example, *trading* offers and requests typically pertain to negotiation on detail, that is, the endgame in the present framework of analysis. In contrast, *comprehensive issue presentation* is likely to be in demand in the process stage of agenda-setting and issue clarification.

Figure 1 implies a number of hypotheses about the conditions that have to be at hand for a state, or organization, to perform as a leader in a multilateral context. These suggestions address the question: What is the necessary *power base* for a multilateral leadership role? The case analyses indicate that the power base consists of at least three different layers. One layer is closely tied to the process of negotiation; its components are called *competencies/resources* in figure 1. The second layer is *issue-specific power*. The third layer, finally, pertains to *general structural power* and is referred to as *status* in figure 1.

Four types of process-related competencies/resources have been tentatively identified in the case analyses:

Diplomatic competence representing a combination of quality and quantity with regard to the human and other resources is directly available for foreign-policy action in a given country. *Administrative resources* include various kinds of back-up and support facilities related to foreign-policy action that are directly available to a nation's government and its central authorities without the employment of special measures of resource mobilization. *Procedural prerogatives,* which potentially condition leadership action in a multilateral negotiation, are essentially of two kinds: a formal assignment (such as a chairperson or rapporteur) given to a national delegate, or the formal task and competence of international organizations involved in the process. *Superior knowledge* represents access to scarce information (such as statistics or technical expertise) needed for the negotiation, or to the resources (such as an advanced national, scientific community) to produce, interpret, or frame such information. *Material resources* is an aggregate of various assets that negotiating parties may "draw from" in order to coerce another party or to trade in stakes.

Issue-specific power stems from the control of the values at stake in a negotiation or other kind of power game. In an old, seminal study, Norwegian analyst Olav Knudsen demonstrated that in the negotiations at the so-called Liner Conferences in UNCTAD about international shipping, the issue-specific power of a nation was indicated by the amount of tonnage that it controlled. According to Knudsen the distribution of controlled tonnage explained why small Norway was one of the most influential countries in the shipping negotiations (Knudsen, 1973). In the GATT/WTO talks the control of trade flows (measured as share of world exports) is a likely indicator of issue-specific power. In the climate negotiations "the total emissions of greenhouse gases" possibly represents a corresponding measure.

Above a certain threshold a country's relative share of a crucial, issue-specific power resource begins to create an exceptional capability of performing a leadership role in a negotiation. The critical threshold corresponds to a situation in which a country's share of the values at stake is so large that an agreement without the acceptance of this country would have only limited value. A classic example demonstrating the potential impact of such *exceptional significance* of a particular nation is the U.S. Senate's refusal to ratify the 1947 Havana treaty concerning the creation of an international trade organization.

It is conceivable that more than one country may be of exceptional significance in the same multilateral negotiation. For example, in the multilateral trade talks it seems that the United States, the EU, and Japan are all of exceptional importance. An agreement in WTO excluding any of these three parties is simply not feasible and is in this sense inconceivable. Various groupings of states are also likely candidates for exceptional significance in WTO, for example the large coalition of free-trading agricultural exporters. A united Group of 77 also has a potential to block negotiation in WTO. The situation is similar in the negotiations on climate change. The economic Great Powers are of exceptional significance, and possibly a few other countries as well. It is, however, easier to block a negotiation than to lead it in line with a certain objective. Superior issue-specific power may be a prerequisite for a leadership role but it does *not* represent a sufficient condition for it.

Structural power is usually considered to be a function of the possession of a military capability. The (Neo-) Realist proposition about the usability of structural power is unconditional; it is supposed to be valid for all sorts of state interaction in all sorts of situations. The implication is that military strength is a key determinant also of the outcome of multilateral negotiations. It is, indeed, not unreasonable to believe that military resources are relevant in negotiation on disputes related to, say, borders, territory, or other hard security issues. In such cases war may represent the best alternative to a negotiated agreement, BATNA. It is, however, also clear that in many other conflicts concerning, for instance, economic issues the use of military force would be either excessively costly or simply not instrumental. In such cases issue-specific power is evidently much more important as a source of influence than general structural power. However, it cannot be excluded that structural power does have some significance also in negotiation on trade and environmental issues. The hypothesis implied in figure 1 is that structural power is associated with the *status* of a nation, which influences how other actors perceive and treat it. It has been suggested that the higher the status of a nation the more willing are other countries to listen to its proposals.

The cases of trade and climate negotiation indicate that under some conditions a particular sub-leadership role may be bolstered by a particular competence or resource in figure 1. For example, the *superior knowledge* of IPCC was evidently sufficient to accomplish *comprehensive issue presentation* in the climate talks. Likewise *procedural prerogatives* made it possible for the GATT Secretariat to relaunch the Uruguay negotiations after the failure of the 1990 ministerial meeting in Brussels.

Such simple couplings between a particular pattern of leader performance and power base element seemingly open the way for a variety of actors to perform a constrained leadership role in multilateral processes that is restricted to a particular situation or phase of a negotiation. For example, international organizations may have a superior knowledge, like the IPCC has had in the climate negotiation, that may give guidance to the development of a negotiation. An actor—or state organization—with a constrained leadership capacity is not able to move the process forward for long periods of time, but there is a possibility that a distribution of work may be established with other actors endowed with a leadership capacity that is constrained in another way. Thus, in theory it would be possible for a number of actors with limited although complementary partial leadership capability to substitute for a hegemon able to lead multilateral negotiation from start to end.

However, collective leadership by means of combination of complementary capabilities is likely to be difficult to attain "in real life":

1. Usually, the effective performance of a given pattern of leadership seems to require a combination of several competencies/resources *at the same time* (for example, diplomatic competence/superior knowledge for the determination of joint interests). Often a particular pattern of performance needs to be combined with another leadership sub-role; one lesson from the climate case is that a problem definition based on superior scientific knowledge may represent a sufficient motive to begin pre-negotiation, or even real negotiations. But it needs to be combined with the determination of critical joint interests if a politically feasible negotiation is to be produced in the process.

2. Process control, which is very demanding, is necessary to brake an impasse or to move the negotiation from one stage to another—from formula to detail, for example. It seems that process control to a great extent depends on issue-specific power, perhaps underpinned by structural power of Great Power dimensions.

We cannot conclude unequivocally here what conditions would allow Middle Powers and state coalitions to take on a leadership role in multilateral negotiation. However, the results of the analysis indicate that leadership should not be regarded as an attribute that a country can—or cannot—have. Leadership can be broken down into functional components and may be regarded as a variable capability that may shift from one situation to another and change over time. Role analysis seems to be a promising approach to further elucidate how leadership functions are conditioned by external circumstances.

NOTES

1. GATT, IMF, and other international organizations supported by Washington were certainly constructed in such a way that the United States retained a dominant role in decision making. The point is, however, that the United States could probably have employed its own power resources more freely if they had built up a system of political command and control based on bilateral deals with individual countries.

2. These conditions need to be clarified by means of research. The propositions in the text should be regarded as indicative and hypothetical.

3. This delimitation is somewhat arbitrary. There are reasonable arguments that vetoing, too, should be included in a leadership role, although the opposite decision has been taken here.

4. For a summary descriptions of the Uruguay Round see, for example, Hampson with Hart, 1995; Sjöstedt, 1994; Winham & Kizer, 1993; and *GATT Activities*, 1986–1994.

5. The description of the case of climate change draws heavily from Michel, 1996. For other general descriptions see Hart, 1995; and Houghton et al., 1990.

6. The analysis of *leadership activities* relates to the above descriptions of the two cases. Furthermore, the analysis is also based on data, which have been gathered in two still unreported research projects, in which the author is currently involved. One project concerns the processes that changed GATT into WTO. The project is carried out in collaboration between the Swedish Institute of International Affairs and the Swedish universities in Lund and Umeå. The second project is joint effort of the Swedish Institute of International Affairs and the universities of Uppsala and Umeå in Sweden and the Johns Hopkins University in Washington DC. The project analyses international environmental governance. Michel's 1996 work was produced within this project.

7. For a description of the process stages and a clarification of the distinctions between *formula* and *detail* see Zartman & Berman, 1982.

8. An *observer* country was not fully integrated into the GATT regime. It could either represent a country incapable of honoring all the obligations of the General Agreement on Tariffs and Trade or a country that was still in the process of becoming a Contracting Party.

9. In the two earlier multilateral negotiations, the Kennedy and Tokyo Rounds, developing countries had been virtually excluded from initiation and agenda-setting negotiations.

10. The Cairns group was created in the Australian town of the same name. It consisted of a fairly large group of countries that wanted to treat agricultural products in the same way as manufactured goods in the international trade negotiations.

11. Some participating developing countries remained virtually passive in the negotiations.

REFERENCES

Ahnlid, A. 1996. "Comparing GATT and GATS: Regime Creation under and after Hegemony." *Review of International Political Economy,* 3 (Spring), 1.

Antrim, L. 1994. "Dynamics of Leadership in UNCED." In Spector, Sjöstedt, & Zartman, *Negotiating International Regimes: Lessons Learned from the United Nations Conference on Environment and Development.* London: Graham & Trotman/Martinus Nijhoff.

Baldwin, D. 1993. "Neoliberalism, Neorealism and World Politics." In Baldwin, *Neorealism and Neoliberalism: The Contemporary Debate.* New York: Columbia University Press.

Bordo, M. 1992. *The Bretton Woods International Monetary System: An Historical Overview.* Cambridge, MA: National Bureau of Economic Research.

Chayes, A., & Chayes, A. 1993. "On Compliance." *International Organization,* 47 (2).

Croome, J. 1995. *Reshaping the World Trading System: A History of the Uruguay Round.* Geneva: World Trade Organization.

Deland, M. 1991. *America's Climate Change Strategy: An Agenda for Action.* Washington, DC: White House.

Edwards, G., & Spence, D. 1994. *The European Commission.* Harlow: Longman Current Affairs.

GATT Activities (selected years). Geneva: The GATT Secretariat.

Gilpin, R. 1987. *The Political Economy of International Relations.* Princeton: Princeton University Press.

Gould, J., & Kolb, W., eds. 1964. *A Dictionary of the Social Sciences.* London: Tavistock Publishers.

Hart, M. 1995. "Multilateral Trade Negotiations." In Hampson with Hart, *Multilateral Negotiations: Lessons from Arms Control, Trade and the Environment.* Baltimore: Johns Hopkins University Press.

Houghton, M. et al., eds. 1990. *The IPCC Scientific Assessment.* Cambridge: Cambridge University Press.

Hudec, R. 1988. *Developing Countries in the GATT Legal System.* London: Trade Policy Research Centre.

Imber, M. 1989. *The USA, ILO, UNESCO, IAEA: Politicization and Withdrawal in the Special Agencies.* London: Macmillan.

Keohane, R. 1980. "The Theory of Hegemonic Stability and Changes in International Economic Regimes." In Holsti, *Change in the International System.* Boulder, CO: Westview.

Keohane, R., & Nye, J. 1977. *Power and Interdependence: World Politics in Transition.* Boston: Little, Brown.

Key, S. 1997. *Financial Services in the Uruguay Round and the WTO.* Washington, DC: Group of Thirty.

Kindleberger, C. 1973. *The World in Depression, 1929–1939.* Berkeley: University of California Press.

Knudsen, O. 1973. *The Politics of International Shipping.* Lexington, MA: Heath.

Krasner, S., eds. 1991. *International Regimes.* Ithaca: Cornell University Press.

Krueger, A. O. 1997. *Whither the World Bank and the IMF?* Cambridge, MA: National Bureau of Economic Research.

Lake, D. 1988. *Power, Protection and Free Trade: International Sources of US Commercial Strategy, 1987–1939.* Ithaca: Cornell University Press.

Michel, D. 1996. "The Story of the Climate Change Negotiations." Unpublished paper. Washington, DC: The Johns Hopkins University.

Olson, M. 1965. *The Logic of Collective Action.* Cambridge: Harvard University Press.

Secretary of State. 1990. *The Activities of UNESCO since U.S. Withdrawal: A Report.* Washington, DC: State Department.

Sjöstedt, G. 1993. "Negotiations on Nuclear Pollution: The Vienna Conventions on Notification and Assistance in the Case of a Nuclear Accident." In Sjöstedt, *International Environmental Negotiation.* Newbury Park, CA: Sage.

Sjöstedt, G. 1994. "Negotiating the Uruguay Round of the General Agreement of Tariffs and Trade." In Zartman, *International Multilateral Negotiations: Approaches to the Management of Complexity.* San Francisco: Jossey-Bass.

Underdal, A. 1994. "Leadership Theory. Rediscovering the Art of Management." In Zartman. *International Multilateral Negotiations.*

United Nations Centre on Transnational Corporations. 1990. *New Issues in the Uruguay Round of Multilateral Trade Negotiations.* New York: United Nations.

Winham, G. 1986. *International Trade and the Tokyo Round Negotiations.* Princeton: Princeton University Press.

Winham, G., & Kizer, K. 1993. *The Uruguay Round: Midterm Review, 1988–1989.* Washington, DC: Foreign Policy Institute, School of Advanced International Studies, the Johns Hopkins University.

Young, O. 1984. *International Governance: Protecting the Environment in a Stateless Society.* Ithaca, NY: Cornell University Press.

Zartman, W. 1994. "Introduction: Two's Company and More's a Crowd: The Complexities of Multilateral Negotiation." In Zartman, *International Multilateral Negotiations*.

Zartman, W., & Berman, M. 1982. *The Practical Negotiator*. New Haven: Yale University Press.

PART III

VALUES

CHAPTER 9

JUSTICE, FAIRNESS, AND NEGOTIATION: THEORY AND REALITY

CECILIA ALBIN

Is there a place for justice and fairness in international negotiation?[1] Can such values be reconciled with the very nature of negotiation, as a decision-making process used only as long as it benefits the parties as much or more than other alternatives available to them?

Most of us agree that our interpersonal relations are subject to moral evaluation and some moral constraints. We know from experience that concepts of justice and fairness have an impact on the dynamics and results of many negotiations that we conduct with other individuals. Such notions influence the positions and expectations brought to the table, the exchange of concessions and evaluation of alternative solutions in the bargaining process, and the ultimate satisfaction with and stability of the outcome. In order to avoid constant confrontations and foster good relations for future dealings, we must normally consider what could be regarded as a fair bargain and moderate any inclination simply to maximize gains at the expense of the other side. The social-psychological literature highlights that concepts of justice and fairness serve these functions in interpersonal negotiations (Deutsch, 1973; Bartos, 1974; Lind & Tyler, 1988; Benton & Druckman, 1973).[2]

The study of justice and fairness in international negotiation is relatively new and much debated. Some analysts are skeptical that international bargaining does (or should) take account of such concerns: They sometimes raise seemingly insoluble questions and entrench parties in deeply confrontational positions, and thus become serious obstacles to "effective" bargaining. Indeed, vicious cycles of violence and reprisals in many regions of the world remind us that ideas about justice may lead to war as well as peace (see Welch, 1993). Much systematic work on empirical cases remains to be done, to illuminate the circumstances under which concepts of justice and fairness play a role and how this role is affected by factors such as power asymmetry, culture, the nature of the issues for negotiation, and the presence or absence of audiences (a public versus confidential setting). We cannot, of course, simply assume that social-psychological research findings apply to conflicts and negotiations among states, nor that justice and fairness influence all international negotiations.

The predominant notion from the time of Plato to the present has been that the bounds of justice coincide with state boundaries and that justice is not an issue in relations between or across states. Principles of distributive justice supposedly apply to the contemporary members of a single group or society with shared values and opportunities for mutually beneficial cooperation, and specifically to the distribution of the cooperative gains among those members (Rawls, 1971). Given the absence of one community of states bound together by enforceable norms, governments are often seen as complying with international norms only when this serves their own particular interests and goals (Nardin, 1983).

Do states genuinely allow ethical considerations to constrain their behavior? A number of international negotiations lend empirical support to the positive answers given to these questions in works on political theory and political philosophy (Barry, 1989a, 1989b; Frost, 1986; Morgenthau, 1971).[3] International negotiators often do formulate their positions and legitimize agreements based on principles of justice or fairness, for reasons that may overlap rather than conflict with self- or national interests. The fact that such values have tactical worth, which parties seek to exploit in negotiations, underlines the genuine significance generally attached to them. It is on the subject of *the circumstances* under which justice and fairness play a role in international negotiations that scholarly research diverges the most.

A widespread assessment traceable back to Plato's *Republic* is that power equality enhances concerns about justice and that extreme power inequalities exclude any role for such norms. The perceived reasons for this, however, vary. The acceptance of principles of justice is often viewed as a necessary compromise between egoistic, self-serving parties who are too equal to pursue their interests without regard for the other or to do injustice without suffering unacceptable costs. Thus adherence to moral constraints depends on the existence of a balance of forces (Gauthier, 1986; Rawls, 1971): "We care for morality, not for its own sake, but because we lack the strength to dominate our fellows or the self-sufficiency to avoid interaction with them. The person who could secure her ends either independently of others or by subordinating them would never agree to the constraints of morality. She would be irrational—mad" (Gauthier, 1986, p. 307). Another perspective is that concern about justice is not egoistic in a narrow sense, but driven by a desire to justify one's actions on impartial grounds that cannot reasonably be rejected by others and that can elicit voluntary agreement and cooperation. Such desires and habits of considering the interests of others are more likely to be cultivated in largely equal parties owing to their experience of interdependence and their need to secure the collaboration of others (Barry, 1989a).

It is a consensus view that power equality facilitates the negotiation of just and fair agreements, and that such agreements are more likely to be implemented and durable. They create a state of equilibrium in which every party feels that it received its "fair share" and that likewise the other parties got neither more nor less than that. Some of the sharpest differences concern whether approximate power symmetry is *required* for just and fair bargaining and whether or what kinds of inequalities, notoriously pervasive in international affairs, may legitimately be reflected in agreements that are to be taken as just. At one end of the spectrum, Rawls's argument that principles of justice are only those selected and agreed upon by parties who are ignorant of their own identity, position, and interests is exactly meant to purge the bargaining process of *all* inequalities—in individual qualities and skills as much as in power and strategic advantages (Rawls, 1971, 1958). Discussion and negotiation remain essential in the choice of these principles. However, behind such a "veil of ignorance" negotiation clearly takes a form radically different from any common practice and appears particularly inapplicable to real international encounters, which would fail to meet Rawlsian criteria of a fair selection situation.[4] At the other end of the spectrum, self-interested bargaining with the use of power and tactical advantages is seen as an activity that can produce perfectly just and fair agreements (Nash, 1950; Zartman, 1995).[5]

This chapter begins by articulating several partly conflicting propositions that arise from the literature on justice and fairness in international negotiation. The applicability of these propositions is then examined in two cases of very different kind: one of regional environmental negotiations (the European acid rain negotiations conducted since the mid-1970s within the UN Economic Commission for Europe) and one of bilateral autonomy negotiations (the Israel-Palestine Liberation Organization [PLO] interim talks conducted from 1993 to 1997 under the Oslo Declaration of Principles). It will be argued that in both these cases, issues of justice and fairness have been central and unavoidable. However, they have played very different roles in European acid rain negotiations and the Israel-PLO interim talks, for which the power inequality present in the latter case is a principal reason. Although propositions from the research literature contribute important insights, each paradigm by itself takes too narrow a view and notably fails to specify the conditions under which justice and fairness play the roles it describes.

FOUR SETS OF PROPOSITIONS

1. The Dynamics and Outcome of International Negotiations Reflect the Distribution of Bargaining Power Between Parties. Justice Lies in Complying with Negotiated Agreements.

This is a classic paradigm according to which a party's negotiating behavior, such as readiness to make concessions and accept a particular deal, is based on a calculation of its relative strength vis-à-vis the other side. In a situation of power asymmetry, the stronger side tends to behave exploitatively and to make the greater gains in rough proportion to its power advantage, while the weaker party has to concede the most. Parties thus bargain to secure all they can acquire given their power, rather than their "just" or "fair" share, which may be more or less. The resulting agreement will largely reflect relative bargaining strength rather than any impartial criteria, particularly in cases of power asymmetry.[6] "Power" is sometimes defined independently of particular situations in terms of structural, such as military and economic, resources.[7] More commonly a wide range of resources and abilities, including the skillful use of tactics, is taken into account that can effectively move the other side in a desired direction (Rubin & Brown, 1975; Swingle, 1970; Zartman, 1983). A key element of bargaining power is certainly the value of a party's best alternative to a negotiated agreement, or "BATNA" (Fisher & Ury, 1981). The higher that value the less dependent the party is on reaching an agreement and the more it can afford to concede little, take risks, and "wait out" the other side. A party that is stronger in this sense cannot be so abusive as to remove all incentives to negotiate, but may appease the weaker one simply by offering some advantage over a continued state of conflict on unequal terms.

The exploitation of power advantages and the constant striving to maximize self-interest do not imply that international negotiations are necessarily considered amoral or unprincipled. Firstly, the classic Realist view holds that the selfishness of states is grounded in and justified by a moral responsibility of national leaders to the security and well-being of their own populations. Even if state action is subject to certain universal moral principles, no leader can be required to adhere to such principles (or help another leader fulfill her duties) if this would compromise on his primary moral obligations toward his own people (Morgenthau, 1971, 1948). Secondly, even the staunchest Realist would hold that the voluntary conclusion of an agreement creates an obligation to honor it. Justice is achieved when parties comply with terms to which they have agreed freely and rationally.

The intellectual roots of this minimalist view of justice are found foremost in the moral theory of Thomas Hobbes.[8] In the Hobbesian "state of nature," men as selfish competitors for scarce resources share an interest in agreeing to constrain their behavior, to avoid mutually destructive conflict. Until such an agreement on mutual constraints has been reached, men are effectively at war and have no obligations: They possess unlimited "natural rights" and liberties to do whatever they can to preserve and please themselves, including at the expense of the lives and property of others. The concept of natural rights, and Hobbes's argument that there are no independent criteria of justice or fairness, mean that ethical considerations are inapplicable to processes of negotiations and to the terms of any agreement. Until an agreement is concluded, there are no constraints on what a party may do or take to better its own situation other than the limits of its own strength. However, an agreement automatically creates obligations of compliance, for supposedly free parties have themselves chosen to conclude it and to constrain their actions accordingly, in the expectation of mutual benefit. It is not only morally binding but also "rational" (self-serving) to implement an agreement concluded for mutual advantage.[9] This assumes that all or most parties honor their commitments under it, so that its raison d'être and benefits are not eroded.[10]

In sum, this first paradigm holds that negotiated agreements are legitimate and valid by virtue of having been agreed and that justice lies in adhering to them whatever the terms. There can never be conflict between justice and power (or self-interest) for negotiated agreements will reflect the balance of power, and justice as much as rationality requires that they be honored. Undoubtedly this approach has some explanatory power: Prevailing power relations influence many international negotiations. The question is whether we can, and whether parties generally do, possess such a limited notion of justice in negotiation. The idea that only the post-agreement phase of implementation is subject to moral judgment, while processes of bargaining and the content of agreements fall outside the domain of ethics, is incompatible with most scholarly and popular views of the meaning of justice. Parties to international or other agreements will rarely separate the duty to comply from the *terms* of what has been agreed or the *process* by which it was agreed: If either is seen as illegitimate or unfair, there is a considerable risk of noncompliance (including as a result of domestic political pressures) both in the immediate and long terms. Particularly in situations of power asymmetry, this paradigm does not coincide with broadly accepted or intuitive notions of justice (Barry, 1989a). These would rather, as we shall see, insist on some *constraints* on the exercise of power and the relentless pursuit of self-interest: A stronger party could not simply in the name of justice more or less impose its will, especially if it initially acquired its powerful bargaining position by taking advantage of the now weaker side (Shue, 1992; Gauthier, 1986).[11]

2. Negotiations Are Guided and Facilitated by Shared Notions of Justice or Fairness.

Another paradigm holds that negotiators are driven not only by divisive interests in maximizing individual gains, but also by a coordinating desire to reach a just or fair solution (Bartos, 1974). The concession-convergence model has been particularly influential. It views negotiation as a progression of moves, consisting of exchanges of concessions based on opening positions. The exchanges are usually governed by a notion of *procedural* fairness—namely, the principle of reciprocity (mutual responsiveness to the other's concessions)[12]—and a notion of outcome fairness defined as a compromise agreement at some point between the initial positions. These notions, presumably shared by parties, serve as functional referents that guide and facilitate the negotiations: They help parties to coordinate expectations and concessions, avoid constant confrontations and stalemates, and forge durable and timely agreements that can be justified to important constituencies in ambiguous situations of multiple alternatives (Lax & Sebenius, 1986; Schelling, 1960). The shared notion of outcome fairness is frequently described as a "focal point" or "salient solution" that emerges as obvious and relevant, above other possible options, because of factors such as precedent, custom, analogy, or prevailing norms. A common salient solution is to split the difference, for it requires parties to make equal concessions on their initial positions.

The concession–convergence model certainly captures the dynamics of some international negotiations; for example, over territorial boundary disputes and arms control (Druckman & Harris, 1990; Jensen, 1963). In the Strategic Arms Limitation Talks (SALT) and other U.S.-Soviet arms control negotiations during the Cold War, equal ceilings or freezes and equal percentage reductions based on existing (unequal) weapon arsenals were usually endorsed. However, justice and fairness can play such a coordinating and facilitating role only under certain conditions. Most essential is approximate equality, a condition widely known to foster effective negotiation and mutually satisfactory agreements (Rubin & Brown, 1975). It is when parties perceive themselves as largely equal—for example, in dependency on or gains to be had from a negotiated agreement—that they tend to hold similar or compatible notions of justice and fairness, and realize the need to search for a balanced solution. They acquire the motivation to practice procedural equality through reciprocal concessions to arrive at such a solution (Zartman, 1991), for their equality implies that attempts to forge some other type of agreement may cause costly delays and even fail.

The assumptions of power equality, compatible ethical notions, and a shared commitment to negotiate on basis of them explain the inapplicability of this paradigm to a large number of international negotiations. To the extent that the behavior of parties is influenced by notions of justice or fairness, a complicating reality is that these are often sharply opposing as a result of differences in cultural norms, resources, historical experience, responsibility for the problems under consideration, and so forth. Such conflicting concepts inevitably become part of the dispute itself and cannot guide or facilitate any negotiation; in fact, they may lead to intransigence and deadlock (Albin, 1995a). If there is power asymmetry, the stronger side may not recognize any need to consider alternative perspectives on a just and fair solution or to compromise on its own principles. These are only some of the difficulties that the Israel-PLO interim talks, which I will discuss, illustrate all too well.

3. Concepts of Justice and Fairness, Often Conflicting, Are Part of the Bargaining Itself and Must Be Balanced and Reconciled in a Negotiated Agreement.

More recently negotiation has become viewed as an exercise in which opposing principles of justice and fairness (or interpretations of them) are, and indeed must be, reconciled in an agreement. The task of determining what norms should underlie an agreement becomes a central part of the bargaining itself. The initial concepts of fair concessions and just or fair solutions held by the parties are modified and combined in the process of exploring options, and somehow balanced in any agreed outcome. This results from the presumed refusal of parties to forgo their own principles. In addition, they may acknowledge that norms other than their own are valid and important. In many contexts a range of criteria must be utilized to weigh all pertinent factors, and to produce an outcome that is fair to each individual party and just in a wider sense (Albin, 1995a; Young & Wolf, 1992; Young, 1994). It has even been argued that no deal can be negotiated or implemented unless parties first accept a formula for a solution that incorporates an agreed notion of justice (Zartman, 1995; Zartman et al., 1996). This notion may involve a single criterion, or a compromise or combination of different principles.

Justice and fairness clearly play this role in many international, including environmental, negotiations in which the parties embrace opposing ethical principles. However, once again it applies poorly to sharply asymmetrical negotiations. In these, the more powerful party may not have much to gain from considering a "just" or "fair" solution, and the weaker party may have no choice but to accept what it is offered. If conflicting notions of justice are to form a serious part of the bargaining and are to be reconciled in the outcome, all parties must have the strength to uphold their respective principles and reject any unbalanced solution.

4. What is a Just and Fair Outcome? Internal, External, and Impartial Criteria.

How do we assess if a negotiated outcome is just and fair? What characterizes such an outcome? A fourth set of propositions arising from the research literature addresses these questions. The set differs on the criteria used, including the extent to which an agreement may legitimately reflect power inequalities. Many paradigms, including game-theoretical, rely on *internal (contextual) criteria* and point to the absence of one overarching standard or of universal values by which to judge an agreement (Zartman, 1995, 1983, pp. 38–41). They stress the "rational" or self-interested grounds for negotiating, and the non-agreement point (the value of each party's BATNA) as the basis for determining the nature of a just and fair agreement. A widespread notion is that the mere fact that something has been negotiated and agreed is a strong indication that it is just and fair. Negotiation is a form of joint decision making that takes place when every party to a problem prefers an agreed solution. Even the weakest party is supposedly empowered to veto an outcome that it views as unfair or unfavorable, and to break off the talks (Zartman, 1991). So just agreements are based on principles that parties themselves have, by their own will, agreed to honor. These must be mutually beneficial, since parties strive to maximize their own gains. There is no place for justice or rationality outside the context of reciprocity and mutually beneficial cooperation; for example, for purely redistributive arrangements or for agreements with a party unable to contribute to the cooperative gains (Gauthier, 1986). In the broadest notion *any* outcome is taken to be just by virtue of having been negotiated and agreed, with no constraints imposed on standards or methods used. For if it has been agreed rationally, it must also leave every party better off than in a state of noncooperation. All parties benefit in this sense from a "just" outcome, and it can cover a wide range of options (Barry, 1989a).[13]

However, specific criteria internal to the bargaining process are commonly endorsed. One group of criteria, while too precise to be perfectly applicable in practice, is based on the premise that parties should gain (or lose) to about the same extent from a negotiated agreement. The principle of "equal excess" allocates to each party resources corresponding to the value of its best alternative to an agreement plus half of the remaining resources. Another norm holds that a just solution should give parties the value of their respective non-agreement points, and then divide the remaining benefits from cooperation in proportion to the worth of their contributions (Gauthier, 1986). The norm of "equal sacrifices" holds that parties should accept burdens or make other concessions proportionally to their resources and ability to do so (Pruitt, 1981). "Equal shares" divides resources in equal amounts irrespective of variations in claims, needs, or other considerations, while the principle of "splitting the difference" does so in reference to the stated positions of parties. In Nash's famous concept, a fair solution is one that yields to each party one-half of the maximum gains it can rationally expect to receive (Nash, 1950).

On rare occasions these contextual approaches restrict the conditions under which negotiation can result in just agreements, including the types of leverage and other advantages that may be used in formulating them.[14] The initial bargaining positions, the starting point for negotiations, and any leverage or power inequalities exploited in bargaining may in these cases only reflect a party's own legitimate endowments and efforts to better itself, without taking advantage of another. Strategic advantages or strong BATNAs resulting from resources acquired through activities that worsened the bargaining position or overall situation of another party may *not* be used or define a party's stake in negotiations (Gauthier, 1986; Shue, 1992). Any such past injustices and illegitimate acquisitions must be corrected or compensated before bargaining can result in just, and indeed rational and stable, agreements.[15] Unlike the case in most game-theoretical approaches (see Braithwaite, 1955; Nash, 1950), the use of threats and coercion to bolster the non-agreement point or bargaining positions is rejected: When effective they redistribute benefits regardless of contributions or desert at the expense of the threatened party, and undermine cooperation in the long term.

The use of ethical criteria that are entirely impartial and external to particular situations and interests is as rare in the literature as it is in actual negotiation practice. An important exception is Rawls's notions of justice and fairness, discussed earlier. Paradigms emphasizing impartial and external standards tend to view these as complementing rather than replacing internal and contextual norms. One common proposition is that just outcomes are based on well-recognized, external principles of distributive justice whose general content is independent of particular bargaining situations. These include norms such as equality, equity (proportionality), need, and compensatory justice, which certainly underlie many international agreements (Young, 1995; Albin, 1995c). The task of negotiation is to produce agreement on what principles are applicable and how they may be interpreted and implemented fairly under the circumstances.

Rather than focusing on external criteria, an "impartial" approach delineates general requirements that a negotiation process and outcome must fulfill in order to be taken to be just and fair. It is probably impossible to create (or even identify the meaning of) parity in bargaining power in most international encounters. However, this approach stresses that there can be no place for justice and fairness in negotiations that take place in a coercive or otherwise manipulative context. Agreements held in place by force are clearly unjust, and only principles and agreements that elicit *voluntary* consent without the use of threats or rewards are just (Barry, 1989a, 1995; Rawls, 1971). These can be defended on impartial grounds. They may reflect some power inequalities as well as mutual benefit, but take account of all interests and do not simply reflect the prevailing balance of forces. They cannot be reasonably rejected by an outside observer or by any party to the conflict that examines the situation beyond its own narrow self-interests. Thus the principal measure of justice or fairness here is not the content of particular distributive norms, the contributions of the parties to the cooperative gains, or the value of their best alternative to a negotiated agreement.[16] Rather, it is the parties' voluntary acceptance of the norms, and their general acceptability from any viewpoint, that makes them just. Negotiations that are just in this sense can clearly materialize only when all the parties, by necessity or choice, are prepared to abandon some partiality and consider a balanced solution.

THE CASE OF EUROPEAN ACID RAIN NEGOTIATIONS

"Acid rain" has come to refer to transboundary air pollution generally. Several kinds of air pollutants can travel over long distances in the atmosphere before they are deposited on the earth's surface. The chief ones are sulfur dioxide (SO_2), nitrogen oxides (NO_x), volatile organic compounds (VOCs), ammonia (NH_3) and carbon dioxide (CO_2). Scientific understanding of such emissions has deepened dramatically: their sources (notably coal- and oil-fired power and heating stations, combustion plants, machines, and road and off-road vehicles); their transport across national boundaries; and their damage to forests, freshwater, agricultural crops, ecosystems, buildings, and human health. In the last two decades, multilateral cooperation has become essential in the attempts to eliminate harmful emission levels in Europe.

The acid rain problem lends itself particularly well to an empirical examination of the role played by justice and fairness in international negotiations. First, there is now a rich record of the nature of the problem and of the negotiations conducted within the United Nations Economic Commission for Europe (UNECE) since the mid-1970s to tackle it.[17] Second, the acid rain problem involves indisputable questions of distributive justice and fairness similar to those at the heart of many other regional and global environmental negotiations. These questions arise from differences in contributions to the problem between heavy polluters (such as Poland, Germany, and the UK) and countries that are predominantly importers of pollution (including Sweden, Finland, and Norway); in sensitivity to the problem (given variations in ecosystems and proximity to polluting sources) and gains to be had from regulatory agreements; and in economic, technological, and political ability to accept and implement control measures. Under current schemes for further acid rain emission reductions in Europe based on economic and environmental efficiency criteria, some of the poorest countries with the least resources are required to invest in the most costly abatement measures, to the benefit of richer countries with lower emission reduction costs (Klaassen, Amann, & Schöpp, 1992). Without a negotiated agreement redistributing the benefits and burdens involved, such strategies are unlikely to elicit the necessary political support.

Negotiations over transboundary air pollution in Europe first got underway in the mid-1970s, driven by Sweden, which had proved that foreign sources of SO_2 emissions were primarily responsible for the acidification of its lakes. The 1979 Convention on Long Range Transboundary Air Pollution

(LRTAP), signed by 32 states and the European Community (EC) within the UNECE, established vague obligations to limit and, "as far as possible," gradually reduce and prevent transboundary air pollution. The LRTAP Convention, together with EC environmental legislation, has provided the main frameworks for subsequent negotiations over specific controls and reductions in SO_2 and NO_x emissions. These include the 1985 Helsinki Protocol on the reduction of SO_2 emissions, the 1988 Sofia Protocol on the control of NO_x emissions, the 1988 EC Large Combustion Plant (LCP) Directive, the 1991 Geneva Protocol on the control of VOCs emissions, and the 1994 Oslo Protocol on further SO_2 emission reductions. Some of the reviewed propositions provide powerful explanations of the role played by justice and fairness in the lengthy negotiations that resulted in these agreements.

NEGOTIATIONS ARE GUIDED AND FACILITATED BY SHARED NOTIONS OF JUSTICE OR FAIRNESS

A shared acceptance and reliance on the principle of equality facilitated getting acid rain talks underway. This notion served as a "focal point" coordinating expectations and guiding the emission reductions undertaken by European countries. Equality came to mean equal shares of rewards and burdens for all parties regardless of differences in resources, contributions to the problem, or other particular circumstances. The application of the principle has been reflected in plans for ceilings on, and freezes and equal percentage reductions in, current SO_2 and NO_x emission levels with fixed time frames. Calls for such agreements based on equality were first made, unsuccessfully, in the mid-1970s by net importers of acid rain—notably Sweden, Finland, Norway, and Canada. In March 1984, however, a group of nine West European states and Canada formed the "30 Percent Club." They committed themselves to unilateral cuts of at least 30 percent in their 1980 levels of SO_2 emissions over a ten-year period. In the eyes of many, the Club set a fair standard for undertaking and evaluating abatement efforts, in the sense that all countries would reduce their individual emission levels by an identical percentage. Its formation was a symbolically significant act that created political pressures on other countries to follow suit. Six months later, another eight West and East European countries had joined the Club.

The 30 Percent Club set the stage for the talks leading to the 1985 Helsinki Protocol on the Reduction of SO_2 emissions. It was signed by 21 states, including several such heavy polluters as West Germany, the Soviet Union, Italy, and France, which previously had vetoed proposals for specific emission controls. In these negotiations, across-the-board 30 percent cuts in SO_2 emissions (by 1993, based on 1980 emission levels) emerged again as the acceptable formula to most participating countries among the many divergent positions advanced.[18] A major hurdle in the talks was the argument of the United States and Great Britain that an earlier base year be selected so as to credit them for emission reductions prior to 1980, thus requiring few if any further reductions. Most participating countries viewed these pre-1980 reductions as insufficient and rejected the demand. The final protocol was not signed by three major exporters of acid rain: the United States, Great Britain, and Poland (for its lack of abatement technology). Yet at a later European Economic Community (EEC) environmental meeting Great Britain suggested the same idea of a uniform 30 percent reduction in SO_2 emissions by 1993 (Regens & Rycroft, 1988). Agreements driven by the equality norm have contributed to a net 15 percent decline in overall emissions in Europe since 1980. Many countries reached the 30 percent target of the Helsinki Protocol before the 1993 deadline.

There are important advantages that explain the frequent reliance on variations on the equality principle in European acid rain and other international negotiations. These include intrinsic appeal, simplicity, and explicitness. First, the equality principle converges with common intuitive ideas about "intrinsic" or "impartial" justice ("all countries should be treated the same") and about the proper basis for concession-making if fair agreements are to result. Second, it is relatively unambiguous in both concept and application. It has helped European countries to coordinate expectations and accelerate concession-making in situations of deeply opposing positions on acceptable measures.

However, a closer examination reveals that the principle (as interpreted and applied) establishes justice and fairness only in a restricted sense. It does not account for, and even less seeks to rectify, inequalities in the particular situations of parties. National emission levels of a particular year are taken at face value as the only relevant information and as the just starting points on basis of which "equal concessions" are then exchanged. Through the formula of the 30 Percent Club, for example, countries are apportioned equal shares of the emission reduction costs, expressed in percentage reductions of their individual polluting outputs. But as national emission levels are in fact unequal, reduction requirements in absolute terms differ. Wide divergences in economic and technological resources and in responsibility for and vulnerability to the acid rain problem further contribute to the actual inequality of the distribution of collective burdens and gains. Basing emission controls on the equality principle is also relatively inefficient in environmental terms. The same requirements are imposed on all countries irrespective of their pollution levels or the sensitivity of their ecosystems. In sum, the insufficiency of this approach from the viewpoints of fairness, environmental effectiveness, and economic efficiency has caused it to lose support.

CONCEPTS OF JUSTICE AND FAIRNESS, OFTEN CONFLICTING, ARE PART OF THE BARGAINING ITSELF AND MUST BE BALANCED AND RECONCILED IN A NEGOTIATED AGREEMENT

Divergent norms of justice and fairness have been at the core of European acid rain negotiations in recent years, and have had to be balanced and combined in complex agreements on further emission reductions. A prime concern has been to take better account of the varied conditions of countries by including norms of equity (proportionality); for example, ability to pay for abatement measures as reflected in national income, willingness to pay as indicated by costs of national plans for emission reductions, contribution to the acid rain problem in terms of current and/or past national emission levels, and susceptibility to ecological damage from acid rain as measured by "critical loads."[19]

The difficult negotiations preceding the adoption of the 1988 Sofia Protocol on the Control of NO_x Emissions are illustrative in this respect. They evolved extensively around conflicting positions on fair and acceptable abatement strategies, which in turn caused impasses and prevented agreement on specific reductions. On the one hand, a group of five countries—Austria, the Netherlands, Sweden, Switzerland, and West Germany—insisted on a uniform 30 percent reduction in NO_x emissions by 1994. On the other, the United States demanded credit or some exemption corresponding to its emission reductions prior to the suggested reference year of 1985 (Fraenkel, 1989). The final document, signed by 25 states, reflected a combination of norms. The equality principle underlay the call for a freeze in NO_x emissions by the end of 1994, using as the baseline the year 1987 or any previous year, thus leaving room for crediting pre-1987 emission reductions. If a country selected a year prior to 1987, its average annual NO_x emissions in the period from 1987 to 1996 could not exceed its 1987 emission levels.[20] Twelve parties to the protocol committed themselves to unilateral 30 percent reductions in their NO_x emissions. Also endorsed was the criterion of "critical loads," entailing differentiated percentage reductions in relation to the vulnerability of each country's ecosystem(s) to acid deposition. In subsequent discussions within the UNECE, two additional criteria were adopted as the basis for negotiating new protocols on SO_2 and NO_x reductions: the relative costs of reducing emissions in different countries; and the relative contribution of a given country's emissions to acid deposition in other countries, or "source-receptor relationships."[21] Together, these three criteria tend to impose greater percentage reductions on heavily polluting states, save states with excessive pollution control costs from undertaking extensive reductions, and reward control and reduction measures undertaken previously.

Another illustrative example is the arduous negotiations resulting in the European Community's Large Combustion Plant (LCP) Directive of 1988. The eventual success of these talks is largely explained by the adoption of a mix of norms reconciling the opposing British and German positions, which had dominated the negotiations. The initial drafts of the Directive were modeled on German legislation, and called for emission limits based on best-available technology only (Haig, 1989). Such limits won the support of environmentally activist countries for removing the unfair conditions of competition and unfair allocation of emission reduction costs resulting from their own higher and more costly levels of environmental protection (Boehmer-Christiansen & Skea, 1991). However, the formal EC Commission proposal of 1983 over which negotiations began called for equal percentage reductions by all member states. It stipulated a 60 percent reduction in SO_2 emissions, and a 40 percent reduction in emissions from NO_x and particulate matter, from large combustion plants by 1995 based on emission levels in 1980. The United Kingdom, supported by less industrialized states, found this proposal one-sided and unfair: It was viewed as failing to take account of (1) the high costs of compliance for countries with a dependency on the coal industry or with otherwise high emissions, (2) emission reductions achieved in the 1970s, and (3) cuts in emissions from smaller plants. The ensuing stalemate was partly overcome by a Dutch proposal that countries undertake different percentage reductions based on an elaborate set of criteria. The Directive as finally adopted ruled that all new power plants must be fitted with the best available abatement technology. NO_x emissions were to be reduced first by 20 percent and then by 40 percent no later than 1993 and 1998, respectively, with adaptations made for individual states as needed. The UK was to reduce its SO_2 emissions in two stages, to reach the 60 percent target by 2003. A number of exceptions cut the costs of agreement for less industrialized member countries and the UK. For example, the emission limits could be renegotiated or surpassed for a transitional period in cases of excessive costs of control technologies, technological problems with plants, difficulties with the use of indigenous or essential sources of fuel, and unforeseen and substantial changes in the supply of certain fuels or energy demand.[22]

The preceding discussion has already pointed to how *a combination of internal, external and impartial criteria* has been used in the last few years to forge agreements. The need for such formulas is obvious, if further acid rain emission cuts in Europe are to be at once environmentally effective and sufficient, economically efficient, and fair in the distribution of gains and burdens. A wider range of factors must be considered than a single type of criteria can possibly capture. Recent proposals for achieving greater emission reductions through "cost-sharing" thus combine external principles (proportionality, compensatory justice) with internal criteria (notably the idea that countries should gain to about the same extent from regulatory agreements).[23] It has also demonstrated that in this case the "Hobbesian" notion of *justice as rooted solely in compliance with power-based agreements* is inapplicable. European acid rain negotiations have certainly reflected prevailing power relations to some extent, but ethical considerations have also shaped their course and outcome. Moreover, the parties appear never to have regarded the duty to comply as separate from the terms of the agreements or from the process by which they were reached.

In sum, negotiations over acid rain and many other environmental problems involve central and unavoidable issues of justice and fairness. An important condition underpinning this reality is the interdependence stemming from the transboundary nature of these problems and the absence of sharp power asymmetries. National initiatives can rarely attain targets that are sufficient environmentally on a regional scale or for several victim countries. If coordinated multilaterally, abatement strategies can also be implemented at much lower cost for Europe as a whole and for several individual states. It is an area in which conventional sources of power and coercive measures often prove to be of little use in inducing compliance from "weaker" (economically less developed) countries. Many of these countries exercise veto power since their noncooperation as heavy polluters or potential polluters threatens to render any agreement ineffective. They have much interest in using negotiation to secure new financial and technical resources in exchange for undertaking abatement measures. Thus virtually all parties to the European acid rain negotiations are required or motivated to consider each others' perspectives on fair and acceptable options, and to accept balanced agreements.

THE ISRAEL-PLO INTERIM NEGOTIATIONS

Force and the predominance of power have determined much of the course of the Arab–Israeli conflict to date. Throughout the history of the Middle East peace process, the international community and the parties themselves have also stressed the need to negotiate a permanent solution based on justice and mutual consent. The last few years of arduous negotiations between Israel and the Palestine Liberation Organization (PLO) within the framework of the Oslo Declaration of Principles, signed by Yizhak Rabin and Yassir Arafat on the White House lawn in September 1993, is no exception. The text of the Oslo Accords and the subsequent interim agreements, and statements by Israeli and the PLO officials alike, assert the importance of several principles of international law and justice, including those endorsed in United Nations Security Council 242 and various General Assembly resolutions. Former Israeli prime minister Shimon Peres, a key architect and driving force behind the Oslo Accords, has emphasized that only a solution that does justice to all parties, and avoids rectifying one side's wrongs at the expense of the other side's rights, can be durable (Peres, 1993). At the same time Jewish and Muslim extremists, responsible for the assassination of Yizhak Rabin and the surge in suicide bombings inside Israel, respectively, have proved their determination to derail the peace process, convinced that negotiation and compromise cannot serve the cause of justice.

The Oslo Declaration of Principles, based on the secret Israel-PLO agreements worked out in Norway, established a staged approach and a timetable for reaching a permanent settlement. First, negotiations would result in Israeli military withdrawal from Jericho and the Gaza Strip, the transfer of power to a nominated Palestinian National Authority, and the beginning of a five-year period of interim Palestinian self-government under this authority. Second, a Palestinian Council would be elected and early "empowerment" achieved for the Palestinians in the rest of the West Bank, through self-government in five spheres. Third, negotiations on a permanent solution—including to the issues of Jerusalem, Jewish settlements, refugees, and final borders—would begin by April 1996 (they have since been delayed). The negotiations leading to the signing of the Gaza-Jericho Agreement in May 1994 achieved the first objective. The signing of the Taba Agreement (Oslo II) in September 1995 set the stage for a partial implementation of the second goal: Palestinians gained full control over six main West Bank towns and administrative responsibility for almost the entire Palestinian West Bank population, and a Palestinian Council was elected in January 1996.[24]

Have the Israel–PLO interim talks merely been dictated by the sharp power asymmetry between the two sides, and confirmed references to principles of justice and fairness as empty commitments for public consumption? Have these negotiations been devoid of moral content and largely witnessed the weak capitulating to the demands and interests of the strong, as some analysts argue (Said, 1995; Usher, 1995; Ashrawi, 1995)? If the terms of the Oslo Accords and the interim agreements reflect imbalance in bargaining power, does this mean that they are unjust? As the reviewed literature suggests, the answer is far from obvious: It depends on what measuring rods and particular conceptions of justice are applied.

The interim talks raised both narrow (contextual) and broad (external) issues of justice and fairness. The narrower ones concerned fair and reasonable interpretation and application of the principles set out in the Oslo Declaration serving as the framework for the talks. They naturally influenced the course of the negotiations considerably, and help to explain both the deadlocks and the eventual outcome. And they became prominent owing to the vagueness or silence of the Declaration on several core questions, some of which inevitably arose in the interim talks while formally deferred to the final status negotiations. The Declaration holds that the interim arrangements may not prejudice the outcome of the permanent status negotiations. The parties knew, however, that exactly the opposite would be true for what was agreed in many instances. The broader ones involved principles of international law and distributive justice, which were incorporated into the texts of the Oslo and interim agreements. These principles led the Palestinians to question the legitimacy of the Oslo peace process itself, but barely influenced the actual course or outcome of the interim talks.

THE DYNAMICS AND OUTCOME OF INTERNATIONAL NEGOTIATIONS REFLECT THE DISTRIBUTION OF BARGAINING POWER BETWEEN PARTIES. JUSTICE LIES IN THE COMPLIANCE WITH NEGOTIATED AGREEMENTS

In the interim talks over the implementation of the Oslo Declaration, which endorsed Israel's de facto control over the West Bank and Gaza as the starting point for negotiations, Israel conceded considerably on a few issues. The declared right of Palestinian Jerusalemites to "participate in the election process" became a right not only to vote but also to stand as candidates if they had a second address outside the city. The original Palestinian demands regarding the size and powers of the elected Palestinian Council were largely met.[25] Despite Israel's earlier objections the Taba

Agreement accorded Palestinian villages in the Jerusalem area the same status as other West Bank villages by placing them under Palestinian civil rule. On the whole, however, the asymmetry in bargaining power between Israel and the PLO became apparent. A most contested issue was Israel's conservative understanding of the nature of its military redeployment required under the Declaration. Apart from the withdrawal from Gaza, the Jericho area, and several other population centers in the West Bank, which was undertaken, article XIII, paragraph 3 of the Declaration called for "[f]urther redeployments to specified locations . . . commensurate with the assumption of responsibility for public order and internal security by the Palestinian police force. . . ."[26] It also held that the interim period should preserve the integrity of the West Bank and Gaza as a single territorial unit. In fact, the areas from which Israeli forces redeployed and over which the Palestinians gained control in the Taba Agreement were scattered and constituted only 4 percent of the land of the West Bank. With regard to Hebron, Israel enforced the view that it be exempted from the principle of redeployment outside Palestinian population centers, owing to the small Israeli settler community living in the heart of the town.

Among numerous questions covered in the Israel-PLO interim talks, the negotiations over water resources are particularly indicative of their treatment of justice and fairness issues. Since 1967, owing to its own limited supplies, Israel has taken maximum advantage of its control over the natural water supply in the West Bank. Over-pumping from Israeli wells, including newly created ones, combined with restrictions on pumping from Palestinian wells and on the drilling of new Palestinian wells, has led to a steady decline in the volume of usable water available to the Palestinians (over one million people) in favor of Jewish settlers in the West Bank (about 100,000 people) and the Israeli population as a whole. Currently Palestinians receive about 110 million cubic meters (mcm), or less than 20 percent of the West Bank water supply, while Israel draws about 490 mcm and has a three to four times greater per-capita consumption. The severe shortage has forced the Palestinians to buy additional water from Israelis at a high price (higher than that given to Israelis), hampered the development and productivity of Palestinian agriculture and the Palestinian economy in favor of Israel, and thus contributed to unfair competition and unfair trade relations.[27]

The importance of cooperative and sustainable management of scarce water resources to Middle East peace and security is indisputable. The Oslo Declaration of Principles called for an Israeli-Palestinian committee to work out arrangements for "cooperation in the management of water resources in the West Bank and Gaza Strip and . . . the equitable utilization of joint water resources" in and beyond the interim period.[28] Water became a central issue in the negotiations leading up to the 1995 Taba Agreement. It was agreed that a joint committee be established to manage the water resources in these territories and thus protect "the interests of both parties."[29] One of the most difficult issues in the talks concerned water allocation. In early September 1995, Shimon Peres, then Israel's foreign minister, made some decisive concessions. Following media exposure of the grossly unequal water distribution between the 120,000 Palestinians and 400 Jewish settlers living in Hebron, Peres agreed to allocate an additional 2,000 mcm daily to the former. Overall he undertook to increase the annual water allocation to Palestinians by 28 mcm. Furthermore Israel expressed an intention to ensure long-term growth in the availability of water resources for Palestinians, specifying that it would have to come from new supplies developed with international assistance rather than from a reallocation of existing supplies reserved for Israeli consumers.[30]

It may thus appear as if the talks on water were influenced by concepts of justice and fairness. However, as in other phases of the Israel-PLO interim talks, the existing situation was through the framework of the Oslo Declaration endorsed as a legitimate starting point for negotiations and the exchange of concessions. Therefore the interim agreements on water and many other issues barely took account of or compensated for past events and activities that contributed to the predominance of Israeli power. Among these are Israeli practices in the territories occupied since 1967 that are illegal according to international law and prevailing international opinion, such as the exploitation of water and other natural resources and Jewish settlement on confiscated land to the detriment of the indigenous Palestinian population (Quigley, 1995). The Palestinians stressed the applicability of legal principles under the Hague and other conventions to matters such as their own water rights (Al Musa, 1996). In the Taba negotiations Israel consented to joint management and "equitable distribution" of water resources located in the occupied territories only, at a low cost to itself. Palestinians agreed to share these resources once taken from them and from Jordan by force, even after the end of the Israeli occupation, not because of a change in their notion of justice but because of the need to improve their current status of having no say at all.

Key Israeli participants do not consider the interim talks unprincipled or amoral. Their notions, which pervaded the negotiations, are reminiscent of some of the discussed Hobbesian and Realist arguments about justice. The Oslo Declaration of Principles is considered legitimate by virtue of having been agreed by Palestinians and Israelis acting in their own interest. Moreover, the principles reflect a situation that was largely brought about by Israel's acting in self-defense against Arab armed aggression, and it should be maintained until Israeli security requirements can be guaranteed by other means (Hirsch et al., 1995, pp. 15–16; O'Brien, 1991). The Oslo principles thus provided a rightful framework for the interim talks. The genuine issues of justice and fairness arising in the talks concerned matters of applying and adhering properly to the letter and intent of the Oslo Declaration (Singer, 1996). They did not and could not in Israel's view concern matters on which no definite commitments were made in the Oslo Declaration, such as the questions of continued Jewish settlement in the occupied territories and Israeli exploitation of West Bank water resources. An influential Israeli participant throughout the interim talks, the lawyer Joel Singer, maintains that they were unique and that there are no clear international legal norms by which they could be judged. Moreover, interpretations of international law are politically biased.[31] To recall a Realist notion of morality, a sense of national duty and concern about Israel's security interests certainly drove the behavior of Yizhak Rabin and his negotiating team, and the initial decision to negotiate with the PLO (Slater, 1993; Makovsky, 1996).

WHAT IS A JUST AND FAIR OUTCOME?
INTERNAL, EXTERNAL, AND IMPARTIAL CRITERIA.

Israel thus held and promoted internal and contextual notions of justice and fairness in the interim talks, defined within the existing Israel–PLO power relations. Israeli negotiators stress how much the Palestinians have already gained from the Oslo peace process.[32] Whether the Oslo Declaration of Principles and the bargaining positions of the parties were indeed a legitimate starting point from which just and fair outcomes could result is debatable. If the only criteria are mutual agreement and mutual gains over a state of noncooperation, objections are unlikely. However, if conditions are placed on the structure and process of negotiations that can be taken to be legitimate, the Israel–PLO interim talks may not fulfill them.

It is precarious to try to assess the extent to which the talks violated particular conditions endorsed in the literature (such as Gauthier, 1986; Shue, 1992). Part of the Israel–PLO power inequality has certainly resulted from Israeli activities and resource acquisitions that made the Palestinians weak, vulnerable, and dependent. It is far more difficult to determine exactly which activities, if any, were necessary under the circumstances (for example, to avoid a deterioration of the Israeli security and economic situation); which of the captured resources had a legitimate owner in the first place; and of what kind of compensation would be appropriate. The continuation of Israeli settlement and land confiscations in the territories contributed an element of threat and coercion to the talks, thus transgressing the discussed impartial criteria: These activities constantly increased the costs of non-agreement to the Palestinians and limited their actual ability to counter Israeli proposals (Khalidi, 1996). Unless they accepted certain terms and did so soon, Palestinians risked being even worse off than they were before negotiations started while Israel would have further fortified its position.[33] However, if negotiation can correct past injustices only as far as it still affords *all* parties net benefits from an agreement (and if pragmatism is essential to any meaningful notion of justice), the interim talks appear far more legitimate.

Palestinians have criticized the Oslo Accords and the interim talks on impartial grounds. They hold that continued Jewish settlement in the occupied territories violated international law and the spirit of the Oslo principles, prejudiced future bargaining over the final status of these lands, and constantly pressured them to give in to Israel's demands. To them, fair negotiations would have required a freeze on settlement activity. For both genuine and tactical reasons, Palestinians have also emphasized principles external to the mandate of the interim talks in presenting their claims (Sayigh, 1996). Virtually all Palestinians agree that a truly just solution requires a reversal of the creation of the state of Israel in 1948 and the establishment of a binational state in Palestine. This notion is based on their historical presence in Mandatory Palestine, and Israel's perceived usurpation of their national rights through military conquest and territorial expansion. All major PLO factions agreed to compromise on this conception of justice when they endorsed the 1988 Algiers Declaration of Palestinian Independence and a two-state solution. In the hope of regaining some rights most Palestinians thus accepted the existence of the Jewish state and the formula of "trading territory for peace" in UN Resolution 242, which was adopted after Israel's capture of new Arab lands in the 1967 Six-Day War. However, Palestinians believe that even if they can no longer be restored, the situations prior to 1948 and prior to 1967 should be used as references in the negotiations for appreciating how their positions already reflect large losses and concessions to Israel over time (Said, 1995). Instead, the Oslo Accords endorse Israel's occupation of the West Bank and Gaza as the legitimate starting point for negotiations and compromise. Palestinians perceive this point of departure as unjust historically and legally and as unfair exploitation of their weakness. It fails to take account of past events and activities that contributed to Israel's superior power at their expense.

These external criteria of justice and fairness are essential in explaining the unprecedented splits within the Palestinian community that the Oslo Accords and the interim agreements have created, and hence some fragility inherent in these achievements. However, they do not explain well the negotiating behavior of the Palestinians who participated in the interim talks. The question of what a just and fair solution would require did not guide their crucial moves. Despite frequent tactical and rhetorical references to legal and ethical principles, the Palestinian negotiators were ultimately driven by pragmatic considerations of what they could achieve given their weakness (Sayigh, 1996; Singer, 1996; Khalidi, 1996). They were acutely aware of the need to make large concessions to move the Israelis. Insisting on their criteria of justice, or on a fairer interpretation of some of the Oslo principles, would have been likely to result in further losses and even greater injustice. Palestinian disadvantages included Israeli control over the resources being negotiated, a constantly deteriorating BATNA, and (related to this) the deferral to the permanent-status talks of the issues most significant to them. Other significant factors were poor coordination, consultation, and bargaining strategies among Palestinian negotiators; fragile support within their own community and the financial crisis of the PLO; and their lack of a powerful patron to offset the largely unconditional U.S. support of Israel's approach to the peace process (Sayigh, 1996; Makovsky, 1996).

The Israel–PLO interim negotiations is a thus case in which there were *no shared notions of justice or fairness to guide the discussions.* Ethical issues were both underlying currents and central questions in these, but were defined very differently by the parties. *These conflicting concepts of justice and fairness were not part of the decisive bargaining, or balanced and reconciled in the agreements.* The result came to reflect largely Israeli principles and interests and, at least according to much of the international community and the Palestinians, past and present injustices inflicted upon their people. It is virtually impossible to measure precisely the extent to which the interim agreements merely mirrored the asymmetries between the two sides. Israelis and Palestinians came to interpret and evaluate the same concessions differently, and their actual significance will not become clear until the permanent-status talks have progressed further.[34] The baseline (time period) in reference to which the gains, losses, and concessions of each party should be assessed is also questionable.

Concluding Comments

In the international negotiations here discussed, there was a definite place for justice and fairness given the nature of the questions covered. But justice and fairness have played very divergent roles in European acid rain negotiations and the Israel–PLO interim talks. Among the numerous differences between the two cases, the sharp power asymmetry in the latter case provides a major explanation. In the former instance, the notions of justice and fairness of all parties have been at the heart of the negotiation process, and have overlapped with mutual interest and mutual gains in arriving at effective agreements. In the latter, Israel's interests and principles have dominated the negotiation process and the agreements: The Palestinians have been too weak to infuse their notions of justice and fairness into the crucial bargaining, and in part also unwilling given that an implementation of them would remove all incentives for Israel to take part.

Contrary to much of the theoretical literature, both cases suggest that a single or precise measure of a just and fair outcome is rarely used in international negotiations. The parties to the European acid rain negotiations and the Middle East interim talks have relied on a combination of internal, external, and impartial criteria in forging, judging, and accepting or opposing agreements. To the extent the actual notions of parties practicing negotiation provide important information about the meaning of justice, the use of internal criteria alone appears particularly unsatisfactory in a situation of power asymmetry. In such a context negotiation cannot be assumed to produce just or fair outcomes in any meaningful sense unless certain requirements are fulfilled (or justice and fairness are simply defined in terms of the prevailing balance of forces). The positions and BATNAs of the parties, accepted at face value as the referents against which the fairness of particular concessions and bargains is assessed, are likely to reflect relative strength rather than differences in entitlements to or need for the disputed resources. And the actual veto power of a weaker party may be insufficient to secure a principled or balanced settlement. Similarly, as the Israel–PLO case demonstrates, a situation of sharp power inequality may leave little motivation for a solely impartial approach. Finally, the exclusive use of external standards may conflict with the basic requirement that successful negotiation be mutually beneficial.

For those concerned with gaining a better understanding of justice and fairness in international negotiations, propositions from the theoretical literature contribute useful suggestions and general insights (descriptive and prescriptive). The vast majority are too demanding to examine empirically with precision or certainty. While relevant to some cases, they either claim universal applicability or fail to specify the conditions under which justice and fairness play the proposed roles. Further study of practice is essential if we are going to improve our knowledge in two central, overlapping areas. The first concerns when and how ethical values actually affect international bargaining: What conditions allow or promote a role for justice and fairness? How do such values interact with other key factors that are known to affect the process and outcome of international negotiations, including culture and the distribution of power? The second concerns how the role played by justice and fairness could be strengthened, so as to enhance the will and sense of obligation among parties to implement and honor their agreements. This must be achieved without eroding the element of mutual gains that motivates and drives all international negotiations. In this regard, the widespread phenomenon of bargaining between unequals poses particular challenges.

NOTES

1. There are no generally accepted definitions distinguishing "justice" from "fairness" (see Barry, 1965; Rawls, 1971). It is nevertheless useful to think of these concepts as existing at the macro- and the micro-levels, respectively. Justice here refers to *distributive justice;* to general standards for allocating collective benefits and burdens among the members of a community (local, national or international). Such standards typically exist independently of any particular allocation problem, but their exact meaning and application in specific contexts are often ambiguous. Notions of *fairness* are individual judgments of what is reasonable under the circumstances, often in reference to how some principle of justice regarded as pertinent should be understood. Parties naturally tend to view and refer to their own notions of fairness as "justice"—as criteria reflecting some higher ethics going beyond partisan perceptions and interests, and situational factors. An outcome may be just in being in accordance with a general distributive principle, but unfair in how the principle has been applied; or fair to a group of parties at the micro-level but unjust in a wider (for example, international) sense.

2. An overview of this literature can be found in Albin, 1992.

3. This literature maintains persuasively that typical "Realist" arguments about the inapplicability of morality and justice to state conduct and interstate relations do not hold. These arguments point to the different rules of conduct and notions of morality among states (the absence of a shared moral purpose and of agreed ethical criteria), the absence of a supranational authority ca-

pable of enforcing or ensuring compliance with norms, and states' inevitable tendency to serve their own interests and define moral obligations narrowly in terms of duties to their respective peoples. Barry (1989b) notes that such arguments are based on real conditions in international affairs that exist also in interpersonal and intersocietal relations, without, for that matter, eroding the actual role that morality plays in those relations; and that widely accepted international norms (moral and legal) are indeed generally observed in the international arena. States usually adhere to norms because doing so rarely interferes with the pursuit of their own ends. Rather, it tends to serve their interests in an age of international interdependence.

4. These criteria effectively remove differences in interests and power from negotiations. Unlike many negotiation scholars, game theorists in particular, Rawls argues: "We cannot take various contingencies as known and individual preferences as given and expect to elucidate the concept of justice (or fairness) by theories of bargaining" (Rawls, 1971, pp. 134–135). The need for a "veil of ignorance" arises from the assumption that parties are driven by a narrow interest to maximize their own gains.

5. Equality in power is difficult to calculate, and has even been termed "a myth" (Barry, 1965). As discussed, it is defined differently across different conceptions of justice. A minimalist view would hold that each party must lack the capacity to achieve its interests by unilateral means at acceptable costs, and has more to gain from cooperating and accepting some moral constraints than remaining in a Hobbesian "state of nature" (Gauthier, 1986). A maximalist view would require perfect equality. For example, it is difficult to envision that the principles of justice that in Rawls's argument (Rawls, 1971) are chosen behind a "veil of ignorance" would be selected or adhered to under different conditions. In the international arena, the inequality of states often means that cooperation must be on unequal terms to benefit and attract the interest of well-endowed states. A middle position holds that moderate power inequalities must not exclude a role for justice and fairness, and may be reflected to some extent in negotiated agreements (Barry, 1989a). In this study power equality refers broadly to a situation in which each party feels that there is sufficient equality to secure a "fair share" of the disputed resources.

6. Some approaches define justice and fairness contextually within a given power relationship, as further discussed in this chapter.

7. These approaches recognize poorly that effective power in negotiation is often issue- or area-specific. Thus they cannot explain how a structurally weak party can gain more or even "win" over a stronger party, as has happened in many international negotiations. Zartman (1983, pp. 120–121) suggests, based on a number of cases, that the greater the structural imbalance between parties, the more likely it is that nonstructural elements will determine the outcome. These elements may include a firm commitment to cer-

tain values and goals, organizational unity, and such tactics as persuasive references to moral principles.

8. See Thomas Hobbes, 1991.

9. Any gains to be had from "cheating" (benefiting unfairly from the compliance by others) will be undermined by the long-term consequences of being excluded from future cooperative ventures. According to Hobbes, however, humans are unable to internalize this logic and to abandon voluntarily the short-term maximization of self-interest. Hence the need for a sovereign ruler to formulate moral codes, and enforce agreements on mutual constraints that leave all parties better off than in a state of noncooperation.

10. "Common-sense" morality upholds an obligation to adhere to norms only if and as long as enough people do so to keep the norms effective in serving their goals, while "utilitarianism" supports a greater obligation to comply as long as this benefits the purposes of the norms at all (Barry, 1989b). Hobbes held that compliance with an agreement is morally binding and rational only as long as the sovereign can ensure that *all* contracting parties in fact comply with it.

11. Shue (1992) expresses a similar view in discussing the meaning of justice between developed and developing countries.

12. Each party will thus make concessions based on the other's tendency to concede, rather than on calculations of relative power as in the "Hobbesian" paradigm. Different interpretations and applications of the reciprocity norm include *equal concessions,* whereby comparable concessions are exchanged in reference to initial positions (Bartos, 1974); *equal sacrifices,* whereby concessions are made so that parties will suffer equally in their respective eyes (Kelley, Beckerman, & Fisher, 1967); and *tit-for-tat,* whereby a party matches the other's move in substance and scope, responding to toughness/softness with the same toughness/softness (Pruitt, 1981). In the case of *responsiveness to trend* each party makes concessions based on its evaluation of a series of moves by the other side (Snyder & Diesing, 1977), whereas with *comparative responsiveness* each party acts based on a comparison of its own and the other's tendencies to concede. The latter corresponds best to several actual cases of international negotiation (Druckman & Harris, 1990).

13. This approach overlaps considerably with the "Hobbesian" view discussed earlier, but we will recall that the latter regards ethical values as inapplicable to the terms of a negotiated agreement.

14. Note that any proposed restrictions ultimately depend on the particular conception of justice that is adopted. Those discussed here are derived from the notion that justice only concerns the distribution of gains from mutually beneficial cooperation. By contrast Rawls considers all differences in power and strategic advantage as illegitimate influences on negotiation, which may (re)distribute justly also the benefits from endowments originally held and resources acquired legitimately by parties.

15. Gauthier (1986) suggests certain circumstances under which "past injustices" as here defined may legitimately be reflected in agreements. Firstly, one party may exploit another party's resources if this is absolutely necessary to avoid *worsening* his own situation, or if adequate compensation is provided. Secondly, *mutual gains* from negotiation is viewed a practical necessity that ultimately must *override all other considerations whenever they are conflicting.* Thus, "past injustices" should be corrected only as far as it is consistent with affording *all* parties net benefits from an agreement compared to a situation of nonagreement (Gauthier, 1986, p. 229). For the confiscation of resources to be considered unjust in the first place the deprived party must be the legitimate owner of them (having acquired them through his own labor), and must have been using (or intended to use) them and have been affected negatively by their being taken away.

16. In his notion of "impartial" justice, Barry (1989a) forcefully rejects the idea that the value of nonagreement points (BATNAs) should play any role in determining the nature of just distributions.

17. See, for example, Fraenkel, 1989; Schneider, 1992; Alcamo, Shaw, & Hordijk, 1990; Boehmer-Christiansen & Skea, 1991; Chossudovsky, 1988; and Carroll, 1988. The discussion here draws partly on Albin, 1995a.

18. "Positions and Strategies of the Different Contracting Parties to the Convention on Long-Range Transboundary Air Pollution Concerning the Reduction of Sulphur Emissions or their Transboundary Fluxes," August 6, 1985. Document ECE/EB.AIR/7.

19. The last-mentioned standard refers to deposition levels for sulfur and nitrogen above which significant harmful effects on specified sensitive elements of the environment (including forests, freshwater, and fish) do not occur, according to present knowledge. See "Economic Principles for Allocating the Costs of Reducing Sulphur Emissions in Europe." Report submitted by the delegation of the Netherlands to the Group of Economic Experts on Air Pollution, Executive Body for the Convention on Long-Range Transboundary Air Pollution, UN Economic Commission for Europe, fifth session, Geneva, June 26–28, 1989. EB.AIR/GE.2/R.26, May 19, 1989; and "Protocol to the 1979 Convention on Long-Range Transboundary Air Pollution Concerning the Control of Emissions of Nitrogen Oxides or Their Transboundary Fluxes (November 1, 1988)," article 1, para. 7 (reprinted in *Register of International Treaties and Other Agreements in the Field of the Environment,* 1991).

20. "Protocol to the 1979 Convention on Long-Range Transboundary Air Pollution Concerning the Control of Emissions of Nitrogen Oxides or Their Transboundary Fluxes (November 1, 1988)." (Reprinted in *Register of International Treaties and Other Agreements in the Field of the Environment,* 1991.)

21. "The Critical Load Concept and the Role of Best Available Technology and Other Approaches." Report of the Working Group on Abatement Strategies, September 1991. Economic Commission for Europe EB.AIR/WG.5/R.24/Rev.1.

22. "Council directive on the limitation of certain pollutants into the air from large combustion plants." Commission of the European Communities (December 7, 1988), 88/609/EEC. Brussels: *Official Journal of the European Communities,* L336.

23. These cost-sharing schemes involve redistribution of financial and technological resources from richer to poorer polluting countries. They seek to make additional reductions in SO_2 and NO_x emissions, particularly in Eastern Europe, both fairer and more realistic. One such scheme suggests that GDP, GDP per capita, and national abatement costs determine contributions to and receipts from an "Acidification Fund" (Sliggers & Klaassen, 1992). France, Germany, and the UK, among others, would through the fund compensate for some of the high costs of emission reductions in countries such as Poland, Ukraine, and Romania. The latter would cover the remaining "reasonable" costs themselves in proportion to their GDP per capita. The plan would presumably motivate polluting countries to participate, but it might elicit support only from those major financial contributors that stand to gain on a national scale from emissions reductions being undertaken abroad, such as the Scandinavian countries. In another proposal the distributive criterion is by contrast relative gains from participation in a European cost-sharing fund, and every member therefore stands to gain (Bergman, Cesar, & Klaassen, 1992). The losses or gains of all member states from further emission reductions are estimated, and they would receive money from the fund or contribute to it accordingly.

24. "Declaration of Principles on Interim Self-Government Arrangements" (Israeli Ministry of Foreign Affairs, 1993); "Israeli-Palestinian Interim Agreement on the West Bank and the Gaza Strip—September 28, 1995" (Information Division, Israeli Ministry of Foreign Affairs, Jerusalem, November 1995); *Middle East International,* October 6, 1995, pp. 2–5; Boutwell & Mendelsohn, 1995.

25. As far back as in the Washington Peace Talks (1991–1993), Israel insisted on the election of a 12-member Palestinian "administrative council" with limited municipal functions that would not come anywhere close to a Palestinian parliament. Elections eventually took place for an 88-member and far more empowered Palestinian Council with both legislative and executive powers, which at present includes seven Jerusalemites.

26. "Declaration of Principles on Interim Self-Government Arrangements" (Israeli Ministry of Foreign Affairs, 1993), p. 26. The major Israeli argument was that the Palestinian police force had failed to assume such responsibility adequately.

27. *Middle East International,* 8 September 1995, p. 6; Boutwell & Mendelsohn, 1995; Sayigh, 1996.

28. "Declaration of Principles on Interim Self-Government Arrangements" (Israeli Ministry of Foreign Affairs, 1993), p. 31.

29. "Israeli-Palestinian Interim Agreement on the West Bank and the Gaza Strip—September 28, 1995" (Information Division, Israeli Ministry of Foreign Affairs, Jerusalem, November 1995).

30. *Middle East Monitor,* Vol. 5, No. 10, October 1995, p. 2. The fact that Israel's interpretations and terms largely prevailed on the redeployment issue and caused extensive Palestinian resentment may explain its greater flexibility on the water issue, as well as on the questions of the Palestinian Council and East Jerusalemites in the elections (Sayigh, 1996; Khalidi, 1996).

31. Singer recognizes that a permanent solution to the water issue should take account of some common principles for the equitable distribution of water resources, such as proportionality and need. He stresses that such a solution can be worked out and that such principles can be considered only in the final status talks once population sizes, the ultimate fate of the territories, and borders are better known (Singer, 1996). However, while the Oslo Declaration states that the interim agreements may not prejudice the outcome of the final status talks, they will in practice be influential and constrain the range of likely solutions to a number of questions.

32. Singer (1996) argues that the outcome of the interim talks do not simply reflect the distribution of gross power between the two sides. Indeed, a lesson to be learnt from this case is supposedly that the weak can turn their feebleness into strength by arguing, as Arafat did on several occasions, that further concessions or costs would be fatal to their survival.

33. This would frequently be defined as a bargaining situation involving unfair threats and coercion (see, for example, Barry, 1965, p. 86). In order for coercive tactics to have a place in fair bargaining, it is often argued that both parties must be in a position to use them and must recognize them as part of the game (see Lax & Sebenius, 1986).

34. For example, the concessions to East Jerusalemites in the interim talks can be viewed as a mere continuation of Israel's old strategies to appease them through limited political rights that do not undermine its sovereignty over the city. By contrast, some Israelis regard the concessions as a dangerous tampering with the status quo and even as the prelude to the establishment of a Palestinian capital in Jerusalem. Palestinians themselves have taken many opportunities to assert their political presence and national claims to the city, partly through institution-building.

REFERENCES

Albin, C. 1992. "Fairness Issues in Negotiation: Structure, Process, Procedures and Outcome." *Working Paper WP-92–88,* December. Laxenburg, Austria: International Institute for Applied Systems Analysis.

Albin, C. 1995a. "Rethinking Justice and Fairness: The Case of Acid Rain Emission Reductions." *Review of International Studies,* April.

Albin, C., ed. 1995b. *Negotiation and Global Security: New Approaches to Contemporary Issues.* Special issue of *American Behavioral Scientist,* 38 (6).

Albin, C. 1995c. "The Global Security Challenge to Negotiation: Towards the New Agenda." In Albin, *Negotiation and Global Security.*

Albin, C. 1997. "Securing the Peace of Jerusalem: On the Politics of Unifying and Dividing." *Review of International Studies,* April.

Alcamo, J., Shaw, R., & Hordijk, L., eds. 1990. *The RAINS Model of Acidification. Science and Strategies in Europe.* Dordrecht, The Netherlands: Kluwer Academic Publishers.

Al Musa, S. 1996. Interview with Sherif Al Musa, member of the Palestinian delegation to the Washington Peace Talks on the Middle East in 1991–1993, February 9.

Ashrawi, H. 1995. *This Side of Peace: A Personal Account.* New York: Simon & Schuster.

Barry, B. 1965. *Political Argument.* London: Routledge & Kegan Paul.

Barry, B. 1989a. *Theories of Justice.* Berkeley: University of California Press.

Barry, B. 1989b. "Can States be Moral?" In Barry, *Democracy, Power and Justice—Essays in Political Theory.* Oxford: Clarendon Press.

Barry, B. 1995. *Justice as Impartiality.* Oxford: Oxford University Press.

Bartos, O. 1974. *Process and Outcome of Negotiations.* New York: Columbia University Press.

Benton, A., & Druckman, D. 1973. "Salient Solutions and the Bargaining Behavior of Representatives and Nonrepresentatives." *International Journal of Group Tensions,* 3, 28–39.

Bergman, L., Cesar, H., & Klaassen, G. 1992. "Efficiency in Transboundary Pollution Abatement: A Scheme for Sharing the Costs of Reducing Sulphur Emissions in Europe." In Krabbe & Heyman, *National Income and Nature: Externalities, Growth and Steady State.* Dordrecht, Boston, and London: Kluwer Academic Publishers.

Boehmer-Christiansen, S., & Skea, J. 1991. *Acid Politics: Environmental and Energy Policies in Britain and Germany.* London: Belhaven Press.

Boutwell, J., & Mendelsohn, E. 1995. *Israeli-Palestinian Security: Issues in the Permanent Status Negotiations.* Cambridge, MA: American Academy of Arts and Sciences.

Braithwaite, R. B. 1955. *Theory of Games as a Tool for the Moral Philosopher.* Cambridge: Cambridge University Press.

Carroll, J., ed. 1988. *International Environmental Diplomacy.* Cambridge: Cambridge University Press.

Chossudovsky, E. 1988. *"East-West" Diplomacy for Environment in the United Nations: The High-Level Meeting within the Framework of the ECE on the Protection of the Environment: A Case Study.* New York: United Nations Institute for Training and Research (UNITAR).

Commission of the European Communities. 1988. "Council Directive on the Limitation of Certain Pollutants into the Air from Large Combustion Plants." *Official Journal of the European Communities* (Brussels), December 7.

Deutsch, M. 1973. *The Resolution of Conflict: Constructive and Destructive Processes.* New Haven: Yale University Press.

Druckman, D., & Harris, R. 1990. "Alternative Models of Responsiveness in International Negotiation." *Journal of Conflict Resolution,* 34 (2).

Economic Commission for Europe. 1985. "Positions and Strategies of the Different Contracting Parties to the Convention on Long-Range Transboundary Air Pollution Concerning the Reduction of Sulphur Emissions or their Transboundary Fluxes," August 6.

Economic Commission for Europe. 1991. "The Critical Load Concept and the Role of Best Available Technology and Other Approaches." *Report of the Working Group on Abatement Strategies,* September.

Economic Principles for Allocating the Costs of Reducing Sulphur Emissions in Europe. Report submitted by the delegation of the Netherlands to the Group of Economic Experts on Air Pollution, Executive Body for the Convention on Long-Range Transboundary Air Pollution, UN Economic Commission for Europe, for the 5th Session, Geneva, June 26–28, 1989. EB.AIR/GE.2/R.26, May 19, 1989.

Fisher, R., & Ury, W. 1981. *Getting to Yes—Negotiating Agreement Without Giving In.* New York: Penguin Books.

Fraenkel, A. 1989. "The Convention on Long-Range Transboundary Air Pollution: Meeting the Challenge of International Cooperation." *Harvard International Law Journal,* 30, 447–476.

Frost, M. 1986. *Towards a Normative Theory of International Relations.* Cambridge: Cambridge University Press.

Gauthier, D. 1986. *Morals by Agreement.* Oxford: Clarendon Press.

Haigh, N. 1989. "New Tools for European Air Pollution Control. *International Environmental Affairs,* 1, 26–37.

Hirsch, M., Housen-Couriel, D., & Lapidoth, R. 1995. *Whither Jerusalem? Proposals and Positions Concerning the Future of Jerusalem.* Dordrecht, the Netherlands: Kluwer Law International.

Hobbes, T. 1991. *Leviathan.* Cambridge: Cambridge University Press.

Israeli Ministry of Foreign Affairs. 1993. "Declaration of Principles on Interim Self-Government Arrangements," September.

Israeli Ministry of Foreign Affairs, Information Division. 1995. "Israeli-Palestinian Interim Agreement on the West Bank and the Gaza Strip," November.

Jensen, L. 1963. "Soviet-American Bargaining Behavior in Post-War Disarmament Negotiations." *Journal of Arms Control,* 1, October.

Kelley, H., Beckman, L., & Fischer, C. 1967. "Negotiating the Division of a Reward under Incomplete Information." *Journal of Experimental Social Psychology,* 3, 361–398.

Khalidi, A. S. 1996. Interview with Dr. A. S. Khalidi, Palestinian senior advisor on security issues to the Israel-PLO interim negotiations in Cairo and Taba and currently Research Associate at the Royal Institute for International Affairs, London, February 8.

Klaassen, G., Amann, M., & Schöpp, W. 1992. "Strategies for Reducing Sulfur Dioxide Emissions in Europe Based on Critical Sulfur Deposition Values." Background paper prepared for the UN/ECE Task Force on Integrated Assessment Modelling, November 30–December 2, Geneva, Switzerland. Laxenburg, Austria: International Institute for Applied Systems Analysis.

Lax, D., & Sebenius, J. 1986. *The Manager as Negotiator—Bargaining for Cooperation and Competitive Gain.* New York: The Free Press.

Lind, E. A. & Tyler, T. R. 1988. *The Social Psychology of Procedural Justice.* New York: Plenum.

Makovsky, D. 1996. *Making Peace with the PLO.* Boulder, CO: Westview.

Middle East International, September 8, 1995; October 6, 1995; November 3, 1995.

Middle East Monitor, October 1995.

Morgenthau, H. 1948. *Politics among Nations.* New York: Knopf.

Morgenthau, H. 1971. *Politics in the Twentieth Century.* Chicago: University of Chicago Press.

Nardin, T. 1983. *Law, Morality, and the Relations of States.* Princeton: Princeton University Press.

Nash, J. F. 1950. "The Bargaining Problem," *Econometrica,* 18.

O'Brien, W. 1991. *Law and Morality in Israel's War with the PLO.* New York and London: Routledge Publishers.

Peres, S. 1993. *The New Middle East.* Shaftesbury, Dorset: Element Books.

Pruitt, D. 1981. *Negotiation Behavior.* New York: Academic Press.

Quigley, J. 1995. "Jerusalem in International Law." Paper presented at a conference on "The Current Status of Jerusalem and the Future of the Peace Process," organized by the International Campaign for Jerusalem, London, June 15–16.

Rawls, J. 1958. "Justice as Fairness." *Philosophical Review,* 67, 164–194.

Rawls, J. 1971. *A Theory of Justice.* Cambridge: Harvard University Press.

Regens, J., & Rycroft, R. 1988. *The Acid Rain Controversy.* Pittsburgh: University of Pittsburgh Press.

Rubin, J. Z., & Brown, B. 1975. *The Social Psychology of Bargaining and Negotiation.* New York and London: Academic Press.

Said, E. 1995. *Peace and Its Discontents.* London: Vintage (Random House).

Sayigh, Y. 1996. Interviews with Dr. Yezid Sayigh, advisor to the Palestinian delegation to the Washington Peace Talks on the Middle East in 1991–1993 and participant in the negotiations over the implementation of the Gaza-Jericho agreement in 1994, February 7 and 15.

Schelling, T. 1960. *The Strategy of Conflict.* Cambridge: Harvard University Press.

Schneider, T., ed. 1992. *Acidification Research: Evaluation and Policy Applications.* Proceedings of an International Conference, Maastricht, The Netherlands, October 14–18, 1991. Amsterdam: Elsevier Science Publishers.

Shue, H. 1992. "The Unavoidability of Justice." In Hurrell and Kingsbury, *The International Politics of the Environment*. Oxford: Clarendon Press.

Singer, J. 1996. Interview with Joel Singer, Legal Advisor of Israeli Ministry of Foreign Affairs and member of Israeli delegation to interim talks, 1993–1996, March 18.

Slater, R. 1993. *Rabin of Israel. A Biography*. London: Robson Books.

Sliggers, J., & Klaassen, G. 1992. "Cost sharing for the Abatement of Acidification in Europe: The Key to a Protocol." Draft paper prepared for the session of the UN/ECE Task Force on Economic Aspects of Abatement Strategies, Geneva, December 3–4.

Snyder, G. H., & Diesing, P. 1977. *Conflict Among Nations*. Princeton: Princeton University Press.

Swingle, P., ed. 1970. *The Structure of Conflict*. New York and London: Academic Press.

United Nations Commission for Europe. 1985. "Protocol to the 1979 Convention on Long-Range Transboundary Air Pollution on the Reduction of Sulphur Emissions or Their Transboundary Fluxes by at least 30 Percent." In *Executive Body for the Convention on Long Range Transboundary Air Pollution*, August 6.

United Nations Environment Programme. 1991. "Protocol to the 1979 Convention on Long-Range Transboundary Air Pollution Concerning the Control of Emissions of Nitrogen Oxides or Their Transboundary Fluxes (November 1, 1988)." In *Register of International Treaties and Other Agreements in the Field of the Environment*, May.

Usher, G. 1995. *Palestine in Crisis. The Struggle for Peace and Political Independence after Oslo*. London: Pluto Press.

Welch, D. 1993. *Justice and the Genesis of War*. New York: Cambridge University Press.

Young, P., & Wolf, A. 1992. "Global Warming Negotiations: Does Fairness Matter?" *The Brookings Review*, Spring, 46–51.

Young, P. 1994. *Equity. In Theory and Practice*. Princeton: Princeton University Press.

Young, P. 1995. "Dividing the Indivisible." In Albin, *Negotiation and Global Security*.

Zartman, I. W., ed. 1983. *The 50% Solution*. New Haven: Yale University Press.

Zartman, I. W. 1991. "The Structure of Negotiation." In Kremenyuk, *International Negotiation. Analysis, Approaches, Issues*. San Francisco: Jossey-Bass.

Zartman, I. W. 1995. "The Role of Justice in Global Security Negotiations." In Albin, *Negotiation and Global Security*.

Zartman, I. W. et al. 1996. "Negotiation as a Search for Justice." *International Negotiation*, 1, 79–98.

CHAPTER 10

JUSTICE IN NEGOTIATION*

I. WILLIAM ZARTMAN

Power is not all in determining the outcome of negotiation. If it were, the structural dilemma—whereby the weak negotiate with the strong and gain favorable (even asymmetrically favorable) outcomes—would not exist. Yet the structural dilemma is an interesting analytical problem, since many negotiations involve asymmetries that require explanation (Wriggins, 1987; Zartman & Rubin, 1999; Habeeb, 1991). Some of these can be artificially eliminated by manipulating definitions of power. Thus, the standard behavioral definition of power as the ability to move a party in an intended direction (Tawney, 1931; Simon, 1953; Dahl, 1957; Thibaut & Kelley, 1959) brooks no dilemma, since it is conclusionary or outcome-directed; the existence of power is proved by the outcome and therefore the most powerful must always win, because the winner is always most powerful, that is, most able to move the other party.

The other common definition of power, which identifies it with resources, poses the structural dilemma most clearly. Actors with an overwhelming imbalance of resources frequently do well (Morgan, 1994, p. 141) but also frequently do poorly in negotiation, and indeed, contrary to common wisdom, negotiations among unequals tend to be more efficient and satisfying than negotiations among equals (Pruitt & Carnevale, 1995; Rubin & Zartman, 1995). A more behavioral basis or source of power that is common to many approaches is the value of alternatives, variously termed security points (Zartman, 1987, pp. 12–13); damage (Harsanyi, 1977, pp. 179); reservation prices (Lax & Sebenius,

1986, p. 51); threat potentials (Rapoport, 1966, p. 97); security levels (Rapoport, 1966, p. 101); resistance points (Walton & McKersie, 1965, p. 41); best alternative to a negotiated agreement, or BATNA (Fisher & Ury, 1981), among others. Here too, however, the power of alternatives leaves many negotiated outcomes unexplained (Hopkins, 1987). Power alone, by any but a tautological definition, does not always account for the maintenance of a veto over conflict-resolving proposals; conflict is often preferred over a negotiated order by weaker parties under great pressure.

An alternative explanation revives the element of justice as a basis for acceptable orders or as a criterion for conflict termination (Zartman, Druckman, Jensen, Pruitt, & Young, 1996; Zartman, 1995). In the process of negotiating the exchange of division of items contested between them, the parties come to an agreement on the notion of justice that will govern this disposition; if they do not, the negotiations will not be able to proceed to a conclusion. Individual notions of justice act as a substantive veto on agreement, and must be coordinated and accepted as the first stage of negotiation. This notion of justice constitutes a formula on the basis of which parties then proceed to the disposition of details. The formula can be a procedural rule for establishing terms of trade, or one or more principles of justice on which such terms can be based (Zartman, 1978; Zartman & Berman, 1982). Inherent in this argument is the recognition that power alone cannot either produce or explain agreement and cannot substitute for justice determination in the process of negotiation (Young, 1994; Zartman, 1995; Zartman, Druckman, Jensen, Pruitt, & Young, 1996). The analytical questions then become: What is the meaning of justice in negotiation, and how is it determined? What alternative outcomes and explanations of outcomes are provided by power and justice?

The most prominent notion of justice is that of equality or impartiality. Equal treatment is seen as fair treatment, and equal outcomes are just deserts. Equality in its many forms is a common point of agreement for combining competing claims, forming a floor (and hence, bilaterally, a ceiling) on relative gains, and providing an acceptable formula for agreement as split-the-difference in the end when other criteria have run out. It is also the basic element in the entire procedural ethos under which negotiation takes place, that of reciprocity or the equal exchange of equal concessions (Keohane, 1986; Larson, 1988). Where equality is desired but cannot or need not be determined, a looser form known as equivalent justice is often used. The basis of justice in these cases is simply an exchange deemed appropriate or roughly similar, and justice is to be found not in the relative size of the shares but in the mere fact of the exchange, as opposed to one-sided concessions.

Yet there are also well-established principles of inequality that serve notions of justice in particular circumstances—equity (or merit or investment), in which the party that has or contributes the most receives the most, and compensation (or need or redistribution), in which the party that has the least receives the most. Even inequalities are equalizing measures, however, exchanged for some past or future equalizer, in the case of equity or compensation, respectively. Compensation is based on equalizing payments to one side; and "entitlement" and "deserving" are brought about through exchange for some external or intangible good (such as responsibility or rectitude) from the receiving side, or for a good somewhere else on the time dimension (past or future). Thus, permanent seats on the UN Security Council were given to the five Great Powers as a down payment on future security, not because the powers had nuclear weapons; merit scholarships are not given because of entitlement for intelligence but as a trade-off for future contribution to society (or to alumni funds); and developing countries receive compensation for reduction of ozone-depleting substances in exchange for future development (or as indemnification for past mistreatment) (Benedick, 1991, pp. 152–157).

Without recognition of such exchanges, unequal divisions are unacceptable and negotiations stalemate. Thus, unequal justice norms can also be interpreted as a different kind of equality, not in exchange for the other party's contribution but in exchange for one's own contribution. The justifying criterion shifted from an interactional (between-party) to an internal (within-party) exchange. Such equalizing is the meaning and purpose of equity in the legal sense, in which various instances of compensatory justice are invoked to temper the severity of partial-justice principles (Deutsch, 1985; Homans, 1961; Adams, 1965; Messe, 1970). Furthermore, starting positions of unequal as well as equal justice may yield equality as the distribution rule through a negotiating process.

A third type of justice principle is equal only in that it is to be equally applied ("equality before the law"), although it designates a winner, according to an established rule or generalized formula. Priority (partial) justice refers to principles from external sources that decree a particular outcome—"First come first served"; "Finders keepers"; "Winner take all"; "Polluter pays"; "Riparian rights"; "Noblesse oblige"; "Primogeniture"; and many others. These principles are usually absolute, incontrovertible; they indicate total allocation, not sharing. Since they are principles that favor one side, they are usually adopted to justify opening positions or the wants, needs, and interests of each side, but they may also be used as the basis of agreement under the equal-application principle.

Thus, as illustrated, there are many principles of justice but they can all be grouped into three categories—*priority* (sometimes called partial); *equality* (sometimes called parital or impartial), including equivalence; and *inequality* (sometimes called proportional), including equity and compensation (Young, 1994; Aristotle; Deutsch, 1985; Zartman, 1987; Cook & Hegtveldt, 1983; Stolte, 1987). All variations can be reduced to these three types, and any kind of outcome—final or proposed—can be classified in one or a combination of these principles. Outcomes are negotiated first among expressions of these principles, until deductively or inductively a formula developed to govern the negotiated agreement. Sometimes the stakes are such that a single, simple principle can constitute that formula; in other circumstances, they may be complex enough to require a formula of compound justice, involving a pairing or combination of principles to constitute the agreement.

The process of arriving at an agreed principle of justice in negotiation can be seen as evolving through three stages: absolute, comparative, and jointly determined. Different parties may initially have different notions of justice (often priority justice) that favor their positions (were they to decide the outcome unilaterally). However, they must place their own position ("justice for me") within a social context ("justice for me compared to you") relating to relative gains and losses. While a party acting alone would most likely adopt a self-serving notion of justice ("I deserve the goods"), the fact that it has to negotiate means that winning outright is not an option, and a different notion of justice is needed; all things being equal, equality is the most frequently held norm ("I deserve to do at least as much as you"). When the two comparative or social evaluations of justice are combined, a jointly determined outcome is (or is not) produced, and the negotiation can go on to apply it. It should be remembered that these are analytical stages, and their neat, discrete quality is not always reflected in the messy world of reality.

Determining the agreeable, applicable one among the three principles of justice is only one step in establishing the negotiation in justice; the other step concerns the referent or application of the principle: equality, inequality, or priority of what? If parties want to maintain their parity or equality in arms, they must decide which of many parts or measures of armaments they will use. When the UN Security Council enunciated the equivalence formula of "territory for security" for the Middle East in Resolution 242 in 1967, it only started the process of determining what was territory and what was security in each of the occupied territories along the Israeli border, which was in turn the necessary prelude to the detail question of how much territory for how much security. When the Serbs, Croats, and Bosnians came to an understanding about the semi-federative relation within Bosnia at Wright Patterson Air Base in late 1995 (the referent question first), they then had to decide the type of justice that would govern relations within and between the parts (the principle question). When legislators on a tax reform bill establish the new code on the basis of equality (flat rate), equity (regressive), compensation (progressive), or some priority principle, they still have to decide what is to be the referent of the principle (income, sales, head, or other).

The propositions, or hypotheses, to be tested, then, can be stated in the form of a necessary proposition, "If there is a final agreement, then there was a prior agreement on justice;" the stronger necessary and sufficient form, "If there is an agreement on justice, then there will be a final agreement;" and its converse, "If no agreement on justice, no final agreement." As in many hypotheses, it is important that the two variables be kept separate and that separate evidence be found for each, lest the statement become an identity and lest agreement itself be taken as evidence for the existence of a shared sense of justice. Like war and peace, justice does not always wear a badge and is not present only when declared. Thus evidence in this inquiry may require interpretation, without thereby diluting its strength. Evidence may come in one of three forms. There may be explicit statements, either invoking justice itself or referring to its principles, such as equality or need or equity. There may be statements of position or policy that refer to principles of justice without explicitly naming them, and yet using them as justifications. And there may be policy or position statements that contain principles presented as self-justifying, for which the analyst may be required to point out the justice principle. Thus, like M. Jourdain, negotiators may be "speaking justice" without knowing it, although like any good diplomats they may also speak justice implicitly and indirectly but perfectly consciously. Like any good diplomats, negotiators may also speak justice explicitly but perfectly insincerely, using the term to cover its opposite. Such subtleties are no less present here than in any other research on power, interest, or preferences, which are the more common terms of negotiations analysis.

The following analysis will examine the role of justice and fairness in the negotiation process. The first task is to seek to establish the proposition by looking for the separate, coincident, and causal existence of the two variables, by examining a number of cases of negotiations that are relatively diverse and important and are deemed successful because they have achieved a final agreement. Was that agreement preceded by a joint agreement on the sense of justice that would govern the outcome? Was there an absence of agreement until that common principle of justice was established? Would power alone have produced different outcomes and different explanations? These cases, chosen because they provide interesting and diverse illustrations of the propositions, include the negotiations over southwestern Africa (Namibia and Angola) between 1977 and 1988, over disarmament in Europe between 1984 and 1986, and over missiles during the 1962 Cuban Crisis.

NAMIBIA AND ANGOLA

Negotiations over Namibian independence pitted South Africa against the Namibian national liberation movement, the South-West African Peoples Organization (SWAPO); Angola; and Cuba in the presence of a number of mediators, including the Front Line States (FLS), the Western Contact Group, the United States, and the Soviet Union (Crocker, 1993; Zartman, 1989, Ch. 5).

South Africa consistently proclaimed that a just solution was to be found in procedural terms, through a general election, although it attached a number of conditions—no external pressure, no violence—that would insure that a friendly neighbor could be assured. This was stated as a self-justifying principle of priority justice on many occasions. Said Prime Minister B. J. Vorster to the South African senate in 1967, "There is only one solution . . . , namely, that the people of South West Africa should be allowed to decide their own future unhindered and without interference."

As South Africa began to lose control of who "the people" were (the referent question), however, its spokesmen began to add the second priority principle of friendliness, stability, or peacefulness, also presented as self-evident. The new prime minister P. W. Botha declared on August 5, 1979, "The South African government, as well as the leaders of South West Africa, attach great value to an internationally acceptable solution; . . . however, . . . if an eventual choice should be between stability or [sic] chaos, we shall choose stability." The South African position was to trade in its rule of Namibia (South West Africa) for independence in such a way as to install a minimally friendly government, but it was couched in terms of priority principles of justice—free and fair elections under conditions of peace and stability.

SWAPO's position was simpler but also presented in terms of priority justice: "It's ours, we fought for it," repeated SWAPO leader Sam Nujoma on many occasions. FLS allies finally brought SWAPO around to agreeing to UNR 435 providing for one-person-one-vote elections under paired UN and South African auspices that SWAPO, which had already been declared "the sole legitimate representative of the Namibian people," felt were unnecessary. "South Africa's only role," said SWAPO's UN observer Theo Ben Gurirab (*New York Times,* June 12, 1977), "is to announce publicly that it accepts all UN resolutions on South West Africa and that means withdrawing from the territory, agreeing to UN-controlled elections, and releasing political prisoners."

The priority justice positions of each side did little to satisfy the other, and it is little wonder that the negotiations deadlocked. Even more striking was the fact that the mediators also clung to a principle of priority justice, rejecting any notion of division, exchange, or sharing. UN ambassador "Andrew Young and Vice President [Walter] Mondale have said that the U.S. is no longer committed to linkage policy with South Africa, as pursued by [former secretary of state] Henry Kissinger. 'Under his approach, the United States agreed in effect to limit its pressure on South Africa to largely philosophical criticisms in exchange for Mr. Vorster's cooperation with regard to Rhodesia and South West Africa.' Officials now explain that 'the State Department is no longer willing to hold back on South Africa in the hope of obtaining action on majority rule in Rhodesia and a new status for South West Africa.'" (*New York Times,* May 18, 1977). The United States supported the UN position that the answer to the conflict lay in the priority principle of one-person-one-vote under UN auspices. Although this position was softened slightly a year later to allow paired UN - South African auspices in hope of extracting a South African agreement to UNR 435, it remained the essential basis of U.S. policy, "the Carter Administrating in effect [taking] the position that South Africa should cooperate on South West Africa and Rhodesia for its own good. . . ." (*New York Times,* December 3, 1978). While a single, well-chosen principle of priority justice may well attract the adherence of both sides in some cases, in others, such as the Namibian instance, it is not seen as just by both parties and so raises unreal hopes on one side while alienating the other.

It was a new linkage by the succeeding mediator that provided a principle of equivalence if not of equality. The objections of each side to the other's principle were to be met by a paired withdrawal of Cuban troops from Angola and South African troops from Namibia, after which the free and fair elections could be held. As Assistant Secretary of State Chester

Crocker explained in a Voice of America interview on June 23, 1982, "The relationship that exists between these two issues was not invented by the Reagan Administration or by the United States—it's a fact, it's a fact of history, of geography, of logic. It's also a fact that no party can lay down prior conditions or preconditions to any other party. . . . The South Africans cannot be threatened into leaving Namibia—excepting on terms which are in some minimal sense acceptable to them. . . . The same applies the other way. And given the history, and the lack of confidence that exists on both sides of that border, we believe that it's unrealistic for any side to say to the other, 'You go first.' What we're seeking is parallel movement on the two questions—South African withdrawal from Namibia as provided under the UN plan, Resolution 435, and Cuban withdrawal from Angola." The new formula was facilitated by a change in parties, the state of Angola replacing the movement of SWAPO in dealing with South Africa. The confrontation of two sovereign states with their own national interests helped the applicability of an equality principle of justice, with the referent question still to be specified.

The equality (or equivalence) principle of a paired withdrawal formed the basis of the eventual solution in 1988 and, perhaps as important, guided in its spirit the search for just and equivalent implementing details for the final agreement—"a reasonable and balanced" set of conditions, in the words of one side's spokesman, and "a just and fair settlement" in the words of another (*New York Times,* August 31, 1988; *Washington Post,* August 12, 1988). Angolan president Eduardo dos Santos finally indicated on July 24, 1986, that "We believe the time is right for negotiation of a just political solution" (*FBIS Africa,* July 24, 1986), and Cuban president Fidel Castro stated in the midst of the final negotiations, "If the agreement is completed and respected, Angola and Cuba will carry out a gradual and total withdrawal of all the [Cuban] internationalist contingent in Angola. There is a real possibility of a just and honorable solution to the war" (*New York Times,* July 27, 1988). The formula was specific enough to be considered an instance of equality, rather than simply equivalence, since the items exchanged—the withdrawal of foreign troops—were the same, and even the number of troops—90,000 South Africans and 80,000 Cubans—was nearly identical, even if their distance and their timetable for withdrawal was not fully coincident; most importantly, of course, South Africa gave up colonial sovereignty with its withdrawal, whereas Cuba gave up contracted assistance. The formula was based not merely on "getting something" in exchange for independence but rather on a matched and balance trade-off that provided the guide for further details. It is noteworthy that the one missing element in the application of equal justice to both areas was the holding of elections in Angola, parallel to those in Namibia; this item, not part of the Washington Agreement of December 1988, was the basis of the complementary Estoril and Lusaka Agreements of May 1990 and November 1994, respectively, which provided for the settlement of the internal Angolan conflict. The shift from priority to equality principles of justice to which both sides could subscribe provided the basis for the negotiated agreement in southwestern Africa.

CONFERENCE ON DISARMAMENT IN EUROPE

The Stockholm Conference on Disarmament in Europe (CDE) represents a very different test for the notions of justice in negotiation. It shows (1) that a common notion of justice (the principle question) can be identified early on but can run up against the referent question; (2) that additional principles of justice may be required to keep negotiations moving; and (3) that that internal changes in the parties and in their relations with each other may be required in order to complete the principle and resolve the referent questions, so as finally to arrive at an agreement.

The 1975 Helsinki Final Act contained, among other things, both a "no use of force" (NUF) declaration and a few limited but instructive confidence-building measures (CBMs). In 1978, France proposed a European disarmament conference "from the Atlantic to the Urals" (in a Gaullist phrase), initially to focus exclusively on CBMs. The relationship between the conference and the measures was debated at the Madrid meeting of the Conference on Security and Cooperation in Europe (CSCE) in 1983, resulting in the Madrid Mandate for "a process of which the first stage will be devoted to the negotiation and adoption of a set of mutually complementary [confidence and security building] measures . . . [over] the entire continent of Europe." The conference began in Stockholm on January 17, 1984.

The careful wording of the mandate represented both a clear agreement on the principles of justice and a troublesome ambiguity on its application. The "mutually complementary measures" were to be an exercise in equal justice, since they were to be equally applied to all parties within the area. This equality of treatment was a crucial rule of standing and treatment for the CSCE members, but most particularly for the NATO and Warsaw Pact partners. Yet the referent question recognized that equality was hard to find in reality, for several reasons. CPSU general secretary Leonid Brezhnev expressed the clash between principle and referent quite succinctly in an interview with *Der Spiegel* on November 2, 1981: "We naturally expect reciprocal [equal] steps from the West. Military preparations in the European zone of NATO do not start from the continental edge of Europe" (Borawski, 1992, p. 28). The same problem was analyzed in careful detail by U.S. ambassador James Goodby (1988, pp. 164, 154):

> The value of confidence-building measures is greater for the United States than for the Soviet Union . . . because greater openness in military activities should better serve the interests of the United States. . . . In addition to this well-known problem, the Soviets faced another dilemma peculiar to the Stockholm Conference—how to reconcile their interest in a European security conference with their instinct that any agreement emerging from it should apply to U.S. forces and territory with no less rigor than to Soviet forces and territory. . . . The asymmetrical geographical coverage probably caused real concerns in some quarters in Moscow, however, and the Soviet delegate sought to compensate for this by making proposals that affected the West to a greater extent than the East (. . . ceiling on exercises, . . . high threshold on notification, . . . naval activities on the high seas, [and] . . . air activities). Thus they sought to achieve not only a geographic offset to the unequal treatment they tried to portray in the outcome of the Madrid mandate, but also to provide for coverage of those U.S. forces that they perceived to be a special threat to themselves. A third category of obstacles common to many of the issues above stemmed from the asymmetries in the way U.S. and Soviet forces are structured and trained.

The negotiations faced a dilemma: How to implement the agreed principle of equality when its implementation could not be accomplished with equal interest and equal effect? Either the principle had to be changed, from equal to unequal justice, as the Soviets tried by seeking compensation for the asymmetries, or ways had to be found to apply the mandated principle of equality. As Soviet ambassador Grinevsky said (or was instructed to say) as late as March 22, 1985, in round V, "Most of the [NATO] proposals . . . continue to be aimed at laying bare the military activities of the Warsaw Treaty countries, at securing unilateral military advantages. As before, they do not meet the requirements of equality of rights, balance and reciprocity, equal respect for the security interests of all participating states" (Borawski, 1992, p. 65). Until the referent question could be answered satisfactorily, the principle question remained abstract and negotiations were stuck.

The negotiators were working on the problem, however. A little-publicized Walk on the Wharf in Stockholm by Ambassadors Goodby and Grinevsky produced the suggestion of a new and complementary principle of equivalence—Soviet agreement to CSBMs (confidence and security building measures) in exchange for U.S. agreement to a renewed NUF declaration. The suggestion was conveyed to President Reagan, who included it as an apparent "precipitating act" (Saunders, 1988, p. 437) in his speech to the Irish parliament on June 4, 1984. Equivalence of issues did not replace equality of application as the governing principle of justice; it only facilitated it, and other changes were needed to make the latter acceptable.

These changes came with the leadership succession in the Soviet Union, not as a matter of personality or idiosyncrasy, but as a matter of the redefinition of Soviet interests that made the application of the equality principle possible. Confidence-building leading to arms reduction in Europe became a prime Soviet interest, therefore allowing a focus on "the whole of Europe" without implying asymmetry. The Europeanness of the Soviet Union was a historic Russian theme of importance to Gorbachev, overriding perceptions of geographical imbalance. In the midst of Round VIII, the first summit meeting between Reagan and Gorbachev in Geneva produced a final statement that "reaffirmed the need for a document which would include mutually acceptable confidence- and security-building measures and give concrete expression and effect to the principle of non-use of force" (Borawski, 1992, p. 77).

Acceptance of the two principles of justice—equality and equivalence—allowed the negotiators to move ahead to the details of the agreement, translating the principled formula into specific measures for the first time. The informal structure that took over by Round VII and characterized proceedings through 1986 testified to the effect of agreement on the formula, allowing parties to work together in search of agreeable provisions (Borawski, 1992, p. 76). In the end, Ambassador Barry, Goodby's successor, judged, "We gave away more than we wanted, but we got . . . a fair bargain. . . ." (*Washington Post,* Sept. 22, 1986).

Power alone could not have produced and could not explain the agreement. Even though the agreement on terms close to the American position came after the weakening (as prelude to the eventual collapse) of the Soviet Union, it was not the pressure of that asymmetry that caused the Soviet Union to agree. The key to that agreement was its formulation in acceptable terms of justice, and until that was accomplished, the negotiations were stuck.

CUBAN MISSILE CRISIS

The third case is the well-known Cuban Missile Crisis of October 1962, on which much has been written, particularly as a case of national security and of cold war confrontation. It was also an almost-textbook case of negotiation, involving a few simple moves. Countervailing power was used to carry the crisis into stalemate, from which war, capitulation, and a negotiated deal were the only ways out. Insistence on capitulation, which was within the grasp of U.S. power, would have produced war; negotiation was necessary to produce a way out that avoided war, or what Khrushchev termed "untying the knot" (Khrushchev, 1962, p. 642). Even though the result reflected the unbalanced distribution of resource power, it became possible only when a notion of justice was addressed and resolved, and the process of resolving involved a number of attempts to create the appropriate balance by criteria of justice.

The installation of Soviet missiles in Cuba was decided in June 1962 (Khrushchev, 1970, pp. 493–494) and discovered by the United States on October 16 (R. Kennedy, 1969, p. 1). The Soviet action was later justified as a deterrent against American invasion of Cuba, based on an absolute priority principle of collective defense, equally applied: "We had the same rights and opportunities as the Americans . . . governed by the same rules and limits. . . ." (Khrushchev, 1970, pp. 496, 493–495; Khrushchev, 1974, p. 511) For the United States, the right of self-defense against an aggressive move received very little mention in the Executive Committee and was assumed as the legitimate expression of an absolute priority principle of justice (Rusk in Trachtenberg, 1985, p. 171; R. Kennedy, 1969). Discussions centered on the choice of an appropriate American response between air strike and blockade, neither of which would have resolved the issue and removed the missiles (J. F. Kennedy & Dillon in Trachtenberg, 1985, p. 195). The quarantine was chosen as the first response to force withdrawal from the Soviet Union; air strikes were left as the second response, in a threat position (R. Kennedy, 1969, pp. 32–33; Rusk & McNamara in Trachtenberg, 1985, pp. 173, 182; R. Kennedy in Trachtenberg, 1985, p. 200). It was early decided that the quarantine around Cuba would not be traded against a Soviet blockade of Berlin (Trachtenberg, 1985, pp. 178–179). The purpose of the quarantine was to impose a stalemate that would force a decision and would provide an item for trade against the removal of the missiles, as the expression of a priority justice principle but one that was uninteresting to the Soviet Union.

After other unsuccessful stabs at an exchange, the appropriate referents for equivalent justice limited to the Cuban area were offered by Khrushchev in his letter of October 26: a U.S. promise not to invade Cuba in exchange for missile "demobilization" (Khrushchev, 1962, pp. 642, 645). The second Khrushchev letter, the following day, repeated equivalence in more nearly equal terms but no longer limited it to the Cuban area: Soviet missiles out of Cuba in exchange for U.S. missiles out of Turkey (Khrushchev, 1962, p. 648). The president considered that this might "make a good trade" whereas the State Department, in rejecting it, proposed the rejection of any equivalence ("no trade could be made" [J. F. Kennedy in Trachtenberg, 1985, pp. 199, 201; R. Kennedy, 1969, p. 79]). The Executive Committee instead opted to take up the previous offer: Soviet offensive weapons out of Cuba in exchange for U.S. removal of quarantine and assurances against invasion (Khrushchev, 1962, p. 649).

Justice is never mentioned in the Kennedy-Khrushchev exchanges. However, there was much discussion of terms of trade, the ingredients of equivalent justice. In the debate over the two Khrushchev letters, President Kennedy clearly indicated that "we have to face up to the possibility of some kind of trade over missiles" (J. F. Kennedy in Trachtenberg, 1985, p. 199). Grudgingly, Khrushchev—who, having less to crow about, crowed more—indicated that "by agreeing even to symbolic measures, Kennedy was creating the impression of mutual concessions" (Khrushchev, 1974, p. 512). Before his assassination, Robert Kennedy planned to conclude his book with a chapter on justification (R. Kennedy, 1969, p. 106). Despite a lack of explicit references to please researchers, there is no doubt that the last days of the crisis and the bulk of the bargaining were spent in an intense search for terms of trade that would justify the withdrawal of the missiles, the lifting of the quarantine, and the negotiation of an agreement.

CONCLUSIONS

Negotiation analysis has been presented here in order to show the interaction of conflict and order. Conflict occurs when interest-based positions rooted in absolute priority (or other) principles of justice are incompatible with similarly based and rooted positions held by other parties. Order through conflict resolution is provided when the incompatibility is overcome, either by the mutual acceptance of a priority principle and its referents or by the joint determination of a principle or equality or inequality and its referents. It is not yet clear what governs the choice of original

Table 1   Principles of Justice

Case	Initial Principles	Referents	Principle of Agreement
Namibia	SA: priority (conditional elections) SA: priority (friendly relations) SWAPO: priority (liberation) US: priority (one person one vote)	Who votes?	US: equality/equivalence (paired withdrawal from Namibia and Angola)
CDE	CSCE: equality (CBMs by all of Europe)	What is Europe?	US–SU: Equivalence (CSBMs for NUF)
Cuba	SU: priority (collective defense) US: priority (self defense, remove missiles) SU: equality/equivalence (remove missiles— Cuba for Turkey)		SU: equivalence (remove missiles for no invasion in Cuba)

principles nor the acceptance or determination of mutually agreeable principles, beyond the obvious (but basic) notion that original notions of absolute justice are chosen to favor the interests of the holder and that mutual positions are chosen to preserve those interests in combination in the best way perceived. It is clear, however, that power alone, in any non-tautological definition, does not explain why a particular notion of justice is adopted or why a particular outcome is reached independent of justice considerations. The selection of an agreed sense of justice, however, does allow the parties to move on to a more detailed settlement of their conflict, and in its absence no such settlement is possible.

Political practitioners, including negotiators, are neither philosophers no theorists. They therefore do not observe the niceties of analytical sequencing nor the neatnesses of analytical concepts. Identifying such concepts and sequences is therefore a matter of interpretation, as always. But the evidence of the role and importance of justice in conflict and order is clear, in both the decisions and words of the actors. Political analysis has long compartmentalized its treatment of political phenomena according to discrete variables, so that discussions of power, order, and institutions rarely meet discussions of justice, principles, and motivations, or meet only in glancing encounters. Without more sustained meetings, the analysis of conflict and order is incomplete. A new type of analysis of negotiation has been presented here that brings normative considerations back in and put them in their place.

NOTE

* An expanded version of this chapter appeared as Zartman 1997, and is adapted with permission.

REFERENCES

Aristotle. *Nicomachaean Ethics.* New York: Dutton, 1911.

Bartos, O. 1987. "How Predictable are Negotiations?" In Zartman, *The 50% Solution.*

Borawski, J. 1992. *From the Atlantic to the Urals.* New York: Pergamon.

Brams, S. J. 1990. *Negotiation Games.* London: Routledge.

Crocker, C. A. 1993. *High Noon in Southern Africa.* New York: Norton.

Cook, K., & Hegtvedt, K. 1983. "Distributive Justice, Equity and Equality." In Inkeles, *Annual Review of Sociology* (Vol. 9). Palo Alto, CA: Annual Reviews.

Dahl, R. 1957. "The Concept of Power." *Behavioral Science,* 2 (2), 201–215.

Deutsch, M. 1985. *Distributive Justice.* New Haven: Yale University Press.

Edgeworth, F. Y. 1881. *Mathematical Physics.* London: Keegan Paul (Reprinted—New York: Kelly, 1967).

Fisher, R., & Ury, W. 1981. *Getting to Yes.* Boston: Houghton Mifflin.

Ghebali, Y. 1989. *La diplomatie de la détente.* Bruxelles: Bruylant.

Goodby, J. 1988. "Stockholm Conference." In George, Farley, & Dallin, *U.S.-Soviet Security Cooperation.* Boulder, CO: Westview.

Habeeb, M. 1988. *Power and Tactics in International Negotiation.* Baltimore: Johns Hopkins University Press.

Harsanyi, J. 1977. *Rational Behavior and Bargaining Equilibrium in Games and Social Situations.* New York: Cambridge University Press.

Hicks, J. R. 1932. *Theory of Wages.* New York: Macmillan.

Homans, G. C. 1961. *Social Behavior.* New York: Harcourt, Brace & World.

Hopkins, R. 1987. "The Wheat Negotiations." In Zartman, *Positive Sum: Improving North-South Negotiations.* New Brunswick: Transaction.

Iklé, F. C. 1964. *How Nations Negotiate.* New York: Praeger.

Keohane, R. 1986. "Reciprocity in International Relations." *International Organization,* 40 (1), 1–28.

Kennedy, R. F. 1969. *Thirteen Days: A Memoir of the Cuban Missile Crisis.* New York: Norton.

Khrushchev, N. 1962. "Messages exchanged by President Kennedy and Chairman Khrushchev during the Cuban Missile Crisis 1962." *Department of State Bulletin* (November 19).

Khrushchev, N. 1970. *Khrushchev Remembers.* Boston: Little, Brown.

Khrushchev, N. 1974. *Khrushchev Remembers.* Boston: Little, Brown.

Larson, D. W. 1988. "The Psychology of Reciprocity in International Relations." *Negotiation Journal,* 4 (3), 281–302.

Lax, D., & Sebenius, J. (1986). *The Manager as Negotiator.* New York: The Free Press.

Leatherman, J. 1996. *Principles and Paradoxes of Peaceful Change.* Syracuse, NY: Syracuse University Press.

Messe, L. 1971. "Equity in Bilateral Bargaining." *Journal of Personality and Social Psychology,* 17 (3), 287–291.

Morgan, T. C. 1994. *Untying the Knot of War.* Ann Arbor: University of Michigan Press.

Mosca, G. 1939. *The Ruling Class.* New York: McGraw Hill.

North, D. 1990. *Institutions, Institutional Change, and Economic Performance.* New York: Cambridge University Press.

Pruitt, D. G., & Carnevale, P. 1993. *Negotiation in Social Conflict.* Pacific Grove, CA: Brooks/Cole.

Rapoport, A. 1966. *Two-Person Game Theory.* Ann Arbor: University of Michigan Press.

Rubin, J. Z., & Zartman, I. W. 1995. "Asymmetrical Negotiations: Some Survey Results That May Surprise." *Negotiation Journal,* 11 (4), 349–364.

Saunders, H. 1988. "Looking Ahead: Reconstituting the Arab-Israeli Peace Process." In Quandt, *The Middle East: Ten Years after Camp David.* Washington, DC: Brookings Institution.

Schelling, T. 1960. *The Strategy of Conflict.* Cambridge: Harvard University Press.

Simon, H. 1953. "Notes on the Observation and Measurement of Power." *Journal of Politics,* 15 (3), 500–516.

Stolte, J. 1987. "The Formation of Justice Norms." *American Sociological Review,* 52 (4), 774–784.

Tawney, R. H. 1931. *Equality.* London: Unwin.

Thibaut, J. W., & Kelley, H. H. 1959. *The Social Psychology of Groups.* New York: Wiley.

Trachtenberg, M., ed. 1985. "White House Tapes and Minutes of the Cuban Missiles Crisis." *International Security,* 10 (1), 164–203.

Walton, R., & McKersie, R. 1965. *A Behavioral Theory of Labor Negotiations.* New York: McGraw Hill.

Wriggins, H. 1987. "Up for Auction: Malta Bargains with Britain, 1971." In Zartman, *The 50% Solution.*

Young, H. P. 1994. *Equity.* Princeton: Princeton University Press.

Zartman, I. W. 1974. "The Political Analysis of Negotiation: Who Gets What When How?" *World Politics,* 17 (3), 33–37.

Zartman, I. W., ed. 1978. *The Negotiation Process.* Newbury Park, CA: Sage.

Zartman, I. W., ed. 1987. *The 50% Solution.* New Haven: Yale University Press.

Zartman, I. W. 1995. "The Role of Justice in Security Negotiations." *American Behavioral Scientist,* 18 (6), 889–903.

Zartman, I. W. 1997. "Justice in Negotiation." *International Political Science Review,* 18 (2), 121–138.

Zartman, I. W., & Bassani, A. 1987. *The Algerian Gas Negotiations.* Washington, DC: Foreign Policy Institute, School of Advanced International Studies, The Johns Hopkins University.

Zartman, I. W., & Berman, M. 1982. *The Practical Negotiator.* New Haven: Yale University Press.

Zartman, I. W., Druckman, D., Jensen, L., Pruitt, D. G., & Young, H. P. 1996. "Negotiation as a Search for Justice." *International Negotiation,* 1 (1), 1–20.

Zartman, I. W., & Rubin, J. Z., eds. 1999. *Power and Negotiation.* Ann Arbor: University of Michigan Press.

Zeuthen, F. 1930. *Problems of Monopoly and Economic Welfare.* London: Routledge and Kegan Paul.

CHAPTER 11

NEGOTIATING WITH VILLAINS

BERTRAM I. SPECTOR

"No-negotiation" is the guiding principle in some extreme international conflicts.[1] In fact, when the other side has been elevated to the role of villain, demon, rogue, or pariah, policy generally dictates that negotiation is not a valid conflict-resolution option. But why? Is negotiation seen to be a benefit for the villain? Is negotiation viewed as a sign of weakness or appeasement by the one who proposes it? Are there fears of double-cross by the villain? Will the party suggesting negotiation lose face? Or is a no-negotiation policy simply a tactic of incapacity, indicating that all bridges to a peaceful dialogue have been burned and the only option to resolve the impasse is for the villain to comply with the offerer's demands?

In a September 9, 1994, "op-ed" article in the *Washington Post,* the former foreign minister of Israel, Abba Eban, argued forcefully that national leaders have an *obligation* to their constituents to negotiate directly and early with even their most detested villains to achieve pragmatic compromises. The no-negotiation principle should not be an option. Eban asserted that leadership needs to adopt normative goals to avert violence, save lives, and allow people to live peaceful lives, regardless of the roots of the conflict. Too often, according to Eban, leaders view extreme conflicts in self-righteous, ideological, morally superior, and emotional terms, based on concepts of virtue, justice, and legitimacy that may be misplaced given the situation. While an adversary may, in fact, pose a real risk to the established order, leaders ought to be obliged to find ways to mitigate the threat through peaceful negotiation, even with the most unthinkable of villains.

Some leaders (such as de Klerk and Mandela in South Africa; Rabin, Peres, and Arafat in Israel; and Major and Adams in Northern Ireland), after spending most of their political careers painting their opponents as unspeakable villains, somehow were able to reframe problems and negotiate mutually acceptable compromises based on pragmatic self-interest. In doing so, they succeeded in convincing their attentive publics that their shift in negotiation policy was reasonable. This "new diplomacy," as Eban calls it, is what diplomacy traditionally has always been about: finding accommodation among intrinsically self-interested parties. The sometimes successful search for such accommodation can take the form of direct and official face-to-face talks or informal, back-channel discussions that test the waters on possible proposals. The unofficial route often allows leaders to villainize *and* negotiate at the same time, offering an easy path for denial if the negotiation attempt fails or yields unfavorable outcomes.

How were the leaders mentioned here capable of the decision to negotiate despite the villainization of the opponent and their longstanding feuds? What keeps other leaders from following in their footsteps? Despite recent examples, negotiation is sometimes perceived as appeasement of an illegitimate aggressor, a villainized adversary. The memory of Chamberlain appeasing Hitler in Czechoslovakia remains remarkably fresh, despite the passage of nearly 60 years. Negotiating with aggressors can be seen as validating their aggression (Laqueur, 1980). It can be viewed as a sign of weakness by the initiating party and a willingness to accept a solution dictated by the aggressor. Negotiating with such opponents is often avoided for fear of encouraging further violent reactions by that group and others. National leaders do not decide easily to negotiate in extreme conflict situations because they want to avoid the negative public opinion that labels them as appeasers and because they are fearful of the real disruption to the established order posed by the adversary.

Fisher, Ury, and Patton (1991), like Eban, encourage leaders to negotiate with terrorists and other villains, even ones as heinous as Hitler, unless they have a better alternative to a negotiated agreement (BATNA). Increasing communication with such foes, they believe, will offer the opportunity to exert meaningful influence over them. Only through active negotiation, not by closing off the negotiation option, can one learn enough about the villain's interests to find a viable formula. Moreover, negotiating with villains should not be viewed as an ethical question. "[N]egotiating does not require compromising your principles," they write (1991, p. 164). If a substantial number of national interests can be achieved through pragmatic negotiations, it is worthwhile. If negotiations can facilitate pragmatic accommodation that yields results better than the BATNA, it benefits the country.

Other negotiation literature on pre-negotiation (Stein, 1989), ripeness of conflict (Zartman, 1989), turning points (Druckman, Husbands, & Johnston, 1991), and creativity (Spector, 1995) seeks to explain the factors that stimulate parties to accept negotiation as the appropriate means of resolving their conflicts. However, this literature deals with normal diplomatic situations—that is, mixed-motive conflicts or problems that can be managed through established negotiation procedures and be maintained at low-conflict levels (Jentleson & Lund, 1994). When extreme, prolonged, and ideological conflicts and villainized enemies are involved, it is not clear that the same factors are sufficient to explain this decision-making process. Affective reasons play an important role, as well as the need for a complete reconstruction of the problem and a subjugation of principles.

The very decision to negotiate in such circumstances instead of continuing a violent struggle often requires a step-level change. In South Africa, Israel, and Northern Ireland, national leaders appear to have undergone a metamorphic process, though at a much later stage in the dispute than Eban would have wanted, after their countries sustained intensive conflict and trauma. Such a change involves an essential frame-breaking pre-negotiation decision, a decision that must overcome the ideology, partisanship, and long-term hatred and emotion characteristic of these conflicts. Moreover, the decision must overcome the very designation of the other party as a villain, the socialization of villainization, and, most importantly, the problem of saving or protecting face. Without this pre-negotiation decision, real negotiation will never occur.

VILLAINIZATION

Enemies are persons, groups, or countries perceived to be threatening or harmful, whether that perception is based on fact or on a projection of fears (Finlay, Holsti, & Fagen, 1967; Klare, 1995). But not all enemies are the same. Enemies who are "low-salient," for example, may present a risk, but are passive, weak, or minimally threatening to basic beliefs and norms. "High-salient" enemies, on the other hand, may be viewed as the incarnation of evil, symbolizing the antithesis of a country's core values and beliefs.[2] High-salient enemies are thus portrayed and perceived as villains, demons, rogues, rebels, outlaws, or pariahs. A villain is the most extreme of enemies, one who is seen as believing and acting in contravention of or in a manner that is totally indifferent to accepted norms of specific societies and, sometimes, the international community. Important to remember is the fact that villains are designated as such by others; villainy is in the eye of the beholder.

Overt support for terrorist groups, trafficking in illegal drugs, blatant disregard for human rights, exporting revolution to unstable regions, explicit deception in international affairs, and illicit trade in banned weapons are all grounds for labeling a nation or group a villain, inviting certain punishments and sanctions *and* providing the pretense for other countries to refrain from negotiating with them. Certain actions or policies exercised by a government that are purely domestic in nature can also cause a government to be labeled as a villain; for example, a so-called villainous regime may govern by force and fear or may be ruled by leaders considered to be criminal and morally unfit.

Actors are usually villainized for their past behavior. The United States, for example, maintains several categories, most defined by national laws or international agreements, by which it officially designates villains. These include

- countries that *sponsor terrorism* (currently Cuba, Iran, Iraq, Libya, North Korea, Sudan, and Syria [U.S. Department of State, 1995a]) as defined in the U.S. Export Administration Act of 1979;
- *drug-producing and/or drug-transiting countries* (currently Afghanistan, Burma, Iran, Nigeria, and Syria [U.S. Department of State, 1995b]) as defined in the 1988 UN Convention Against Illicit Traffic in Narcotic Drugs and Psychotropic Substances;
- countries with which diplomatic relations have been broken unilaterally because of deeply rooted political conflicts with the United States or its allies (for example, during the Cold War, divided states such as East Germany, North Korea, and North Vietnam [Berridge, 1994]);
- countries that develop and export weapons of mass destruction, as defined in the Chemical Weapons Convention, the Nuclear Non-Proliferation Treaty, and other agreements; and
- countries that have demonstrated major violations of human rights of their own citizenry, as defined in the 1984 UN Convention Against Torture.

Rogue states or groups usually do not view what they are doing as unacceptable or wrong; they do not define themselves as villains, but are designated as such by others. The so-called villain may be following an internally logical policy (for example, sponsoring liberation movements or unsettling Western hegemony in a region). It may view its cause as righteous and its position as defending "the cause." However, within the context and norms of the international community, its actions may be viewed as perverse.

From the designator's perspective, villains are created and unmade for opportunistic reasons. They can serve to foster in-group strength. Some suggest that a country may need enemies—especially heinous enemies—to serve as scapegoats on which to displace frustration, to justify improper actions, and to make the country seem morally superior (Finlay, Holsti, & Fagen, 1967; Volkan, 1988). Demonization and dehumanization of the enemy are strong psychological motives that help countries clarify their purpose and demarcate their goodness from others' badness. Villains may be designated as part of power ploys to gain leverage in the international context and to rally domestic sentiment, perhaps forcing negotiation in the end, but at a risk of threatening lives and promoting conflict and struggle in the short term.

IMPLICATIONS OF VILLAINIZATION

As a result of being villainized, the designated states or groups bear the brunt of certain sanctions and restrictive actions. For example, they may lose diplomatic relations with key countries, they may be subject to particular export controls, their trade and financial transactions may be controlled, and their citizens and leaders' ability to travel may be limited. Ostracism and the breaking of formal and informal channels of communication can create harsh conditions for the villain. One of the major consequences of villainization is the closing off of the negotiation option and the peaceful settlement of disputes. The goal of all of these sanctions is to change the behavior of the villainous country. Sometimes these tactics succeed over time, but often the immediate response of the villain is further rigidity in its position and an escalation of the conflict.[3]

Designator states are motivated to initiate the process of villainization for various political reasons. Some reasons are for export and some for domestic consumption. From the perspective of export, villainization is meant to weaken the leadership of the villainized state or group in the eyes of its people. The process is intended to indicate to the citizenry that their leaders have fallen from grace in the international community and, as a result, that the people will suffer certain negative consequences. They will no longer be viewed as legitimate partners in the international community. Allies of the villainized country or group are also put on alert that they may suffer similar sanctions. Aside from the negative words and press, the sanctions themselves—restricted trade and travel, embargoes, boycotts, severing of diplomatic relations, and so on—may have a concrete and direct impact on the well-being of the villainous state or group and its members.

The villainization process is also intended to influence the domestic population in the designator state. It seeks to mobilize domestic perceptions against an outrageous enemy, to portray the other as not just an enemy but a rogue that must be undone. Socialization of the domestic population through the villainization process prepares them for any potential military action against the enemy. Friedman (1992), McKersie (1992), and Wheeler (1992) assert that to make "going to war" palatable to the American public in the Gulf crisis of 1990, the Bush administration was compelled to villainize Saddam Hussein. Hussein was equated with Hitler, the stakes were simplified and moralized, and emotions were aroused about his demonic and aggressive nature. A no-negotiation principle was espoused by President Bush, enforced by the villainization of Hussein, and motivated by the fear of appeasement.

Villainization may be able to achieve its objectives with some enemies, resulting in their acquiescence. But with other enemies, the process of villainization may be counterproductive. In some cultures, such as in China, public denunciation as manifested by removing "most favored nation" treatment in the face of human rights violations, for example, may only invigorate resistance to external demands for human rights reform. Rather, quiet negotiations out of the public glare may be more effective in these types of cultures.[4]

Does villainization always yield intractability and limit the negotiation options? Commonly practiced by all sides in ethnopolitical struggles, villainization is often viewed as one of the major reasons for stalemate. However, Gurr (1992) concludes that these types of conflict are usually negotiable. Historically, some form of negotiation often yields peaceful solutions in the short run between feuding ethnic groups and the ruling government, although new conflicts, backlashes, and subversions of agreements may arise later. Even if these deeply rooted disputes are not entirely resolvable, but only manageable over the long term (Richardson, 1992), the negotiation process is a viable and available mechanism if leaders can only unleash themselves from rigid policies of no-negotiation with their villains and find ways of saving face to avert charges of appeasement.

DECIDING TO NEGOTIATE

The decision to negotiate with villains—through either official or unofficial channels—requires a reversal of the villainization process. Despite the repulsive actions and values attributed to the villain, the designator country may decide that it is better to take a pragmatic road and negotiate rather than continue the struggle. Idealistic motives may prevail—leaders may see it as their duty to protect and ensure the peace and security of their citizens and therefore to negotiate. But this conversion from villainizer to devillainizer does not necessarily imply that ideological differences are abandoned or compromised. Israel's decision to negotiate directly with the Palestine Liberation Organization, for instance, did not usher in a total collapse of Israel's quest for security. It may just indicate a realization that short-term goals can be better achieved through negotiation than through a continued struggle.

But there is a risk in devillainizing the enemy for the designating country's leaders. At a minimum, they can be accused of being hypocritical; they turn the demons of last week into the legitimate and respectable partners of this week. At its worst, leaders directing a devillainization campaign can be accused of being appeasers and traitors.

Jimmy Carter, for example, was vilified as "a collaborator in evil," an "amoral" person, and "a menace" for negotiating as a private citizen with the Bosnian Serbs in December 1994 to achieve a ceasefire.[5] He was called "naïve" (Mollins, 1994) and "soft on dictators" (Rose, 1995), and accused of "making pacts with oppressors" and "wheedling 'respect' for torturers" (Schorr, 1994) for his interventions on behalf of the U.S. government in North Korea and Haiti. He was castigated for negotiating in "the lair of 'thugs'" and for "declaring (dictators) to be men of honor" (Kramer, 1994).[6]

Despite these accusations, Carter has been willing to negotiate with villains, but only once his presidency was over, when there could be no reprisal at the voting booth. Ironically, as president, Carter elevated the cause of human rights in U.S. foreign policy and took the high moral road, never to negotiate with immoral leaders. His reversal is based on the belief that communication, respect, trust, and granting legitimacy are essential to ending conflicts (Rose, 1995). Carter believes that, in a crisis, it is critical to address the decision maker directly, even if that decision maker has been painted as a villain. By listening to the villain's interests, it may be possible to devise a formula that can resolve the crisis; without communication—by closing off the negotiation option through villainization—a meaningful and peaceful solution usually cannot be found.

Villains, once designated, are usually denied the privilege of negotiating with other countries directly to resolve the problem. However, without this channel for negotiation, the designator country also limits its own options, relying entirely on sanctions to resolve the conflict. Herein lies the "villainizer's dilemma." By villainizing a group or state, the designator country seeks to punish and pressure the villain to change its behavior. Sanctions and negative incentives are mobilized. But in so doing, the villainizer greatly limits the possible ways of finding a solution. Responsibility for resolving the crisis is shifted almost entirely to the villain, who *must* comply with the sanctions imposed and change its villainous behavior before anything else will be forthcoming from the designator country.

The villainizer's dilemma lies in initiating a peaceful resolution to a crisis with a villain if the villain does not comply with the sanctions within a reasonable time frame. During their defiance of the sanctions, villains can continue, for example, to abuse human rights at home, terrorize their own populations, and export terrorism overseas. With the continued loss of life and human suffering, and in the absence of a cease-fire, for example, designator countries might feel pressured by the international community and their home constituencies to do something beyond the current sanctions to get the villains to comply.

Under these circumstances, there are at least three options for the designator country. One decision is to escalate the sanctions regime—to impose yet harsher punishment on the villain—in the hope that it will break the villain's defiance. However, harsher sanctions—stricter embargoes on trade, restrictions on civil aviation, and so on—may only serve to invigorate the villain's will to defy and generate a greater sense of loyalty within the villain's group or state. Moreover, such harsher sanctions would not only punish the leadership, but would also likely increase the hardship facing innocent people. Another decision, also escalatory, that could be made by the designator is to take limited strategic military action. Terrorist training camps, nuclear reactors, or military headquarters could be targeted, for example. But such military action truly escalates the crisis to a war, which may not be in the interest of the designator country.

The third option is to negotiate with the villain. There are obvious risks involved for the designator country to reverse the process and decide to communicate and negotiate. However, if the designator state finds that the policy of villainization does not yield the desired results in a reasonable time frame or if it wishes to become proactive in resolving the conflict, it may eventually decide to negotiate.

FOUR EXAMPLES

Four recent international examples illustrate the decision to negotiate with so-called villains under a variety of circumstances.[7] In two of these examples, regimes with questionable legitimacy challenged the more powerful United States in confrontational episodes to extract concessions. In the other two examples, insurgent groups were involved in often prolonged violent struggles with a government to achieve step-level changes in governance and socioeconomic relations. In all four cases, the conflicts can be characterized as the weak versus the strong, and the decision to negotiate served to level the playing field between the parties. Parenthetically, it would not be difficult to imagine similar situations in entirely different contexts—in bitter labor-management disputes or in divorce or child-custody proceedings—in which the parties have been demonized, villainization reversed, and successful negotiations conducted.

ISRAEL'S DECISION TO NEGOTIATE WITH THE PALESTINE LIBERATION ORGANIZATION: MAY 1993

One of the most emotional, deeply rooted, and persistent conflicts of this century has been that between the Israelis and Palestinians. A hundred years of violent conflict between Israelis and Palestinians have resulted in a difficult combination of fear, hatred, revenge, and dehumanization. These emotions have long been taught to their populations, encouraging demonic stereotypes and irrational perceptions, and giving rise to Palestinian terrorism and a heritage of hatred.

However, over a short period of time in the early 1990s, many of the barriers to negotiation were dropped and halting progress was made toward achieving an accommodation between the protagonists. One of the major stumbling blocks to direct negotiation was the extreme villainous status accorded by the Israeli government to the Palestine Liberation Organization (PLO), the body deemed to represent the majority of Palestinians.

The Israeli government "go-ahead" to conduct direct and official negotiations in May 1993 was preceded and catalyzed by four months of unofficial and secret talks conducted by Israeli and PLO-affiliated academics through what has been called "the Oslo channel."[8] Because of their unofficial nature, these talks could be plausibly denied if there were leaks or if the talks ended in failure. However, sufficient progress was made to convince the Israeli leadership that authorized and official negotiations were a reasonable next step.

Analysis

Devillainization on both sides—by Israel of the PLO and by the PLO of Israel—was accomplished in a pragmatic way. Neither side denied the fact that it still considered the other an enemy of the worst kind. However, both sides agreed that peace could only come when the negotiation option was made available. Rabin said, "peace is not made with friends. Peace is made with enemies, and some of them—I will not specify their names—I abhor enormously" (FBIS, 1993, p. 17). Elsewhere he said, "Arafat carried out what I considered to be atrocities. But I've said more than once in the context of the Arab-Israeli conflict, we make peace, or we negotiate meaningful steps toward peace, with enemies. Sometimes bitter enemies" (Gibbs, 1994, p. 22).

The devillainization process that lead to the decision to negotiate involved arguments that drew on pragmatism, power relationships, trust, and initiative.

Pragmatism. Rabin accommodated his view of Arafat as a terrorist and murderer with his belief that Israel could "do business" with him. There were other Palestinian leaders and organizations, but Arafat, especially at this point in time, was most favorable from the Israeli perspective and most likely to be able to deliver on his promises. Rabin said, "I came to the conclusion that it's in their interest as well as our interest. It is not based on any feeling of affection or affiliation" (Gibbs, 1994, p. 22). Specifically, the Intifadeh was a constant negative pressure and drain on the Israelis and there was no sign that it would end anytime soon. From the PLO perspective, with no visible progress toward the goal of a Palestinian homeland, the Hamas fundamentalists were winning over converts, and the PLO was strapped for cash as the Russians and the oil-rich states stopped or reduced their payments.

Power Relationships. Both parties seemed to have realized that it was critical to talk directly with those who had the power to influence the conflict situation, not through proxies or emissaries. Rabin said, "I realized that everything is dictated by the PLO. . . . It's about time we took off the masks at the masked ball and talked to the man in charge" (Gibbs, 1994, pp. 21, 24). Arafat concurred by saying, "He [Rabin] is the boss, and without him, the accord will not work" (Gibbs, 1994, p. 22).

Trust. Both Rabin and Arafat, despite their mutual villainization, had confidence that the other would fulfill his word with appropriate deeds after the negotiation. Arafat described Rabin as "my enemy, but . . . a man who fulfills his commitments" (Gibbs, 1994, p. 22). Once the process began, each was dependent on the other to keep it going and, importantly, to maintain the public image that devillainization was not appeasement or "giving in" to the enemy—that devillainization would pay off for both sides in the form of a real peace. As the negotiation progressed, perceptions of commitment on both sides were generated naturally. Moreover, the leaders had confidence at the outset that both had the capacity to deliver on their promises.

Initiative. To start the process of devillainization took initiative. To break the frame, each leader had to be willing to take the necessary risks—had to have the courage—to surprise and do something unexpected to open the negotiation channel after so many years of villainization. Rabin said, "I hope that Arafat learned a lesson, as I have learned the lesson, that you have to be more forthcoming" (Gibbs, 1994, p. 24).

The Israeli public that had given the Labor Party a mandate to seek peace was also strongly pragmatic. They were tired of the conflict and the violence and the burden of controlling a hostile population. Their support enabled Rabin to take the steps toward opening the channels for negotiation that he did.

The advancing age of the leaders of both Israel and the PLO also may have stimulated movement toward negotiation. If a more peaceful world were to be handed on to the next generation by Rabin and Arafat, negotiations had to begin soon.

In the end, it might be concluded that Rabin decided to negotiate when he did because the PLO was never weaker and needed the "Declaration of Principles" agreement to survive. By saving the PLO, Israel took on only a small risk; if it stood by silently and allowed Hamas to take over, that would be an opening to a much more palpable threat. By supporting Arafat, Rabin would get a partner to help manage fundamentalist and terrorist violence. And Rabin could always tout Israel's superior power to protect himself from the charge of appeasement—that while he might compromise with the villain, he was acting on Israel's behalf from a position of power. He always maintained the military might to protect Israel's security if the deal went sour or if Arafat did not live up to his promises.

UNITED STATES DECIDES TO NEGOTIATE WITH NORTH KOREA: JUNE 1994

In June of 1994, Western fears over the North Korean nuclear weapons program had built to a crescendo, with North Korea's extracting fuel rods from its reactor that could be reprocessed into weapons-grade material, withdrawing from the International Atomic Energy Agency (IAEA), threatening to expel IAEA inspectors, and leaving itself isolated from any communication with the West. North Korea had long been condemned in the United States as an outlaw state and its leader, Kim Il Sung, portrayed as a criminal. North Korea had consistently shown indifference to established norms of international behavior. It had sponsored terrorist acts against South Korea since the 1980s. North Korea also had a record of selling intermediate-range missiles to Iraq, Syria, Libya, and Iran; and it was feared that it would more likely sell than use nuclear weapons in the future to obtain dearly needed foreign exchange.

Former president Jimmy Carter was granted permission by the U.S. government to travel to North Korea in June 1994 as a private citizen representing the Carter Center of Emory University. The purpose of Carter's trip was to meet with President Kim Il Sung and discuss the reopening of negotiations with the United States concerning the nuclear program in North Korea. As an unofficial party, Carter presented the U.S. position in two days of meetings with President Kim. According to Carter, the North Korean leader readily conceded to all demands, affirming that his country would freeze its nuclear program, refrain from refueling its reactors or reprocessing spent fuel, permit IAEA inspectors and surveillance equipment to remain, and agree to restart negotiations with the United States. As a sign of good will, he promised to allow joint U.S.-North Korean teams to search for and recover the remains of American soldiers who were buried in North Korea during the Korean War.

In return, President Kim received a resumption of the dialogue with the United States, recognition that North Korea is a legitimate nation, an end to the threat of universal condemnation as an outlaw country, and assurance that the West would support North Korea's efforts to get light water reactor technology.

Analysis

The U.S. administration felt that it needed to be proactive. In the post - Cold War world, nonproliferation had been elevated to a high priority in the foreign policy of the United States. As a well-established rogue state,

North Korea could challenge the renegotiation of the Nuclear Nonproliferation Treaty, actively export nuclear and missile technology to other
states, and seriously threaten South Korea and U.S. troops there. The
United States had three basic options: sanctions, force, and diplomacy.

At the time of the decision to send Carter's negotiation mission to North
Korea, there was still a very real question as to whether agreement could
have been reached to approve international sanctions at the United Nations.
The Russians wanted to delay the decision, the Chinese did not want to
place pressure on their allies, the Japanese did not want to place sanctions
that could restrict remittances to North Korea from Koreans living in Japan,
and the South Koreans were fearful that sanctions could trigger a war.

Some counteraction needed to be taken toward North Korea's challenges. Sanctions were a real threat, but there was still a major problem in
mobilizing the international community to agree to impose them. A military strike against the nuclear complex at Yongbyon was one scenario, but
it could catalyze a retaliatory response leading to major military conflict on
the Korean peninsula. Carter's mission was a last-ditch diplomatic option,
which, at a minimum, could serve as a delaying tactic for the U.S. administration to cobble together a consensus in favor of the sanctions or some
other strategy. Little could be lost by trying the diplomatic route in the
short run; the fuel rods could not be reprocessed into plutonium for several weeks, when their radioactivity reached safe levels.

With the imposition of international sanctions imminent, Carter's mission was seen as fulfilling a final attempt by the U.S. administration to conduct good-faith negotiations to resolve the problem. If these negotiations
succeeded, the world would be saved from the uncertainty of North Korean actions in the aftermath of sanctions. If they failed, the sanctions could
be imposed, which would overshadow any blame for attempting to deal
with the villain. In fact, failure of the talks would merely reinforce the villainous status of North Korea and its leaders.

Upon Carter's return with President Kim's promises to accede to all of
the United States' requests, Carter was confronted by his critics as having
appeased the North Koreans. He was labeled as naïve and gullible for having believed Kim's words. He was lambasted for allowing the North Koreans to achieve all of their short-term objectives and for characterizing
Kim Il Sung as an "honest statesman committed to a peaceful reconcilia-
tion with his neighbors" (Weinberger, 1994). In fact, Clinton himself re-
frained from meeting with Carter personally when he returned to the
United States. It was only a week later, on June 22, when the North Korean government officially confirmed to the U.S. government all of the

agreements as presented to Carter and affirmed its desire to renew negotiations with the United States in July, that Carter was congratulated publicly by Clinton.

From the beginning, the U.S. administration made a conscious effort to
distance itself from the Carter mission until it was viewed as a success. If it
had been left to the State Department, Carter would not have gone to
North Korea at all, and he certainly would not have represented the U.S.
position. Clinton, however, appears to have been persuaded that Carter's
intervention as a private citizen might possibly serve to avert the impending crisis; but he needed a way to repudiate the intervention if it did not
succeed.

Carter ascribed the success of his mission to the confidence-building
that is inherent in maintaining direct communications even with villains,
for the most despised of leaders are often the ones who have the power to
actually resolve the problem (Cable News Network, 1994). Sometimes it
is difficult to maintain that communication on official levels, according to
Carter, but those are the circumstances in which unofficial channels must
be forged. Outlawed leaders are often cooperative when treated with respect, according to Carter. He asserts that the element of distrust can be
moderated by holding direct discussions on a very pragmatic basis with
those that have the authority and power to make decisions; one must treat
such leaders with respect despite one's feelings of repulsion toward them.

At the same time, the threats of international sanctions were probably
potent inducements for the North Korean leader to reach an agreement
quickly. North Korea would be isolated even more than before: Russia was
no longer a strong ally and China had already recognized South Korea.
Thus, this "last chance" effort—extending an olive branch in the context
of impending sanctions—appears to have been viewed seriously by the
North Korean leadership. This type of brinkmanship—allowing for one
small, unofficial opening to negotiate at the eleventh hour within the context of a tough strategy with visible punishments for noncompliance—appears to have worked for the U.S. administration, averting charges of
appeasement and achieving the desired objectives.

THE UNITED STATES DECIDES TO NEGOTIATE WITH THE MILITARY LEADERS OF HAITI: SEPTEMBER 1994

Haitian military leaders were villainized by the Clinton administration because of their illegal coup in 1991, which toppled a democratically elected
leader, President Jean-Bertrand Aristide, from power; human rights abuses;

a reign of terror that reportedly claimed over 3,000 deaths; and the resulting tide of Haitian refugees seeking to enter the United States illegally.

On September 15, 1994, President Clinton placed an ultimatum before the three leading Haitian commanders, General Cedras, General Biamby, and Colonel Francois: Leave now or we'll force you from power. However, at the eleventh hour on the very next day, President Clinton agreed to dispatch a high-level delegation to Port-au-Prince to negotiate with the generals in the hope that they would step down voluntarily and thereby avert the need to resort to force. The delegation was headed by former president Carter and included former Joint Chiefs of Staff General Colin Powell Jr. and Senate Armed Services Committee chairman Sam Nunn, whom Carter had recruited. The express purpose of these negotiations was solely to discuss the means of departure of the generals—their departure from office, not necessarily their departure from the country.

Analysis

The success of the diplomatic mission was aided handily by the imminent threat of U.S. military force. Much of the discussion centered around the inevitability of the arrival of U.S. troops in Haiti, and the fact that the timetable was already set and could not be altered. Haitian detection of the actual launch of the military operation as the negotiations proceeded served to make the consequences of a negotiation success or failure very real to the Haitian generals. It set a real deadline in the talks that could not be changed.

Very clearly, the villains in Haiti were the military generals who were labeled by the United States one week as dictators and murderers, and the next week officers with honor who should be treated with respect. They were leaders who were viewed as having broken previous agreements—in particular, the Governor's Island Agreement—and thus, as individuals who could not be trusted. However, the United States struck an agreement with these villains that relied on our confidence in their compliance with the basic provision, their departure from office. Moreover, the chief villain, General Cedras, was treated generously and respectfully. This apparent flip-flop and, some would say, hypocrisy, in U.S. policy was questioned strenuously in the press: How can you negotiate with villains that are both contemptible and untrustworthy?

Carter, in fact, was portrayed by some in the media as an appeaser, posing with "thugs," declaring them to be men of honor, trusting that their words would be borne out by compatible deeds, granting them legitimacy, and making demonized dictators into de facto leaders (Kramer, 1994). He

was seen as "wheedling respect for torturers and making pacts with oppressors" (Schorr, 1994) and for settling for less than the Clinton administration had demanded of him. By deciding to negotiate with villains
through the Carter delegation after successfully villainizing them, Clinton
was also accused of having few principles, being incoherent in his policies,
believing in the religious salvation of even the worst demons, and, ultimately, leading the United States in retreat (Kramer, 1994).

Senator Nunn justified the decision to negotiate with the Haitian villains by indicating that it enabled the United States to carry out its chosen
policy while greatly reducing the loss of life on both sides (Rose, September 26, 1994). In such cases, he believes that negotiating with villains is justifiable. While the generals may, in fact, be the unsavory and dishonorable
characters that had been painted by the United States, one tries to appeal
to the better instincts of the person with whom one is negotiating. In
order to gain agreement from Cedras, for example, it was necessary to gain
his understanding and appeal to *his* sense of right and wrong, whether or
not it conformed to U.S. understanding or beliefs. In his memoirs (1995,
p. 602), Powell said, "What happened to the junta was inconsequential. Because of what we accomplished, young Americans and probably far more
Haitians, who would have died were still alive. That was success enough for
me." Playing on the honor of dishonorable men, men who had been officially condemned by the United States, was acceptable if the direct consequence was the saving of lives.

The decision to negotiate with the generals was part of a brinkmanship
policy to balance unbearable and unstoppable pressure on the villains that
threatened their military defeat with an honorable way out through negotiation. If the negotiation failed, the U.S. administration would make good
on its threats to invade the island and achieve its goals through military
force. If the negotiation succeeded, U.S. troops could enter the country
safely and prepare for the exit of the generals and the return of Aristide.
Little would be lost and much would be gained by limiting negotiations
under the shadow of an invasion. Negotiation also allowed the administration to dodge a possible vote on the matter and the resentment of Congress for not having been consulted on the Haitian plan.

American credibility in international crisis situations had been on the
line, especially after fresh and continuing memories of the yet unsolved
problems in Somalia and Bosnia. Making a stand in Haiti, the weakest crisis, provided the opportunity for a success. But with the sensitivity of the
American public to possible casualties, the lack of public sentiment for an
intervention in Haiti, and the bitterness of Congress to the entire mission,

the administration found that a tough military posture balanced by a diplomatic escape channel was the optimal strategy. It could appear strong and resolute and get what it wanted, while avoiding nasty military encounters.

GREAT BRITAIN AGREES TO NEGOTIATE WITH SINN FEIN: DECEMBER 1994

The current conflict involving the British government, the Catholic minority, and the Protestant majority in Northern Ireland dates back twenty-five years and has resulted in more than 3,000 deaths. One could say that this conflict began much earlier, and some historians even trace it back to the twelfth century invasion of Ireland by the Anglo-Normans. The main Catholic protagonist in the contemporary conflict, the Irish Republican Army and its political wing, Sinn Fein, had been clearly designated for years by the British government as an outlawed terrorist group.

The British government agreed to engage in direct discussions with Sinn Fein on December 9, 1994. The cease-fire declared by the Irish Republican Army (IRA) on August 31, 1994, had held for three months, and that was the required time period specified by the government as necessary to establish a stable and trustworthy cessation of hostilities.

An entire year before, on December 15, 1993, British Prime Minister John Major and Irish Prime Minister Albert Reynolds had signed the "Downing Street Declaration," which constructed a formula for commencing negotiations that included Sinn Fein. That formula (similar to a failed formula designed in 1985) sought to (1) reassure the Catholic minority by including the Irish Republic as a player in future all-party negotiations, (2) reassure the Protestants by suggesting that the Irish Republic would accept a solution that maintained the status quo of Northern Ireland's standing in the United Kingdom, and (3) offer a place at the negotiating table to Sinn Fein conditional on a three-month IRA cease-fire. By October 29, 1994, Britain's Major had announced that the government was ready to start talking with Sinn Fein, under the presumption that the cease-fire would continue uninterrupted. At that time, Major also promised that troop levels on the streets of Northern Ireland would be reduced and border crossings with the Irish Republic would be opened in line with the reality of the diminished terrorist threat. Additional government promises of private economic investment and European Union funding of new projects in Northern Ireland were held out as carrots for maintaining the cease-fire. Major's statement was clearly a preliminary government reciprocation to the IRA, encouraging it to hold fast to the cease-fire.

Analysis

Movement to the negotiation table on the part of the government came
as reciprocation for the IRA's cease-fire initiative. Without that initiative,
the government probably would not have commenced negotiation activity in December 1994. The government had been demanding a cease-fire
from the IRA for a long while and stood firm in its policy to refuse the
negotiation option until such a cease-fire was not only declared but proven
to be long lasting.

Why did the IRA cease military operations in August 1994?

- The Downing Street Declaration sought to isolate the IRA from its
  constituency and prod it to commit to a cease-fire by reassuring the
  more moderate Catholic factions in Northern Ireland.
- John Hume, a member of the British and European Parliaments and
  leader of the predominantly Catholic Social Democratic and Labor
  Party in Northern Ireland, concluded at least six years of private
  talks with Gerry Adams, president of Sinn Fein, in early 1994 with
  a declaration of principles that established a framework for developing peaceful relations between the Catholic and Protestant communities and between Britain and Ireland. This agreement
  moderated the position of the more radical Catholic nationalists.[9]
- Perhaps it had something to do with the opening and recognition
  afforded to Gerry Adams by the U.S. government in March 1994
  when Adams was granted a visa to attend a conference in the
  United States. During that visit, Adams was reportedly impressed
  by the support of the Irish-American community for a negotiated
  settlement and the implied economic support that the United
  States would make available to Northern Ireland if a negotiated
  peace was achieved. Not long after that trip, the IRA cease-fire
  was announced.

From the British government's perspective, it had to be made clear for
the public that a cease-fire was "permanent"; a three month peace was seen
by the government as the minimal time necessary to create the public
image that the villains had indeed ceased their terrorist activity for good.
While it was probably evident to all that a resumption of violence was lurk-
ing just below the surface, the veneer of peace and the trappings of nor-
mality were sufficient after three months to open the way for negotiations
with the villain. Actions are more compelling than mere words, and only
with this public image that the villain had abandoned its villainous ways

could the government agree to negotiate with them and not lose face. In the atmosphere of the cease-fire, any future government concessions to Sinn Fein would not appear to be surrendering to violence or terrorism.

Thus, the government had pronounced its simple incapacity to negotiate dependent upon compliance by the villain group with its demand. The government was prepared, as it had been for over two decades, to "wait it out." When the villain decided to make the move to devillainize itself in the public mind, the government was prepared, in lock step, to open the door to negotiation.

Later in the process, when the talks got bogged down on the issue of Sinn Fein's entrance into all-party talks, and the IRA broke the cease-fire, thus reasserting its villainous status, the negotiation process did not get derailed. The government was able to push the negotiations forward despite these setbacks without being labeled as an appeaser or being viewed as succumbing to the villain's tactics. The IRA was still a villain, but the government had demonstrated the overwhelming benefits of peace negotiations to the public, enough to withstand future storms and maintain the talks without losing face.

THREE MODELS OF DECISION

Three models emerge from these examples to describe how and why designator countries decide to negotiate with their villains.

MODEL 1: PUTTING THE DECISION IN THE VILLAIN'S HANDS

In the British - Sinn Fein case, negotiation was not initiated by the government. It was a consequence of certain conditions being met by the villain. The British government had declared Sinn Fein a villain and held true to its word not to negotiate until the cease-fire conditions were satisfied.

The villain, in fact, was forced to change *its* ways and tactics—to appear not to be a villain anymore in a very public manner—before the government was willing to accede to direct negotiations. Thus, the villain needed to "devillainize" itself in a public and credible manner. Once that reversal occurred, the British government was shielded from the accusation of appeasement and agreed to negotiations.

But this simple incapacity on the part of the government to withhold its decision to negotiate ensured a very passive government role. The government not only eliminated negotiation as an option when it villainized

Sinn Fein, but it also abrogated its own power to open the negotiation option until Sinn Fein decided it was ready.

MODEL 2: BRINKMANSHIP

In both the Haitian and North Korean cases, the U.S. government was well along in setting a course to implement harsh sanctions on the villains. In the Haitian case, a military invasion was imminent. In the North Korean case, UN-backed international sanctions were about to be implemented. All official communications had been severed. In both situations, Jimmy Carter, as an unofficial mediator with official U.S. government approval, was sent in at the eleventh hour to open the communications channel. Although the press labeled both of these initiatives ad hoc and last-minute, they share several attributes that suggest a consistent stylistic approach.

First, a mediator who had the trust of the villainous rulers was introduced. However, the mediator was a private citizen who, although a former president briefed by the U.S. government before his departure, did not represent the government in an official capacity. As a result, in the event of failure or an outrageous proposal, the intervention could be repudiated. Second, the mediator was given a very narrow agenda on which to conduct talks and find agreement with the villain. All issues were not out on the table. The designator sought to hold all of the cards, including harsh punishment if agreement was not reached. Third, the mediator was dispatched just before the onset of strong sanctions. Imminent punishment was threatened if the mediation efforts failed. These would be unacceptable costs from the villains' perspectives. And fourth, the mediation missions were publicized and timed as last-ditch efforts to avert the onset of sanctions. There was a very narrow window for agreement. Thus, there were very real deadline pressures, consciously developed by the U.S. government as part of its decision to negotiate. Overall, brinkmanship was the principal characteristic that motivated success in the Haiti and North Korea cases.

MODEL 3: BUSINESS MODEL

The Israeli-PLO rapprochement is an example of a model characterized by businesslike interactions. Much more could be done in secret informal settings—away from the media, and the opposition, and in the absence of public posturing—than could ever be done in an open, public forum. In secret, the taboos of noncommunication could be broached and overcome. In private, villainized personalities could be listened to, questioned, understood, and dealt with on a very human level. Reports from firsthand participants suggest that a collegial atmosphere was generated and a sense of affiliation developed among the participants.

This model also demonstrates pragmatism. If you want to resolve a problem, you must deal with the actors who have the authority to decide, even if they are the ones you have villainized. From a pragmatic perspective, pride must be swallowed and necessary business accomplished. This model operates under the assumption that both parties understand their own self-interests; seek to maximize them; and will be motivated by their interests, not ideology to make the negotiation decision.

There is also a pragmatic need to work with the other side as your partner, a partner who can deliver on promises, who will not renege, and who is strong and will not bend to opposition forces. More than the other two models, this one depends on trust—trust in the villain to take initiatives and assume risks to the same degree as the designator country.

MOTIVATING THE DECISION TO NEGOTIATE

The scholarly literature suggests that the decision to negotiate is motivated by certain factors under normal circumstances. Such factors include the perceived negotiability of the issue (Iklé, 1964; Zartman & Berman, 1982); reaching ripe moments and critical turning points (Zartman, 1989; Druckman, Husbands, & Johnston, 1991); introducing creative heuristics that reframe the problem (Spector, 1995); finding perceived power symmetry between the parties (Rubin, Pruitt, & Kim, 1994); and favorable assessments in the prenegotiation phase (Stein, 1989).

When deciding to negotiate with villains, additional factors appear to be influential, as demonstrated in the four illustrations. Following are brief descriptions of these factors.

- All four examples seem to share *the sense of a great historic moment* (suggested in Stein, 1989). The drama of a cease-fire, the meeting of old warriors, the unseating of military generals, and the freezing of nuclear-weapons production are part of what makes this kind of breakthrough decision different from negotiation decisions under normal circumstances. The leaders sense these historic moments, grab them, and seek maximum credit for them.

- The leaders who make these decisions are usually perceived as being *tough and unyielding actors or as having developed a tough strategy* that presents the villain with overwhelming costs to motivate compliance or, at a minimum, the willingness to negotiate (suggested in Rubin & Brown, 1975).

- The decision makers are also *risk takers* who are willing to break the established mold in a crisis and make new and historic decisions to resolve it (suggested in Zartman & Berman, 1982).

- The leaders are *astute and practical* politicians; they find a way to make the risky decision and shield themselves and their governments from potential negative fallout. For example, the use of *unofficial mediators and facilitators* is usually an important element in such face-saving strategies. These intermediaries are positioned as convenient *scapegoats* in the event that the negotiations fail or public opinion changes (suggested in Sherif, 1967).

- *Principles, values and ideology must be temporarily suspended* in favor of the decision to negotiate (suggested in Kelman, 1996). Convictions need not be compromised, but a dogged and pragmatic outlook must be developed.

- *Negotiation goals are usually very limited and incremental* (suggested in Fisher, Ury, & Patton, 1991). Achieving agreement on very narrow, pragmatic interests needs to be the focus of talks with villains to achieve short-term goals that can end imminent bloodshed.

- While constraining ideology could be suspended, *deeply rooted hatreds and animosities were not forgotten or dealt with directly* in any of these cases. The pragmatism of the negotiations ignored many of the underlying emotional issues of the conflicts. The hope is that such feelings will recede over time as relations normalize.

- It appeared that some progress was made in *reframing the conflict and the image of the villain,* particularly for the long-term insurgencies; less progress was made in this regard in the rogue challenges that confronted the United States (suggested in Finlay, Holsti, & Fagen, 1967; Volkan, 1988).

- *Overwhelming incentives* proved to be powerful and, perhaps, catalytic factors influencing the decision to negotiate. In the two rogue challenges, extreme negative costs were threatened if negotiations were not successful. In the two insurgencies, positive incentives—the cessation of violence—were promised as an element of the decision to negotiate. Without these major rewards or punishments, the decisions to negotiate may not have been successful in achieving their ends. In fact, the punishments needed to be an integral part of the negotiation decision strategy for the leaders to take the risk, in the event of negotiation failure or loss of face.

ETHICAL PRAGMATISM

Finally, obvious ethical questions are posed by the idea of negotiating with villains. Is it the duty of leaders to negotiate no matter what? Can one really negotiate with the likes of a Saddam Hussein?

The decision to negotiate with villains to stop human rights abuses and possible bloodshed can be seen as a principled decision. Abba Eban, Jimmy Carter, and others advocate a morally neutral approach in such negotiations, one that does not excuse the villain's crimes, but is committed to keeping pragmatic, businesslike communication channels open, so that conflicts and crises can be averted through good-faith negotiations. Their approach effectively separates the present from the past, while not forgiving or forgetting the past; thus former hatreds do not cast a pall over opportunities for conflict resolution in the present or the future.

This position, however, leads to some ethical dilemmas. The agreement with Haiti's generals, brokered by Carter, rewarded the perpetrators of human-rights abuses. Carter's goal was to negotiate any agreement that would ensure the removal of the generals. He succeeded in that limited goal, but as a result, the military leaders escaped accountability and were granted waivers from prosecution for their human-rights violations (Williams & Petrie, 1995).

Mediators are also faced with a painful balancing act. Is it better to save lives in the short term through brokering a cease-fire with villains, even though they may remain in power and can continue to perpetrate human rights abuses on the public? Or is it better to take the longer road and avoid "collaborating" with the villains, promoting actions that will not only drive them from power but establish a more stable and longer lasting peace settlement (see Touval, 1995)? Negotiating a cease-fire may save lives in the short run, but at the cost of accepting horrific abuses that have already been perpetrated. On the other hand, negotiating a longer-term solution—a real peace—that rights the injustices of the past may yield a more stable and long-lasting settlement, but requires more time during which more lives may be lost.

What these cases suggest is that leaders need to practice an *ethical pragmatism* in negotiation. On one hand, such a policy implies an ethical perspective, far removed from any ideology that has perpetuated a struggle and villainization. It is an ethical perspective that is based on humanistic precepts that place the saving of lives and the cessation of bloodshed as the highest priority. On the other hand, ethical pragmatism emphasizes a businesslike approach to solving conflicts—putting aside taboos that limit communication and interaction in favor of direct discussions with those who have the authority to make decisions and the power and resources to carry them out. This may mean negotiating with villains.

NOTES

1. The research upon which this article is based was supported by the United States Institute of Peace under Grant No. SG-37-95. The conclusions reported in this article do not necessarily represent the views or opinions of the institute. Portions of this chapter were previously published in *Negotiation Journal* 14 (1), January 1998. The author would like to thank an anonymous reviewer for his/her valuable comments and suggestions.

2. "Low-salient" enemies tend to be nonideological opponents. Disputes with such enemies may concern important, though not strongly emotional issues. "High-salient" enemies, on the other hand, are often described in ideological terms by the designating state. Disputes with these enemies are more likely to deal with such deeply rooted interests as identity, security, or ethnicity.

3. Perhaps the best-known example of such a case for American readers is the relationship between the governments of the United States and Fidel Castro's Cuba for the past thirty-five years. Cuban resolve to stand as a bulwark of opposition to the U.S. seems to have only been reinforced by the maintenance of American sanctions, including the no-negotiation policy (though this policy has sometimes been relaxed to allow for emergency talks in recent years).

4. The release from prison and apparent exile of Chinese human rights activist Wei Jingsheng in November 1997 occurred shortly after President Clinton held high-level talks with President Jiang Zemin in Washington. Wei's release appears to be in response to the U.S. policy of "constructive engagement" toward China rather than a no-negotiation approach. The Chinese were able to save face by claiming the release was to obtain medical treatment, while their action enables Clinton to deflect charges that he is too soft on China.

5. The January 9-16, 1995, issue of *The New Republic* reports this criticism in an editorial titled "Merry Christmas, Mr. Karadzic" (p. 7).

6. Prime Minister Tony Blair has similarly been derided as a traitor for meeting and shaking hands with Gerry Adams, the Sinn Fein leader (*Washington Post*, October 14, 1997, p. A1). Blair stated that, from his point of view, it is

important to treat members of Sinn Fein as human beings, not villains, for only then can a peaceful settlement be negotiated.

7. For the detailed case analyses and source materials on each of the four examples mentioned here, see Spector, 1996.

8. See the special issue of *International Negotiation* 2 (2), 1997, entitled "Lessons learned from the Middle East peace process" for details and analysis of the Oslo channel.

9. Hume is quoted as taking the principled route of negotiating with villains. He said, "I sat down and thought it through, and I decided if after twenty-five years and 20,000 troops that if I could save even one life by talking to one man, I would do it" (Kelly, 1994, p. 5).

REFERENCES

Berridge, G. R. 1994. *Talking to the Enemy: How States without Diplomatic Relations Communicate.* New York: St. Martin's Press.

Cable News Network. 1994. Text of Carter Interview on North Korea Progress. Breaking News, Transcript No. 421, Segment No. 3, June 22.

Druckman, D., Husbands, J., & Johnston, K. 1991. "Turning Points in the INF Negotiations." *Negotiation Journal,* 7 (1), 55–67.

Finlay, D., Holsti, O., & Fagen, F. 1967. *Enemies in Politics.* Chicago: Rand McNally.

Fisher, R., Ury, W., & Patton, B. 1991. *Getting to YES,* 2nd ed. New York: Penguin Books.

Foreign Broadcast Information Service (FBIS). 1993. "Rabin Explains Decision to Talk to PLO." *Near East and South Asia Report, Daily Report* (FBIS-NES-93–170), September 3, p. 17.

Friedman, R. 1992. "Negotiating with the Public." *Negotiation Journal,* 8 (1), 33–36.

Gibbs, N. 1994. "Yitzhak Rabin and Yasser Arafat." *Time,* January 3, 20–25.

Gurr, T. 1992. "Transforming Ethnopolitical Conflicts: Exit, Autonomy or Access?" Unpublished manuscript.

Jentleson, B., & Lund, M. 1994. "Preventive Diplomacy: An Idea in Search of a Strategy." Unpublished manuscript.

Kelly, M. P. 1994. "The Men behind the Peace: Hume to Gore to Clinton." *Commonweal,* 21 October, 4–5.

Kelman, H. 1996. "Negotiation as Interactive Problem-solving." *International Negotiation,* 1 (1), 99–123.

Klare, M. 1995. *Rogue States and Nuclear Outlaws: America's Search for a New Foreign Policy.* New York: Hill and Wang.

Kramer, M. 1994. "The Carter Connection." *Time,* October 3, 30–32.

Laqueur, W. 1980. *The Political Psychology of Appeasement.* New Brunswick, NJ: Transaction Books.

McKersie, R. 1992. "Getting to 'No.'" *Negotiation Journal,* 8 (1), 31–32.

Mollins, C. 1994. "Trust and Respect: Jimmy Carter's Personal Diplomacy in Haiti Averts a Bloody Showdown with the Country's Dictators." *Maclean's*, October 3, 26–28.

Powell, C. 1995. *My American Journey.* New York: Random House.

Richardson, J. 1992. *Democratization and Ethnic Conflict.* Washington, DC: American University. Unpublished manuscript.

Rose, C. 1994. "The Haitian Envoy: Sam Nunn." *The Charlie Rose Show,* Transcript No. 1212, broadcast by PBS, September 26.

Rose, C. 1995. "Always a Reckoning." *The Charlie Rose Show,* Transcript No. 1293, broadcast by PBS, January 17.

Rubin, J. Z., & Brown, B. 1975. *The Social Psychology of Bargaining and Negotiation.* New York: Academic Press.

Rubin, J. Z., Pruitt, D., & Kim, S. H. 1994. *Social Conflict: Escalation, Stalemate and Settlement,* 2nd ed. New York: McGraw-Hill.

Schorr, D. 1994. "Peanut Diplomacy in Haiti." *The New Leader,* 77 (9), 3–5.

Sherif, M. 1967. *Social Interaction: Process and Products.* Chicago: Aldine Publishing.

Spector, B. 1996. *Negotiating with So-Called Villains: Duty or Appeasement.* Final Report. Washington, DC: U.S. Institute of Peace.

Spector, B. 1995. "Creativity Heuristics for Impasse Resolution: Cognitive Processes to Help Reframe Intractable Negotiations." *The Annals of the Academy of Political and Social Science,* 542 (November), 81–99.

Stein, J. G. 1989. "Getting to the Table: The Triggers, Stages, Functions, and Consequences of Prenegotiation." In Stein, *Getting to the Table: The Processes of International Prenegotiation.* Baltimore: Johns Hopkins University Press.

Touval, S. 1995. "Ethical Dilemmas in International Mediation." *Negotiation Journal,* 11 (4), 333–338.

U.S. Department of State. 1995a. *Patterns of Global Terrorism, 1989–1994.* Washington, DC: State Department.

U.S. Department of State. 1995b. *International Narcotics Control Strategy Report.* Washington, DC: Bureau for International Narcotics and Law Enforcement Affairs.

Volkan, V. 1988. *The Need to Have Enemies and Allies: From Clinical Practice to International Relationships.* Northvale, NJ: Jason Aronson.

Weinberger, C. 1994. "Mr. Carter goes to Pyongyang." *Forbes,* 154 (2), 33.

Wheeler, M. 1992. "Fighting the Wimp Image: Why Calls for Negotiation Often Fall on Deaf Ears." *Negotiation Journal,* 8 (1), 25–30.

Williams, J. A., & Petrie, J. N. 1995. "The Carter Mission to Haiti: Unintended Consequences for Human Rights Law." *The Fletcher Forum of World Affairs,* 19 (2), 95–114.

Zartman, I. W. 1989. *Ripe for Resolution,* 2nd ed. New York: Oxford University Press.

Zartman, I. W., & Berman, M. 1982. *The Practical Negotiator.* New Haven: Yale University Press.

CHAPTER 12

THE ROLE OF EMOTIONS IN INTERNATIONAL NEGOTIATIONS

FRED CHARLES IKLÉ

The topic of this chapter may seem both ambitious and ambiguous. After all, emotions affect every conscious action of an individual—and many of the unconscious ones as well. But this ambiguity and lack of boundaries serves a good purpose here.

The broad concept of "emotions" is useful for two reasons. First, it forces us to focus on real people. A nation, a government, or an international organization does not have emotions; only people do. Yet, so much of academic writing—at least in the United States—uses such expressions as "Germany *fears* that . . . ," "the U.S. Government *is angry* at Japanese trade practices," or "Beijing *feels strongly* that Taiwan belongs to China." Strictly speaking none of these expressions make much sense. More importantly, by using such language we tend to overlook significant psychological processes that affect the behavior of diplomats and other government officials involved in negotiations.

My second reason for exploring the role of emotions in international negotiation is that this broad approach stimulates us to inquire into a wider range of issues. The very vagueness of the question allows us to come up with some new and perhaps interesting answers. In particular, I hope that by seeing negotiators as real people—people with emotions—we can shed some light on the changing role of nation-states and national governments in world affairs. By contrast, if we see sovereign countries as the ultimate international "actors" we will never notice how much the capacity of sovereign (or national) governments to act on any-thing depends on people and their sentiments and emotions. What en-ables a nation-state to be a so-called actor is the people who serve in its government as well as all the men and women who support the govern-ment as workers and warriors, scientists and artists, merchants and farm-ers. And it is all these people who together shape the actions of a nation-state and who are influenced by their hopes and fears, their feel-ings of loyalty or alienation, their sense of enthusiasm or despair.

Those who have had the patience to read some of the specialized aca-demic literature from the United States dealing with international relations may have come across the debate between the so-called realist theory and the liberal or institutional theory. The realist theory emphasizes the ten-dency towards anarchy in international affairs and the reliance on balance-of-power arrangements. The institutional and "liberal" theories stress the possibility that international institutions can overcome the tendency to an-archy and that truly cooperative relations among liberal democracies are likely to overcome the risk of war. During the Cold War, the East-West confrontation and the U.S.-Soviet military balance of power imposed an order on the world that fit with the realist theory. The most famous states-man who sought to act in accordance with the "liberal" theory was U.S. president Woodrow Wilson. But as a manifestation of a liberal-institutional concept of international order the European Union (which is regional, of course, not global) has been far more successful than President Wilson's League of Nations.

These few sentences, to be sure, cannot do justice to the richness of re-cent international relations writings on realist versus liberal-international-ist views. For a recent sampling of contributions see Baldwin (1993). A stimulating discussion is offered by Stanley Hoffmann (1995), who makes several observations that are in agreement with a thesis of this chapter; namely, his points on the importance of "emotional bonds of allegiance that tie the society to the state" and on the loosening or severing of these ties in current ethnic and separatist crises.

For our purposes here it is useful to distinguish two types of emotions: on the one hand, emotions that refer to, or are animated by, something in the future; on the other hand, emotions that refer to, or are animated by, something in the past. We will, however, pay little attention here to emo-tions that are linked to something that happens in the immediate present. For example, it will not interest us here that a diplomat may get angry be-cause his opponent has just used offensive language. Similarly, it will not interest us that a negotiator may be more willing to make some concessions because he feels relaxed and in good spirits, having just enjoyed a fine lunch and imbibed lots of sake.

EMOTIONS ANIMATED BY IDEAS ABOUT THE FUTURE

Let us first look at emotions referring to an event that is expected to occur in the future. These are the emotions of hope or fear, the emotions of yearning for some future success or of worrying about some future failure. In complex international negotiations these images about future outcomes and their follow-on consequences consist of many variables. For example, in trade negotiations these variables may include tariff levels for different goods, rules restricting government subsidies, adjustments of patent rights, agreed volumes of trade, and so forth. Most of these variables are not commensurable, that is to say, the outcomes agreed for each of the variables cannot be added up to get a measurement for the overall outcome. Hence, the negotiators have to attach more or less arbitrary weights to these variables. They must decide, for example, whether their nation would benefit more if its principal trading partner strengthened the enforcement of patent rights, or, instead, if it lowered certain tariffs. The way in which government officials prioritize such different issues depends on their emotional attachment to alternative outcomes—their concerns, hopes, and fears for the future.

In the so-called armistice negotiations that ended the Korean War in 1953, the variety of issues included the return of prisoners of war, restrictions on armaments for North and South, and the structure and composition of an international arms inspection team (the Neutral Nations Supervisory Commission). The American negotiators placed great hopes on this Neutral Nations Supervisory Commission. In their eyes it was an essential element of the armistice agreement that they had to win in order to prevent North Korea from violating the prohibitions against an arms build-up. As Americans soon learned, this commission was worse than useless. It could do nothing about North Korea's arms build-up in violation of the truce agreement, but it inhibited the U.S. response. By contrast, the American negotiators invested much less effort in the dividing line between North and South, which—far from being a temporary armistice line—became a permanent border. Today this line is the most heavily armed border in the world.

This example illustrates an important tendency in American diplomacy. The negotiating tactics of U.S. government officials in the Korean armistice talks reflect an emotional attachment to the liberal-institutional view of world order. The Neutral Nations Supervisory Commission was meant to make sure that the hard-won peace in Korea would last. It was like a miniature version of the Wilsonian dream of the League of Nations, the organization that was meant to prevent another world war. Actually, it became obvious very quickly that this Neutral Nations Supervisory Commission was neither neutral (because Communist Poland and Czechoslovakia together had half the votes), nor supervisory (because the North Koreans could easily block all relevant access).

While setting up this commission seemed to be a goal that the American negotiators valued, drawing the line for the territorial division between North and South Korea was emotionally an unappealing issue for American diplomats, and hence something on which the U.S. negotiators spent less effort and time. In the American view the Korean peninsula was meant to become a unified country at the end of World War II. The division between North and South, hastily arranged, in 1945 was meant to be a temporary compromise only, reached with Moscow to create separate Soviet and U.S. occupation zones.

During the first phase of the negotiations on a nuclear test ban in the late 1950s, U.S. and British diplomats exhibited a similar attachment to institution-building. As if motivated by a strange utopianism, the U.S.-British side sought to superimpose a liberal-institutional structure on the Cold War reality of balance of power. They sought to create an elaborate "impartial" control organization intended to detect and confirm nuclear tests carried out in violation of the treaty. To act as a neutral arbiter, this organization would have had to float above the Cold War cleavage like some heavenly creature. Of course, nothing came of this idea. The Soviet negotiator at that time, Ambassador Tsarapkin, had no such illusions. "If any State were to take the step of violating the treaty and to start a series of nuclear explosions," Tsarapkin said, "such a State would of course never allow any inspection team to enter its territory." We should ask ourselves whether more recent arms control agreements, with all their elaborate international inspection organizations—such as the Chemical Weapons Convention—might not be similarly unrealistic.

In negotiations that might lead to the partitioning of a previously unified country, strong emotional preferences become involved on both sides of the issue. Minorities seeking independence will favor partition; those who wish to preserve an empire, or "national" unity, will fiercely oppose it. Interestingly, in many recent struggles about partition the American political elite has strongly opposed the idea that a previously unified country should be broken up. Some intellectuals have suggested that the American memory of the terribly costly Civil War might explain this tendency; others have argued that the emotional distaste for partition of American diplomats might stem from the realization that the United States itself is a country with many ethnic and racial groups.

Whatever the reason, this American tendency shows itself in many instances. For example, when the Soviet Union broke up in 1991 into its constituent administrative "republics," senior officials in the Bush administration at first hesitated to recognize these newly independent states. In the same year these senior U.S. officials opposed the break-up of former Yugoslavia. And with the unfolding crisis in Bosnia, this aversion to partitioning has manifested itself particularly strongly, even though Bosnia had never been a sovereign state with a unified territory but was merely an administrative division of Yugoslavia and before that, of the Austrian and the Ottoman empires.

The 1995 Dayton Accords on Bosnia produced the detailed map of separation between territories with Serb military forces and under Serb political control, on one side, and territories with Muslim-Croat forces and under the political control of authorities in Sarajevo, on the other side. The negotiations in Dayton, Ohio, in the fall of 1995 that produced this map were inspired, led, and managed by American diplomats. Yet, in these negotiations—as well as during the several years of Bosnian strife and warfare before and since then—the senior U.S. officials unequivocally maintained that the separated territories of Bosnia had to be glued together again. The Dayton agreement provides that a single unified government is to be set up and that the dividing line between Serbs and Muslims (as well as Croats in Bosnia) must be erased. That is to say, a constitutional structure is supposed to bridge and heal the chasm that has been opened up by four years of brutal religious warfare. At this time it seems unlikely that the unification of Bosnia will succeed just because it has been mandated by the Dayton Accord. History, however, might yet show the Dayton agreement to be a significant accomplishment of American diplomacy, either because it led to a peaceful integration of Bosnia, or—more likely—because it led to a more or less peaceful partition.

History teaches us that in reality, international diplomacy is usually motivated by a mixture of philosophies that could be viewed as a combination of the theory of "realism" and the theory of "institutionalism" (or of a "liberal" order based on consensus). As Henry Kissinger (1994, pp. 21 & 812) wrote, "balance-of-power systems have existed only rarely in human history" and that for American diplomacy the combination of the "moral" and the "strategic" (balance-of-power) elements "cannot be prescribed in the abstract." Sometimes statesmen have sought to create an international organization (or a union of states) to buttress a balance-of-power system, sometimes to advance a Wilsonian world order, sometimes having a combination of these two broad ideas in mind.

Once negotiations are underway to create such a new entity, the diplomats involved often become emotionally attached the institutional edifice they are creating. In the evolution of NATO—surely, one of the most successful alliances in history—the satisfaction with the negotiating progress nourished such an attachment among many NATO diplomats. American and British officials were the principal promoters of the integrated military core of NATO, which greatly enhanced the alliance's military strength and helped build emotional links among the staff.

A parallel example is the creation of the European Union. American diplomacy, using the leverage of the Marshall Plan, helped Western Europe after World War II to overcome its prewar economic protectionism. This provided a favorable environment for French, German, and other West European officials to create the European Common Market. But without the emotional attachment to a larger goal among many of these officials, the enterprise would at best have become a free-trade area. It remained for Jean Monnet and his German, Belgian, and Dutch colleagues to articulate the idea of building a united Europe and to keep alive a sentimental attachment to this vision. Although a great many interesting books and articles have been written about the dramatic success of the movement to unite Europe, only a minority of the authors have fully recognized the importance of this emotional dimension. Jean Monnet's own story (1955) does, of course, reflect the power of emotions in shaping the approach to European integration. Is it possible that in the next century today's European Union will evolve into a single sovereign state? The continuing negotiating process in Brussels has not been without setbacks from the point of view of those who favor greater integration. But a certain momentum and sense of direction has been created during the past four decades, with the gradual construction of more powerful central institutions to which the member states agreed.

The growth and eventual fragmentation of centrally governed sovereign states is a mysterious process for which human history offers many puzzling and conflicting examples. The sense of national belonging, or what is sometimes called nationalism, is only part of the story. As Elie Kedourie (1993, p. 73) reminds us, "the Ottoman Empire was not a 'nation', the Roman Empire was not a 'nation', and yet they were able, as few contemporary states have shown themselves able, to continue for centuries, to maintain the cohesion of the social fabric and to attract the loyalties of men." Sometimes, a national sentiment emerges suddenly and motivates soldiers and diplomats to fight and bargain for a nation that they had never dreamt of before. E. J. Hobsbawm (1992, p. 47) points out that "while the Jews, scattered throughout the world for some millennia, never ceased to identify themselves, wherever they were, as members of a special people . . . at no stage . . . does this seem to have implied a serious desire for a Jewish political state, let alone a territorial state, until a Jewish nationalism was invented at the very end of the nineteenth century. . . ."

Equally puzzling can be the breaking apart of nations or sovereign states. Very few of the academic and government experts on the Soviet Union thought before 1990—let alone before the mid-1980s—that Russia might be separated from such entities as Ukraine (including the Crimea!), Belarus, and Kazakhstan. A previously unified state may break apart even without any ethnic, linguistic, or religious differences that would seem to justify the separation. The secession of Norway from Sweden in 1907 was not proposed by anyone until the 1890s (Hobsbawm, 1992). How can such things be anticipated? And if the state is inherently an unstable entity, what does that say about the sense of loyalty and emotional attachment of the officials who serve the government of "their" state? This leads us to the question of the influence of emotions that are rooted in past events.

EMOTIONS ANIMATED BY REMEMBRANCE

The main purpose of international negotiations is to shape relations between governments or within public organizations (such as the UN, EU, WTO) for the near or more distant future. As noted above, negotiators are therefore influenced by "forward-looking" emotions, such as hope and fear. But people's emotions are also influenced by the memory of events that occurred in the past, or that people imagine to have occurred in the past. These emotive recollections influence human behavior in many situations; in particular, in diplomatic negotiations—a context in which precedents and history play a large role.

Several "backward-looking" emotions are relevant for international negotiations:

Anger, resentment, or hatred because of misdeeds, treachery, or wanton attack committed by the opponent's government or its predecessors. This sentiment has considerable impact on many diplomatic relationships. It seems to affect, for example, South Korea's diplomacy toward Japan. It has also influenced Japan's diplomacy toward the Soviet Union because of the latter's violation of the Japanese-Soviet neutrality pact and its retention of the Northern Territories. This unpleasant memory appears to influence Japanese negotiators even when dealing with today's Russia. It is more easily understandable that the diplomacy of the Baltic states and Poland towards Russia should be influenced by the remembrance of the Soviet depredations suffered during the Stalin period.

Emotional attachment to pieces of national territory. Territorial disputes tend to be the most difficult issues in international negotiations. When two countries desire to exert sovereignty over one and the same piece of territory, negotiations between them will be prolonged. And if influential people on each side feel emotionally attached to the contested territory—no matter how small and worthless it might be—the risk of war is often imminent. Clearly, the tenacity with which government officials seek to hold on to or reclaim a piece of territory is not proportional to its value. It is not just economic assessments or strategic calculations about the future value of a piece of land, but an emotional attachment rooted in history that determines the stubbornness and sacrifice with which the conflict is pursued.

British officials easily gave up the port of Aden which could have become a valuable strategic base in the Gulf region (much better located than the British-U.S. base on Diego Garcia). But they continued to hold on to the Falkland islands, which are strategically and economically worthless. In 1982, Prime Minister Margaret Thatcher was so strongly motivated to undo the Argentine aggression and occupation of the islands that she accepted the risks of an extraordinarily difficult military operation 8,000 miles from the United Kingdom because a negotiated Argentine withdrawal could not be obtained. Many senior British officials, but by no means all, shared this emotive emphasis on reestablishing British sovereignty over these barren islands inhabited by only 2,000 British citizens. Sir Nicholas Henderson (1983), British ambassador in Washington at the time of the Falkland crisis, wrote in an essay: "There could scarcely have been an issue since 1939 upon which the British felt so strongly, and this feeling ran across party lines. No government in Britain could possibly contemplate a negotiation involving the Argentines while they remained in occupation of the islands." The Argentine leader, General Galtieri, was even more motivated by emotions rooted in the past and deaf to calculations about the future. He rejected possibilities for a compromise that had emerged from frantic

U.S., Latin American, and United Nations efforts to mediate the conflict, even though some of the final compromise formulas might well have led to eventual Argentine possession of the Falklands.

One can think of many more examples of negotiations over some slice of territory in which negotiators feel they cannot "surrender an inch" even though the overall relations with the other side to the dispute are far more important than the contested piece of land. The strong insistence of Japanese officials that Russia must return the Northern Territories is a case in point. This insistence is matched by Russia's stubborn position to refuse negotiations about a return of these impoverished islands.

Recent history, however, provides a few noteworthy exceptions to this tendency to become emotionally attached to pieces of territory. Most of the senior officials of the Russian Federation, it seems, became resigned to the loss of the Crimea despite Russia's strong historic claims and the emotional attachment of many Russians to the Crimean peninsula, where Russian ethnics dominate. All the more puzzling is the inability of Russian diplomats to exploit the strong emotional interest of Japanese officials in recovering the Northern Territories. Russia might negotiate a substantial (albeit perhaps disguised) compensation by agreeing to return these islands to Japan.

Another example of overcoming the emotional attachment to a piece of territory is provided by the U.S.-Panamanian negotiations over the Panama Canal. Starting with the Johnson administration, U.S. officials have been quite willing to negotiate the surrender of the Panama Canal and the Canal Zone to Panama, despite the fact the United Sates had good legal title to keep the canal "in perpetuity" and even though the government of Panama had never exercised sovereignty over the canal and its U.S. zone. (The state of Panama came into existence only as a result of U.S. intervention and as part of a bargain by which it agreed to give the United Stated control over the Canal Zone.)

Trust and Bonding. Diplomats who participate in prolonged conferences often develop emotional bonds with each other as well as a certain attachment to the ongoing conference. The conference becomes "their" institution; and the diplomats representing governments that might have opposing positions begin to feel like colleagues engaged in a noble common enterprise. A reasonably satisfactory experience in dealing and working with these "colleagues" can engender mutual trust. An excellent analysis of the interactions that build up trust in such situations is to be found in Zartman & Berman, *The Practical Negotiator* (1982). Agreements that were hammered out together will nourish a sense of jointly achieved accomplishment. Such personal bonding and collegiality are important in prolonged multilateral arms control negotiations and in complex trade negotiations.

An interesting associated development of this personal bonding and sense of collegiality is the creation of a common intellectual culture. A set of shared concepts and a common vocabulary usually emerge in arms control and trade negotiations long before the work of the diplomats has culminated in an agreement acceptable to their governments. Indeed, the negotiating process in prolonged multilateral conferences is greatly influenced by the common culture of ideas that serve to structure the issues, a culture toward which the participants develop an increasing emotive affinity.

In a way, these conferences become nonviolent arenas for a contest among competing ideologies that seek to establish values and goals for ordering international relations. Thus, the goal of a comprehensive test ban has now emerged, after decades of argumentation and dispute, as a cultural norm that is almost taken for granted by most nations. It is the associated conditions, not the goal itself, that remain under dispute. Similarly, on human rights a common culture has emerged for the norms on racial persecution and discrimination. Today, these are strongly emotional issues in international negotiations and no diplomat would dare to disagree that racism is bad. On other aspects of human rights, however, one can now observe a continuing, lively debate, especially between European and American negotiators, on one hand, and Chinese and Southeast Asian ones, on the other. That is to say, a common culture of terms and concepts has not yet emerged. (A recent American view of the differences is provided by Hitchcock [1994], and a Japanese view is offered by Mitsuta [1993].)

Whether one wishes to expand or to limit the influence of common norms and concepts for international diplomacy depends on one's preference for giving priority either to full national sovereignty or to a more uniform international order. Clearly, members of the so-called international staffs of multilateral organizations (such as the United Nations or the European Union) are supposed to work together as colleagues on the achievement of the organization's goals, not as negotiators on behalf of the nations from which they were recruited. The people who serve on international staffs, however, have differed greatly in their willingness and ability to serve the common goals of the international organization rather than the preferences or instructions of the country from which they came. In past decades, it is fair to say, those who came from Western Europe, North America, and Japan have acted more as truly "international" officials than those who came from other countries. The selection process in Western countries tends to recruit individuals who are already emotionally predisposed in favor of international cooperation. By contrast, "international" officials who had been recruited from the Soviet bloc were kept under tight supervision and formidable pressure by their home governments to support the policy of the Soviet Union.

Feelings of loyalty and related sentiments. No government can function unless the people who serve it—or at least the key people—are motivated by feelings of loyalty. A feeling of loyalty is part of a larger cluster of feelings, or sentiments, that enable people to work together in competition with or in opposition to other groups. This cluster includes feelings of belonging to a group (being part of "we" in opposition to "them"); a sense of trust towards colleagues; an emotional attachment to unifying common values and symbols (such as the national flag and anthem); a code of honor, historic traditions, and religious beliefs. Evidently the emotions involved here are largely rooted in the past. They may have been nourished by a common education, memories of past common achievements, or positive feelings toward parents and ancestors that blend into a sense of attachment toward the national patrimony.

In Moscow in the autumn of 1991, representatives of the administrative divisions of the Soviet Union—the so-called Soviet republics—negotiated with senior Soviet government officials about the relationship of their republics with the center. Most of the senior Communist (or former Communist) officials in the central Soviet government wanted to keep the Soviet Union together. Despite the failed coup in August 1991, they felt a sense of loyalty toward the larger Union in which they all had grown up and lived, and for which many of them had fought in World War II. To be sure, Boris Yeltsin chose to enhance his own political role by promoting a sovereign, independent status for the Russian Republic. That assertion of independence, in itself, was not particularly startling. However, what surprised most experts who had studied Soviet affairs and Soviet history for decades, was the sudden evaporation of a sense of loyalty toward the single unified country among all the delegates who negotiated about the future relationship between these administrative entities (the Soviet republics) that they represented. Even though most of these administrative units had not existed as independent sovereign nations in the lifetime of these delegates, or the lifetime of their parents, and even though the borders of most had been arbitrarily drawn by Stalin, these delegates managed to defend a new independence for their republics and to abandon their loyalty toward that larger country that had been held together and ruled for many generations from St. Petersburg (in tzarist times) and from Moscow (in Soviet times).

EMOTIONS THAT WILL SHAPE THE WORLD ORDER

Is it conceivable that negotiators representing the Prefectures of Japan or the Départements of France would some day meet in Tokyo or Paris, respectively, to make their administrative units into newly independent states? We are approaching here some important questions about the emotions of people who are in a position to structure the relationships among states, among the sub-units of existing states, and within international organizations. The sense of loyalty toward an existing nation and the desire to preserve the integrity and independence of that nation can be destroyed by a radical upheaval in political ideology. It is political ideology—in many cases intertwined with religious beliefs—that provides the glue that makes national loyalty a powerful force. For seventy years the Soviet Union was dominated and politically inspired by the Communist Party. When that party lost its cohesion, power, and legitimacy, there was nothing left to hold the country together since the Communists had gone to great lengths to erase all legitimacy of the tzarist tradition. An excellent assessment of the end of Soviet Communism can be found in the special issue of *The National Interest,* "The Strange Death of Soviet Communism" (1993). Charles H. Fairbanks, Jr. wrote in that issue: "Having undermined its own legitimacy at the February [1990] Plenum, the Party voted at its Twenty-Eighth, and last, Congress in July 1990 to destroy itself organizationally by giving up the Party's supervision of the government, by removing all government officials except Gorbachev from the Politburo, and by filling that body with non-entities" (Ibid., p. 54). Then, after the failed coup in August 1991, Gorbachev was totally discredited, and Yeltsin promoted, for his own reasons, the independence of the largest unit within the USSR. That left nothing in the center toward which the representatives of the other Soviet republics could feel a sense of loyalty.

The Communist Party in China is losing its power, ideological relevance, and cohesion far more slowly and less dramatically than did the Soviet Communist Party. Nonetheless, the process of weakening the center has gone so far that the authorities in Beijing now continuously have to negotiate with provincial authorities on tax revenues, economic policy, and other issues. After a future succession crisis in Beijing, some officials representing provincial power centers might feel greater loyalty to their local constituency than to a fractured and ideologically bereft national government. Beijing's adamant position on Taiwan may reflect a sense of insecurity about national cohesion.

The recent breaking-up of several sovereign countries into smaller sovereign states has been the result of negotiation, in most instances, not of wars fought for secession. In addition to the Soviet Union, the break-up of Czechoslovakia was a negotiated outcome, as was the separation of Macedonia from Yugoslavia. And if Quebec should separate from Canada, that outcome would also be reached through negotiation. At the same time, other independent nations have engaged in prolonged and complex negotiations to form a larger union. The most notable case, of course, is the European Union. The more recent North American Free Trade Agreement represents a far more limited from of integration than the European Union. Slowly, however, the world of today is becoming enmeshed in a global web of trade and financial networks, communications links, environmental interdependence, and cultural interactions that restrict national sovereignty to some degree and lead to mixed emotions among the diplomats and officials of all the governments involved. Many British government leaders and officials, for example, seek to limit the process of European integration. In the United States, opinion is divided on whether to strengthen international organizations or to protect and reaffirm America's sovereign independence.

In recent decades, many political scientists and international-relations experts have written about the growing global interdependence caused by the environmental impact of industrialization, security problems, demographic pressures, and an increasingly integrated world economy. German, Scandinavian, and American writers, especially, have suggested that the role of nation states will diminish and that the emerging worldwide problems will require global political structures that can develop common policies and seek to implement new solutions.[1]

What most of these writings neglect, however, is the emotional dimension of the political process that seeks to build government structures for the world as a whole that would increasingly have to perform functions now the responsibility of nation states. By and large, the advocates of stronger global organizations are motivated by emotions that concern the future—fear of nuclear proliferation, concerns about population pressures, hopes for controlling global warming, and so on. By contrast, the statesmen and diplomats who seek to preserve the untrammeled national sovereignty of their countries are motivated by emotions that relate to things in the past—a sentiment of national belonging, a desire of people to preserve their cultural environment, a sense of loyalty toward the existing national government.

In the normal flow of international negotiations, these conflicting emotions nudge decisions almost imperceptibly. At one point they might induce a diplomat to support a small step toward greater international cooperation, at another point they might motivate a diplomat to oppose a decision that would detract from his nation's freedom of action. The clash of these emotions becomes more apparent only in a crisis. And in most crises, the emotions animated by things in the past tend to win out over the emotions animated by ideas about the future. It takes a leader of extraordinary forcefulness—and often ruthlessness—to prevail with his vision about the future against colleagues or opponents who are motivated by emotions that are rooted in the past. Lenin was such a person when in 1917 he seized power, engineered the destruction of the tzarist traditions, and imposed upon Russia a totally new social and economic order.

By contrast, the socialist parties in Europe in 1914 were too weak to promote the principles of the Second International (the program approved by European socialist leaders) that called for halting the outbreak of World War I. The socialist parties of the European states could not negotiate a united position in August 1914 against the war. Each party rationalized in its internal deliberations that its own nation was embarking on a *defensive* war, and according to previous socialist peace resolutions defensive wars were permissible (Waltz, 1954). This crisis illustrates that the emotions of nationalism and of things of the past can prevail over the hopes for a new, peaceful future.

In June 1940, days before the final defeat of France by Nazi Germany, British prime minister Winston Churchill tried to negotiate with the French premier Paul Reynaud a deal inspired clearly by emotions and visions about the future. Churchill proposed to the French government an "indissoluble union" of France and Great Britain; but the French government (at that time huddled in Bordeaux, its last refuge from the advancing German army) could not embrace the future-oriented sentiments of Churchill. The emotions rooted in past things prevailed and the French Council of Ministers rejected Churchill's proposal. Churchill (1949, pp. 213–213) wrote after the war: "Rarely has so generous a proposal encountered so hostile a reception. . . . Most [French ministers] were wholly unprepared to receive such far-reaching themes." Some of the French complained that it was a scheme to put France in tutelage, or to carry off her colonial empire. Remarkably, after World War II it was the British who refused for more than ten years to join with France in the integration of

Europe, the endeavor that has since become—with British participation—the European Union.

International negotiation as a subject of scholarly inquiry is rich in ambiguities and spreads over a vast terrain with blurred boundaries. The extensive literature on negotiation that has grown up during the last thirty years illustrates the diversity of the topic and the difficulty of imposing a rigorous structure on it. The fact that the emotional dimension is so important for an understanding of the negotiating process makes scholarly analysis all the more difficult, since emotions represent a highly elusive force influencing human interaction. In the decades to come, negotiations between sovereign states and within international organizations will greatly influence the evolving world order, and in this process it is precisely the force of emotions that will shape the future of our world.

NOTE

1. A small selection of these writings includes The World Commission on Environment and Development, 1987; Commission on Global Governance, 1995; Hoffmann, 1995; Knieper, 1991; Kaiser & Schwarz, 1995; and Dror, 1995.

REFERENCES

Baldwin, D. A., ed. 1993. *Neorealism and Neoliberalism: The Contemporary Debate.* New York: Columbia University Press.

Churchill, W. S. 1949. *The Second World War: Their Finest Hour.* Boston: Houghton Mifflin.

Dror, Y. 1995. *Ist die Erde noch regierbar?* Munich: Bertelsmann.

Fairbanks, C. H., Jr. 1993. "The Strange Death of Soviet Communism." *The National Interest,* Spring.

Henderson, N. 1983. *Economist.* November 12.

Hitchcock, D. I. 1994. *Asian Values and the United States: How Much Conflict?* Washington, DC: Center for Strategic & International Studies.

Hobsbawm, E. J. 1992. *Nations and Nationalism since 1780.* Cambridge: Cambridge University Press.

Hoffmann, S. 1995. "The Crisis of Liberal Internationalism." *Foreign Policy,* no. 98, Spring, 159–177.

Kaiser, K., & Schwarz, H. P., eds. 1995. *Die neue Weltpolitik.* Bonn: Bundeszentrale für Politische Bildung.

Kedourie, E. 1993. *Nationalism.* Oxford: Blackwell.

Kissinger, H. 1994. *Diplomacy.* New York: Simon & Schuster.

Knieper, R. 1991. *Nationale Souveraenitaet.* Frankfurt: Fischer.

Mitsuta, A. 1993. *Chuka no hasso to Nihonjin* [The Chinese Way of Thinking and the Japanese]. Tokyo: Kodansha.

Monnet, J. 1955. *Les Etats-Unis d'Europe ont commencé.* Paris: Laffont.

Waltz, K. N. 1954. *Man, the State and War.* New York: Columbia University Press.

World Commission on Environment and Development. 1987. *Our Common Future.* Oxford: Oxford University Press.

World Commission on Global Governance. 1995. *Our Global Neighborhood.* Oxford: Oxford University Press.

Zartman, I. W., & Berman, M. R. 1982. *The Practical Negotiator.* New Haven: Yale University Press.

Contributors

Cecilia Albin (Ph.D., Johns Hopkins University) is Lecturer and Director of the Centre for International Security and Non-Proliferation in the Graduate School of European and International Studies at the University of Reading, United Kingdom. She was previously Deputy Director of the Global Security Programme at the University of Cambridge, and has been a research fellow at the Hebrew University, Harvard, and Stanford, and at the International Institute for Applied Systems Analysis (IIASA). Dr. Albin is the author or coauthor of numerous articles and book chapters on negotiation, conflict resolution, and the Middle East. She is the editor of and a contributor to *Negotiation and Global Security: New Approaches to Contemporary Issues* (special issue of the *American Behavioral Scientist*); *Negotiating Effectively: The Role of Non-Governmental Organizations;* and *Sinai II: The Politics of International Negotiation.* From 1997 to 1998, she directed a research project funded by the United States Institute of Peace on the role of justice and fairness in international negotiations. E-mail: c.a.albin@reading.ac.uk

Peter Berton (Ph.D., Columbia University) is Distinguished Professor Emeritus of International Relations at the School of International Relations, University of Southern California, where for thirty years he was Coordinator of the Asia-Pacific Regional Studies Program. He also taught at Stanford and UCLA, and in Japan, England, and Germany; and held research positions at Harvard, Columbia, and Tokyo universities, and the International Research Center for Japanese Studies in Kyoto. He served as consultant to the Library of Congress, the Ford Foundation, the Social Science Research Council, and the American Council of Learned Societies. He is the author, coauthor, or editor of well over one hundred publications on Asian and Soviet/Russian affairs, including *The Japanese-Russian Territorial Dilemma; The Russian Impact on Japan; The Fateful Choice: Japan's Advance into Southeast Asia, 1939–1941; The Russo-Japanese Boundary; The Secret*

Russo-Japanese Alliance of 1916; and a number of articles and symposium chapters on psychological and psychoanalytic dimensions of Japanese, Chinese, and Soviet/Russian negotiating behavior. E-mail: berton@usc.edu

MICHAEL BLAKER (Ph.D., Columbia University) is a Fellow, East Asian Studies Center, University of Southern California, specializing in Japanese domestic politics and foreign relations. He has taught at Columbia, USC, the Fletcher School of Law and Diplomacy, and most recently Harvard University where he was Senior Research Associate at the Program on U.S.-Japan Relations. An Abe Fellow, he was also the initial holder of the Japan Chair at the Center for Strategic and International Studies in Washington, DC. His published work includes *Japanese International Negotiating Style, Japan at the Polls, The Politics of Trade,* and many articles on Japanese diplomacy and Japanese-American relations. In 1996–98, he received a grant from the United States Institute of Peace to continue his research on Japanese negotiating behavior, and the Institute will publish his forthcoming book-length study, *Negotiating by the Numbers: Contemporary Japanese Bargaining Behavior.*

GUY OLIVIER FAURE is Professor of Sociology at the Sorbonne University, Paris, where he teaches international negotiation. He is also associated with the China-Europe International Business School in Shanghai. He is a member of the editorial boards of the three major international journals on negotiation theory and practice: *Negotiation Journal, Group Decision and Negotiation,* and *International Negotiation.* He is a member of the Steering Committee of the Process of International Negotiation (PIN) at the International Institute of Applied Systems Analysis (IIASA). He has authored or coauthored *La negociation: situations et problematiques; Conflict, Cooperation, and Justice; International Multilateral Negotiations; Culture and Negotiation; International Environmental Negotiation; Entre savoirs, l'interdisciplinarite en actes; International Negotiation; Conflits et negociations dans le commerce international; Evolutionary Systems Design, Policy-making under Uncertainty;* and the forthcoming *Economic International Negotiation, Power and Negotiation,* and *Traditional Conflict Medicine.* E-mail: gofaure@worldnet.fr

ROBERT L. FRIEDHEIM (Ph.D., University of Washington, Seattle) is Professor, School of International Relations, University of Southern California (USC). He acted as the Director of the School of International Relations (1992–1995), and the Director of the USC Sea Grant Institutional Program (1980–1989), and Associate Director of the Institute for Marine and Coastal Studies (1976–1989). He also served in the Center for

Naval Analyses (1966–1976) where he was the director of a research project that served the U.S. Delegation to the Third United Nations Law of the Sea Conference (1969–1975). He is the author of seven books, including *Negotiating the New Ocean Regime, Japan and the New Ocean Regime, Making Ocean Policy,* and *Managing Ocean Resources.* He has written more than seventy articles, papers, and book chapters, among which is a chapter in I. William Zartman, ed., *Positive Sum: Improving North-South Relations.* Dr. Friedheim is currently editing a book, *Toward a Sustainable Whaling Regime.*

JOHN L. GRAHAM (Ph. D., University of California, Berkeley) is Professor of International Business and Marketing, and Associate Dean (1994–95) at the Graduate School of Management at the University of California, Irvine. He has taught at Georgetown University School of Business, Madrid Business School in Spain, and the University of Southern California. He is the author, coauthor, or editor of *Smart Bargaining: Doing Business with the Japanese* (2nd ed.); *International Marketing* (10th ed.); *Global and International Marketing* (2nd ed.); and more than fifty articles and chapters for publications such as the *Harvard Business Review,* the *Sloan Management Review,* the *Journal of Marketing,* the *Journal of International Business Studies,* the *Journal of Consumer Research, Marketing Science,* and the *Journal of Higher Education.* Excerpts of his work have been read into the Congressional Record; his research of business negotiation styles in twenty cultures was the subject of an article in the January 1988 issue of *Smithsonian;* and his 1994 paper in *Management Science* received a citation of excellence from the Lauder Institute at the Wharton School of Business. E-mail: jgraham@uci.edu

FRED CHARLES IKLÉ was Undersecretary of Defense for Policy in the Reagan administration, and served Presidents Nixon and Ford as Director of the U.S. Arms Control and Disarmament Agency. Since 1989 he has been affiliated with the Center for Strategic & International Studies. He is also a Director of the National Endowment for Democracy and serves on the advisory boards of RAND's Drug Policy Research Center and of the Center for Security Policy. Between 1977 and 1981, Dr. Iklé served as Chairman of the Republican National Committee's Advisory Council on International Security, and as Coordinator of Governor Reagan's Foreign Policy Advisors. He was Professor of Political Science at M.I.T. and held positions with the RAND Corporation (head of Social Science Department), the Center for International Affairs at Harvard University, and the Bureau of Applied Social Research at Columbia University. Dr. Iklé is the author of several books, including *How Nations Negotiate* and *Every War Must End,* and has published many articles on foreign policy and defense.

HIROSHI KIMURA (Ph.D., Columbia University) is a Professor at the International Research Center for Japanese Studies in Kyoto and serves as First Vice-President of the International Council for Central and East European Studies (ICCEES). He was a Fulbright-Hays Visiting Professor at the Institute for Sino-Soviet Studies, George Washington University, and a visiting professor at Stanford University. He was also a special research fellow at the Japanese embassies in Vienna and Moscow. Before assuming his present post, he was a Professor and Director of the Slavic Research Center at Hokkaido University. His recent research has focused on Russian foreign policy toward Japan. His major publications in English include *Prospects for East-West Relations; Gorbachev's Reform: U.S. and Japanese Assessments;* and *Beyond Cold War to Trilateral Cooperation in the Asia-Pacific Region: Scenarios for New Relationships between Japan, Russia, and the United States.* He was a Visiting Scholar at the Harriman Institute for Advanced Russian Studies, Columbia University from August 1998 to May 1999. E-mail: kimura@nichibun.ac.jp

FRANK R. PFETSCH (Ph.D., University of Heidelberg) is professor of political science at the University of Heidelberg. He also studied economics and political science at the universities of Karlsruhe, Paris, and Turin, and at Harvard. He was visiting professor at the University of Pittsburgh, Kyung Hee University in Korea, the University of Leipzig; and Halevy Professor and Alfred Grosser Professor at the Institut d'Etudes Politiques in Paris. He also worked in research institutes and was a consultant to the West German Ministry for Scientific Affairs and to UNESCO for various science-policy administrations in South America, Africa, and Asia. He is Member of the Steering Committee of the Standing Group on International Relations and of the Executive Committee of the European Consortium for Political Research. His recent books include *West Germany: Internal Structures and External Relations; Urspruenge der Zweiten Republik. Prozesse der Verfassungsgebung in den Westzonen; Die Aussenpolitik der Bundesrepublik. Von der Spaltung zur Vereinigung. Erweiterte Neuauflage; Internationale Politik* and *La politique internationale; Handbuch nationaler und internationaler Konflikte; Dimensionen des Politischen* (3 vols.); and *Die Europaeische Union. Eine Einfuehrung.*

GUNNAR SJÖSTEDT (Ph.D., University of Stockholm) is a senior research fellow at the Swedish Institute of International Affairs, where also he held the position of Director of Research. He previously taught political science at his alma mater, and is working with doctoral students at the universities of Lund and Umeå, and at the Royal Institute of Technology. He is a consultant on non-military security issues for various Swedish governmental agencies. Dr. Sjöstedt serves on the Steering Committee of the Process of Negotiation Project at the International Institute of Applied Systems Analysis, and on the International Advisory Board of *Negotiation Journal* since 1990. His publications include *The External Role of the European Community; Free Trade—Managed Trade? Perspectives on a Realistic Trade Order; Power, Capabilities, Interdependence—Problems in the Study of International Influence; International Environmental Negotiation; Environmental Aid to Eastern Europe: Area Studies and Theoretical Applications; Sweden's Free Trade Policy. Process, Issues and Contexts;* and *Negotiating International Regimes: Lessons Learned from the United Nations Conference on Environment and Development.*

BERTRAM I. SPECTOR (Ph.D., New York University) is Executive Director of the Center for Negotiation Analysis, in Potomac, MD, a nonprofit group providing research, training, and advisory support in negotiation, mediation, and other forms of dispute resolution for government agencies, international organizations, and foundation programs. He is also Senior Associate of Management Systems International, Washington, DC. Dr. Spector served as the Director of the Process of International Negotiation (PIN) Project at the International Institute for Applied Systems Analysis (IIASA) and was a Fellow at the Foreign Policy Institute of the School for Advanced International Studies at the Johns Hopkins University. His current research projects include a NATO-sponsored study concerning the use of international and regional negotiation processes to reduce and prevent serious escalation of environmental threats to security, and a book on post-agreement negotiations and international regimes. He is also Editor-in-Chief of *International Negotiation: A Journal of Theory and Practice.* E-mail: negocenter@email.msn.com

I. WILLIAM ZARTMAN is the Jacob Blaustein Professor of International Organizations and Conflict Resolution and Director of the International and Conflict Management Program at the Paul H. Nitze School of Advanced International Studies of the Johns Hopkins University in Washington, DC. He is a member of the Steering Committee of the Process of International Negotiation (PIN) Project at the International Institute of Applied Systems Analysis (IIASA), and convenor of the Washington Interest in Negotiation (WIN) Group. He was Visiting Professor at American

University of Cairo, Olin Professor at the U.S. Naval Academy, Halevy
Professor at the Institute for Political Studies in Paris, and Visiting Distin-
guished Fellow at the United States Institute of Peace. His many books on
negotiation include *Elusive Peace: Negotiating an End to Civil Wars; Ripe for
Resolution: Conflict and Intervention in Africa; Cooperative Security: Reducing
Third World Wars; Positive Sum: Improving North-South Negotiations; Interna-
tional Multilateral Negotiation: Approaches to the Management of Complexity;
The Practical Negotiator;* and *The 50% Solution.*

INDEX

AUTHOR INDEX